Gatekeeping in BSW Programs

Gatekeeping in BSW Programs

Edited by Patty Gibbs
and Eleanor H. Blakely

Columbia University Press
New York

Columbia University Press
Publishers Since 1893
New York   Chichester, West Sussex

Sections of chapter 9 include revised material from the following article: Madden, R.G. "Protecting All Parties: A Legal Analysis of Clinical Competency and Student Dismissals," *Journal of Law and Social Work* 3, no. 1 (1993): 1–13. Reprinted by permission of the *Journal of Law and Social Work.*

Chapter 10 was originally published by the Association of Baccalaureate Social Work Program Directors in the premier issue of *The Journal of Baccalaureate Social Work* 1, no. 1 (October 1995). Copyright © 1995 National Association of Baccalaureate Social Work Program Directors. Reprinted with permission of *The Journal of Baccalaureate Social Work.*

Some of the data reported in chapter 16 were reported earlier in Reeser, L. C., and Wertkin, R.A. "Sharing Sensitive Student Information with Field Instructors: Responses of Students, Liaisons, and Field Instructors," *Journal of Social Work Education* 33 (1997): 347–362. Reprinted by permission of the *Journal of Social Work Education.*

Library of Congress Cataloging-in-Publication Data
Gatekeeping in BSW programs / edited by Patty Gibbs and Eleanor H. Blakely.
    p. cm.
  Includes bibliographical references and index.
  ISBN 0–231–11050–2 (cloth)
    1. Social work educaton—United States. 2. Peer review—United States. I. Gibbs, Patty.
II. Blakely, Eleanor H.

HV11.7 .G37 2000
361.3'2'071173—dc21   99–045382

Casebound editions of Columbia University Press books are printed on permanent and durable acid-free paper.

Printed in the United States of America
c 10 9 8 7 6 5 4 3 2 1

Contents

Foreword

Baccalaureate social work education has served as a gateway to the profession for diverse student populations: ethnic minority students, immigrant students, students with low incomes, returning adult students, and students from rural areas. As baccalaureate social work educators, we are responsible both for gatekeeping and for preserving this gateway. We fail the profession when we graduate unsuitable social workers. We also fail when, for lack of financial or academic support, gifted prospective social workers do not enter the profession.

In the professional literature, we educators have supported the BSW gateway by presenting research on recruiting and retaining ethnic minority students, on teaching culturally competent practice, and on infusing human diversity through the curriculum. At the same time, we have shown increasing interest in gatekeeping, in narrowing access to the profession. At conferences for social work educators, sessions on gatekeeping attract overflow crowds. I view this trend uneasily. In choosing sessions on gatekeeping, we may be avoiding discussions of other, more basic issues in social work education.

Does gatekeeping mask our difficulties in teaching students from various cultural, ethnic, and economic backgrounds; students with weak academic preparation (preparation often related to their economic status); students with English as a second language; or students with learning or other disabilities? In the name of gatekeeping, we can design admissions policies to screen out those students whom, regardless of their potential for social work, we do not know how to teach.

Does gatekeeping mask our difficulty in teaching values? Although social work education includes affective outcomes, such as respecting the positive value of human diversity, we do not have empirical evidence that social work education significantly influences students' attitudes toward diversity or oppression. In the name of gatekeeping, we can deny admission to those students who do not already demonstrate the attitudes and values we hope to teach.

Does gatekeeping mask our difficulties in conducting evaluative research? Social work has not made a commitment to sustained, consistent evaluation of education or practice. As a result, we do not have an empirical basis for predicting which students will succeed as baccalaureate social work students or as practicing social workers. In the name of gatekeeping, we can use admissions criteria without concern for their predictive validity.

With this book, Patty Gibbs and Eleanor H. Blakely have brought together resources for a responsible study of gatekeeping in BSW education. They make no attempt to simplify the discussion, to reduce gatekeeping to a two-sided debate with a single resolution. From screening-in to screening-out, the papers collected here represent the wide range of current opinion, research, and practice on gatekeeping issues.

How should baccalaureate social work education reconcile its responsibilities for affording and for restricting access to the profession? This collection challenges our tacit values as educators and as social workers. It makes a distinct contribution as a catalyst for further research and honest thought.

Lorrie Greenhouse Gardella, J.D., A.C.S.W.
Saint Joseph College
West Hartford, Connecticut

Preface

Frustration provided the impetus for this book. Social work educators and field instructors often express unrelenting frustration with attempts to carry out their gatekeeping responsibilities. Spurred by a series of sessions and workshops on gatekeeping presented at annual conferences of the Association of Baccalaureate Program Directors (BPD) and the Council on Social Work Education (CSWE), in 1993 a group of volunteers from across the country decided to do something about this frustration by gathering information on the "state of the art" in social work education gatekeeping. This book grew out of the work of these social work educators, who proceeded with courage and determination into relatively uncharted waters. Because the history of this project's evolution is somewhat peculiar, as group efforts go, it seems well worth highlighting.

During my sabbatical leave in the spring semester of 1993, as I sat pondering the stacks of projects before me, I found myself returning to a study on gatekeeping I had previously carried out. Having resolved to bring this particular study to a logical conclusion, I revised and polished both of the articles the research had yielded and shipped the two manuscripts off to publishers; nonetheless I had a nagging sensation of unfinished business.

Like other social work educators across the country, I had spent several years attending all of the sessions on gatekeeping issues offered by the Association of Baccalaureate Social Work Program

Directors at their annual BPD conferences, as well as those scheduled at the annual program meetings of the Council on Social
Work Education. Many of us who attended these sessions began
to recognize each other and continue the discussions outside of
each conference session. Over time, a network of sorts was
formed, which led to my eventual participation as one of several
speakers during gatekeeping panel presentations at BPD and
CSWE conferences.

I was always struck by the enormous number of conference
attendees who gravitated to these sessions, given the many other
choices that were available during the same time slots. The chairs
were always filled and the room jammed past capacity as people
stood shoulder-to-shoulder in the aisles. I was equally struck by
the lively discussions and the widespread concern that unanimously was expressed about gatekeeping issues. These sessions
usually drifted into the bogs of "we can't—though I wish we
could, but we don't know how, and what about legal implications
and potential legal repercussions?" Nonetheless, I would come
back from the conference sessions full of steam, only to find
myself drifting into those same bogs as my home faculty and I
unsuccessfully struggled with the problems and issues associated
with our gatekeeping responsibilities. At my school much disagreement prevailed about all aspects of gatekeeping, and little
progress was made in developing effective policies that would
guide our gatekeeping efforts.

So during that frigid January of my sabbatical leave, I searched
out the names of everyone who had published or presented anything on BSW gatekeeping in the recent past. I sent them letters,
asking if they would like to form a national task group on bac-
calaureate-level gatekeeping, which would collaborate to develop
"something" in writing, although I wasn't sure what. I included in
my letter a request for names of other social work educators who
might be interested in undertaking this (loosely structured, ill-
defined, but absolutely essential) project.

Miraculously, more than a dozen social work educators
responded to my initial call, although membership fluctuated as
people drifted in and out of the group during the more than six
years it took to complete this work. Because the group grew out
of the Baccalaureate Program Directors Association, we called

ourselves the National Task Group on BSW Gatekeeping Standards. Twice when the task group was scheduled for a meeting at BPD conferences, the room filled with other conference attendees who thought the meeting was a general session on gatekeeping. A few of these folks became new task group recruits.

Despite the absence of both grant monies to facilitate the effort and release time at my home institution to give concentrated attention to the work, I facilitated the banding together of this trailblazing group of social work educators who pooled their expertise and collaboratively saw this project through to completion. Although hazards in my own life delayed completion of the book for two years, the release time I was given during the fall of 1998 enabled me to finalize the manuscript and get it off to Columbia University Press.

The materials developed by the National Task Group on BSW Gatekeeping Standards represent the only collective thinking to date on gatekeeping issues and standards in social work education. The task group, of which I am the chair, offers this book to our social work colleagues in hopes that it becomes a candle that will partially illuminate the shadowy corners of gatekeeping in programs across the country.

Patty Gibbs, Chair
National Task Group
on BSW Gatekeeping Standards

Acknowledgments

The National Task Group on BSW Gatekeeping Standards that collaborated to shed light on the topic of BSW gatekeeping comprised the core group of individuals who brought this project to fruition. However, without the support, assistance, and influence of many people, both the substance and presentation of this work would have been dramatically different.

I (Patty) am deeply indebted to Eleanor, "Ellie," Blakely, who deserves rich praise for joining the project as coeditor when it was well into its second year. In addition to her excellent critique of manuscripts and help with the myriad tasks associated with such a massive undertaking, her high energy level, commitment to gatekeeping, and pleasant collegiality made very tedious work a lot more enjoyable.

Because the project was not funded, the School of Social Work (more recently the Division of Social Work) at West Virginia University shouldered much of the cost associated with the development of this book over the years. We (Patty and Ellie) give special recognition to Karen Harper and Barry Locke, both of whom have held leadership positions in the school/division and have supported this project in direct and indirect ways.

We extend appreciation to Robert Madden from Saint Joseph College's Department of Social Work in Connecticut for graciously lending his expertise in order to ensure that the sample policies, as well as the chapter content, advanced in this book are on firm ground legally. We give special recognition to Jerry Blakely from West Virginia University (WVU) for the various ways he assisted in this project. We wish to acknowledge the technical assistance offered by Cherie Hawkins, a former WVU BSW student, during the early years of this project.

I (Patty) express deep gratitude to my family for bearing with me for more than six years of "burning the midnight oil" while I completed this time-consuming but gratifying project. I give thanks and praise to my youngest son Brian for his good-natured acceptance that my fingers seemed to be glued to the computer keyboard during most of his waking hours for so many years of his young life. I lovingly thank my adult son Shaun for his unfailing belief in my abilities and, in particular, for his strong emotional support during a shattering family crisis when work on this book was in its final stages. I additionally extend deeply heart-felt appreciation to my lovemate and lifemate, Jim Wahlberg, who tenderly patched up my broken wings and enabled me to reclaim my strength when strength was not an operative part of my life. His love and support are more central to the completion of this book than he will ever understand or would even willingly acknowledge.

Both Patty and Ellie are extremely appreciative of the consistent enthusiasm of John L. Michel, Columbia University Press' associate executive editor, who gave us strong support from the time we first approached him about publication of this project. His belief in and support of our work meant a great deal.

It seems that from the moment I (Ellie) walked in the door of the School of Social Work here at WVU, Patty and I began discussing gatekeeping issues. Being a member of the school's admissions committee and a faculty member who teaches across both the BSW and MSW programs provides a somewhat unique position from which to view and confront these issues. When Patty asked if I would be interested in working with her on a book she had underway, I jumped at the chance, not only because I knew I would enjoy working with Patty but also because I optimistically believed this would answer all those thorny gatekeeping questions that continue to occupy our thoughts. On the former issue, I was right; on the latter, I was wrong. In fact, I probably have more questions now regarding our gatekeeping responsibilities than before we began working on this book. However, I am confident that I am better equipped to tackle these issues as a result of this experience. To Patty, all I can say is thank you for believing I was the right person with whom to share this project. I don't think either of us realized what we were undertaking, but it was well worth the effort. To my husband, Jerry, thanks for your patience as you constantly stepped over and around the piles of "book stuff" that have filled our study for the last few years. To our students and alumni, thanks for demonstrating through your dedication, commitment, and professional practice that these gatekeeping efforts lead to positive results.

Last, but certainly not least, the authors and task group members deserve professional accolades for their unflinching commitment to a complex task that was so global and ill-defined at its inception. On blind faith alone they joined the task group and energetically took up the task at hand. Several of the authors were contacted to draft chapters when the project was into its third and even fourth years; yet they willingly and enthusiastically contributed their expertise to improve the value and usefulness of the final product. To our authors, thank you for your insights and your patience as we scrutinized every concept, every reference, every sentence, and every punctuation mark. I (Ellie) hope to meet each of you one of these days. The authors also have my (Patty's) gratitude for exercising great patience when a personal life crisis and subsequent life changes regrettably delayed publication of this book for two years. Both of us are deeply appreciative of the cooperative and collaborative spirit that all task group members brought to the endeavor of sharing their expertise in and experiences with gatekeeping in social work education. This book would not have been possible without each of their valuable contributions.

Contributors

LYNN FRANTZ ADKINS is a professor and BSW program director at Bethany College in West Virginia. She has been associated with undergraduate social work education since 1972 and has directed the program at Bethany College since 1978. She received her MSW from West Virginia University and her doctorate from the University of Pittsburgh. Her specialized areas of study are social welfare policy and substance abuse. She has made numerous policy and substance abuse presentations at the national, state, and local level. At Bethany she developed the senior comprehensive exit exam for the social work major and has worked with other colleges in reviewing their comprehensive examination program. Bethany College, a Liberal Arts I institution, is one of the few undergraduate programs that requires students to pass a comprehensive examination as a graduation requirement.

BILL ALLBRITTEN is the director of the Counseling and Testing Center and professor of guidance and counseling at Murray State University in Kentucky. He has been on the faculty at Murray since 1975. He received his doctorate in college student personnel work from the University of Northern Colorado in 1975. He has published articles and made presentations in the areas of dating violence, computer applications in the human services, and psychological assessment as a tool in program admissions processes. His responsibilities at Murray State University also include supervision of developmental and remedial academic programs.

ELEANOR H. BLAKELY is an associate professor and director of the MSW program in the Division of Social Work at West Virginia University, where she has been a member of the division's Admissions Committee since 1990. She teaches both undergraduate and graduate courses in policy, administration, and child welfare. Her research interests include poverty and hunger, welfare reform, and policy practice issues. In 1995 she received the West Virginia Coalition on Food and Nutrition's first annual award for Outstanding Contributions Toward Food Security in West Virginia. Dr. Blakely received her MSW from the University of Louisville and her Ph.D. from the University of North Carolina at Chapel Hill.

ROSE BOGAL-ALLBRITTEN is a professor and the BSW program director at Murray State University in Kentucky, where she has been a faculty member since 1977. She received her MSW and doctoral degrees from Loyola University of Chicago. She has presented a number of papers and has published a number of articles on issues in social work education, family violence, and date rape. Since 1991 she has shared her program's state-of-the-art admissions, termination, and appeals policy and process with numerous social work educators. She has served as a site visitor for the Council on Social Work Education since 1981.

WANDA D. BRACY is a professor, department head, and the BSW program director at Eastern Michigan University. She holds a master of arts degree in sociology, a master of philosophy in education, and an MSW degree. She recently completed her doctoral degree in education at Northeastern Illinois University, and her dissertation was on the inclusion of diversity in social work education. She has presented many papers and published several articles in the areas of student assessment, student recruitment and retention, collaborative learning strategies, and the inclusion of diversity in higher education and the social work curriculum. She has served as a board member of the Council on Social Work Education (CSWE) and the Association of Social Work Program Directors (BPD). In addition, she has served as conference chair for the annual conferences of CSWE and BPD. She worked closely with the local chapter of the National Association of Social Workers (NASW) and has served on its board for two terms.

KATHY BYERS is an associate professor and coordinator of the BSW program on the Bloomington Campus of Indiana University. She previously taught in the BSW programs of Southwest Missouri State University and Wright State University. She graduated from Wellesley College, received her MSW from Brandeis University, and completed her doctorate at Indiana University. Her practice experience includes work in public welfare, family planning, residential treatment, and consultation with public schools. Her most recent work with practitioners has been in applying strengths perspectives to work with families. Her current research focuses on characteristics and experiences of students as they enter BSW programs, including the influence of family background characteristics on decisions to enter the field and initial orientations toward political activity and social activism. She has taken leadership in recent efforts at Indiana University School of Social Work to refine the BSW admissions process and develop comprehensive procedures for student continuation and review. In addition, she serves as a regional representative on the state NASW board of directors.

CHARLOTTE C. CHRIST is the former BSW program director in the School of Social Work at the University of Southern Mississippi where she taught in both the BSW and MSW programs. She received her BSW from the University of Georgia, her MSW from the University of Southern Mississippi, and is at the dissertation stage of her DSW at the Catholic University of America. Previously she was a project associate of the National Center for Social Policy and Practice while attending Catholic University. Other past experience includes a number of administrative, management, and policy practice positions, including director of Child and Adolescent Service Systems at the MS State Department of Mental Health and director of the MS Governor's Office for Children and Youth. Her publications include an article on students with disabilities and an invited contribution to in *Social Work Processes* (4th ed.).

NORMAN H. COBB is an associate professor in the School of Social Work, University of Texas at Arlington. Since 1994 he has served as chair of the Academic and Professional Standards Committee, which addresses student behavior, ethics, and grade grievances. He received a doctorate from the University of California at Berkeley, an MSW from University of Texas at Arlington, and a

Master's of Divinity from St. Paul School of Theology. He writes and conducts workshops and presentations on student conduct, ethics, dual career couples, clinical practice, and parenting.

BETTIE S. COLE is a professor in the Department of Social Work at East Tennessee State University, where she has been on the faculty since 1986. She received her MSW and Ph.D. degrees from the University of Alabama and was on the faculty at that university for almost six years. She has published several articles related to gatekeeping and other social work education issues. Two of her published articles specifically address legal implications of suitability and admissions decisions in social work. One article focuses on the ADA as it relates to social work education and gatekeeping. She has served on various panels as a presenter at the Council on Social Work Education's annual program meeting and the Baccalaureate Program Directors' annual conference.

PATTY GIBBS, a former professor and BSW program director at West Virginia University, where she was a faculty member since 1976, is now a professor, BSW program director, and chair in the Department of Social Work at East Tennessee State University. She received her MSW and her doctorate in education from West Virginia University. During her 1993 sabbatical leave she formed the National Task Group on BSW Gatekeeping Standards and subsequently chaired the group. She has published a number of articles on topics related to social work education, rural social work, social work licensure, and women's issues. Two of her published articles address BSW gatekeeping. Since 1992 she has served as a panelist and presenter on gatekeeping issues at the Council on Social Work Education's annual program meetings and the Association of Baccalaureate Program Directors' annual conferences. She also has served as a board member of the Council on Social Work Education and is currently a board member of the Association of Baccalaureate Program Directors. Her special area of expertise in her home state of West Virginia is social work values and ethics. She has provided numerous workshops on values and ethics throughout the state to social work practitioners, reaching more than 3,000 licensees to date.

HOPE HAGAR, associate professor emeritus, recently retired as department chair at the University of Wisconsin–La Crosse's

Social Work Program since 1974. She has an MSW degree from the University of Iowa and a doctorate from the University of Wisconsin. Her primary areas of teaching responsibility have included HBSE, practice, and field coordination. She is an active researcher, and she serves as a site visitor for the Council on Social Work Education.

SKI HUNTER is a professor in the School of Social Work at the University of Texas at Arlington. She teaches courses in adult development, close relationships, and human behavior. She participates in the school's Academic and Professional Standards Committee. Widely published, her major recent scholarship is in the areas of midlife and lesbian and gay men issues. She coedited a book, *Myths of Midlife,* and coauthored another book, *Lesbians and Gay Men: Translating Knowledge for Human Services Practice.*

DAVID JENKINS is an associate professor of social work at Texas Christian University. He teaches classes in human behavior, advanced practice, and family intervention. He has published in the areas of gatekeeping, family therapy, and self-awareness. He currently has research interests in the areas of sexual harassment, siblings, diversity issues, and multiple births. The latter interest arose following the birth of triplet daughters in 1993.

NANCY P. KROPF is associate dean and associate professor in the School of Social Work at the University of Georgia. She received her MSW degree from Michigan State University and her doctoral degree from Virginia Commonwealth University in social work/social policy. In addition to her interest in social work education, her area of research and scholarship is gerontology and family caregiving relationships.

ROBERT G. LEWIS recently retired as an associate professor and chair of the Department of Social Work at East Tennessee State University, where he has served as a faculty member since 1967. One of his published articles on gatekeeping addressed legal issues in terminating unsuitable social work students. He has served numerous times as a panelist/presenter on gatekeeping issues at the Council on Social Work Education's annual program meetings and the Association of Baccalaureate Program Directors' annual conferences. He has been an active participant in BPD activities beginning with the first conference in 1983, and he served as a

BPD board member from 1992–94. He has participated in board decisions and strategies designed to strengthen gatekeeping efforts in baccalaureate social work education nationwide.

HARRY J. MACY is a professor of Social Work and has served as the Department of Social Work chairperson at Ball State University, Indiana, since 1977. Formerly, he directed a community-based graduate social work education training center for the School of Social Work at the University of Iowa. He received his MSW degree from Indiana University and completed a master's degree in public affairs and a doctorate in higher education administration. His research, publications, and professional development contributions have focused on instruction methodologies, social work education administration, and effectiveness of social service delivery. Professional service includes board and leadership positions with the Association of Baccalaureate Social Work Program Directors, Council on Social Work Education, and the Indiana Chapter of the National Association of Social Workers.

ROBERT G. MADDEN is an associate professor and the field practice coordinator for the BSW program at Saint Joseph College in West Hartford, Connecticut. He received a BSW from Providence College, MSW from Columbia University, and a law degree (JD) from the University of Connecticut. Professor Madden is the author of *Legal Issues in Social Work Counseling and Mental Health: Guidelines for Clinical Practice in Psychotherapy,* published by Sage. He has written and presented on law and statutes related to social work practice and education. In addition to full-time teaching, he maintains a small law practice specializing in representing social workers on matters of confidentiality, privilege, record-keeping, and other legal issues in practice. His work in the area of gatekeeping has resulted in publications and presentations at the Council on Social Work Education's annual program meetings and the Association of Baccalaureate Program Directors' annual conferences.

LINDA S. MOORE is an associate professor of social work and the director of the social work program at Texas Christian University (TCU). She received her B.A. in sociology from Eastern College in St. Davids, Pennsylvania, her MSW from Virginia Commonwealth

University and her Ph.D. in sociology from Texas Women's University. She has been on the faculty at TCU since 1977. She has published in the areas of gatekeeping in social work education, teen suicide, resources for gay and lesbian students, the emergence of the NAACP, the use of the Myers-Briggs Type Inventory (MBT), and the impact of social work education on student values and attitudes. She also has made conference presentations in these areas. She has been honored with the Dean's Award for Distinguished Teaching, has twice been the Social Science nominee for the Chancellor's Award for Distinguished Teaching, and was the Social Worker of the Year for the Ft. Worth Unit of NASW. She is a member of Alpha Delta Mu, Alpha Kappa Delta, Phi Kappa Phi, Golden Key National Honor Society, and Who's Who Among Human Service Professionals. She is active in CSWE, BPD, and NASW, and has served as president of the NASW Texas Chapter.

THOMAS D. OLLERICH is an associate professor and former chair of the Department of Social Work at Ohio University, where he has been a faculty member since 1970. He received his MSW from Adelphi University and his doctorate from the School of Applied Social Sciences at Case Western Reserve University. He is a member of, and the past secretary and president of, the Ohio College Association of Social Work Educators. He has presented papers on various aspects of undergraduate social work education. His areas of particular interest include child abuse, especially the sexual abuse of children. He was formerly Ohio On-Site Coordinator through the Region V Child Abuse and Neglect Resource Center, University of Wisconsin-Milwaukee. Social work values and ethics are another area of interest. He was awarded two NEH fellowships to develop an interdisciplinary course on dealing with ethical dilemmas in the social services.

PENNY SMITH RAMSDELL is an assistant professor in the School of Social Work at Louisiana State University. She received an MSW and doctorate in administration from the University of Texas at Arlington. Her practice experience following her master's degree was with Planned Parenthood. She has taught in both graduate and undergraduate social work programs and has served as a field coordinator. She has published in the areas of professional ethics, participatory decision making, and social work education.

GINNY TERRY RAYMOND is associate professor, chair of the BSW program, and associate dean at the University of Alabama School of Social Work. She has taught BSW and MSW courses since she joined the faculty in 1975 and Ph.D. courses since 1995. She received the MSW from Tulane University School of Social Work and the Ph.D. from the University of Denver Graduate School of Social Work. She has been active in the Council on Social Work Education as an accreditation site visitor, member of the Commission on Educational Policy and Planning from 1988 to 1993, member of the Board of Directors from 1993 to 1996, and chair of the Membership Committee of the board in 1996. She has also been active in the Association of Baccalaureate Program Directors, having attended every BPD conference from the first in 1983, presenting papers at most and serving on the Conference Planning Committee. She has presented papers at other national and international conferences, including the CSWE annual program meeting, the Congress of the International Association of Schools of Social Work, the European Groupwork Symposium, the Conference of the Association for the Advancement of Group Work, and the International Conference on Women in Higher Education. Many of her published articles and book chapters are on issues in social work education.

LINDA CHERREY REESER is an associate professor and director of field education at Western Michigan University, School of Social Work, where she has been on faculty since 1981. She received her doctorate from Bryn Mawr College and her MSW from Temple University. She has published a number of articles in the areas of field education, professionalism, and activism. She coauthored a book with Irwin Epstein entitled *Professionalization and Activism in Social Work: The Sixties, the Eighties, and the Future.* She made three presentations with Robert Wertkin at CSWE annual program meetings on the topic of sharing sensitive information about students with field instructors.

DAVID ROYSE is a professor, associate dean, and director of graduate studies at the College of Social Work at University of Kentucky. He is the author of over fifty articles and four texts (*Research Methods for Social Workers; Program Evaluation: An Introduction; Field Instruction: A Guide for Social Work Students;*

and *How Do I Know It's Abuse: Identifying and Countering Emotional Mistreatment from Friends and Family Members.*) Since 1972 Dr. Royse has had experience in the fields of mental health, human services, and education. He has conducted research on childhood trauma and its effects, public attitudes toward child abuse, the impact of being in foster care, and on such diverse topics as homelessness, diversion programs for shoplifters, and attitudes about AIDS.

DAN WEISMAN is BSW chair and professor of social work at Rhode Island College, and chair of CSWE's Commission on Social Work Practice. He received his MSW from the University of Michigan in 1969 and his doctorate in social work from Rutgers University in 1986. His practice has included antipoverty community organizing in Kentucky, including Welfare Rights; mental health advocacy in New Jersey, including developing and monitoring community mental health centers, action-research on behalf of former psychiatric patients, and helping to establish a mental health law project; and directing a community council in New York, where he organized an adolescent health center and a self-help/advocacy agency for disabled adults and children. His research and publications address BSW curriculum, civil liberties, and labor issues. He is treasurer of a senior citizens center, producer of a public-access cable TV program for the ACLU, and executive committee member of his faculty union.

ROBERT A. WERTKIN is a professor in the School of Social Work at Western Michigan University, where he has been on faculty since 1981. He has served as the interim director of the School of Social Work and Physician Assistant Department, as well as assistant to the director of the Michigan Department of Social Services. He holds a DSW from the University of Utah and MSW from the University of Kansas. His publications and presentations have focused on job satisfaction, organizational culture, public welfare policy, program evaluation, and victimization theory. He made three presentations with Linda Cherry Reeser at CSWE annual program meetings on the topic of sharing sensitive information about students with field instructors.

Gatekeeping in BSW Programs

PART ONE

Background and Issues

1

Introduction: The Arena of Gatekeeping

Patty Gibbs and Harry J. Macy

In social work education, selective evaluation, screening, and retention of students are decision arenas in which students' rights and interests, faculty's responsibilities, program integrity, institutional policies, professional practice standards, social work's ethical principles, and the legal requirements of higher education converge. Few program operations are viewed as more complex, troublesome, and emotionally charged than the gatekeeping component of the educational enterprise. And few program operations are imbued with more mystery and misunderstanding.

Even the term *gatekeeping* invokes different notions in the minds of those who are responsible for the evaluation, selection, and retention of students. Some see gatekeeping as a process whereby students are nurtured through the educational enterprise in order to ensure that they successfully complete the program and are competent to practice when they graduate. Others think of gatekeeping as primarily a way to selectively "close the gate" at some point in a student's program when she or he is found to be unsuitable for practice in the field of social work, and a student might be seen as unsuitable for any number of reasons related to the inability to function within the parameters of professional expectations.

Those who see gatekeeping as a nurturing process, a perspective based on the students' strengths, are generally uncomfortable with a gatekeeping mentality that ostensibly centers on the need "to close the gate." To view gatekeeping primarily if not exclusively as closing the gate seems somehow anathema to those who want to nurture students up to and through the gate of professional practice. However, gatekeepers who emphasize occasionally closing the gate seldom view this as incompatible with nurturing any given student through the program when that student needs, and responds to, extra supports and attention. For gatekeepers who are social workers both by training and by professional identification, helping students to achieve their goals is second nature, and thus they may not even think of this as one of the functions of gatekeeping: It is just what a good faculty member or field instructor does to help students succeed and to support them in reaching their personal and career goals. These gatekeepers don't disagree with a strengths perspective; in fact, they undoubtedly implement it on a day-to-day basis as they interact with social work students in various capacities. However, their basic stance on gatekeeping as requiring closing the gate when necessary probably stems from unfortunate experiences with students who graduated from the program despite concerns that may have been voiced along the way.

The following example, written by a BSW program director on the BPD (baccalaureate program directors) listserver, eloquently and poignantly illustrates the urgency and critical nature of effective gatekeeping practices, as well as the reasons why some faculty think of gatekeeping as first and foremost a way to selectively close the gate to students whose fit with the requirements of professional practice is questionable.

> I recently received a communication from CSWE regarding academic and nonacademic criteria for dismissal from a BSW Program. Undoubtedly like many of you, our faculty have been having discussions about student performance standards, both for individual courses and overall program completion. We seem torn by conflicting goals. On the one hand, we want to produce well-prepared social workers. On the other, we are reluctant to give low grades or to terminate students who are performing poorly. We may view the student as client—we want to help them, to give them another chance. Or, as one faculty member stated, "Well, even if he graduates, probably no one will hire him anyway." I'd like to share a recent experience that has influenced my thinking on the importance of this issue.
>
> My oldest son, Dave, is now twenty-five. Immediately prior to his senior year in high school, we moved to a distant city, and he had to

spend that senior year in a new high school. It was a traumatic year, but he adapted and made new friends, one of whom was Mike. Mike came from a blue collar family and wasn't interested in attending college. In spite of that, he was bright and would graduate about 10th in his class from a large high school. When my son went away to school, Mike attended the local community college in a skilled trade program. Our home was close by, and he would frequently stop over to mooch a meal or just to talk. He became like a member of the family. I'd come home from work to find he had let himself in the house and was playing computer games, a luxury he did not have at his own home. I joked about adopting him so I could at least use him as a tax deduction. The following year, my son opted to attend the community college too, and so we saw even more of Mike. When Dave returned to . . . [XYZ] University, Mike got a job about 50 miles away, and the boys kept in close contact.

Occasionally Dave told me about the dumb stuff that Mike was doing. He joined a band 60 miles away. He bought a chipping machine to dispose of one little tree in the yard of his rental duplex. Then he bought a large, new car. We dismissed his behavior as growing pains of a sheltered kid who had to learn how to get by on his own. But in retrospect the signs were more ominous. Mike's parents were celebrating their thirtieth wedding anniversary. Mike was supposed to come home to bartend for the celebration. Home is 400 miles away, so when he didn't show up as scheduled, they waited. It wasn't like Mike to miss something like this. They called his apartment. Finally he answered the phone. Mike, the happy-go-lucky kid, was sitting on his bed with a shotgun in his hand ready to kill himself.

After emergency hospitalization, Mike returned home. He was under the care of the local community health center. He made some progress toward recovery but then suddenly left home on a trip through Wisconsin. He was eventually detained by authorities for a traffic offense. During the course of this spree he had been charging hundreds of dollars worth of Green Bay Packer gear and giving it away to kids. Eventually, he was released to his family and returned home. He was diagnosed as bipolar. His concerned parents took him to the Mayo Clinic where the diagnosis was confirmed, but for treatment, Mike would have to depend on the mental health resources of the local community.

For a year or so, Mike seemed to be managing. He had returned to his old grocery store job that he had held before graduating from the community college. He would see the psychiatrist for medication, and he had a case manager. The case manager was Bill, one of my own BSW graduates. I consult with the particular mental health agency on a weekly basis, so I would occasionally see Mike when he came in for appointments with Bill or the psychiatrist. I couldn't discuss the particulars of the case with Bill, but we did talk about his job, and I'd occasionally get comments from other staff. As a student, Bill had been "OK." He missed some classes, it was rumored that he had an occasional substance abuse problem, but his grades were good enough. They liked him in his field placement and even hired him.

Last week, I received a phone message from Mike's mother. She was near tears. Mike was back on the psych unit at the hospital. Would I go see him? I did, and over the last several days the story began to fall into place. Although Mike had been assigned to Bill as his case manager, Bill seldom saw his client. Appointments fell through; they had to be rescheduled. Bill was having "personal problems" of his own. Because Mike didn't demand to be seen, he fell through the cracks. The agency was reorganized; supervisors changed, and no one noticed that Mike wasn't being followed, that he was drinking, and that he wasn't taking his medication. When his behavior again became bizarre, it was his family that got him to the hospital. Fortunately, Mike is still alive, and he has the potential to recover, but I seriously question if this latest episode had to happen. There are multiple reasons, but high quality case management might have prevented the relapse. Now, when I go to see Mike on the psych ward, I see a young man who could just as well be my son, but I also see a person whose very life partially depends on the skill and professionalism of my BSW graduate.

I'm not sure what the answer is, but I know that I cannot be content with gatekeeping as, "Oh well, no one will probably hire him anyway." When you look at your graduates, not just your "star" students, but your run-of-the-mill BSW, are you willing to entrust them with the lives of those you love? Perhaps that should be our standard.

C. DeJong, electronic mail on
bpd listserver, March 2, 1999

As this illustration so clearly shows, avoidance of gatekeeping responsibilities can lead to potentially dangerous outcomes for an unwary public that entrusts the lives of loved ones to professional helpers. Thus, the primary intent of gatekeeping is to protect the public at large, who are left unsuspecting and vulnerable when an unsuitable student is credentialed and sanctioned to practice. Consequently, gatekeeping, at least in part, involves boundary maintenance. Sound gatekeeping policies protect the space between the primacy of public need and trust and the essential nature of professional responsibility. If we as faculty members misunderstand our role as gatekeepers and permit an unsuitable candidate for a degree to obtain that degree, we have abdicated our responsibility to society by minimizing the potential harm that could result.

To put our gatekeeping responsibility in its proper perspective, a short mathematical exercise may be helpful. As of March 1999 there were six hundred accredited and in-candidacy BSW and MSW programs-and the list keeps growing. But let's assume that as of that moment the growth of accredited programs permanently stalled. If annually each of these six hundred programs confers a social work degree on just one student who is ill suited for professional practice, in ten years we will have let loose on an unsuspecting public more than six thousand unsuitable practitioners nationwide. These sobering figures show that if we look at the mathematical ramifications alone, the potential cost of evading gatekeeping responsibilities is staggering. If the number of accredited programs continues to increase at the same pace we have witnessed in the past five to ten years, negligence in gatekeeping could have crushing repercussions on the lives of countless individuals who seek help.

BSW program directors figure prominently in the gatekeeping equation because of their critical role in helping faculty members to overcome their resistance and to move forward with sound gatekeeping policies and processes. Program directors shoulder a series of gatekeeping responsibilities that distinguish this administrative position. Their responsibilities include, at the very least, staying apprised of the legal dimensions that must guide a program's gatekeeping efforts; facilitating the creation of structures, policies, and processes for implementing effective gatekeeping in the program; aiding in the development of appeal (due process) procedures; and monitoring the implementation of gatekeeping standards once they are developed and approved by the faculty body. In addition, program directors also must ensure that institutional administrators are apprised of both the unique legal status of professional schools and the legal precedents that support extension of academic standards to include professional qualities and behaviors.

The growing complexities of gatekeeping, particularly in relation to gatekeeping's legal dimensions, often immobilize faculty. Rather than grapple with the variety of legal, ethical, administrative, professional, and curricular issues in order to establish sound and effective gatekeeping policies, faculty sometimes resort to taking the path of least resistance. They may decide to use grade point average (GPA) as the primary definer of competence and potential for professional success, a position that ignores some obvious pitfalls; for example, it begs the question of students who easily meet scholastic expectations but are ill suited for other dimensions of professional practice. For many faculty members the issue is quite simple: why struggle with the complexities of gatekeeping and go to all this effort when only an occasional student needs to be stopped at the gate? This attitude seems fairly prevalent, and it greatly impedes the development of sound gatekeeping policies and practices.

Gatekeepers and Their Constituencies

From a program director's perspective, selective admission and retention procedures represent a delicate balance of the diverse interests of the various constituencies involved in the enterprise of social work education. These groups include students, faculty, field instructors, academic administrators, quality assurance entities, and the clientele. Each of these constituencies holds key interests related to gatekeeping in social work education, and many face complex issues related to developing and implementing gatekeeping standards.

Students

As consumers of social work education, the admission and retention procedures in social work programs are a gateway to students' personal aspirations, career opportunities, state licensure for practice, and future entrance to advanced education. Also, the use of selective admissions tends to increase students' identification with and commitment to the profession because individual capability and potential for a career in the field are formally recognized and rewarded through sanctioned entry into the professional core classes. Students are proud of this initial accomplishment, and their investment in quality control seems to crystallize as a result.

When the process for selective admissions is somehow flawed and a student who is ill suited for the profession slips through the gate, it is not unusual for other students to express their concerns among each other or even privately to a faculty member. An E-mail from a student representing a University of Kansas (KU) group called Social Work Students Concerned About Retaining Ethics (S.C.A.R.E.) illustrates this point. The message, which was sent to more than forty BSW program directors, explained that S.C.A.R.E. was a new KU campus organization dedicated to safe-guarding and exploring the *NASW Code of Ethics*. The organiza-tion was in the process of reexamining the undergraduate admissions process because group members had some concerns about how to screen out students who appear unable to adhere to social work ethics and values and how to achieve diversity within the program (Martin, electronic mail, January 29, 1998). They put their message on-line in order to find out about admissions processes in other BSW programs and to discover whether or not other programs included standards on values and ethics as part of their admissions screening. This group's efforts illustrate each stu-dent's stake in their program's admission and retention processes. Other variables are also important.

Through sound gatekeeping procedures, students are able to demonstrate achievement of outcomes that lead to professional competence, which is extremely critical in order to effectively practice in a society whose problems have become increasingly severe. The nature of social dysfunction that must be addressed by entry-level social work practitioners has grown in complexity and scope over the two-decade history of accredited BSW programs. This phenomenon requires students to demonstrate higher levels of professional competence, a more extensive knowledge base, and a broader range of practice skills in order to function within the world of contemporary social work realities. Consequently, gate-keeping takes on increased significance in today's society.

Faculty

As the primary evaluators of students' cognitive abilities, affective capacities, value orientations, maturational levels, and mastery of professional competencies, faculty members' gatekeeping functions are highly significant. Our gatekeeping responsibility involves providing academic instruction and assessment of the students' performance in our classes. Additionally, as faculty we make judgments at various points in the program about performance in relation to potential for success, and we give professional counsel and guidance on career matters to every individual who seeks a social work degree.

We are credible and legitimized as gatekeepers because of our practice backgrounds, education, and expert knowledge. By the same token, our backgrounds and expertise in the field of social work give us special understanding of and sensitivity to the students, to their growth and development. If we stay strictly in our role as gatekeepers and thus negate our interpersonal connection to the student and our commitment to the student's development, it becomes easy to dismiss the emotional impact our actions have on individual students and to deny our role in facilitating a student's success. On the other hand, if we divorce ourselves from our commitment to society and focus primarily on our interpersonal connection to students, we may become negligent in our function as gatekeepers. We must achieve a balance, and we must be ever mindful of it as we carry out our charge.

As a logical extension of our gatekeeping responsibilities we must collaboratively develop and implement sound gatekeeping policies, procedures, and processes. It is at this juncture, however, that faculty encounter many stumbling blocks. In an era of mushrooming enrollments, limited fiscal resources, legislative mandates for increased workloads, and increased accountability for both faculty productivity and educational impact, the time-consuming tasks associated with conscientious gatekeeping find scant room on a plate that is already too full.

Many programs are rapidly expanding while resources are simultaneously diminishing, which leads to larger classes as well as increased teaching loads. These factors make it extremely difficult to get to know a large number of individual students other than through the work they produce or the GPA on their transcripts. It is difficult to make accurate assessments of any given student for gatekeeping purposes when the student may be a virtually "unknown quantity" to all or most of the faculty—sometimes to the extent that the student's name may not even elicit a visual image in anyone's mind when faculty meet to make admissions decisions. Consequently, faculty must design application materials that enable students to provide a clear picture of who they are and what their potential is for becoming an effective helper.

Field Instructors

The role of field instructors in gatekeeping efforts is often not explicitly and formally recognized (e.g., in the social work program's written policies). However, on the informal plane, sentiment generally takes a dramatic reversal when a problematic student slips through the admissions gate and into the program. Then, all too often, reluctant faculty gatekeepers suggest that the field will be able to "do something" about the problematic student at a later point in the curriculum, that is, during the field placement. Field instructors, on the other hand, are caught up in the various demands of their workplace and often feel only a tangential connection to the complexities of the educational enterprise. While many field instructors take their educational role during student field placements quite seriously, some become involved with the social work program primarily to acquire additional "staff" to help with the agency's myriad tasks and endeavors. This additional help is needed to ease the workload in the agency or to augment the services provided by employed staff, who are already stretched almost to the limits of their capacity.

The difficulties with gatekeeping during student field placements are further complicated when field instructors substitute their clinical function for their gatekeeping function while working with a student whose performance is weak or unsatisfactory. As practitioners, field instructors assume the roles of nurturer, facilitator, advocate, caregiver, and enabler on a daily basis with their clients. However inappropriate, these professional helper roles often become too prominent when field instructors work with students, or, even worse, these roles may take primacy in the student-supervisor relationship.

While judicious use of these roles in moderation with students helps them gain confidence and develop as professionals, overreliance on a helping relationship dynamic rather than a supervisory-educational dynamic in work with students during the field experience is problematic for several reasons. It blurs the boundaries of the respective functions of each role (i.e., social worker or supervisor) in relation to work with the student. This blurring leads to confusion about what the student can and should expect from the field instructor and about what the field instructor can and should do about a problem student. However, the weak or problem student may come to prefer the helping relationship dynamic with the field instructor because it is less threatening; that is, it probably will neither lead to termination from the placement nor result in an unsatisfactory evaluation for field performance. The field instructor who takes the role of a more traditional helper may be disinclined to "fail" a student because of the inconsistency of that action with the facilitative, enabling, and nurturing roles of the helper, a role that feels more comfortable and "natural" to social work supervisors. Faculty must work closely with field instructors to orient them to their role in the program as gate-keepers.

Academic Administrators

Management issues related to selective admission and retention become more convoluted as higher education faces external demands and controls, such as legal protections, accountability for outcomes, requirements for diversity among students, fiscal constraints, and issues of faculty autonomy. The many pulls and tensions created by external demands and controls force the institution's administrators to assume a conservative posture when it comes to giving guidance and counsel to programs that are trying to establish and enforce academic standards designed to safeguard the profession and its clientele.

When the call for more professionally appropriate standards sounds from the ranks of social work faculty, forward momentum is often met with resistance from the administrators of higher education, who tend to have little awareness of professional programs' special privileges to broadly define academic performance, as established through case law. Thus, administrators tend to favor clear-cut standards and screening criteria, such as grades, over those that address ethical and behavioral expectations, which they fear might leave the institution open to possible litigation. With little or no support from administrators, faculty members find themselves in reluctant collusion with the institution's "don't-rock-the-boat" position. Faculty must take responsibility for educating administrators on case law that applies to professional programs, the mandates of accreditation, and the faculty's role in gatekeeping.

Quality Assurance Entities

As the demands for professional accountability increase, the dictates of many groups external to the institution gain greater influence and control over educational programs within the institution. Some of these external entities include state, regional, and national accreditation bodies; licensure boards; certification groups; and other quality assurance bodies. Although educational programs are often blocked in their efforts to address professional gatekeeping in any but the most basic ways, quality control agencies paradoxically look to the educational program to provide assurance that the program's graduates are morally, ethically, and behaviorally suited for practice.

Clientele

As indirect beneficiaries of academic gatekeeping standards, clients are ultimately impacted by whether or not educational programs are able to screen out or terminate students whose suitability for a career in social work is compromised for any reason. Educators and institutions of higher education cannot and must not evade their professional responsibility or their legal obligation to protect the clientele from future social workers whose personal issues or deficits might interfere with competent social work practice. Only through application of appropriate quality control mechanisms in social work programs can educators carry out their commitment to clients, the profession, and society at large.

An Overview of the Issues

If faculty members' commitment to gatekeeping is a critical function of their role as educators, then what seems to keep them from fully carrying out their obligations? Why is it that faculty who have been in academia for any length of time can cite many cases of students having received their degrees against the better judgment of many of the faculty? What legal issues must faculty be aware of as they develop and implement gatekeeping processes? How do students' rights factor into the gatekeeping equation? How does the issue of achieving diversity in the student body relate to gatekeeping? Does field instruction give rise to any special gatekeeping concerns? What factors might lead to students losing access to professional education? These questions defy easy answers because of the complexities inherent in gatekeeping.

Legal Issues and Student Rights

Most faculty easily identify legal issues as the primary obstacle to effective gatekeeping. Today's litigious society coupled with a conservative political climate in academe dramatically compromises the commitment to gatekeeping. Foremost in this scenario is the fear of lawsuits. Pressures from institutional administrators and their legal counsels are barriers to the development of sound policies and practices that would allow programs to screen out or terminate students who are not suited for a career in social work. Moreover, faculty remain uninformed about legislation, such as the Americans with Disabilities Act and case law, that impact gatekeeping policies. Fear of doing something wrong often keeps faculty from doing anything at all.

Concerns about students' rights present another series of sticky wickets in gatekeeping, not because students' rights are not valued but because students' rights are often misunderstood or misinterpreted. Students, as well as many faculty members and administrators, believe that decisions that negatively impact tuition-paying students violate the students' rights. Access to a degree is seen as entitlement rather than as an opportunity. Carte blanche entitlement to a degree that sanctions professional practice in a human service arena is fraught with dangers that frequently go unrecognized.

Achieving Diversity

As social workers, faculty are committed to promoting social justice and eliminating institutional barriers that negatively impact disadvantaged and oppressed groups. Reconciling commitment to eliminate discriminatory practices against minority groups and commitment to gatekeeping in social work education is a challenging issue that frequently leaves faculty torn and bewildered. Some faculty take the position that affirmative action on behalf of minorities means lowering standards, if necessary, to ensure that minorities can enter the social work program and ultimately the profession. Conversely, some faculty view lowering standards for minorities as reverse discrimination because nonminorities who cannot meet the program's articulated standards are turned away while minorities with comparable or even lesser qualifications gain access.

According to many proponents of inclusionary strategies for achieving diversity in programs, a different perspective is called for with respect to what is meant by the term "excellence," as it relates to the abilities and qualifications of the students. Are we placing too much emphasis on the excellence of the candidate/applicant when we should instead devote our energies to ensuring the excellence of the graduate? A shift in our thinking allows us to conceive of excellence as the high performance of students at *exit from* the program rather than at *entry into* the program. Thus, rather than *students* "measuring up" at entry, the *institution or program* itself must measure up with respect to providing a sufficiently supportive curriculum and learning environment in order for students who are generally underserved and underrepresented to realize success in achieving their academic and career goals.

The issues inherent in achieving diversity illustrate how, in many respects and for obvious reasons, minority issues in gatekeeping are a particularly sensitive area for faculty and students alike.

Institutional Contexts and Program Policies

Gatekeeping does not occur in a vacuum; it is contextual. As previously noted, the context of academe involves a slew of pressures and tensions that sometimes countermand conscientious gatekeeping. In the face of such forces, faculty members may relinquish their gatekeeping responsibilities in favor of tasks that "count" in higher education, namely teaching, research, and service.

Other gatekeeping issues involve setting standards and developing policy. Faculty would like some assurance that the standards they set are, in fact, predictors of success in the program and in the field of practice. Impressionistic information suggests that GPA, for example, may not be as sound a predictor as we might wish, particularly if it is applied without more professionally oriented standards during screening and retention. An intellectually bright student does not necessarily become an effective practitioner who is interpersonally capable of establishing effective helping relationships. In the absence of data to guide the development of appropriate screening and retention policies, faculty either rely on hunches and intuition or establish criteria that are less apt to be challenged, such as GPA, completion of certain courses, standardized test scores, and the like.

Above and beyond setting appropriate and effective standards is the issue of identifying the various gatekeeping points in the program and matching the appropriate standards to those points. For instance, students should not be expected to demonstrate achievement of the expected outcomes at the point of entry into the program. In the same vein, evidence of *potential* for developing effective interpersonal relationships, for adhering to the code of ethics, and for establishing positive working relationships is sufficient at the point of admissions but insufficient at the end of the practicum. By the end of the practicum, that is, near the time of graduation, students need to be demonstrating more than mere *potential*. They must be able to demonstrate competence.

Field Instruction

The role of the field practicum and field instructors in the program's gatekeeping efforts is another thorny gatekeeping issue, although it should not be. Field instructors are essentially more than adjuncts to the program; they are an integral component of the educational endeavor. During field placements students test out classroom learning and demonstrate their abilities not only to apply those learnings but also to perform as a beginning professional. When programs sanction field instructors to supervise students, those field instructors become an extension of the academic faculty and carry comparable gatekeeping functions. However, as previously noted, a paradox sometimes occurs in this context. Academic faculty are inappropriately inclined to surrender gatekeeping responsibilities to field instructors while field instructors are sometimes disinclined to assume a gatekeeping role in their work with students.

Attitudes About Screening Students

An issue noted earlier is the program's basic approach to gate-keeping. Does the program take a basic screening-in or screening-out position during gatekeeping endeavors? A screening-in posture may mean that all students are nurtured through all screening points, whereas a screening-out posture involves stopping some students at any given screening point because they do not meet predetermined criteria and standards or because of some program constraint, such as limited resources. Either posture may be problematic under certain circumstances. For example, programs that consistently screen in students not only fail to meet accreditation standards but also violate the public trust. On the other hand, a screening-in posture may not be problematic if the program has the institutional supports to build student competence in areas where deficiencies exist. In the latter case, faculty are in the enviable position of focusing on the students' strengths at all gate-keeping points. Throughout the program the students' strengths are built upon with the help of various resources and services to awaken in students areas of untapped potential and to enable them to overcome any self-identified or faculty-identified deficits.

Not all programs that screen out students at the point of admission to the program do so because the criteria are not met. Some programs are compelled to screen out students at the point of admissions not because of any deficiency of an individual student, but simply because the number of acceptable applicants to the program exceeds the institutionally enforced enrollment cap on the program. Enrollment caps pose particularly painful issues for faculty because students who are at least minimally acceptable candidates for the degree must be turned away at a time when this country's social problems and social welfare needs are ballooning.

Institutional services and faculty time are finite resources, and at a growing number of institutions there are not enough of either to go around. Programs in these institutions, by necessity, must rely on a deficit model during gatekeeping activities: only the strongest students survive the gatekeeping cuts. For social workers turned academicians, this state of affairs is contrary to the basic tenets of the profession, but it is a reality over which there is little control.

Purpose and Overview of This Book

This book was conceived to equip faculty gatekeepers with the required knowledge, facts, and tools for carrying out their gate-keeping functions in a responsible and fair way. Since knowledge is power, information is the first step toward reaching this goal. Some of the gatekeeping approaches and tools discussed in this book are neither widely known nor frequently employed, such as comprehensive exit exams, psychometric tests, and portfolio assessments. We hope that faculty will explore their merits and their use based on the information we have included.

Because the task group that formed to write this book was an outgrowth of gatekeeping panels and networks that began in the Baccalaureate Program Directors Association, the book unfolded as a work devoted entirely to BSW-level education. However, the issues, tensions, concerns, and policies discussed in this book are not peculiar to BSW programs. They span BSW- and MSW-level education, so faculty in MSW programs also will find this book extremely useful.

There are no pat answers, easy solutions, road maps, or cook-book approaches to gatekeeping, regardless of the program level at which gatekeeping is implemented. In essence, "one size doesn't fit all." Institutional and programmatic policies vary from place to place; some are more restrictive than others. These policies gener-ally vary among programs because of the perspectives of the dif-ferent players at each institution and in each program. For instance, some programs run police checks on students, either at the point of admissions or prior to entry into the field practicum. Others do not run police checks and would not even consider doing so. The same holds true for the use of psychometric tests as part of gatekeeping processes. Some use such tests and swear by them; others find the very idea terribly disconcerting. Differences of opinion flourish even within the same institution. Not infre-quently, for example, tensions exist between the institution's legal counsel and the social work faculty, the former taking a more con-servative stance and the latter taking a more active stance. This dynamic greatly impacts how gatekeeping policies will be framed in that particular program.

Because of differences among institutions and programs varying inclinations of faculty, some of the issues and ideas discussed in this book will be viewed as very controversial. Actually, this book is designed to unveil as many controversial issues and ideas as the editors were able to identify. Faculty members need to have round-table discussions on all issues, exploring the pros and cons of each in relation to their respective institutional climates, program needs, and student populations.

Overview of the Book

This book is divided into four main sections. In this first section, "Background and Issues," the chapters that follow this introduction examine the issues that shape, impact, or obstruct gatekeeping functions and implementation in social work education. Gatekeeping is examined from several different vantage points, including historically, and a variety of gatekeeping approaches and attitudes are discussed. The critical nature of gatekeeping standards that include professional performance standards is a common theme. A topic of special concern, achieving diversity in higher education, stresses inclusionary strategies for achieving both equity and excellence in higher education. A review of the research literature reveals some of the primary issues associated with gatekeeping, and field instruction as a significant component of the curriculum in which gatekeeping problems often manifest is explored.

Whenever gatekeeping concerns are raised at conferences or in other contexts, the most compelling issue articulated with the greatest passion and the least knowledge is the legal dimension of gatekeeping. For this reason, section two of the book is devoted to comprehensive coverage of the "Legal Perspectives" that pervade gatekeeping in social work programs. This section includes a lengthy annotated list of case law that is germane to gatekeeping in professional programs and which will be helpful in working with an institution's legal counsel. The remaining chapters in this section conceptualize the landscape of gatekeeping legalities and provide practical suggestions for policy development and implementation. Actual student case examples illustrate how faculty members have addressed gatekeeping concerns in their home programs.

The third section of the book, "Strategies and Processes," provides practical suggestions and information to aid faculty members as they carry out their difficult charge as the profession's gatekeepers. Included in this section are discussions of drawing on local practitioners as resources during admissions screening, of using psychometric testing to assess the students' readiness and suitability for professional practice, and of developing program policies that permit sharing sensitive information about students with field instructors. Two useful approaches to the evaluation of student performance are examined in chapters on portfolios and comprehensive exit exams. A central feature of this section is a collaboratively written chapter that details the differences between two types of academic standards-scholastic and professional. Listed under each type of standard are illustrative program criteria, outcome statements as evidence of achieving each criterion, and measures useful in evaluating student outcomes.

Part four of the book, the appendixes, provides a wide selection of sample tools and policies that programs may find useful as they develop their own policies, forms, contracts, and guidelines for gatekeeping.

The traditional use of selective admission and retention policies to provide a quality control dimension is emerging as an even more significant concern facing social work education given contemporary fiscal, legal, and political realities. It is imperative that information about gatekeeping policies, procedures, and mandates stemming from case law and legislation become more widely available in order to facilitate gatekeeping efforts across the country. It is equally imperative that the issues implicit in the complex process of policy development undergo continual systematic evaluation, refinement, and discussion by program faculty.

Gatekeeping in social work education should occur throughout the program. It is inseparable from curriculum, faculty, students, field instructors, and institutional auspices. It cuts across CSWE's evaluative standards. Additionally, it converges with other program responsibilities, as illustrated by a not altogether surprising theme that emerged in the book. Chapter discussions of gatekeeping practices and approaches frequently led to discussions of evaluating educational outcomes, showing that the two are not mutually exclusive categories. The intersection of gatekeeping and outcome evaluation occurs primarily due to the use of various tools common to both endeavors, for example, psychometric tests, exit exams, portfolios, skill labs, student self-assessments, and the like.

The remaining chapters of this book are designed to take faculty on a journey of gatekeeping that promotes exploration and development of effective gatekeeping policies in their respective programs. Although the road will sometimes be bumpy, with sharp curves and steep inclines that must be navigated successfully, the outcome of those efforts should be well worth the travel across rough terrain. The National Task Group on BSW Gatekeeping Standards wishes you well as you undertake your individual journeys, which ultimately will serve each program in several ways: to protect students' rights, to attend to diversity concerns, to better meet accreditation standards, to aid in students' successful passage through the program, to meet legal requirements, and to provide assurance to the public that they are protected from helpers who do not belong in the profession of social work for one reason or another.

2

The Ethics of Gatekeeping

David Royse

A Contemporary Fable

A long, long time ago in a university far, far away a student enrolled in a social work program. He was a handsome, personable fellow with one of those gifts for speaking pleasantly and knowledgeably—most everyone was assured of his competence, sincerity, and integrity.

The student traveled many hours from his humble home each day, climbing hills, fording streams, and cutting paths through the woods to reach the fortress of higher learning. Possibly because he was also a full-time knight in an agency serving despairing and discouraged humankind, faculty were understanding and patient when he missed classes because of inclement weather, trolls, or because his steed had an appointment at the smithy.

Brave and hard-working (to hear his accounts), the student seemed destined for greater things—perhaps prince of a small realm of his own some day. He would be an alumnus who would give the learned social work faculty abundant reasons to be proud.

All went well until one day, during a routine midsemester visit to the student's practicum agency, the student's field instructor voiced a small complaint to his learned faculty liaison. Allowed to serve his internship in the evening hours after his supervisor had gone home, the confident and assertive student had been given assignments he could complete on his own. His supervisor trusted that he would faithfully and honestly record his time and perform his work. He was, after all, a student in the noble field of social work.

The field instructor even stayed past her normally scheduled work hours and risked the wrath of an evil husband-gnome so she could meet with the student for his weekly supervision. She hadn't complained that the student-knight missed about as many of these sessions as he kept; she understood that he was busy saving the poor and unfortunate, and he *did* travel a long way.

No, what bothered her more was that his assessments often were so generally written and vague that she felt either his pen was blunt and needed sharpening or, worse, his assessments were an exercise in creative fiction—he had never met with the clients assigned to him. She began checking.

What she found was that the student-knight wasn't meeting personally with his clients, he wasn't even coming to the place of healing and residence when scheduled. Alas, his armor was no longer shiny bright. When the student was confronted by the learned social work faculty, he had a ready excuse: he had been in the cafeteria, or the library, or in one of a dozen different places, always unavailable by phone.

Unfortunately for the student, he could produce no evidence that he had been in the agency on the occasions in question. He seemed to have lied not once, but many times. Ultimately, he received a failing grade in not only one but two field placements, and is no longer associated with the fortress of higher learning.

The Case for Gatekeeping

Part of our job as social work educators is to evaluate students' performance. Whether we like it or not, we are thrust into the role of gatekeeper. It is our responsibility to assess whether all students enrolled in our courses acquire the content necessary to function as social work professionals.

We educators pass or fail students based on criteria that are well reasoned and spelled out in our course syllabi. Students who are unable to complete the requirements for a social work degree and those we counsel out or terminate from our programs can be viewed as unsuitable for the profession. While we may differ on how "wide" or "narrow" the gate that opens to professional practice should be, every educator and every college or university with a social work program must be concerned that their graduates exit with certain minimum competencies and knowledge. The accreditation process is but one means by which we are held accountable for those we graduate as social workers. Other concerned parties may include our alumni, their parents, the agencies that hire and provide our students with field experience, their clientele, state licensing boards, and our college or university administrations. Each of these influential groups supplies, on occasion, feedback about how effective we are as social work educators.

However, we act as gatekeepers even before students are allowed into our classrooms. It is not uncommon for BSW programs to have admission standards. A minimum GPA of 2.0, for instance, is often required. In deciding whom to admit into our programs, we also decide who ought to be excluded. It would be entirely reasonable, for example, to refuse admission to convicted felons. Perhaps even a stronger case could be made against admitting a convicted child molester. Although there would seem to be good grounds for adopting exclusionist criteria based on legal violations (a study by Wellner and Albidin in 1981 found that forty-five of fifty state licensure boards would deny, revoke, or suspend the license of a psychologist for a felony conviction), such matters, as we shall see later, are more complex than they appear.

It would also seem to be very reasonable to keep out of our BSW programs known drug addicts and nonrecovering alcoholics as well as those who are mentally ill or incompetent. But what if someone had a problem in the past and has now recovered? What if the problem is held in check by medication? (See chapter 10 for a complete discussion of the Americans with Disabilities Act as it relates to gatekeeping in social work education.)

Professional mandates established by the National Association of Social Workers (NASW 1996) compel social workers to "discourage, prevent, expose, and correct the unethical conduct of colleagues" (18) and to "prevent the unauthorized and unqualified practice of social work" (25). Thus, the *NASW Code of Ethic* requires us to be gatekeepers—at the entry into a program, during the course of educational instruction, and no less so whenever we are made aware of a violation of our ethical code.

Consistent with that perspective, a Task Force on Quality in Graduate Social Work Education of the National Conference of Deans and Directors of Graduate Schools of Social Work (1984, cited in Hepler and Noble 1990) has stated that excellence in social work and social work education is "essentially a matter of ethical responsibility" that we educators have for protecting the public interest and promoting the general welfare" (126).

The best argument *for* gatekeeping and maintaining firm, uncompromising standards is that without them it is difficult to protect the vulnerable sections of society from dishonest, impaired, and incompetent students who would like to call themselves social workers. Most educators have encountered one or more of these students.

The Case of William, an Antisocial Personality

Consider the student we'll call William. William was not polished, sophisticated, or even very smart. He had shifty eyes that didn't engender trust, and he was inconsiderate, dropping in on faculty at every opportunity to make small talk. On one such visit he remarked that he had been fired from every job he had ever held. That term, he was working part-time at a liquor store.

A short time later, William took a gift, a bottle of wine, to a faculty member's house one evening and left it with his wife. He took a pint of whiskey to another faculty member and something else to a third. Several weeks later William visited again and complained he had been "laid off" because the liquor store owner wasn't making any money. Most likely he was fired for stealing.

William was not the type of student most of us would encourage to enter the field of social work. When an acquaintance, Jack, learned that William was a student in the social work program, Jack told of being invited to William's house and discovering that pornographic movies were playing on the television, although William and his wife had young children who wandered in and out of the room.

Even though program administrators were aware that William posed potential problems, he could not be denied a practicum placement. The reason? There were no charges, no hard evidence that he had violated the *NASW Code of Ethics* (1996). A review of his folder revealed no letters complaining about him or reporting illegal or unethical behavior. Officially, the university doesn't know about his improper, if not illegal acts, and cannot solicit such information to screen William out of the program.

Somehow, after one or two false starts, William completed his practicum requirements and graduated. Within months he experienced some difficulties in his new job; there were allegations of sexual imposition in his dealings with a minor. He retained an attorney and agreed to resign with no charges in his personnel folder. William is not presently working as a social worker and probably never should do so again. However, one wonders if he won't attempt to improve his luck, as an unemployed BSW, by applying to an MSW program.

Because of students like William, we social work educators *must* be vigilant regarding those who would abuse trust and power. We *must* accept the notion that gatekeeping is our responsibility as much as monitoring and documenting instances of poor judgment, fraud, and deception, moral turpitude, incompetence, and values in opposition to commonly accepted practice principles. We must not be naive and believe that *our* students would never do anything inappropriate.

Impaired Helpers

Impairment in professionals resulting from substance abuse, mental illness, and emotional stress is gaining attention. Deutsch (1985), for instance, found that more than half her sample of therapists (including social workers, psychologists, and counselors) reported significant problems with depression: 24 percent had been in therapy because of depression; 11 percent reported substance abuse problems. In a review of studies on the topic, Pope (1988) estimated that about 8 percent of male therapists reported sexual contact with their clients.

Although our social work literature only recently acknowledged the issue of impairment (Reamer 1992), there is no reason to suspect that social work would have fewer problems with impaired professionals than allied fields. We also have a code of ethics that requires that social workers seek consultation and get help if personal problems or mental health difficulties begin to interfere with their professional judgment and performance.

Though few studies document social workers with impairments, there is an increasing amount of data suggesting that traumatic events early in life may be associated with the selection of social work as a career (Black, Jeffreys, and Hartley 1993; Lackie 1983; Marsh 1988; Rompf and Royse 1994; Russel et al. 1993). Similarly, Pope and Feldman-Summers (1992) found that one third of a sample of five hundred clinical and counseling psychologists reported having experienced some form of sexual or physical abuse as a child or adolescent.

As social work educators, we should not allow students whose impairments will interfere with their professional judgment and performance to graduate from our programs. We must not pass the buck and hope that some day a licensing board will stop those likely to be dangerous or harmful. Licensure boards can't do it all. In fact, in some areas they do very little other than conducting examinations and screening applications.

Keith-Spiegel and Koocher (1985) in their chapter on incompetent and troubled psychologists have noted, "the evidence tends to refute the claim that licensing protects the public." They go on to explain, "except for the most populous states, licensing boards are often so overworked and underfunded that disciplinary enforcement is nearly impossible except in the most flagrant cases of abuse or misconduct" (235).

Similarly, Berliner (1989), in a study of individual ethics cases filed with NASW Committees on Inquiry between 1979 and 1985, found that state regulatory boards initiated less than 1 percent of all complaints.

Towle (1954) provided a good case for educators' ethical responsibility to act as gatekeepers: "A professional person's services are sought because he has a competency, a mastery of knowledge and skill, which the recipient of the service does not have" (4). If we educators knowingly allow unqualified and incompetent students to go into our communities and practice as social workers, we are guilty twice: for deceiving the American public and for permitting them to be harmed.

The Ethical Dilemma of Gatekeeping

The thought of screening out, choosing this student and rejecting that one, is distasteful, if not abhorrent, to many social work educators. The main reason, I believe, is that we strongly believe in and adhere to our fundamental values: Every individual has a right to be accepted as he or she is; each one is deserving of consideration and respect. Because of confidentiality, we can't always reveal information that we have in our possession. Most important, maintaining a nonjudgmental attitude means that we avoid passing judgment on people. Our values and code of ethics call upon us to foster maximum self-determination.

Similarly, Peterman and Blake (1986) observe, "We have been socialized into being non-judgmental, fighting for the underdog and the oppressed; however, this may take the form of graduating inappropriate students" (33).

Several years ago, I heard of a female undergraduate student interning as a social worker in a high school. It was her misfortune to be caught "making out" with a high school senior. They were discovered after hours by the principal in his office. This brief example suggests a number of issues. First of all, was the social work program at fault for teaching that sexual misconduct was a behavior in which only *men* could be the offenders? Had it been made abundantly clear that female social workers are equally at fault when they engage in sexual activities with their clients? Indeed, had the program dealt with the issue at all? Second, because there was no harm, no complaining client, should this little indiscretion have been overlooked—attributed to the social work student's lack of maturity? She was, after all, only a few years older than the high school senior. Do we rationalize, saying to ourselves, "She's young; she won't make that mistake again"? Do we give her another chance?

Had the students been sitting in a parked car or in the BSW student's apartment, probably no one would have been the wiser. But because the BSW student was engaging in unprofessional behavior in a place where she was expected to conduct herself as a social work professional, the dilemma is in deciding whether this one incident is a one-time lapse of judgment or the first evidence of a troubling inclination to engage in hedonistic, self-serving behavior.[1] If we knew that the BSW student had previously been considered a "good" student, should we social work educators provide a word of caution but allow her to proceed unimpeded through the social work program? Or should we dismiss her from the program because of a violation of one of the ethical standards in the NASW code: "Social workers should under no circumstances engage in sexual activities or sexual contact with current clients, whether such contact is consensual or forced" (NASW 1996:13)?

If we think of the student as an inexperienced, immature individual deserving special consideration, and we sincerely believe in her worth and potential, we are likely to be very uncomfortable labeling her unfit or unsuitable to practice social work. At best, we might acknowledge that her actions were improper, but with infinite respect for the individual, we may separate a single instance of inappropriate behavior from the whole of her worth. And, as a result, we would likely give her a second chance, overlook this one episode. But should we? Would we be so quick to overlook a violation of our professional standards if the BSW student had been a male and the high school student a female?

In this particular case, the faculty field liaison placed the BSW student in a different practicum agency, and she was not allowed to count the hours previously accumulated at the high school. It meant that the student had to work several weeks after the end of the semester—not much of a reprimand. No note, no letter, nothing "official" went into her folder. However, the faculty liaison could also have given the student a failing grade for that one practicum course, which would have added an additional semester to the amount of time required to graduate. Such an action might have served as the catalyst for the BSW student to examine anew her interest in and motivation for a social work career. Maybe at that point she might have selected herself out of the program.

A more severe measure would have been to discharge the student from the social work program. Such an action would demonstrate to our students, their clients, and the community around us that ethical behavior is a serious matter and that violation of professional standards has major repercussions.

1An excellent resource for untangling issues of professional boundary violations is Marilyn Peterson's *At personal risk: Boundary violations in professional-client relationships* (New York: Norton, 1992).

When we are not serious about ensuring that our students abide by ethical standards, we weaken and dilute the profession by lowering its reputation and prestige. Brighter, superior students don't want to be associated with those they consider less than competent. Students who see violations of professional practices and note our reluctance to enforce standards lose respect for us as faculty and social workers. Our *NASW Code of Ethics* is not just a guide to professional conduct, it is a set of criteria by which social work practice can be evaluated (Cobb 1994; Levy 1976)

We create difficulties for ourselves and are unable to perform the necessary gatekeeping when we view students as our clients. Born and Carroll (1988) argue that practically and ethically our clients are not the students; our clients are the recipients of our graduates' services. While good arguments can be made either way, viewing the public as our clients would likely result in less cognitive dissonance with our values and our purpose as educators and would free us to engage in more spirited and enthusiastic gatekeeping. Ultimately, such a perspective affords the public a much higher degree of protection from those unsuited to practice the profession of social work.

Even if students and not the public were our primary clients, we must not let our interest in producing graduates from our programs interfere with our professional objectivity. As Levy (1976:136) has articulated so well,

> another important ethical principle involves objectivity toward clients. The social worker is enjoined, according to this principle, against letting extraneous interests or biases affect his professional decisions and actions in relation to his client. . . . Any risk of insufficient objectivity may mean less than the best service or less than the unbiased service that the social worker can offer a client and that the client may need.

What Can We Do to Promote Ethical Standards?

At a minimum, the *Code of Ethics* should be distributed to students going into every practice course and every practicum and should be discussed at some length, preferably with some examples or vignettes that prompt students to react and raise questions. Assigned papers should require students to contemplate ethical issues and aspects suggested in their cases and case material. Levy (1976) suggests that "students should have the opportunity in both classes and field instruction to suffer the discomfort of uncertainty with respect to the ethical choices they must make, and of inner and outer tension with respect to the consequences of the ethical choices they will have made" (230).

There is no reason to assume that students are well informed or instructed regarding ethics. Indeed, the few studies available seem to suggest an appalling lack of recognition of ethical dilemmas and usefulness of the *Code of Ethics* as a guide to ethical problem-solving. Holland and Kilpatrick (1991) interviewed twenty-seven practicing social workers to explore the experiences and relationships that shaped their ethical development and value commitments. They found that "not a single respondent offered the profession's code of ethics as a resource for helping to deal with complex ethical issues" (140).

Lindsay (1985, cited in Slimp and Burian 1994) asked psychology graduate students to listen to taped, scripted interviews of therapist-client interactions. Although the students were not prompted to listen for the ethical dilemmas built into the interviews, nearly 50 percent failed to recognize the ethical concerns.

Berliner (1989) states that "anecdotal and other evidence indicates that few NASW members have read or are familiar with provisions of the Code of Ethics" (70). He later argues that the code is "so unfamiliar . . . that it fails to serve as an ethical guide" (71). Clearly, if the code is to guide practice, we educators must give students a working knowledge of it: the *Code of Ethics* cannot be treated as just another class handout.

Content of expected professional behavior must not be left to chance. Congress (1992) speculates that field instructors who received their degrees a number of years ago may not be stressing social work ethics as much as we might want or expect. Obviously, field instructors and faculty need to engage in a dialogue about the importance of teaching ethical decision making to students; they should jointly develop plans to provide students with opportunities for learning about and understanding the ethical conflicts that occur in social work practice. Professional development seminars can help staff and students "sharpen ethical decision-making skills" (Slimp and Burian 1994:44).

If we are serious about enforcing the *Code of Ethics,* we must establish a formal process that outlines how reports of problematic behavior and questions about ethical issues can be documented and conveyed to an academic hearing committee. If there is no standing committee within the program to review allegations of ethics violations, one should be created. Even flagrant violations may be overlooked and forgotten when there is no procedure in place to review allegations. Indeed, of the three case examples presented so far, only in the first case was a special committee appointed to hear the charges. That may help to explain why no action was taken on the other two.

In an article outlining the legal issues involved in dismissing students, Madden (1993) notes that courts expect due process: students are entitled to hearings prior to academic dismissal. However, virtually any form of hearing is sufficient as long as the process is not arbitrary and capricious on the part of the institution. Social work programs must develop their own procedures in such cases.

Cole (1991) also addresses the legal issues associated with gatekeeping and student admissions, pointing out that in our search for "suitable" applicants we cannot exclude students solely on the basis of an admission to a mental hospital or prior chemical dependency. However, schools do have the right to insist upon sobriety and to set minimal standards that must be met by *all* students, regardless of protected classifications or other special circumstances.

Whether or not we are successful in getting our administrators to create standing committees to review instances of unethical and unprofessional practice, each of us can determinedly assess competence in our classes and practicum sections. In the first disguised case that opens the chapter, the polished and sophisticated but unethical student probably could have easily graduated from the program with a high grade point average—had it not been for a field instructor who took seriously her responsibility of overseeing students' performance within the agency. It was her concern about the *quality* of the work produced that led to the discovery of problems in other areas. It was her sense of ethical responsibility to the profession that led her to confront the student and request that his practicum at her agency end.

Unfortunately, this student would have passed through most BSW admission screenings. Probably no amount of vigilance at program entry would have detected him as potentially problematic. However, it is very likely that such students can be detected in their field placements—*if* administrators, educators, faculty liaisons, and field instructors are sincerely interested in assessing competence.

Madden (1993) observes that difficult legal issues do not usually arise from fair and impartial admissions procedures or from the dismissal of grossly inappropriate or unethical students, but from students who pass most of their academic courses and fall short of field expectations. The field experience is the best "window" we have for observing and determining competence. Field instructors and faculty liaisons to the field agencies have a weighty responsibility. Their tasks are made easier with clear behavioral expectations regarding skills and competencies to be acquired by students. (Chapter 6 fully explores the place of field instruction in gatekeeping efforts.)

Finally, we need more research on ethical dilemmas and ethical decision making. According to MacKay and O'Neill (1992) there has been "relatively little examination of exactly what an ethical dilemma is" (227). Dolgoff and Skolnik (1992) reviewed all the issues of *Social Work with Groups* and found only one article focused specifically on an ethical issue. Holland and Kilpatrick (1991) note that "the profession suffers from a lack of systematic studies of ethics in practice. Little is known about how practitioners respond to moral and ethical issues, how they understand and cope with these aspects of their work, and what resources are used or needed for improving performance in this area" (138).

Discretion and Choice in Gatekeeping

Having argued that the ethical position for us as social work educators is to hold firm in our expectation of professional behavior and to be vigilant in monitoring and reporting infractions, let me now address the other side of the coin. For completely altruistic reasons, we may decide to overlook areas of incompetence.

During her junior year in college Daphne survived a multicar accident that fractured her skull and spine. With paralyzed legs and limited use of her arms, she resumed her college education in social work with the assistance of a motorized wheelchair and an attendant twice a day. Unfortunately, traumatic injury to her brain also left Daphne with cognitive impairments. To compound her problems, the emergency tracheotomy and tubes forced down her throat permanently damaged her vocal cords, and Daphne was unable to speak beyond a barely perceptible whisper. In order to make herself heard, Daphne would suddenly arch her back and with great willfulness project her voice toward the ceiling. To an unprepared bystander, she often appeared to be having a seizure.

Daphne desperately wanted to live independently and to finish college; she told one instructor that she would take his course again and again, as many times as it took until she passed it. Her faculty field liaison had a difficult time finding a suitable agency for her internship. One was finally secured that did not require Daphne to have any client contact. Procedures were bent, expectations were lowered, and she was allowed to stay in that placement both semesters. Her perseverance paid off. Daphne graduated at the end of five years with a GPA of 2.16.

The consensus of the faculty was that Daphne would never be hired as a social worker and for that reason "bending" the rules and lowering the expectations regarding Daphne's performance did not seem to trouble any of the faculty. Had the faculty insisted that Daphne demonstrate the same level of competence as other students in the program, it is very likely she never would have received her BSW.

Did the faculty do the right thing in passing Daphne in each course? This is not an easy question to answer. Daphne may or may not ever be employed as a social worker. If she obtains employment, her employer will have decided that she can perform a specific job after closely assessing both her abilities and disabilities. She will not be hired with a quick interview and by merely presenting her BSW diploma, as happens with some graduates.

It could be argued that the faculty did Daphne no favor. If she is unable to find a job as a social worker, is the faculty to blame for leading her to believe that she could function on a professional level? If she is unable to secure employment, would it have been less cruel to have counseled her out of the program? Ethically, our profession expects each practitioner to be competent and for each of us "to act to prevent the unauthorized and unqualified practice of social work" (NASW 1996:25). But we also are called upon to prevent and eliminate discrimination and "to expand choice and opportunity for all people, with special regard for vulnerable, disadvantaged, oppressed, and exploited people and groups" (NASW 1996:27).

Competence and admission standards that are too rigid can come across as the products of uncaring and unsympathetic bureaucracies. Rigid standards don't allow our humanity to emerge; they can hold back and exclude from participation those who are differently abled and those who have the potential to succeed although they have not previously revealed it.

However, there is obviously a difference between making an occasional exception or bending the standards a little and not having any kind of admission or competence standards in the first place. When there is no minimum grade point expectation and no interview to inquire about students' motivations, their prior experiences in helping others, their interests in working in traditional social work fields of practice, we prop open the admission gate so wide that insincere and undesirable students enter.

Moore and Urwin (1991) present a rather comprehensive gatekeeping model for baccalaureate programs that includes an evaluation conference to determine the students' readiness for field placement. Faculty discuss a wide variety of topics with each student, such as academic performance and extenuating circumstances affecting performance, volunteer experience and goals for the field experience, reasons for choosing social work, attitudes and behaviors in need of attention, special interests, and preference of client populations with which to work. Faculty evaluate several areas during the conference: academic performance, sense of responsibility, communication skills, social work values, and ability to handle feedback.

Following the individual conferences and assessments, faculty decisions include approving a student for a particular field site, postponing field education, or removing the student from the program. Postponement may result when students are assessed as immature, academically marginal, in need of more volunteer experience, or when students have changed majors or transferred late in their academic careers. Students with personal issues to resolve may be asked to wait a year before reapplying. Because the decision is made by a committee, students who are dismissed from the program receive the deliberations of the faculty as a group, and a potentially arbitrary individual decision is avoided.

Moore and Urwin caution that their gatekeeping model is time-consuming and intense. Implementation requires the support of faculty and university administrators as well as inclusion of the evaluation process in all program literature. They recommend educating administration officials about the legal precedents noted by Cobb and Jordan (1989) that student "conduct, character, and psychological fitness" (91) can be considered in academic evaluations.

When a program is this diligent in its evaluation process, students cannot help but regard the transition from classroom to field education with great seriousness.

Grades and Test Scores as Screening Criteria

In our university, the social work program is popular with the athletic department. That concerns me—not because I believe that athletes can't become wonderful social workers, but because in a large university being an athlete on scholarship is a full-time job. And sports are not played for fun or recreation, but as a means to acquire wealth. These athletes do not hide the fact that they want to play for the NBA or the NFL. Visions of big bucks dance in their heads; most of these athletes have no interest in becoming social workers. What do they care about the *NASW Code of Ethics*? Some of them don't even care about graduation, it's the professional drafts that have their attention. Do we gatekeepers make it too easy to choose social work as a major? Gibbs (1994) reported on a survey of BSW programs and their screening mechanisms. She found that 88 percent of those programs with a formal admissions process specified that their admissions criteria required an overall GPA of at least a C but less than a B, and 46 percent of these programs required only a C average.

The potential to do well in a program or to perform adequately as a social worker may not always be measured by academic criteria. A colleague argued this point by telling her personal account—of not being in the top 10 percent of her high school class and not having the test scores necessary to get admitted to a noted midwestern university. However, she was admitted to and attended its sister school. Under a reciprocal agreement between the two schools, she took a number of her courses at the more prestigious school. Not only did she do well in those classes, she often did better than the students who had been admitted to the more celebrated of the two schools. Although high academic criteria kept my colleague from attending the prestigious university, these criteria did not measure her desire to obtain superior grades in college or her ability to perform in her chosen career.

Should We Use Values for Screening Criteria?

Several years ago I spent a little time developing an instrument to assess social workers' values. It was my intent to design an objective means for measuring who had the "proper" values to be a social worker and who didn't. Preliminary results indicated that students in an introductory social work course had lower scores than students who had completed several social work courses. Delighted with these findings, I argued for using the instrument to eliminate the athletes and other insincere students from our social work program. An associate on the committee with me, a graduate of a Lutheran seminary and the University of Chicago, looked over my instrument and said, "You know, I don't think I would have passed a values test at the point when I applied to my MSW program."

Even though I think it is possible to assess with some precision whether a student has social work values, my colleague made a good point. After all, students enroll in our programs so we can *educate* them. Screening for inappropriate values at entry into a social work program may be like expecting a calf to give milk. A question we need to resolve is: at what point in the social work program do we administer a values test? Before students enter field placements? Before students exit our programs? I don't know.

Certainly, important learning occurs in field placements. This learning is apt to make social work values come alive for students in a way that classroom discussion of hypothetical cases does not. On the other hand, if a student doesn't have social work values by the end of the last field placement, what recourse do faculty and program administrators have then? Is there some remedial course we could require these students to complete? Screening for social work values is obviously a complex issue and should not be adopted rashly as a means to exclude students from our programs.

Although the issue is complex, we shouldn't avoid classroom discussions of topics like abortion, homosexuality, welfare dependency, racism, capital punishment, and others that will "test" the beliefs and values of our students. This allows them to decide whether they could be impartial and objective in working with persons whose value orientations and lifestyles are different from their own. Indeed, rich and fruitful discussions can help students realize, in some instances, that their attitudes are not consistent with social work's values.

The Gatekeeper: A Lonely Sentry

Because of fear of litigation and charges of discrimination, many social workers are afraid to be candid and put in writing what they know or have observed about improper and illegal actions of social work students. Although it is not possible to share all the details of the cases presented earlier, suffice it to say that *several* social workers had ample opportunity to initiate charges against William and the student-knight for various violations of the *NASW Code of Ethics*. None did.

The conscientious social work educator has a lonely role for reasons other than fear of litigation: universities and their administrators often appear to be more interested in numbers—state appropriations frequently are based on enrollment-than in screening out students who do not aspire to the standards expected of a professional social worker.

Concerns about not weeding out students at admission is a topic beginning to appear with some frequency in the literature: "There is evidence that schools of social work fail to screen applicants adequately" (Hepler and Noble 1990:126). Cole and Lewis (1993:150) state, "The review of professional literature has revealed that limited research on the termination of students has been published, and the few studies available clearly indicate that termination is almost nonexistent." Along this line, Peterman and Blake (1986) surveyed nine BSW programs in New Jersey and found that over a five-year period fewer than 3 percent of the students were dismissed or counseled out of those programs.

At the same time, applications to graduate programs in social work fell between 1975 and 1984 while admission rates increased from an acceptance of 41 percent to a conservative estimate of about 70 percent. The actual acceptance rate could be 80 percent or higher since many individuals apply to more than one program (Born and Carroll 1988). In 1982 Ginsberg reflected, "I have been puzzled over the years by being told that the number of applicants is down but that the quality is better. The explanation for this phenomenon has always escaped me" (9).

If universality in admissions has become normative in BSW programs as well, we educators have an even greater responsibility to monitor students for unprofessional behavior and values than in the past. However, gatekeeping should not be conceptualized as an activity limited to admitting or rejecting applicants to our programs. Born and Carroll (1988) argue that gatekeeping should continue through graduation and licensure.

When I caught two students cheating on an exam at another university, the head of the program informed me that he was uncomfortable with my failing them. Indeed, he would not support me in even giving them even a D. Given several more weeks to prepare for *another* "final" exam, neither student got less than a C. Was this an isolated incident? I think not. At various times colleagues have reported to me that they have been instructed *not* to give low or failing grades to certain students. Sometimes the student is an athlete or a member of a minority group, but that need not be the case. What do you do with a student, the daughter of a powerful state senator, who doesn't attend class or who repeatedly sleeps through it? Do you give her the grade she deserves? Or try to convince yourself that she probably won't ever practice social work and give her the grade she needs to graduate?

In a political bureaucracy such as a university, administrators have been known to advise untenured professors not to "rock the boat" and caution that "the nail that sticks up gets pounded down." In such situations, faculty may not feel it is politically expedient to call attention to themselves by pursuing an ethics violation charge against a student. What happens to the faculty member's reputation if a committee does not uphold his or her charge against a student? And what happens to enrollment when the word gets out that social work students can be kicked out of the program—not because of low grades, but because of just one incident involving poor judgment?

As an educator, I must admit to liking rigid, inviolate standards. Cheating on a test, for instance, should always result in a failing grade. Students who engage in or who attempt to engage in sexual activities with clients violate the *NASW Code of Ethics* and should *always* be dismissed from a social work program. Life is made simpler when there are rules and boundaries demarcating appropriate and inappropriate behavior. Unfortunately, more than standards are required: it takes courage to confront students who violate ethical standards, to refuse admission to marginal students, and to fail those who lack competence.

Gatekeeping is not just difficult for social work educators. In a study of clinicians, 42 percent reported offering help or referring impaired colleagues to therapists, but only 8 percent had ever reported an impaired colleague to a regulatory body (Wood et al. 1985).

The last case I want to present is illustrative of the ethical dilemmas attendant on gatekeeping. A BSW program received an application from a man, a convicted felon, who had served two years in prison for child molestation. Attached to his application was a poignant letter in which he professed his innocence, explaining that he and his wife had been going through a divorce and that in an act of anger she had accused him of molesting his stepdaughter during a bath. The letter went on to explain that after he was sent to prison his exwife attempted to recant her testimony, but the judge would not allow it. Even his daughter protested that she had not been abused. After he served his time, husband and wife were remarried and the daughter chose to live with them instead of with her biological father and stepmother. It was at this point that the application was made to the BSW program. Two members of the faculty interviewed both the prospective student and his wife. She verified his version of events as elaborated in his letter, specifically stating she did not believe that he had ever sexually abused her daughter.

The faculty of that university went through a process for making ethical decisions that is instructive for others. They identified the parameters of the problem, fleshing out all the potential issues involved. They discussed existing university and program admission standards as well as the relevant values. Then they debated their alternatives and the consequences of each course of action. Ultimately, they decided to admit the student.

Ralph was a model social work student and did so well in his final field placement that the agency offered him a job. However, the offer was quickly rescinded once agency management learned that he was a convicted felon. Several years later Ralph was still unable to find employment. Even though the BSW program faculty made the very best decision they could—consulting others, asking for additional information, discussing their values and concerns, and brainstorming the consequences of their final decision—the faculty had no guarantee that Ralph wouldn't be arrested a second time for child molestation.

Morally, if we follow Loewenberg and Dolgoff's (1988) ordering of social work values, protecting life and vulnerable populations is a higher good than facilitating the autonomy and self-determination of an individual (in this case, the convicted felon). Philosophically, allowing a student such as Ralph into a BSW program bestows trust and power (particularly if the degree requirements are completed) that place him in a position to do greater harm than might occur if he were urged to find another career. However, it cannot be said that the faculty did anything unethical. Indeed, there was strong sentiment among faculty that it would have been unethical *not* to admit this man.

Was he really guilty? We'll never know, but that's not the point. Our profession obligates us to engage in a *process* though which we attempt to discern the best possible course of action whenever we face two conflicting decisions. When we go through a deliberate process that is objective and impartial like the one used by the faculty in this example (others have been suggested by Loewenberg and Dolgoff 1988; Tymchuk 1982), then we have discharged our ethical obligation—no matter whether the final decision is to admit or to reject.

How do we know when we are doing the right thing? We don't always know, and in some cases we may never know. Sometimes we're proven wrong. A basketball player whom I failed in one course and never would have admitted into the program has returned on several occasions to talk to me about his job as a social worker in Chicago. A student with severe physical impairments, very much like those of Daphne described earlier, was hired by a branch of the government to review the completeness of employment applications. I'm glad to admit that sometimes I'm wrong. These little discoveries force me to examine my own biases and prejudices.

Because I know that not all of us may share the same value orientations, I trust an open process that attempts to be impartial, where different views and arguments can be expressed. As we struggle with the complex issues of gatekeeping, let's understand that none of us have to make these decisions alone. All of us do, however, have a responsibility not only to teach about the *NASW Code of Ethics*, but also to act as role models, demonstrating ethical professional behavior, and to become involved whenever we detect inappropriate, incompetent, or unethical students. We can do little more—and must do no less.

References

Berliner, A. K. (1989). Misconduct in social work practice. *Social Work* 34:69–72.

Black, P. N., Jeffreys, D., and Hartley, E. K. (1993). Personal history of psychosocial trauma in the early life of social work and business students. *Journal of Social Work Education* 29:171–180.

Born, C. E., and Carroll, D. J. (1988). Ethics in admissions. *Journal of Social Work Education* 24 (1): 79–85.

Cobb, N. H. (1994). Court-recommended guidelines for managing unethical students and working with university lawyers. *Journal of Social Work Education* 30:18–31.

Cobb, N. H., and Jordan, C. (1989). Students with questionable values or threatening behavior: Precedent and policy from discipline to dismissal. *Journal of Social Work Education* 25:87–97.

Cole, B. S. (1991). Legal issues related to social work program admissions. *Journal of Social Work Education* 27:18–24.

Cole, B. S., and Lewis, R. G. (1993). Gatekeeping through termination of unsuitable social work students: Legal issues and guidelines. *Journal of Social Work Education* 29:150–159.

Congress, E. P. (1992). Ethical decision making of social work supervisors. *The Clinical Supervisor* 10 (1): 157–169.

Deutsch, C. (1985). A survey of therapists' personal problems and treatment. *Professional Psychology: Research and Practice* 16:305–315.

Dolgoff, R., and Skolnik, L. (1992). Ethical decision making, the NASW Code of Ethics, and group work practice: Beginning explorations. *Social Work with Groups* 15:99–112.

Gibbs, P. (1994). Screening mechanisms in BSW programs. *Journal of Social Work Education* 30:63–74.

Ginsberg, M. I. (1982). Maintaining quality education in the face of scarcity. *Journal of Education for Social Work* 18 (2): 5–11.

Hepler, J. B., and Noble, J. H. (1990). Improving social work education: Taking responsibility at the door. *Social Work* 35:126–133.

Holland, T. P., and Kilpatrick, A. C. (1991). Ethical issues in social work: Toward a grounded theory of professional ethics. *Social Work* 36:138–144.

Keith-Spiegel, P., and Koocher, G. P. (1985). *Ethics in psychology: Professional standards and cases.* Hillsdale, N.J.: Lawrence Erlbaum.

Lackie, B. (1983). The families of origin of social workers. *Clinical Social Work Journal* 11:309–322.

Levy, C. S. (1976). *Social work ethics.* New York: Human Sciences Press.

Lindsay, R. T. (1985). Moral sensitivity: The relationship between training and experience. Paper presented at the annual meeting of the American Psychological Association, Los Angeles.

Loewenberg, F. M., and Dolgoff, R. (1988). *Ethical decisions for social work practice.* Itasca, Ill.: Peacock.

MacKay, E., and O'Neill, P. (1992). What creates the dilemma in ethical dilemmas? Examples from psychological practice. *Ethics & Behavior* 2:227–244.

Madden, R. (1993). Protecting all parties: A legal analysis of clinical competency and student dismissals. *Journal of Law and Social Work* 3 (1): 1–13.

Marsh, S. R. (1988). Antecedents to choice of a helping career: Social work vs. business majors. *Smith College Studies in Social Work* 58:85–100.

Moore, L. S., and Urwin, C. A. (1991). Gatekeeping: A model for screening baccalaureate students for field education. *Journal of Social Work Education* 27:8–17.

National Association of Social Workers (NASW). (1996). *NASW code of ethics.* Washington, D.C.: NASW.

National Conference of Deans and Directors of Graduate Schools of Social Work. (1984). *Towards excellence in graduate social work education in the United States* (Report of the Task Force on Quality in Graduate Social Work Education). New York: National Conference of Deans and Directors of Graduate Schools of Social Work.

Peterman, P. J., and Blake, R. (1986). The inappropriate BSW student. *Aretê* 11 (1): 27–34.

Pope, K. S. (1988). How clients are harmed by sexual contact with mental health professionals: The syndrome and its prevalence. *Journal of Counseling and Development* 67:222–226.

Pope, K. S., and Feldman-Summers, S. (1992). National survey of psychologists' sexual and physical abuse history and their evaluation of training and competence in these areas. *Professional Psychology: Research and Practice* 23:353–361.

Reamer, F. G. (1992). The impaired social worker. *Social Work* 37:165–170.

Rompf, E. L., and Royse, D. (1994). Choice of social work as a career: Possible influences. *Journal of Social Work Education* 30:163–171.

Russel, R., Gill, P., Coyne, A., and Woody, J. (1993). Dysfunction in the family of origin of MSW and other graduate students. *Journal of Social Work Education* 29:121–129.

Slimp, P. A. O., and Burian, B. K. (1994). Multiple role relationships during internship: Consequences and recommendations. *Professional Psychology: Research and Practice* 25 (1): 39–45.

Towle, C. (1954) *The learner in education for the professions: As seen in education for social work.* Chicago: University of Chicago Press.

Tymchuk, A. J. (1982). Strategies for resolving value dilemmas. *American Behavioral Scientist* 26:159–175.

Wellner, A. M., and Albidin, R. R. (1981). Regulation/enforcement/discipline of professional practice in psychology: Issues and strategies. *Professional Practice of Psychology* 2:1–16.

Wood, B. J., Klein, S., Cross, H. J., Lammers, C. J., and Elliott, J. K. (1985). Impaired practitioners: Psychologists' opinions about prevalence, and proposals for intervention. *Professional Psychology: Research and Practice* 16:843–850.

3

The History of Gatekeeping

Linda S. Moore and David A. Jenkins

Gatekeeping is not new to social work education; it was a component of social work's earliest venture into preparing workers for effective practice (Moore and Urwin 1990, 1991). Since the late 1800s the profession has attempted to provide relevant education to adequately train professional social workers. It also has emphasized guarding the gate to the profession to ensure that there is evidence that students have internalized instructional material before they graduate and begin to practice.

In this chapter, we will trace the background and history of gatekeeping in social work education in order to emphasize that the charge to guard the gate of the social work profession has a long and valuable history. This history provides a rationale for gatekeeping at the undergraduate level and also indicates strategies that can be used in the process.

Early Gatekeeping Efforts

According to Trattner (1989), neither volunteer service nor good intentions alone could dispel the complex problems emerging in the 1800s. The need for trained workers to confront the social problems brought about by industrialization, urbanization, and immigration was apparent. These workers needed knowledge about the problems they were tackling and specific skills to address them effectively.

The earliest forms of gatekeeping appear to be the screening and training of friendly visitors through the Charity Organization Societies (COS). The Boston COS held weekly conferences in order to enhance the experience of friendly visiting and to provide suggestions for effective visiting. The COS agents also carefully assigned cases to friendly visitors to best utilize their skills and to guard against inappropriate behavior (Smith 1961). By the early 1900s, the COS, in response to the focus on "scientific charity" and the inadequacy of friendly visitors to investigate and to address the problems of families, began to direct their attention to preparing professionals who could adequately cope with the demands of their clients' misfortune (Axinn and Levin 1992). In order to reach this goal, they delivered lectures and provided information about readings that could enhance practice (Trattner 1994).

At the same time, the Settlement House movement emphasized providing support primarily for immigrants (although they also served other clients) within their own community and enabling them to assess their own needs. The early settlement leaders were convinced that the most effective services for people in need were provided in their own neighborhoods. Leaders of the settlements trained social workers to provide professional service from a humanitarian perspective, respecting cultural and personal differences (Moore 1994). Settlement training was done through supervision and social study but was deemed necessary to ensure that workers were able to enhance the social functioning of their clients and to improve communities (Woods and Kennedy 1922).

Most of this early training for social workers took place informally in staff meetings and group discussions, but the focus was consistently on ensuring the competence of workers (Popple and Leighninger 1990; Pumphrey and Pumphrey 1961). In a paper presented to the National Conference on Charities and Corrections in 1897, Mary Richmond eloquently argued that better service could be provided if workers were trained. The response to her plea was the development of formal social work education with the establishment of the New York School of Philanthropy in 1898 (Popple and Leighninger 1990; Trattner 1979).

Formal Social Work Education

The formalization of education was a major step toward establishing gatekeeping in social work education. From its earliest days, the mission of social work education was to guard the gate of the profession by training qualified practitioners (Moore and Urwin 1991). Both settlement and COS workers understood that professionalism developed from education, which served as the means to transfer knowledge, values, skills, and standards to practitioners (Trattner 1994). The COS argued that work with the needy should be scientific, and it could become scientific through the "development of professional skill, professional schools, and authoritative standards of entrance and excellence" (Trattner 1989:215). Mary Richmond (1899) agreed, stating that since social work was both an art and a science, there should be training, and excellence must be its focus. Her book *Social Diagnosis,* published in 1917, was the first textbook used in the professional education process, and it established "scientific casework" as the foundation of social work practice (Popple and Leighninger 1990:67).

Throughout the late 1800s and early 1900s, a "persistent theme was that the paid, full-time careerist, with background knowledge, training, and experience, was best fitted to give service" (Pumphrey and Pumphrey 1961). The Richmond School for Social Economy's first annual announcement in 1917 noted, "Philanthropy in all its phases . . . has come to be recognized as dangerous in the hands of the uninformed" (Carlton 1987:10). More important, excellence and expert knowledge were emphasized as the only way to avoid paternalism (Cabot 1909). Cannon (1924) further argued that using untrained people indicated a lack of standards that could undermine the entire profession. This was probably best demonstrated by the prestige of medical social work, which emphasized a high level of training and screening for that particular specialty (Popple and Leighninger 1990). Even those outside the profession recognized that training was vital to dealing with the complex problems of the day. In 1914 the commissioner of labor said, "The unintelligent, untrained charity worker can . . . often cause . . . havoc [with the needy]" (Trattner 1989:212).

While there were many struggles among the members of the social work profession over methods and fields of practice, the emphasis during the 1920s and 1930s was on developing a professional subculture with norms and beliefs that could be transmitted through the educational process (Lubove 1975). As social work education evolved, it gradually moved from a six-week training course to a two-year program of study. The focus shifted from agency-based training to affiliation with universities in order to provide training in casework techniques, research, and, most important, in field work that would enable students to become more than "routine technician[s]" (Abbott 1931:13). Edith Abbott (1931) stated that "the practice of social work demands character as well as education; and proper service can be given only by those who are trained for the responsibilities of action" (47–48). Here, the assumption was that the effective social worker was one who loved learning, yet who also possessed the appropriate skills for practice. The goal was "to professionalize social programs by credentialing their staff in training programs" (Jansson 1988:96).

As schools proliferated, the need for curriculum standards became apparent in order to ensure consistency in the preparation of students. Although schools of medical social work were the first to set such standards, other programs soon followed suit (Lubove 1975). The Association of Training Schools of Professional Social Work (the forerunner of the Council on Social Work Education [CSWE]) was formed in 1920 to develop standards for social work education (Trattner 1994). The association emphasized that the main focus of education and standard-setting should be to prepare students who believed in the values of the profession, who were skilled in the roles of the social worker, and whose prejudices, which could negatively affect practice, were eliminated through the educational process (Lubove 1975). During this time, agencies such as the Boston Children's Aid Society developed written policies requiring workers to be trained in social work because "natural endowments alone could not insure the kind of skilled professional service" necessary to work effectively with clients (Lubove 1975:44).

Up to this time, some social work education programs had accepted African-American students, but attendance was very difficult for the majority. Moreover, services for African-American clients were scarce due to the lack of trained African-American social workers. In order to address both issues, George Haynes, the first executive director of the National Urban League and a teacher at Fisk University, set up a field program with the Urban League so Fisk students could enter the social work profession and serve African-American communities (Popple and Leighninger 1990). Haynes believed selection was one key to providing a cadre of competent African-American social workers, and he also emphasized gatekeeping through setting standards for practice. Haynes maintained that competent African-American social workers were vital to solving the urban problems of African-Americans (Carlton-LaNey 1992).

Organizational Gatekeeping

The 1920s and 1930s brought about the development of professional organizations that, according to Trattner (1994), provided another form of gatekeeping. Through them, the connections between educators and practitioners could serve to raise levels of both education and practice and to promote the socialization of novices into the profession (Lubove 1975). Professional organizations were able to support the concept of educational gatekeeping by helping to set and maintain standards that must be met before a person could engage in professional practice. Through their educational and practice requirements, they also provided a means to exclude untrained people from the profession.

Until the 1920s, it appeared that most social workers supported the role of gatekeeping because of their quest for professionalization. However, there were some who disagreed. Bertha Capen Reynolds was one of the few who argued that schools of social work should be used as "educational, rather than gatekeeping institutions" (Reisch 1992:69). Nevertheless, in 1929, Porter Lee's famous paper acknowledged that the increase in social work jobs was generating a greater effort toward professionalism. Lee argued that the growth of the social work profession would be accompanied by greater demands for accountability and ethical standards. This further increased the need for the profession to police itself (Gilbert and Specht 1976).

The role of foundations in influencing social work curricula, particularly by emphasizing agency collaboration and identifying the role of professionals in solving social problems, also originated during the 1920s. Funding students' education allowed foundations to have an impact on the educational content and to require foci relevant to their major concerns (e.g., the Commonwealth Fund emphasized educating social workers to work in mental health). The most significant of these foundations was the Laura Spellman Rockefeller Foundation, which had a major impact on the development of generic content with a social science base and the expansion of educational programs west of the Mississippi River. This foundation influenced the growth of social work education from the 1930s to the present (Stuart 1995).

Even with the thrust toward educating social workers, the Milford Conference in 1929 and several studies done during the 1930s indicated that many agency staff delivering social work services were not professionally trained. As a result, schools of social work were urged to increase the number of graduates in order to staff agencies. However, they also were challenged to do so without sacrificing standards. In response, the Association of Professional Schools of Social Work (APSSW) began to emphasize admission standards and curriculum requirements in order to restrict entry to practice to those who were adequately trained and who espoused the values of the profession (Lubove 1975). By 1932 these APSSW standards emphasized the gatekeeping role of social work education, stressing the need to eliminate biases, preferences, and perspectives that were inconsistent with effective social work practice.

In the early 1950s CSWE commissioned a study of social work education based on the concern that the profession was growing rapidly without clear principles and guidelines for education. The report, known as the Hollis-Taylor Report, indicated that, despite the actions resulting from the Milford Conference, the majority of social work activities continued to be performed by people who were not trained social workers, most of them having been trained in disciplines other than social work. As a result, the report focused on developing the objectives of social work education

(Hollis and Taylor 1951). There was concern that unless the profession was clear about the knowledge, values, and skills needed for effective practice, no evaluation of practice could take place. The report emphasized that social work "served a social purpose . . . and its internal self-disciplinary measures have been formalized in order to insure continued development of the profession" (Pumphrey 1959:10).

Educators were seen as the key to raising the standards of practice by screening out unsuitable students. Pumphrey argued that because social work is a practice profession, educators must assess how effectively students can apply the values and ethical principles to their practice with clients. Charlotte Towle's famous comment that "a profession's leaders cannot advance it beyond the common practice" (Towle 1954:5) generated increased emphasis on the role of education. Gardner (1961) stated that social work education is a sorting out process and argued that "success involves more than talent" (59). Social work educators were encouraged to use their assessment skills to determine which students had the potential for social work practice and to screen out those who did not. Such screening, even though difficult, was necessary because a profession that did not emphasize quality would not achieve excellence. In discussing the educational objectives of the casework curriculum, Boehm (1959) listed the behaviors (classified as knowledge, values, and skills) the educational process should address. Students were expected to change their behaviors to meet these standards of the profession.

Moore (1970:121) reiterated that professional schools serve as the first formal gatekeepers by setting admission and graduation standards; he called the faculty the "collective conscience" of the profession. Bartlett (1970) argued that the characteristics of skilled helping and sensitivity to clients' needs must remain the core of social work practice despite growth in the profession. She felt that a common base of social work practice would provide a means to "define professional competence" (193). The 1968 National Association of Social Workers (NASW) Commission on the Study of Competence identified the four major components of competence that would provide the basis for evaluation of students: "(1) professional knowledge and understanding, (2) professional qualities and attributes, (3) professional practice, and (4) work management and relationships" (Bartlett 1970:201). These were the components that the profession accepted as the basis for evaluation of students.

Undergraduate Education

During the 1950s and 1960s, recognition of the shortage of trained social workers in the social welfare arena led to heightened emphasis on undergraduate education. Discussion and debate about the purposes of baccalaureate (BSW) education and its curriculum requirements went on for over a decade. The emphasis remained on "foster[ing] an identity with the profession (Witte 1965:27). In 1971 a group of social work educators met at Allenberry Inn in Pennsylvania to discuss undergraduate curricula and standards. The participants at this meeting, known as the Allenberry Colloquium, reaffirmed the importance of gatekeeping: "educators have to be prepared to move the student, even the well-meaning student, out of the program if he [or she] is not competent to enter the profession" (Feldstein 1972:65). As chair of CSWE's Commission on Accreditation, Rothenberg (1975) stressed that educators must be willing to make professional assessments of students, even when those assessments indicated the need to dismiss students from social work programs. This was a challenge to social work education.

The changes in social work education during the 1970s increased the significance of gatekeeping at the undergraduate level (Arkava and Brennan 1979). Baccalaureate accreditation standards, developed in 1974, identified the importance of screening students. Licensing at the baccalaureate level, the development of advanced standing for graduates of baccalaureate programs who enter MSW programs, and continued pressure from the practice community to provide graduates with the appropriate values and skills for practice increased the focus on gatekeeping (Moore and Urwin 1991). During the late 1970s and early 1980s, in the wake of an emphasis on gatekeeping, social work enrollments decreased, partly as a reaction to the political climate. Some schools responded to this decrease with open enrollment of students, many of whom would have been screened out in the era of larger enrollment figures (Born and Carroll 1988; Carbino and Morganbesser 1982).

In the 1980s enrollments for undergraduate social work education increased. However, while enrollments were up, social work graduates encountered the exigencies of program cutbacks, funding loss, and burnout because of increased caseloads. Because there was some indication that many students were choosing social work for reasons other than social work's historic commitment to the poor and needy, the students' values, attitudes, and skills remained important gatekeeping issues (Moran 1989; Wilkerson 1987; Zimmerman 1987).

The resurgence of emphasis on gatekeeping began partly as a result of increased enrollment, yet also as a result of the perceived change in students' motivation for social work. According to the 1984 CSWE Curriculum Policy Statement (CSWE 1984), an underlying assumption of educational programs was that "student self-selection and program admission processes combine to bring to programs of social work education people who are committed to the basic values and ethics that shape social work practice" (125). Although gatekeeping historically emphasized the shaping of the students' values and attitudes, some research indicated that values and attitudes were set when students selected the social work profession, and major changes in those values and attitudes rarely occurred (Enoch 1988). However, educators argued that if increased enrollments indicated a desire for economic opportunity rather than a commitment to "individual and institutional arrangements that will have a humanistic impact on clients" (Howard and Flaitz 1982:11), gatekeeping was even more important.

It was clear in the 1980s that faculty were desperate for strategies to guard the gate without legally jeopardizing their programs. Several articles appeared about the issue (Born and Carroll 1988; Cobb and Jordan 1989; Moore and Urwin 1990, 1991; Moran 1989), and attendance at special gatekeeping sessions at the Association of Baccalaureate Social Work Program Directors (BPD) and the Council on Social Work Education's Annual Program Meeting was high (Gibbs 1994a). The concern at the undergraduate level was strong because many of the traditional methods of gatekeeping used at the graduate level either were not appropriate for baccalaureate educators or had to be modified to match the university requirements for undergraduate educational programs and the development needs of the undergraduate student population. Throughout the decade of the 1980s and into the 1990s gatekeeping strategies have been developed and organizational structures established to provide support for BSW faculty struggling to maintain standards of education (Gibbs 1994b).

A major issue that emerged during the gatekeeping resurgence of the 1990s was the distinction between termination of students for "academic" and "nonacademic" reasons. Obviously, addressing ethical issues is a crucial component of gatekeeping efforts. However, while social work values and ethics were (and are) components of both the classroom and the field practicum, they have not been consistently handled as gatekeeping issues in all programs. Some social work educators were reluctant to view professional competence, adherence to the code of ethics, and appropriate values and attitudes as academic issues that could be legally validated. Others argued that addressing ethical issues allowed educators to make professional assessments that are part of the nature of gatekeeping (Cobb 1994; Moore and Urwin 1991) and stressed that "an unethical student is likely to be an unethical practitioner" (Saunders 1993:231).

According to Cobb (1994:23), judicial decisions have supported universities "where students knew the criteria for dismissal" and have given professional programs more latitude in defining their academic standards than traditional academic disciplines. If programs specify academic violations and make clear that decisions based on violations of the code of ethics and on value conflicts are a part of the academic arena of social work, the courts generally uphold such decisions (Cobb 1994; Moore and Urwin 1991). Several judicial decisions have supported dismissal from professional programs based on academic criteria related to professional behavior, ethics, and client relationships.

Accreditation standard EVS 5.8, however, makes it difficult for BSW and MSW programs to frame professional expectations as *academic* performance expectations because it requires programs to have policies and practices for "terminating a student's enrollment in the social work program for reasons of academic and *nonacademic* performance" (CSWE 1994:89, 127, italics added).

In trying to iron out this problem with the accreditation standards, CSWE inadvertently added fuel to the fire in August 1996 with the issuance of a memo entitled *Guidelines for "Nonacademic" Termination Policies and Procedures*, which reaffirmed that in accordance with EVS 5.8, programs must define academic and nonacademic performance differently in their policies. The memo explained that "knowledge, value, and skill expectations are all *academic in a professional program* as they relate to a student's 'likely performance as a social work practitioner'" (CSWE 1996). This statement is in line with court decisions on what constitutes academic standards in professional programs. However, the memo also stated that knowledge, skill, and value expectations are *nonacademic* as they relate to the language of the accreditation standard, "to differentiate between termination for deficiencies in academic standing (e.g., a student whose GPA is less than the required minimum or who has earned more unsatisfactory grades than allowed in the program) and inadequacies in student ability to demonstrate professional conduct and relationship skills and behavior consistent with the values and ethics of the profession." The latter statement in essence cancels the first and leads faculty to continue to make artificial distinctions between performance and behaviors that are academic (i.e., scholastic in the traditional sense) and nonacademic, or of a more professional nature. Such distinctions will not serve programs well in case of litigation.

In February 1999 CSWE distributed an updated memorandum on academic and nonacademic standards (see appendix 13), but the only difference between this memo and its predecessor involved a change in the title. The memorandum is now entitled *Guidelines for Termination for Academic and Professional Reasons* (CSWE 1999). Until Evaluative Standard 5.8 and its interpretive guideline are revised (CSWE 1994:89, 127), CSWE's hands are tied in resolving the problems associated with professional standards being characterized as an area of "nonacademic performance."

As we approach a new century, social workers are again facing a critical time in American society when social problems often appear overwhelming. Social workers are called on to solve problems and provide effective services just as in the 1890s. Recent court cases raise the possibility that social work educators and social work institutions may be legally liable for the performance of their graduates (Custer 1994). Faculty must be willing to make hard decisions, acknowledging that their professional assessments are appropriate for screening students, thus safeguarding the social work profession. "The credibility of the [social work] graduate rests on the assumption that social work educators are responsibly monitoring the quality of their graduates" (Arkava and Brennan 1979:4).

We have monitored quality in the past; the lessons generated throughout the past one hundred years of gatekeeping in social work education may provide insight into how to continue to ensure that our gatekeeping works today. Our gatekeeping heritage also may provide insights for our continued development as a profession and our ongoing efforts to serve clients (Moore and Urwin 1991). "Where it is commonly supposed that anyone can do social work, anyone is likely to do it" (Hollis and Taylor 1951:270). Gatekeeping ensures that educators have met their charge to allow only those who have demonstrated competence to pass through the gate of the social work profession (Feldstein 1972).

References

Abbott, E. (1931). *Social welfare and professional education*. Chicago: University of Chicago Press.

Arkava, M., and Brennan, E. C. (1979). Quality control in social work education. In M. Arkava and E. C. Brennan (eds.), *Competency-based education for social work*, pp. 3–21. New York: Council on Social Work Education.

Axinn, J., and Levin, H. (1992). *Social welfare: A history of the American response to need*. 3d ed. New York: Longman.

Bartlett, H. M. (1970). *The common base of social work practice*. New York: National Association of Social Workers.

Boehm, W. W. (1959). *The social casework method in social work education*. New York: Council on Social Work Education.

Born, C., and Carroll, D. (1988). Ethics in admissions. *Journal of Social Work Education* 24:79–85.

Cabot, R. C. (1909). *Social service and the art of healing*. New York: Macmillan.

Cannon, I. (1924). History and development of social work. *The Family* 4:250–255.

Carbino, R., and Morganbesser, M. (1982). A national challenge: The decline in MSW admissions applications. *Journal of Education for Social Work* 15:13–22.

Carlton, T. O. (1987). History of the school of social work. *VCU Magazine* 15 (4): 10–12.

Carlton-LaNey, I. (1992). George Edmund Haynes' impact on social work education. In J. Andrews (ed.), *From vision to action: Social workers of the second generation*, pp. 21–42. The College of St. Catherine, The University of St. Thomas.

Cobb, N. H. (1994). Court-recommended guidelines for managing unethical students and working with university lawyers. *Journal of Social Work Education* 30:18–31.

Cobb, N. H., and Jordan, C. (1989). Students with questionable values or threatening behavior: Precedent and policy from discipline to dismissal. *Journal of Social Work Education* 25:87–97.

Council on Social Work Education (CSWE), Commission on Accreditation. (1984). *Handbook of accreditation standards and procedures.* New York: CSWE.

Council on Social Work Education (CSWE), Commission on Accreditation. (1994). *Handbook of accreditation standards and procedures.* 4th ed. Alexandria, Va.: CSWE.

Council on Social Work Education (CSWE), Commission on Accreditation. (1996). *Guidelines for "nonacademic" termination polices and procedures.* Alexandria, Va.: CSWE.

Council on Social Work Education (CSWE), Commission on Accreditation. (1999). *Guidelines for termination for academic and professional reasons.* Alexandria, Va.: CSWE.

Custer, G. (1994, November). Can universities be liable for incompetent grads? *Monitor* 7:n.p.

Enoch, Y. (1988). Why are they different: Background, occupational choice, institutional selection, and attitudes of social work students. *Journal of Social Work Education* 24:165–174.

Feldstein, D. (1972). *Undergraduate social work education: Today and tomorrow.* New York: Council on Social Work Education.

Gardner, J. W. (1961). *Excellence: Can we be equal and excellent too?* New York: Harper & Brothers.

Gibbs, P. (1994a). Screening students out of BSW programs: Background, issues, and strategies. Paper presented at the 12th Annual Conference of the Association of Baccalaureate Social Work Program Directors, San Francisco, Ca.

Gibbs, P. (1994b). Gatekeeping issues in BSW programs. *Aretê* 19:15–27.

Gilbert, N., and Specht, H. (1976). *The emergence of social welfare and social work*. Itasca, Ill.: Peacock.

Hollis, E. V., and Taylor, A. L. (1951). *Social work education in the United States*. New York: Columbia University Press.

Howard, T. U., and Flaitz, J. (1982). A scale to measure humanistic attitudes of social work students. *Social Work Research and Abstracts* 18:11–18.

Jansson, B. S. (1988). *The reluctant welfare state: A history of American social welfare policies*. Belmont, Cal.: Wadsworth.

Lee, P. (1937). *Social work as cause and function, and other papers*. New York: Columbia University Press.

Lubove, R. (1975). *The professional altruist*. New York: Atheneum.

Moore, L. S. (1994). Interorganizational linkages: Social workers and the development of the NAACP. *Journal of Sociology and Social Welfare* 21:125–137.

Moore, L. S., and Urwin, C. A. (1990). Quality control in social work: The gatekeeping role in social work education. *Journal of Teaching in Social Work* 4 (1): 113–128.

Moore, L. S., and Urwin, C. A. (1991). Gatekeeping: A model for screening baccalaureate students for field education. *Journal of Social Work Education* 27:8–17.

Moore, W. E. (1970). *The professions: Roles and rules*. New York: Russell Sage Foundation.

Moran, J. R. (1989). Social work education and students' humanistic attitudes. *Journal of Social Work Education* 25:13–19.

National Association of Social Workers (NASW). (1994). *NASW code of ethics*. Washington, D.C.: NASW.

Popple, P. R., and Leighninger, L. H. (1990). *Social work, social welfare, and American society*. Boston: Allyn and Bacon.

Pumphrey, M. W. (1959). *The teaching of values and ethics in social work education*. New York: Council on Social Work Education.

Pumphrey, R. E., and Pumphrey, M. W. (1961). *The heritage of American social work*. New York: Columbia University Press.

Reisch, M. (1992). Linking client and community: The impact of Bertha Reynolds on social work. In J. Andrews (ed.), *From vision to action: Social workers of the second generation*, pp. 58–74. The College of St. Catherine, The University of St. Thomas.

Richmond, M. (1899). *Friendly visiting among the poor*. New York: Macmillan.

Richmond, M. (1917). *Social diagnosis*. New York: Russel Sage Foundation.

Rothenberg, E. (1975). Teaching is our business. Paper presented at the 21st Annual Program Meeting of the Council on Social Work Education, Chicago, Ill.

Saunders, E. J. (1993). Confronting academic dishonesty. *Journal of Social Work Education* 29:224–231.

Smith, A. D. (1961). Country help for city charities. In R. E. Pumphrey and M. W. Pumphrey (eds.), *The heritage of American social work*, pp. 214–218. New York: Columbia University Press.

Stuart, P. H. (1995). Foundations and social work education: The 1920s. Paper presented at the 41st Annual Program Meeting of the Council on Social Work Education, San Diego, California.

Towle, C. (1954). *The Learner in education for the professions.* Chicago: University of Chicago Press.

Trattner, W. (1979). *From poor law to welfare state.* 2d ed. New York: Free Press.

—. (1989). *From poor law to welfare state.* 4th ed. New York: Free Press.

—. (1994). *From poor law to welfare state.* 5th ed. New York: Free Press.

Wilkerson, I. (1987, November 9). Schools of social work swamped by applicants. *New York Times,* p. A18.

Witte, E. F. (1965). Articulation between graduates and undergraduate education for the social services: Observations on undergraduate social welfare education. New York: Council on Social Work Education.

Woods, R. A., and Kennedy, A. J. (1922). *The settlement horizon.* New York: Russell Sage Foundation.

Zimmerman, A. (1987, December 1). The new social workers: Students again ponder their debt to society. *Dallas Times Herald,* pp. E1, E3.

4

Gatekeeping in BSW Programs: A Review of the Research

Nancy P. Kropf

Baccalaureate programs in social work education have the responsibility to provide educational experiences, socialization, and opportunities to prepare students for entry into social work practice. In addition to the educational function, programs are also expected to serve as "the keeper of the gate" to the social work profession (Moore and Urwin 1990:114). Under BSW accreditation standards, all programs must have procedures to determine the suitability of the students for entry-level practice (Council on Social Work Education [CSWE] 1994). Gatekeeping involves two different processes: restricting entry to a program (i.e., denying admission) and termination of the educational process (i.e., dismissal, screening a student out of the major). The issues related to gatekeeping are important but complex and continue to generate much concern and debate in the profession.

In an effort to begin exploring these issues in more detail, this chapter provides a review of the research and literature on gatekeeping in baccalaureate social work education. The first section describes the emerging reasons for an increased interest in gatekeeping. The second section identifies gatekeeping points in the curriculum. Finally, implications for programs and further research are presented to provide additional consideration and clarification about this important educational and professional responsibility.

The Recent Increased Interest in Gatekeeping

Over the past few years, a growing interest in gatekeeping has been emerging in baccalaureate education. One reason is a combination of increasing numbers of students and limited program resources. During the late 1970s and into the early 1980s, programs were forced into the dubious practice of universally accepting students, including some who might not have been accepted previously in order to maintain full-time equivalents (FTEs) (Born and Carroll 1988). During the mid-1980s enrollment trends reversed, which translated into a reemergence of students interested in pursuing a career in social work.

While this phenomenon has many advantages for the profession, budget and program restrictions have caused additional problems in social work education: There is a greater number of students majoring in social work, but few or no additional faculty or program resources. In a study by DeWeaver and Kropf (1995), 64 percent of the BSW programs surveyed experienced an increase in enrollment of 25 percent or more over the past five years. Greater numbers of students often lead to larger class sizes, which leave faculty with less time to devote to other responsibilities besides teaching, such as making admissions decisions or spending time advising students. Projections suggest that the pattern of increasing enrollment will continue due to increased numbers of high school graduates combined with an expected rise in the numbers of nontraditional students and students seeking a second degree (Big Increase 1993). Therefore, gatekeeping mechanisms may be crucial for programs in regulating enrollment in social work courses and in the program.

In addition to fluctuating enrollment patterns, the students' motivation for entering social work programs has also changed. Some authors suggest that student motives are less based on the value of social justice and more on economic factors (Wilkerson 1987; Zimmerman 1987). As stated by Engle (1990:10), "the individual does *not* commence social work education as a tabula rasa, but with a more or less well developed personal construct or meaning system which encompasses some notion of social work and self as social worker." Moore and Urwin (1991) stress the importance of gatekeeping in preserving the mission and values of the profession in this changing professional climate.

While programs are confronted with changing student demographics, problems exist in constructing criteria and structures for gatekeeping. Programs wrestle with the question of what constitutes an "inappropriate" student (Peterman and Blake 1986). Madden (1993) suggests that the problem is not with the blatantly inappropriate student, such as the student who is academically unsuitable. The marginal student, for example, someone who is adequate in the classroom but unacceptable in the field, presents the most difficult situation. Since many programs position the internship in the final quarters or semesters of the curriculum, decisions about appropriateness may not surface until the student has accumulated many credits (and years) in the program.

Implementation of Gatekeeping Functions

Gatekeeping is a dynamic and ongoing process in social work programs (Moore and Urwin 1991), and most undergraduate programs have some formal gatekeeping procedures in place (DeWeaver and Kropf 1995; Gibbs 1994a; Urwin 1992; Wahlberg and Lommen 1990). However, the models of implementation vary considerably. Some programs have multiple screening points and indicators, but others rely on a single point or a particular indicator. A review of the studies on gatekeeping in social work education suggests that gatekeeping periods can be categorized into three phases: at the point of admission to the program, at various points throughout the curriculum, and as students prepare to exit the program.

Admissions

The earliest national study on undergraduate admissions was by Constable (1977). His research suggested that different admission models existed: programs with no admission policy (everyone accepted) as well as those that screened students at multiple points. According to Constable, the programs exerting the greatest control over the process set gatekeeping points furthest along in the curriculum. Establishing decision-making points later in the program of study provides faculty with more data on the applicant, such as performance in a variety of courses and a GPA based on a greater number of credits, all of which facilitate informed decision making about the student's potential for success in the program.

Some programs use various indicators in making decisions about admission into the major. These can include personal interviews, autobiographical statements, references, GPA requirements, standardized test scores (e.g., SAT and ACT), completion of certain prerequisite courses, volunteer experience, and various individual characteristics (e.g., being a member of an underrepresented group, level of enthusiasm for profession, maturity). As can be seen, the variables used by programs to make admissions decisions are a mix between those that are more "scholastic" in orientation and others that tend to measure more "personal" characteristics and experiences of the applicants.

Although a number of indicators for judging a student's fit with the profession may be available at the time of admission, significant issues about screening decisions and standards have been raised. One example is the variation in faculty members' use of admission data to make their decisions. In a study on rater adherence, McClelland, Rindfleisch, and Bean (1991) conclude that admission evaluations may be more a measure of the raters' preferences than of the qualifications of the students. A second issue pertains to the weight, or importance, assigned to the student variables. Wahlberg and Lommen's (1990) findings suggest that BSW programs tend to select more scholastic indicators as screening mechanisms, such as cumulative GPA, completion of certain courses, and written statements. A recent Australian study on gatekeeping also found that academic indicators formed the basis for admissions decisions (Ryan, Habibis, and Craft 1997). In the study of fifteen social work programs, the most highly ranked criterion in the admissions process was academic ability, which was ranked first in two-thirds (67 percent) of the programs. For a complete discussion of academic standards of a scholastic nature versus those of a professional nature, see chapter 13.

Finally, another important question is the effectiveness of admissions criteria in discriminating which applicants are inappropriate. In a national study of the admissions process, Isaac,

Johnson, Lockhart, and White (1993) reported an average acceptance rate of 81 percent in BSW programs. Gibbs (1994a) found that even when programs have admission screening requirements in place, most programs (66 percent) are unlikely to deny students entry to the program based on those standards. Studies of the admission practices of social work programs suggest that admission screening does little in the way of gatekeeping.

Throughout the Curriculum

Gatekeeping functions are often performed at various points as students progress through the curriculum, and they are based on a variety of criteria and strategies. Students may be dismissed or counseled to leave the program for failing to achieve a certain grade in preprofessional courses or for not satisfying requirements needed to enter a field placement. In a study on liability issues in social work education, Gelman, Pollack, and Auerbach (1996) included reasons for terminating students. Over a five-year period, the average number of terminations in BSW programs was 3.3, which was a lower rate than either combined BSW/MSW programs (6.8 dismissals) or MSW only (8.6 dismissals). The most frequent reasons for dismissal were poor academic performance, psychological reasons, request of the field agency, and ethical violations. Students also may be prevented from continuing in the major for conduct-related issues such as inappropriate or unprofessional behavior.

One screening strategy is to evaluate the students' progress after the completion of specific courses or other curriculum requirements. Some programs identify preprofessional courses that must be completed before admission to the major. Often these courses provide an overview of the domain of social work, which allows students to determine the "goodness of fit" between their career goals and the profession. During the preprofessional curriculum, screening decisions may be guided by academic indicators, such as a requirement that students receive a minimum grade in these courses (B or above). Programs may also include ancillary requirements to assist students in determining their career goals and choice of a major. For example, as part of the introduction to the profession, students may be required to complete a certain number of volunteer hours in a social service setting. Students who discover that they do not enjoy working with people during their volunteer experience have an opportunity early in their education to investigate other disciplines that are more compatible with their skills and interests. Through a preestablished feedback loop, experiences in volunteer settings also can provide faculty with some additional data about students' potential for a career in the field of social work.

Another clear demarcation point is the admission process to the field practicum. Most programs identify screening criteria for entry into the field (Gibbs 1994a; Urwin 1992), and these may include maintenance of a minimum GPA, interviews with faculty or field instructors, personal statements, and references. Although screening mechanisms for field placements are in place in most schools, research suggests that students are rarely prevented from entering the field practicum. In one study, fewer than 1 percent of applicants were denied entry to the field experience in over two thirds (68 percent) of BSW programs surveyed (Wahlberg and Lommen 1990).

Students may be screened out of the major during the field practicum, usually for not meeting academic standards related to professional behavior, for example, nonadherence to social work values and ethics, or unprofessional behavior in the practicum setting. Termination of students from the program tends to be a responsibility left to field instructors. According to Gibbs (1994b:25), "when a student 'slips through the gates' of the academic program, academic faculty can count on field instructors to address issues of unsuitability as these emerge during the practicum." The degree to which faculty believe in delegating gatekeeping responsibility to field instructors reinforces the notion that programs are reluctant to make decisions about the suitability of students. A national study by Koerin and Miller (1995) examined nonacademic reasons for termination. Nonacademic reasons were operationalized as those factors excluding academic performance and broader institutional policies (e.g., academic dishonesty, plagiarism, cheating). Most programs (67 percent) had no policy on termination for nonacademic grounds. In programs that did have this type of policy, several different factors were listed as potential reasons for termination. These included violating professional ethics, poor performance in the field, emotional or psychological disorders, conviction of a felony, and disruptive classroom behavior. Although the research was at the MSW program level, many of these reasons would be similar for undergraduate students.

Exit Examinations

Gatekeeping may take place at the end of the curriculum and prior to conferment of a degree via an exit exam. Exit evaluations usually take the form of a comprehensive exam that must be passed in order to graduate. The general goal of exit exams is to have students demonstrate their ability to synthesize content that has been learned throughout the program of study. In actuality, exit evaluations are rarely used as a way to ensure that graduating students meet certain minimum standards to enter professional practice (Dinerman 1982). Gibbs (1994a) reported that only 19 percent of the BSW programs surveyed use exit exams to make determinations about graduation. Those programs using exit exams seemed to favor oral ($n = 35$) over written ($n = 16$) strategies, and programs in private, church-affiliated institutions tended to use exit examinations more frequently than programs in public institutions.

Implications for BSW Programs

If current enrollment trends continue, issues related to the function and implementation of gatekeeping mechanisms will become even more prominent and complex. Past research on BSW gatekeeping suggests several important themes related to these issues.

Gatekeeping Strategies

One way to enhance gatekeeping functions is to promote self-selection by students. Engle (1990) suggests implementing strategies in programs to provide multiple opportunities for students to select or deselect the major. Faculty can facilitate self-selection by giving students feedback at an early juncture on the goodness of fit between the student and the profession. Requiring human service activity is another strategy. If students are given an opportunity to experience the role of "doing social work," those who might otherwise enter the major under false assumptions get an opportunity to change their major prior to immersion in professional-level courses.

The value of practical experience soon after the major is declared cannot be overstated, so BSW programs should structure initial internships or volunteer requirements in the preprofessional curriculum. As a result of these experiences, students may discover that being a social worker is not what they had envisioned and could then opt out of the major. For example, some students select a social work major with the intention of using the profession as a forum for airing or implementing their own particular religious beliefs and converting "sinful and immoral" clients. Other students enter the major as an avenue for healing their own personal life wounds (see, for example, Black, Jeffreys, and Hartley 1993; Maeder 1989). During volunteer work students would receive feedback on the inappropriateness of these behaviors and motivations in the field of social work, which would help them to recognize the fallacy of their thinking. Thus, exposing students to the practice settings and the roles of social workers via volunteer experiences provides them with an opportunity to modify their views of professional roles and to continue in the major or to make the decision that another major is a more appropriate career choice.

If individual students are unable to arrive at these understandings on their own, faculty can use information from the volunteer experience as a springboard for discussions with students or may draw on the information to counsel students into a more appropriate major. Supplemental opportunities for gaining an understanding of the social work profession also enhance the students' understanding of professional social work, for example, career development seminars sponsored by the program, early advising sessions with faculty, linkages of students with practicing professionals through alumni contacts, and mentor relationships between seniors and premajors (Engle 1990).

Responsibility for Gatekeeping

Faculty often view field placements as the "proving ground" for students whose performance in the program has been questionable, and consequently they may rely too heavily on the practicum as a primary gatekeeping point. This situation causes concern for several reasons. One is the perception that gatekeeping is "dumped" onto field instructors, who are left with the responsibility of implementing the program function that is most troublesome for faculty. Another issue relates to the evaluation criteria in core courses. If students who have inappropriate or marginal abilities can adequately complete required courses, does the curriculum prepare students for the actual practice of social work? This discrepancy between classroom and field performance may signal a gap between the outcomes of educational preparation and the actual skills necessary for carrying out professional functions. A third issue relates to the roles of faculty and field instructor as gatekeepers during the educational process. Isaac et al. (1993) question whether faculty and field instructors are able to separate their role as "educators" from their role as "clinicians." Social workers who have a more therapeutic orientation (i.e., take a helping, nurturing, or facilitative role with students) may find the role of gatekeeper incongruous with their basic orientation. The discord that results may create role conflict for faculty or field instructors and cause reluctance to carry out gatekeeping responsibilities.

These issues suggest that the role of the practicum in comprehensive gatekeeping efforts needs to be discussed and researched further. In particular, the role of faculty as field liaisons, which has received limited attention in research to date (c.f. Rosenblum and Raphael 1983; Smith, Faria, and Brownstein 1986) must be examined more closely. Despite the paucity of research in this area, field liaison work is not an inconsequential element in gatekeeping efforts. In many programs liaisons carry important responsibilities, such as setting up and evaluating the students' practicum experiences. The duties and functions of liaisons should be analyzed more fully, including the liaison's role in providing direction to field instructors on the linkage between classroom and practicum expectations during the students' field placements. Additionally, ways that liaisons should be involved with field instructors and other field faculty in gatekeeping decisions need to be explored in greater detail. Chapter 6 examines the dimensions of gatekeeping during the field practicum.

Legal Issues

The implementation of gatekeeping, either barring or dismissing students from programs, can result in legal action. Cole and Lewis (1993) speculate that the resistance of programs to terminate students may be attributed to the fear of possible legal ramifications. Any arbitrary decision making in admissions and dismissal is problematic (Cole 1991; McClelland, Rindfleisch, and Bean 1991) because it makes gatekeeping processes unfair and capricious.

One way a program can respond to this issue is to develop clear policies and information about gatekeeping. Urwin (1992) reported that most programs informed students about procedures through a handbook or program materials (69 percent), but discussions about policies through advising and orientation sessions (49 percent) and classes (27 percent) occurred much less frequently. Policy information about admission and termination procedures is critical and should be discussed with and explained to students. This material should be covered several times and by different methods throughout the curriculum.

Establishing clear guidelines about student conduct is an issue that extends beyond the scope of BSW program responsibilities. In a discussion on guidelines to assist social work educators with gatekeeping decisions, Cole and Lewis (1993) recommend a revision of the *NASW Code of Ethics* (National Association of Social Workers [NASW] 1994) to include a section on academic and behavioral conduct for students. Although the code has since been revised (NASW 1996) and includes some ethical principles related to the educational arm of social work, further strengthening of the code is needed to give additional guidance to social work faculty and field instructors as they carry out their educational responsibilities. In the absence of clearer direction from NASW, individual programs currently are left with the problem of articulating their own set of appropriate standards for students. The recommendation to involve the NASW in setting standards for use in social work programs provides a rationale for a continued and inclusive professional discussion about educational and practice standards at the BSW level.

In summary, a number of issues relating to gatekeeping have been raised by research and scholarship in this area. Literature to date provides a clearer understanding of the reasons that gatekeeping issues have become prominent, including increased enrollment trends, changing demographics of the student population to include greater numbers of nontraditional students, and limited resources in many social work programs. Gatekeeping strategies exist in many BSW programs to help manage and regulate enrollment and also to determine whether students are suited for entry into and progression through the program. While past research has provided greater understanding of BSW gatekeeping, some aspects of the gatekeeping process need further exploration.

References

Big increase in high-school graduates seen. (1993, October 13). *Chronicle of Higher Education,* p. A42.

Black, P. N., Jeffreys, D., and Hartley, E. K. (1993). Personal history of psychosocial trauma in the early life of social work and business students. *Journal of Social Work Education* 29:171–180.

Born, C., and Carroll, D. (1988). Ethics in admissions. *Journal of Social Work Education* 24:79–85.

Cole, B. S. (1991). Legal issues related to social work program admissions. *Journal of Social Work Education* 27:18–24.

Cole, B. S., and Lewis, R. G. (1993). Gatekeeping through termination of unsuitable social work students: Legal issues and guidelines. *Journal of Social Work Education* 29:150–159.

Constable, R. T. (1977). A study of admissions policies in undergraduate education. *Journal of Education for Social Work* 13 (3): 19–24.

Council on Social Work Education (CSWE), Commission on Accreditation. (1994). *Handbook of accreditation standards and procedures.* 4th ed. Alexandria, Va.: CSWE.

DeWeaver, K. L., and Kropf, N. P. (1995). Gatekeeping in baccalaureate social work programs: An empirical investigation. Paper presented at the 41st Annual Program Meeting of the Council on Social Work Education, San Diego, Ca.

Dinerman, M. (1982). A study of baccalaureate and master's curricula in social work. *Journal of Education for Social Work* 18 (2): 84–92.

Engle, P. R. (1990). Values education in undergraduate social work: Collaboration for socialization. Paper presented at the 8th Annual Conference of the Association of Baccalaureate Program Directors, Minneapolis, Minn.

Gelman, S. R., Pollack, D., and Auerbach, C. (1996). Liability issues in social work education. *Journal of Social Work Education* 32:351–362.

Gibbs, P. (1994a). Screening mechanisms in BSW programs. *Journal of Social Work Education* 30:63–74.

Gibbs, P. (1994b). Gatekeeping issues in BSW programs. *Aretê* 19 (2): 15–27.

Isaac, A., Johnson, R. N., Lockhart, L. L., and White, B. W. (1993). Gatekeeping: How effective are social work educators performing this function? Paper presented at the 39th Annual Program Meeting of the Council on Social Work Education, New York, N.Y.

Koerin, B., and Miller, J. (1995). Gatekeeping policies: Terminating students for nonacademic reasons. *Journal of Social Work Education* 31:247–260.

Madden, R. G. (1993). Protecting all parties: A legal analysis of clinical competency and student dismissals. Paper presented at the 39th Annual Program Meeting of the Council on Social Work Education, New York, N.Y.

Maeder, T. (1989). The wounded healer and the helping professions. In T. Maeder, *Children of psychiatrists and other psychotherapists*, pp. 69–93. New York: Harper & Row.

McClelland, R. W., Rindfleisch, N., and Bean, G. (1991). Rater adherence to evaluative criteria used in BSSW admissions. *Aretê*, 16 (2): 10–18.

Moore, L. S., and Urwin, C. A. (1990). Quality control in social work: The gatekeeping role in social work education. *Journal of Teaching in Social Work*, 4 (1): 113–128.

Moore, L. S., and Urwin, C. A. (1991). Gatekeeping: A model for screening baccalaureate students for field education. *Journal of Social Work Education* 27:8–17.

National Association of Social Workers (NASW). (1994). NAS*W Code of Ethics*. NASW.

National Association of Social Workers (NASW). (1996). NAS*W Code of Ethics*. NASW.

Peterman, P. J., and Blake, R. (1986). The inappropriate BSW student. *Aretê* 11 (1): 27–34.

Rosenblum, A., and Raphael, F. (1983). The role and function of the faculty field liaison. *Journal of Education for Social Work* 19 (1): 67–73.

Ryan, M., Habibis, D., and Craft, C. (1997). Guarding the gates of the profession: Findings of a survey of gatekeeping mechanisms in Australian Bachelor of Social Work programs. *Australian Social Work* 50 (3): 5–12.

Smith, H., Faria, G., and Brownstein, C. (1986). Social work faculty in the role of liaison: A field study. *Journal of Social Work Education* 22:68–78.

Urwin, C. A. (1992). Gatekeeping survey of accredited BSW programs. Paper presented at the 38th Annual Program Meeting of the Council on Social Work Education, St. Louis, Mo.

Wahlberg, J., and Lommen, C. (1990). An analysis of admissions and termination criteria in BSW programs. Presentation at the 8th Annual Conference of the Association of Baccalaureate Program Directors, Minneapolis, Minn.

Wilkerson, I. (1987, November 9). Schools of social work swamped by applicants. *New York Times,* pp. 18A.

Zimmerman, A. (1987, December 1). The new social workers: Students again ponder their debt to society. *Dallas Times Herald,* pp. E1–E3.

5

Gatekeeping in Social Work Education: Achieving Diversity and Excellence

Wanda D. Bracy

The need to increase the number of professionally educated persons of color has been discussed in the social work literature for several decades. Much of the literature in social work education on the recruitment and retention of students of color was published more than twenty-five years ago. While this literature has been primarily concerned with graduate education in social work, many of the techniques and strategies can be applied to undergraduate education and remain relevant today. However, since this literature was published, attitudes and laws regarding the use of racial preferences in admissions have changed. While there is extensive literature on this topic in higher education, social work education has been relatively quiet on this issue.

Those who want to end affirmative action believe the use of racial preferences is unfair and unjust and represents outright reverse discrimination. Opponents of affirmative action believe that quantitative measures (standardized test scores and grade point averages [GPA]) determine qualification for admission, and they want admissions decisions to be almost exclusively based on these measures. They believe that the use of racial preference represents social injustice because this practice permits less qualified persons to be admitted over more qualified ones. Qualification, of course, is determined by where an applicant ranks on these quantitative measures.

Supporters of affirmative action defend racial preferences because they believe the goal of diversity in institutions of higher education legitimates the use of race as one among many criteria. They point out to opponents that quantitative measures have never been the only factor considered in the admissions decisions in higher education. First of all, these measures do not tell admissions officers all they need to know about a prospective student. Second, there have been other qualitative factors traditionally used in admissions (e.g., children of alumni, talent or valued attribute relevant to the mission of the university, and residential location of the prospective student). Supporters of affirmative action believe that there has not been any mobilized attempt to eradicate these preferences in admissions because persons with these characteristics are valued. On the other hand, maybe racial preference raises the ire of opponents because they do not value the contribution of marginalized racial groups to institutions.

It appears to be a commonly held belief that if we open higher education to previously excluded persons of color, then we must lower standards. Lowering standards, of course, means admitting those with lower test scores and grade point averages, thus compromising excellence and eroding the quality of education. Inherent in this belief is the assumption that test scores and grades are the most credible form of assessing appropriateness and that persons of color are less qualified on these measures and therefore unable to compete with white students who do qualify.

How to achieve excellence and at the same time attain diversity is a hotly debated question in higher education. The educational reform movement in higher education calls for "maintaining" standards of excellence, and its proponents perceive the movement for equity in admissions as sacrificing traditional scholastic standards. Therefore, they call for a return to GPAs and higher test scores as a basis for admissions.

On the other hand, those who have a commitment to diversity in higher education contend that these traditional standards for admissions assess only a very narrow spectrum of performance, and they question the extent to which these measures predict students' future success (Gardner 1993; Justiz and Kameen 1994; Minnich 1990). This group believes that the overreliance on GPAs and standardized test scores is an obstacle to the full participation by diverse populations, so they call for more inclusive admissions criteria (Justiz 1994). They do not see diminishing the importance of GPAs and test scores as "lowering" of academic standards. However, they support the development of multiple measures, which may include consideration of traditional admissions criteria, believing this alternative approach augments and improves standards for admissions (Minnich 1990).

While accreditation standards require social work education programs to ensure equity for all students in recruitment, admission, retention, and financial aid policies and procedures (Council on Social Work Education [CSWE] 1994), the question is how equity is defined and where social work education stands with respect to the use of racial preferences in the admission process. Previous accreditation standards (CSWE 1988, 1991) required social work education programs to make specific, continuous efforts to reflect racial, ethnic, and cultural diversity throughout the curriculum and in all categories of persons related to the program. This standard was eliminated in the most recent accreditation guidelines (CSWE 1994).

In my opinion, it is imperative for social work education to support the goal of diversity in affirmative action policy and to recruit and retain students who represent diverse backgrounds. This will require social work education to address the issue of access and excellence and to publicly establish its position in this regard. To do this, there must be a critical analysis of this issue and a positioning of social work education in this debate. Consequently, the purpose of this paper is to present recruitment strategies and techniques developed to enhance the enrollment of students of color that have been previously presented in social work literature, to help resolve the issue of access and excellence for social work education by proposing an alternative conceptualization of excellence, and to propose practices that need to be established in social work education to help ensure the retention of students of color. The first section of this chapter presents recruitment techniques and strategies that will assist programs in their efforts to recruit students of color. The second section addresses the issue of access and diversity and presents a conceptualization of excellence based on talent development, a conceptualization that has been proposed as a resolution of the inherent conflict between access and excellence.

The third section focuses on how this conceptualization can inform criteria for admissions to social work education that may be more equitable than quantitative measures and more likely to reflect greater diversity in admissions. The final section addresses the concern about the retention of students of color and presents suggestions for practices that will improve the success of social work education in this regard.

Recruitment Strategies

For several decades social work educators have been extolling the virtues of increasing the enrollment of students of color. It has been proposed that the inclusion of students from diverse racial and ethnic backgrounds can contribute to the solution of critical urban and racial problems and that because of their experiences, lifestyles, and interests these students can enrich the educational program by helping other students and faculty become more sensitive to the needs and demands of "minority" communities (Greenberg and Scott 1970). Over a decade ago some social work educators believed there was a disproportionate number of non-minority social workers serving minority clients, and for this reason they encouraged social work educators to increase the numbers of minority students in social work education programs (Jones and Jordan 1984). More recently, social work education has been challenged to train more minority students because of the demand for professionally trained practitioners who already are sensitive to and understanding of the plight of disadvantaged minority clients (Berger 1989, 1991).

There has been a good deal of literature in social work education reporting on the successful strategies and techniques for recruiting students of color; however, much of this literature was published more than twenty-five years ago (Berger 1989, 1991; Billingsley 1970; Greenberg and Scott 1970; Hall 1974; Jones and Jordan 1984; Kramer and Miller 1974; Levitt 1970; Oliver and Brown 1988; Robertson 1970; and Scott 1971). Even though this literature is dated, the suggestions and recommendations for recruitment and retention are still applicable today. This literature includes descriptions of outreach efforts designed to attract and motivate minority students. Greenberg and Scott (1970) reported survey results on practices graduate schools of social work used in 1969 in their recruitment strategies. Among the successful efforts were working with admissions officers in their outreach attempts, utilizing alumni contacts, and establishing relationships with community organizations. Schools reported that they lowered or waived admissions requirements on an individual basis, reserved a particular number of scholarships or sought special scholarships for minority students, and established a percentage of spaces for students from ethnic minorities in the entering class. While these practices are commendable on the part of social work education, quotas are illegal and using special criteria to enhance diversity is a practice that is currently hotly contested.

Billingsley (1970) reported on the success of recruitment efforts at the University of California at Berkeley. There a special faculty committee for minority recruitment was established, and it was supported by top university administrators and the Dean of the School of Social Welfare. The recruitment program included developing outreach linkages to students from minority groups, providing special counseling and advising to prospective students to assist them in the application process, developing more flexible admissions requirements, developing academic assistance programs, and hiring more faculty members from minority groups. Billingsley indicates that in spite of the misgivings on the part of some faculty about lowering standards, most of the students performed well in the classroom and in the field.

A decade later, Oliver and Brown (1988) presented a plan for the recruitment of minority students and discussed the tasks and strategies that were effective in their school of social work. They first presented what they considered to be basic recruitment principles and then proceeded to describe the tasks in the recruitment process. The principles constitute the philosophical position that should underlie any recruitment effort and are as follows: (a) those in the institution who hold power and who represent the majority populace should be visibly and actively involved in all aspects of recruitment; (b) recruitment programs should develop and facilitate links between and within minority students' social networks; (c) service components that will obviate problems before they negatively affect academic performance and that will enhance access need to be an integral part of the recruitment effort; and (d) retention efforts must be a planned part of the recruitment effort.

A framework for planning and developing a recruitment program is considered essential to the success of recruitment efforts and consists of the following parameters: (a) determining the readiness to effectively mount a recruitment and retention program; (b) developing a support structure to ensure a receptive and supportive environment; (c) designing the recruitment program; (d) engaging in specific recruitment activities; (e) assessing the contributions and limitations of the program; and (f) institutionalizing the program.

Even more recently, Berger (1989, 1991) presented recruitment strategies she considered effective in the recruitment of minority students to undergraduate social work education. She recommended that social work programs work with admissions officers who recruit students from high schools. Even though this group of potential students is perceived as sometimes too immature, they may have special abilities with populations such as children in special settings, the elderly, and physically and mentally impaired individuals. She also suggested developing relationships with community colleges in the area and encouraging students to consider a career in social work. Social welfare organizations in large urban areas are another place to recruit. Targeting minority individuals who hold low-level jobs and using training programs to identify potential students are some recommended strategies. In her most recent article, Berger (1991) describes a collaborative effort of a union, a hospital, and an undergraduate social work program that proved successful in recruiting and retaining minority students. This collaborative effort targeted clerical and technical workers in social service agencies and provided an opportunity for employees to attend college full-time.

It was refreshing to find that as early as 1970 Robertson (1970), in her presentation of social work education's responsibility to enhance the enrollment of students from minority groups, alerted social work educators to keep in mind that there were two distinct groups of minority students, each requiring different recruitment strategies. The first group consists of a large number of minority students who are well prepared for higher education but may not have considered social work as a career or may hold negative perceptions of the social work profession. Recruitment efforts for this group of potential students would focus on changing their perceptions of social work and persuading them that social work is a viable option for pursuing career satisfaction. Too often in the discussion of recruitment of students of color, it is assumed that these students are educationally disadvantaged, and as a result students of color are associated with deficits, which in turn leads to the perceived need to lower standards.

The other group of students to which Robertson (1970) referred are those who may be educationally disadvantaged but not marginal students, and she reminds us that there is a difference between these two characteristics. The disadvantaged student lacks adequate preparation because he or she could not access necessary resources; however, this student has the potential to successfully complete a social work education program. This student can be accommodated in social work education programs only if we alter our concept of intelligence and achievement and reflect this expanded conceptualization in admissions criteria and instruction. Marginal students, on the other hand, lack basic academic skills and/or appropriate characteristics to the extent that it would drain resources to bring them to a required level of performance. Admissions procedures and criteria must be developed so that these two groups of students can be distinguished.

The point to be made here is that there are students of color who would make excellent candidates for undergraduate and graduate social work education programs, and we should not automatically associate students of color with academic deficiency. However, much of the literature in higher education on the inclusion of previously excluded groups has been based on the perception that one has to "lower" standards for admissions and thus compromise excellence for the purpose of inclusion. This perception is at the center of much of the current controversy on diversity and access in higher education. If social work education is truly committed to the inclusion of racial and cultural diversity, then we as faculty must give serious attention to the issue of access and excellence and must critically examine our admissions criteria in social work education.

Equity and Excellence

Admissions Issues in Social Work Education

Admissions procedures and criteria in social work education have been a concern to social work educators for some time. Some social work educators believe that the quality of social work education is being lowered by the presence of academically ill-prepared students. As noted earlier, this perception has led them to propose a more stringent admissions policy requiring higher undergraduate grade point averages (GPAs) and higher scores on standardized tests as criteria for admission to graduate social work programs (Hepler and Noble 1990). Adopting such admissions criteria is seen as "tightening up standards" and "screening out" applicants who are likely to fail in the more demanding academic environment of graduate school (Hepler and Noble 1990).

Other social work educators, no less concerned about quality control in social work education, warn us that gatekeeping should be done to maintain high professional standards, not to eliminate types of people with whom educators are uncomfortable (Moore and Urwin 1990). Access to social work education, according to Moore and Urwin, should be open to students who can contribute their diverse strengths and skills to the social work profession. Social work educators, according to these authors, have the responsiblity to help students identify and apply their strengths. Consequently, the admissions process should examine not only scholastic ability but also each student's potential for growth and change and her or his concern for people.

Several decades ago there was much more open discussion in social work education about making admissions criteria more flexible in order to accommodate students of diverse backgrounds. Among other recommendations for removing obstacles to enrollment of minority students, Scott (1971) advances the idea that schools should reassess their admissions criteria and consider giving less emphasis to grade point average and test scores. Hall (1974) points out that although standardized tests may contribute to admissions decisions, they have some limitations because even the best test cannot measure all of the desired characteristics. Hall further points out that while it may be difficult to distinguish among applicants who have creativity, talent, and ability, admissions procedures should discern those values in the applicant's experiences that are professional attributes. She contends that this cannot be done with the usual measuring tools. Levitt (1970) suggests some modified admissions criteria for social work education that include (a) the importance of drive toward an education possessed by students who are first in their family to receive a college education; (b) the involvement of students in civil rights activities; and (c) weighting grade point average by the extent to which a student had to seek employment.

Since the 1970s the "silent majority" has become the "conservative right," and modifying admissions criteria and procedures for the purpose of inclusion of diverse groups has been severely attacked. Modifying admissions criteria and procedures is seen as lowering standards and compromising quality. Developing more flexible admissions criteria had been seen as equitable and a move toward social justice by those who wanted more inclusion. Now, tampering with admissions criteria is seen as inequitable and socially unjust and as jeopardizing excellence. Supporters of inclusion have proposed a reconceptualization of excellence in higher education and a reexamination of standards as resolution to the ostensibly inherent conflict.

Excellence from a Reputation and Resource Perspective

The reputation and resource conceptualization of excellence in higher education defines excellence in terms of (a) the research productivity and scholarly visibility among faculty, (b) the admission of students with high academic performance who may gain recognition after graduation, and (c) the amount of financial resources an institution can secure from various sources (Astin 1994). These criteria are used to rank institutions and serve to promote fierce competition among institutions to recruit the "best and brightest" faculty and students. To achieve excellence in reputation and resource conceptualization, institutions must establish and maintain "standards" for selective admissions of students, and these generally refer to the performance of students with respect to GPA and scores on standardized tests. Students with high grades and good test scores are so aggressively sought because they enhance the institution's reputation and its ability to secure additional resources.

Universities whose mission incorporates a vision of excellence within this conceptualization based on reputation and resource are concerned with identifying "talent" and developing selective admissions criteria that will help to ensure the institution's reputation (Hollins 1995). Excellence translates into student outcomes that show low attrition rates among students, a high proportion of students attending graduate schools, and large percentages of students making good salaries. The reputation and resource perspective prompts institutions to ensure these outcomes by identifying those students who have the greatest potential to achieve them (Richardson and Skinner 1991). Faculty also must enhance the reputation of the institution within this conceptualization of excellence through their scholarly activity and their ability to secure resources that will further enhance the reputation of the institution. Such faculty endeavors often leave less time to spend on developing academic abilities among students, and as a result fewer resources are required. Admitting students with higher GPAs and standardized test scores reduces the amount of resources that have to be deployed in teaching and the development of the students' abilities. In these institutions most of the responsibility for learning is placed on the student, and diversity among students is restricted by weeding out a majority of those who cannot survive an academic environment that offers only limited learning assistance (Richardson and Skinner 1991).

The reputation and resource conceptualization of excellence and its concomitant high scholastic admissions criteria have been criticized for fostering a unidimensional image of what it means to be a good student (Clark and Garza 1994; Gardner 1993). Formal testing, for example, does not take into account differences in how students learn, nor does it assess the varieties of expertise that may contribute to a student's success (Gardner 1993). Grades also have been criticized as a criterion for admissions to college because they reinforce old exclusivities. According to Hollins (1995), grades are frequently based on undisclosed and implicit criteria and represent a value judgment made by each professor. Hollins views academic grading as the reward for employing acceptable yet implicit conventions for representing knowledge based on the European-American culture.

The "excellence-in-education" reform movement opposes achieving diversity by "lowering" academic standards and admitting students who did not achieve high scores on standardized tests and did not attain high GPAs during their secondary education years. Many educators see this reform movement, which developed in the 1980s with the election of President Reagan, as a backlash against the policies and programs of the 1960s and 1970s that promoted diversity. It is not by mere chance that this reform movement coincides with attacks on multiculturalism, affirmative action, and bilingual education and with severe cutbacks in financial aid for college-bound minorities as well as with a dramatic return to overt racism on college campuses (Halcon and de la Luz Reyes 1991; Thompson and Tyagi 1993).

Excellence versus Equity

In the context of the reputation and resource conceptualization, excellence seems to inherently contradict an equitable distribution of resources. Admission based on criteria other than high test scores or grade point averages is deemed inconsistent with quality and excellence and also inequitable and unfair. For many, equity means giving just rewards for past performance. However, some educators strongly believe that an institution concerned with quality and excellence, as defined within the reputation and resource conceptualization, excludes rather than welcomes diverse populations (Kuh and Whitt 1988; Minnich 1990; Richardson and Skinner 1991; Smith 1989). These educators contend that when educational equity is conceptualized as equal access, one way to measure whether equity has been attained is the enrollment of underrepresented groups in proportion to their representation in the general population.

Attaining equity within the reputation and resource conceptualization of excellence, on the other hand, is a zero-sum game according to Astin (1994). Only so many resources can be distributed within an institution, and if we allocate more resources for the remediation of underprepared students, this leaves fewer resources for the better prepared students. Within the reputation and resource conceptualization of excellence, admitting students who are seen as underprepared dilutes excellence. In the eyes of their critics, institutions promoting access represent poor educational quality, while institutions raising their admissions standards emphasize quality (Richardson and Skinner 1991).

With shrinking financial resources for higher education, the expansion of educational opportunities to disadvantaged students poses the greatest threat to "excellence" within the reputation and resource model. Resources allocated to "underprepared" students come under scrutiny, and in many instances remedial programs are eliminated to preserve resources. Reduction in support programs, accompanied by an increase in GPA and test score requirements, results in exclusionary practices, which pose a dilemma for educational institutions concerned about both equity and excellence. This dilemma accounts for the inherent conflict between equity and excellence within the reputation and resource approach to excellence. This dilemma also has prompted a change in the academic culture (Richardson and Skinner 1991) and a critical examination of the concept of excellence (Minnich 1990). This reexamination of excellence will, according to its proponents, result in a reconceptualization of excellence in higher education.

Excellence: A Mystified Concept

The concept of excellence has become a cultural artifact in higher education although it is embedded in most mission statements. While excellence is a powerful concept in that it undergirds many decisions in institutions of higher education, it is an ambiguous concept, subject to many interpretations. According to Minnich (1990), excellence is a mystified concept—one that is opaque, ambiguous, yet powerful because it serves systemic interests. Mystified concepts, while appearing to be neutral, persist because their opacity veils how they serve the interests of the dominant culture in the academy, which locks everyone into old hierarchies and forms of thought; further, mystifying concepts tend to be mind-numbing because they are fraught with emotion (Minnich 1990). The concept of excellence is considered a prime example of a mystifying concept, and Minnich's perspective on this matter is summarized below.

Excellence is invoked with great frequency in discussions of the mission of higher education, especially when discussions are provoked by considerations of possible changes in how the mission should be understood and carried out. It is rare, however, for those who invoke excellence in these discussions to identify what they actually mean by it. A call to "return to excellence" or to "maintain excellence" is actually a call to solidify one's loyalty to tradition; in fact it is a defense of tradition that serves to solidify the "rank and file." Commitment to excellence means adherence to traditional measures of excellence, and this, according to Minnich, is where the root of the problem lies. These measures become *the* representation of excellence, and the fact that these standards as representations of quality lack neutrality and are overgeneralized is ignored. In essence, the means have become the ends within the dominant tradition insofar as what has already been judged excellent by these measures becomes the standard for anything else to be judged excellent.

Traditional measures of excellence are not neutral tests of abilities, but rather serve to protect exclusivity by weeding out those who fall short of these narrow measures of excellence. Those who defend the use of traditional tests of abilities believe that any change in how these measures are used to determine excellence leads to a lowering of standards to achieve inclusion. Advocates for inclusion, however, maintain they are not lowering standards but rather augmenting narrow measures of excellence, because a call to excellence should not be a rush to judgment based on standards that lie along a single plane. Reconceptualizing excellence in higher education as discussed in the following section has implications for access by diverse populations.

Talent Development Perspective of Excellence

The current hierarchy of institutions of higher education, based on the reputation and resource conceptualization of excellence, has resulted in a system of education in which institutions on the upper end of the hierarchy are accessible to those who are deemed capable and worthy of the resources and benefits of these institutions; institutions on the lower rungs are the only ones accessible to those who are less prepared and thus less worthy of the resources of higher education (Halcon and de la Luz Reyes 1991). This hierarchical system would be inverted if we defined excellence on the basis of the talent development conceptualization, wherein the focus is on how well the institution performs in bringing students to expected levels of competency by the time of graduation.

The talent development approach to excellence measures excellence in terms of how effectively an institution develops educational talent among its students and, according to Astin (1994), depends less on which students are admitted by institutions and more on what is done for students once they are admitted. The approach emphasizes performance at exit rather than at entry. When an institution wants to maintain standards and enroll a greater proportion of underprepared students, a greater share of resources must be deployed to deal effectively with those students and more time must be given to students to reach performance standards. Consequently, such an institution must shift its paradigm for excellence from one in which academic standards are determined at admissions to one in which academic standards are achieved by the time of graduation. Thus an institution focuses on what it does to achieve academic standards and to maximize the number of students who reach minimum performance levels by graduation.

In the talent development perspective of excellence, quality is judged more by the program's offerings than by its admissions standards. Quality and access (excellence and equity) are both addressed when institutions accommodate the growing diversity on college campuses by emphasizing teaching and support strategies and, at the same time, by ensuring fair representation of previously underserved populations. Assessment focuses on identifying the strengths and weaknesses of students in order to design a more appropriate learning environment as opposed to identifying how to reconcile the students to the prevailing pedagogy and curriculum. Richardson and Skinner (1991) point out that when information about performance levels of entering students and desired exit competencies are used to alter pedagogy and curriculum for diversely prepared students, this strategy serves to provide a "level playing field" and thereby addresses equity issues. (Further discussion of such practices takes place later in this chapter in the section on student retention.)

Developing Talent

Academic standards within the talent development conceptualization of excellence relate more to the teaching and learning process than to the skills and abilities students have at entrance to support exit performance. Thus, excellence relates to the quality of the curriculum and the learning environment.

According to Hollins (1995), the increasing multiculturalism in the population and the pool of students from which the institution must select make talent development an imperative rather than an option, and this requires a change from a Eurocentric paradigm of operation to one that is more responsive to cultural diversity in the student population. Hollins further contends that to rely on grades as the primary criterion for admissions is not a good measure of academic abilities because traditional grading practices are based on value judgments and undisclosed criteria. The students who receive favorable grades are those who have acquired cultural norms, values, and ways of perceiving the world that are consistent with those of European-Americans. Students from different cultural and ethnic backgrounds who have not acquired these norms, values, and perceptions may receive lower grades even though they may not be less capable of complex thought and creative endeavors (Hollins 1995).

A talent development conceptualization of excellence can be utilized in social work education to assist in developing admissions criteria that will reflect excellence and maintain diversity. Preparation of students in both scholastic and professional academic areas is critical to the success of social work education. There is some concern that criteria addressing professional qualities and behaviors are not given sufficient attention in both the admissions process (Gibbs 1994) and at termination (Koerin and Miller 1995); however, I contend that a talent development conceptualization of excellence directs us to more inclusionary measures, which take into account the complete range of academic performance criteria.

Excellence and Equity in Social Work Education

Talent Development in Social Work Education

Conceptualizations of excellence in social work education reflect both the reputation and resource and the talent development perspectives. In the early 1980s quality in social work education was seen primarily from the reputation and resource perspective (Ginsberg 1982). A decade later, however, when Munson (1994) queried social work educators through focus groups, he found indicators of excellence consistent with both the reputation and resource and the talent development perspectives. Indicators reflecting the talent development perspective included such measures as the ability to enhance learning as well as the professional and personal growth of students, the ability to equip students for success, the development of a climate fostering diversity, and the capacity to instill higher aspirations in students.

A talent development perspective in social work education focuses our attention on the identification of characteristics essential to the development of professional competence and the deployment of resources to ensure the development of this competence. While the talent development perspective suggests that given sufficient motivation, time, and resources, any student can reach the desired level of competence, Astin (1994) warns that there are negative consequences for professional programs that admit all applicants. Some characteristics commensurate with professional competence are more amenable to development than others, and therefore, if a program is concerned about diminishing resources, efforts should be directed at developing those characteristics more amenable to change. Although there should be minimum levels of performance related to all areas of professional competence, minimum performance levels for those characteristics less amenable to change should be higher than those for characteristics more amenable to change.

Social work educators should be concerned with both professional and scholastic academic standards during the admissions process; however, admissions decisions are almost exclusively based on academic criteria of a strictly scholastic nature (Gibbs 1994). Academic criteria for BSW programs generally consist of GPA in nonsocial work courses in addition to evidence of sound skills in written and oral communication (Gibbs 1994). Academic criteria of a professional nature consist of emotional and mental stability, adherence to social work values and ethics, and congruence between personal values and social work values (Gibbs 1994). Criteria also include an absence of criminal and illegal behavior, ability to make use of self, absence of personal problems that significantly interfere with learning, adequate interpersonal skills, and responsible and appropriate behavior suitable for professional practice (Koerin and Miller 1995). Academic criteria of a professional nature seem to pose the greatest difficulties for social work educators during admissions and termination processes. Koerin and Miller indicate that screening out applicants who are academically able but otherwise unsuitable during the admissions process is complicated by the subjective nature of the definition and assessment of professional qualities. Even when there is an attempt to assess professional suitability, admissions accouterments such as essays and the like do not adequately reflect an applicant's professional qualities (Gibbs 1994).

I contend that to address the issue of equity and excellence in social work education we should give greater attention to characteristics related to professional behaviors and modify our emphasis on criteria related to scholastic achievement. In my opinion, this would make admissions criteria more inclusive, resulting in a more diverse student population, and it would be more congruent with the talent development perspective of excellence. Resources would be allocated to areas of performance that are more amenable to change.

Social work literature provides some evidence that values, attitudes, and personal qualities are not greatly affected by education (Frans and Moran 1993; Judah 1979; Merdinger 1982; Moran 1989; Varley 1963, 1968); therefore, it may be unwise to direct resources to bringing about a change in these characteristics. On the other hand, there is some evidence that academic skills are amenable to change given an understanding of how students learn. It is my position that when we are talking about raising standards, we should consider raising the level of expectations related to professional characteristics and devote sufficient resources to bringing students to appropriate levels of scholastic performance. This suggests that we must identify admissions criteria that clearly set minimum levels of performance and/or skills in all facets of academic expectations in order to   utilize our resources more efficiently. Therefore, social work educators must devote more attention and resources to the conceptualization, identification, and assessment of the desired professional characteristics for the purposes of admission and retention.

Bringing students to acceptable performance levels in a professional program requires a tremendous investment in resources. Social work programs communicate this investment of additional resources needed for professional programs to university administrators in their self-study reports. When faculty almost exclusively use scholastic criteria to determine admissions and become concerned about raising those criteria to "weed out" unsuitable applicants, they have decided that they do not want to put resources into the development of students. It is my contention that a more efficient and appropriate investment of resources would be to develop criteria of professional competence, such as the students' personal and interpersonal characteristics, skills, values, and attitudes. Since it is much easier to develop scholastic skills than it is to transform the students' values, attitudes, and personal and emotional characteristics, I think we would use fewer resources and enhance goal attainment if we focused on "weeding out" inappropriate students on the basis of these latter characteristics. From the talent development perspective, faculty are compromising excellence and using up tremendous resources when they focus on developing characteristics less amenable to change.

I do not believe that we are "lowering" admissions standards when we admit students who may have a lower GPA and/or standardized test scores but who may possess the characteristics and attitudes central to professional development. Admitting a student whose scholastic achievement is lower than that of another student but whose emotional intelligence and social attitudes are more congruent with professional social work does not constitute a "lowering" of standards. While I recognize that prospective students *must* possess a minimum level of scholastic ability to perform effectively, more inclusive admission criteria are needed. GPA and standardized test scores can be considered as long as measures of personal characteristics such as emotional intelligence and social attitudes also are used. Social work educators should broaden their conceptualization of admissions criteria and not view this strategy as a lowering of standards. We are lowering standards when we fail to identify minimum professional behaviors and performance levels and assume that if we get students with high grades and standardized test scores, we are getting the "best and brightest" who are appropriate for the social work profession.

Social work educators have lamented the difficulty of changing students' attitudes and values and have expressed concern about graduating students who excel academically but nonetheless have values and attitudes that are inconsistent with the profession. However, admitting students who may not possess appropriate values is not considered a compromise in "excellence" and "quality" of social work education; at least a movement to raise these standards is not evident.

I contend that it is far easier to develop students scholastically than it is to change students' basic attitudes, values, and personal characteristics, which may impact their future professional effectiveness. Would it not be a more efficient use of resources to develop minimum criteria in the area of professional characteristics and then direct more resources into developing students' scholastic abilities? Would it not be more inclusive to relax the level of scholastic performance required for admissions and raise the level of criteria that we consider critical to the development of a professional social worker? I find it hypocritical for social work educators to cry "foul" when scholastic criteria are "relaxed" for the purpose of admitting students who may be more suitable for professional practice than students who perform well by scholastic standards but may not possess appropriate professional characteristics. If social work educators viewed excellence within the talent development perspective, more attention would be given to the development of admission criteria that better reflect the professional behaviors critical to effective practice and measures for assessing these criteria could be developed.

Currently, social work education is preoccupied with measures that reflect the reputation and resource perspective of excellence with its inherent assumption that higher test scores and GPAs determine who might be a more effective future practitioner. In other professional programs, however, this does not hold true.

Teacher education programs have already begun to acknowledge the limitations of test scores as indicators of preparation for entry to higher education (Justiz and Kameen 1994). National leaders, according to Justiz and Kameen, are posing questions to the educators of future teachers about the meaning of standardized test scores as an admissions criterion, maintaining that standardized tests measure the ability to take standardized tests, rather than the ability to acquire knowledge. This position has led to a call for a more comprehensive perspective on assessing prospective teachers that will include valid measures of the affective as well as the cognitive factors essential to the development of effective teachers.

What is needed is deployment of more resources for the development of students' scholastic skills, which, as noted, are more amenable to change than emotional and social characteristics. Additionally, we need to develop measures for use during admissions that can assess the level of students' emotional intelligence and social attitudes.

Conceptualization of Multiple Intelligences

Howard Gardner (1993), in his book *Multiple Intelligences: The Theory in Practice*, presents the idea that there are multiple intelligences. His theory is conceptualized within the purview of cognitive and developmental psychology, building upon biological and evolutionary roots of cognition and cultural variations in cognitive competence. He defines intelligence as the ability to solve problems or to create products that are valued within one or more cultural settings (15). The intelligences identified by Gardner include linguistic, musical, logical-mathematical, spatial, bodily-kinesthetic, and personal. Personal intelligence includes both intra- and interpersonal intelligence and is the form of intelligence that would be most useful in terms of more inclusive admissions criteria and academic standards.

Gardner argues that educators primarily focus on logical-mathematical and linguistic intelligence in testing and expectations for performance. Hence, most resources have been devoted to assessing and developing these intelligences to the exclusion of other forms of intelligence. While these aspects of intelligence may be important, personal intelligence, which was later conceptualized by Goleman (1995) as emotional intelligence, is an aspect of intelligence that is more central to social work professional competence. In the following sections, I present the basic characteristics of this conceptualization and suggest how it can be used to inform the development of criteria and measures for admissions and retention in social work education.

Intrapersonal Intelligence

Intrapersonal intelligence is the capacity to access one's own range of affects or emotions, to discriminate among these feelings, label them, and then to draw upon them as a means of understanding and guiding one's behavior. Through this type of intelligence comes the capacity to form an accurate model of oneself and the ability to use that model to operate effectively in life. Self-identity and the ability to transcend the self are components of intrapersonal intelligence. At its most advanced level, intrapersonal knowledge allows one to detect and symbolize complex and highly differentiated sets of feelings. A developed sense of self is seen as the quintessential manifestation of intrapersonal intelligence that emerges from a fusion of one's intrapersonal and interpersonal knowledge.

Self-awareness—the ability to engage in introspection and know oneself—is a characteristic we deem essential to effective practice, and we invest a good deal of resources to develop self-awareness in our students. The inability to access one's own emotions and be able to draw upon them to better understand oneself is certainly a deficiency that would negatively affect professional practice. The literature devotes a good deal of attention to how we go about helping students develop this capacity through the use of journals and other types of written assignments and classroom exercises, and we recognize that the inability of some students to successfully engage in this level of introspection presents a problem.

I believe we could and should assess a student's level of intrapersonal intelligence at admission. Because this characteristic can be measured, minimum levels of performance can be set for the purposes of admission and retention. Some useful exercises have been developed to help educators access and amplify intrapersonal intelligence (Lazear 1991). These exercises can be modified for social work education's use in the admissions process, and they could also be used during an introductory course in social work. Lazear maintains that intrapersonal intelligence can be awakened by any exercise or activity that causes self-reflection and raises questions about self-identity. While he has described a number of exercises to tap into different aspects of intrapersonal intelligence, exercises that access a transpersonal sense of self, awareness and expressions of different feelings, and tracking one's thinking may be useful in social work education. These exercises generally set up a scenario, guide students through the reflection process, and ask them to record reflections and insights. Criteria can then be developed to determine the extent to which a student has been able to access his or her self.

Interpersonal Intelligence

Interpersonal intelligence is the ability to understand other people: what motivates them, how they work, and how to work cooperatively with them. It is the capacity to notice and distinguish among the moods, temperaments, motivations, and intentions of others. This intelligence in its advanced form permits a skilled adult to read the intentions and desires of others even when they have been hidden. Interpersonal intelligence also includes the capacity for genuine empathy for another's feelings, fears, anticipations, and beliefs.

To access this form of intelligence Lazear (1991) developed exercises that require an individual to become involved in structured situations in which he or she must rely on others for the completion of a project. The individual is required to "listen deeply" to others and focus on what they are saying as well as on what they might be thinking or feeling based on various nonverbal cues. In one exercise designed to access sensitivity to another person's moods, temperaments, and feelings, an individual is asked to read something to another individual who is instructed to react normally without verbal comment. The reader's task is to carefully watch the partner's reaction and try to sense his or her feelings precipitated by the reading. The reader then tells the partner his or her perceptions of the partner's thoughts and feelings.

The reader also tells the partner what cues prompted the reader's interpretation of the partner's thoughts and feelings.

In another exercise that is useful in assessing an individual's social skill of understanding and appreciating a perspective that is quite different from his or her own, the individual is asked to intentionally place himself or herself in a situation where he or she strongly disagrees with another person. While conversing with this other person, the individual must attempt to understand where the other person "is coming from" by listening carefully to the other person's perspective. The individual can ask questions but must not share his or her own opinions. After this encounter, the student then writes a statement describing how his or her own perspective has been informed by the conversation and what social skills were learned as a result of the experience. Criteria for assessing responses could be developed that would determine the extent to which a student is able to discern the perspectives of others, which indicates the student's empathic capacity.

These exercises on intrapersonal and interpersonal intelligence can be built in as part of an introductory course in social work or in a prepractice skills course. Many programs require students to complete introductory courses prior to official admissions into the social work major. For those programs that require a prepractice skill development course these exercises are ideally suited. Programs can determine the criteria for assessing performance and decide on the minimum level of performance a student must attain in order to be admitted to the program. Of course, it is assumed that a variety of measures will be included in admission decisions. A program can assess students in multiple ways: via measures of intelligences, scholastic measures such as GPA and test scores, and measures on values and attitude instruments. A composite measure could be developed and a minimum composite score could be identified.

Empathy is another dimension of interpersonal intelligence and is also a critical component of professional competence. While a good deal of attention is devoted to the development of students' empathy, it would be informative to assess a student's capacity for developing empathy at admission. There are a number of scales that could be used to assess empathy, including the Hogan Empathy Scale and the Questionnaire Measure of Emotional Empathy

(Wortman 1989). Videotapes can also be used to increase levels of emotional and expressed empathy (Vinton and Harrington 1994).

Values and Attitudes

In addition to considering personal-emotional intelligence in admission and retention, attitudes and values consistent with those of the profession should also be taken into account as critical. Some of the measures used by social work educators to assess aptitudes, to determine the extent of socialization to values, and the consistency of personal values with social work may be used for admission and retention efforts after minimum levels of performance are established. The values and attitudes assessed by these instruments are presented below.

Social and Economic Justice. Social and economic justice is now one of the nine foundation areas in the most recent Curriculum Policy Statement (1994). A student's beliefs about social justice are an important consideration. The Belief in a Just World Scale and a Social Justice Advocacy Scale were used by Van Soest (1996) in her attempt to assess the impact of social work education on students' attitudes. Social justice attitudes also have been assessed by Moran, Frans, and Gibson (1995) using a Social Humanistic Scale developed by Howard and Flaitz (1982, cited in Moran, Frans, and Gibson 1995). A scale measuring attitudes toward poverty has also been developed and tested by Atherton and others (1993) and could be used as a measure of attitude toward economic justice.

Attitudes Toward Social/Cultural Diversity. Carrillo, Holzhalb, and Thyer (1993) assessed the attitudes of social work students to cultural diversity and identified a number of measures that could be used for this assessment. Racial attitudes, for example, were measured using such scales as The Acceptance of Others, The Modern Racism Scale, and the California F-Scales. The Acceptance of Others Scale seems particularly relevant to social work education in that it measures diversity, one of the nine foundation areas in CSWE's Curriculum Policy Statement. This scale assesses the students' ability to tolerate and value diversity and to accept others on their own terms. Inventories and questionnaires designed to assess gender role attitudes also are described by Carrillo, Holzhalb, and Thyer. These measures identify the extent of the respondents' categorical thinking about sex roles, the extent to which a person's expectation of another person's behavior are based on gender stereotypes and attitudes toward female sex-role equality. (Readers can secure more information regarding the various scales utilized from the article.)

Values. The socialization of students to the values and ethics of the profession is of critical importance in social work education. As indicated earlier, there is considerable evidence that the social work education curriculum has little, if any, significant impact on changing a student's basic values, and the need to assess suitability at admission is underscored by social work educators such as Cobb and Jordan (1989). A value orientation compatible with professional ideals includes, for example, beliefs in (a) the individual as the primary concern of society, (b) the democratic process and use of the democratic process for the realization of full potential for each individual, and (c) a pluralistic society and respect for diversity (Judah 1979).

An instrument used to measure two dimensions of ethical decision reasoning, which are linked to personality structures and not related to intelligence or academic achievement, was developed by Hess and Williams (1974). The Social Work Questionnaire (SWQ), which measures four social work values—equal rights, service, psychodynamic mindedness, and universalism—was used by Judah (1979) to assess the extent of change in values over the course of the curriculum, and it also has the potential to assess a student's readiness for entry into the professional program. The Social Humanistic Ideology Instrument, another useful tool designed by Howard and Flaitz (1982, cited in Moran et al. 1995), measures a person's attitude to individual freedom and human nature as well as beliefs about social justice.

Student Retention: Conceptualizing an Approach

Although the previous discussion attempts to identify some of the professional characteristics that should be given serious attention in the admissions process, additional efforts must be devoted to the retention of students to graduation. I believe students must be able to comprehend and retain concepts and ideas in order to benefit from the further enhancement of their critical and analytical thinking. I also believe that students should be able to clearly present their ideas (in writing and orally) and that skill levels in this area should be determined at admission. However, the ability to retain students of color requires a social climate and educational environment that is sensitive to the needs of diverse students.

Creating an environment in which the student feels accepted is critical to the retention of students, especially for previously marginalized students who are sensitive to any cues that may signal a lack of acceptance. Creating a hospitable environment that is welcoming to students does not require much effort or resources on the part of the social work program. It just requires sincerity and a valuing of differences. I have found that being warm and receptive to students in the admissions process as well as being able to reduce anxiety about this process is extremely helpful. This is the first step in opening up access to students, and it is a critical encounter for students of color. This is the time when students are assessing whether they belong and whether the program is really interested in what they have to offer.

The teaching performance of faculty and the provision of a meaningful curriculum are critical factors in student retention. Upholding academic standards means planning and developing student-centered instruction of high quality that facilitates learning among diverse groups of students. Hollins (1995), in his attempt to develop faculty performance, identifies the requirements for improving instruction so as to address academic standards of both quality and equity. The first requirement is to establish links between the students' background knowledge and the new content being presented, because learning takes place when the learner can integrate new knowledge with prior knowledge. Consequently, faculty must have some knowledge of the perspective and background of diverse students. The second requirement is for faculty members to study their individual teaching practices. This includes systematically documenting patterns of failure and successes in reaching course objectives as well as critically reflecting on student feedback. This also requires that faculty routinely conduct student assessments of their teaching and respond to that feedback.

Creating a learning environment that incorporates a variety of stimuli and supports for learning is the third requirement. Options in the learning environment include strategies and activities that encourage both analytical and holistic thinking. Links must be established to encourage natural collaboration among different groups of students. There must also be clear connections between theory and abstract conceptualizations, on the one hand, and the background and experiences of students on the other. Explicit and clearly defined connections between course objectives and personal goals of students also are important.

The fourth requirement addresses managing the learning environment in such a way that a common experience is created that can serve as a reference point when students experience difficulty with technical content. To achieve this, faculty must "get students on the same page," that is, create a common theme throughout the course that supports, illustrates, and advances student learning and that is used repeatedly to reinforce learning. As can be seen, the suggestions advanced by Hollins (1995) are not unique to a talent development perspective but rather represent "plain old good teaching." Utilization of these strategies is consistent with principles of excellence in teaching and is considered effective with a broad range of students in higher education.

There has been much debate and controversy about the idea that preferences in learning styles can be used to characterize entire groups of people. The appropriateness of generalizing about racial and gender groups has been challenged (Green 1989), and we should, therefore, be cautious and not make sweeping and simplistic generalizations in this regard. On the other hand, while there has been no research that establishes definitive links between learning style and race, culture, or gender, there are consistent findings across such disciplines as psychology, sociology, anthropology, and linguistics that suggest some correlation (Anderson and Adams 1992). This research could be informative if we are careful to avoid the danger of stereotyping.

Creating a classroom that is sensitive to diversity and developing quality teaching that provides an intellectual home for culturally diverse students benefits all students (Green 1989). Some principles that can assist faculty in this area are presented by Green and include (a) encouraging student and faculty contact both within and outside of the classroom; (b) encouraging cooperation among students; (c) encouraging active learning; (d) providing prompt and appropriate feedback on student performance; (e) pacing tasks and helping students realize the time needed for tasks; (f) communicating expectations explicitly; and (g) respecting diverse talents and ways of learning.

Faculty who are committed to developing an inclusive classroom must examine their own implicit cultural assumptions that inform their instructional practices. It has been pointed out that the most sacrosanct practices in academe remain unstated, unexamined, and unacknowledged until they are challenged by divergent beliefs from outside the predominant culture (Adams 1992). Those who have been socialized into the traditional academic culture are scarcely aware of these implicit norms; however, those who have not already been socialized into this culture find that their values and beliefs are in conflict with traditional classroom procedures, often characterized as the hidden curriculum. Difference must not be regarded as a greater or lesser departure from the "norm," but rather must be valued in itself. According to Adams, the learning process involves implicit cultural values that define the social interrelations and behavior among instructors, classroom peers, and the individual. Rather than choosing between one teaching strategy or another, an instructor is advised to recognize that instructional design involves the consideration of the learning process from the point of view of the learner and the selection of strategies with the perspective of the learner and the intentions of the instructor equally in view.

This multiculturally responsive teaching does require a commitment on the part of faculty. Some may view this as too time-consuming and emotionally demanding. In addition, some may believe that the efforts put into this multiculturally responsive teaching will not be rewarded when it comes time for promotion and tenure. My response is that this approach requires a paradigm shift about what constitutes good instruction and also requires that time be devoted to developing a better understanding of the teaching and learning process. This initial investment of time is analogous to the time devoted to learning how to use technology in the classroom. After an understanding of how to utilize this technology is attained, the instructional process is much more efficient and effective and requires much less time and effort. Also, as with technology, when the institution and the program value the benefits of such approaches, these efforts are rewarded. Faculty concerned about accumulating publications for promotion and tenure can also produce scholarly publications in the area of multiculturally responsive teaching.

Multiculturally responsive teaching, as any endeavor we undertake, requires commitment and a desire for quality and excellence in social work education. For those who are unwilling to engage in multiculturally responsive teaching because they say that it takes too much time, I ask "How are you currently utilizing the time you devote to teaching?" Developing this approach merely requires a redirection of efforts, not necessarily additional time. For those who currently devote little time to their teaching and believe this takes too much time away from more preferred activities, I have no answer. You must be committed to excellence in teaching and want to reach diverse learners to undertake the approach I presented. Having a better understanding of the learning needs of diverse learners and being able to employ instructional methods to address these needs will result not only in effective instruction but also in more efficient teaching.

This chapter has briefly summarized past attempts at recruiting students of color, addressed the issues of access and excellence, and presented strategies that I think will help in the retention of students of color in social work education. Recruitment strategies that have been successful for social work educators over the past several decades were presented with the expectation that useful strategies could be extracted. In responding to the concern about "lowering" admissions standards for the purpose of enhancing diversity, I attempted to demonstrate that a reconceptualization of excellence resolves this inherent conflict. With regard to retention I have made suggestions for developing an environment sensitive to diversity and have presented strategies for multiculturally responsive teaching.

I believe social work education can achieve the goal of diversity and at the same time enhance quality and excellence. To do this, however, we must become more inclusive in our admissions criteria and develop procedures to assess characteristics not measured by standardized tests and grades. The characteristics and measures I have identified in this chapter are merely suggestions. My intent is to get social work educators to think about the kinds of characteristics we may want to examine and to suggest ways in which we could measure what are traditionally characterized as nonacademic characteristics. I certainly recognize the need for research on the effectiveness of using such measures in admissions and invite social work educators to engage in such endeavors. Also, my suggestions are not meant to be exhaustive; rather, they are intended to get educators to think about how to move in this direction.

Retaining minority students requires an examination of the cultural assumptions in academe and changes in traditional practices to accommodate differences. The development of a culturally sensitive environment that permeates the entire educational program is necessary for the retention of students. We must be careful not to view differences as a euphemism for deficits but must instead value differences for their contribution to the enhancement of the program. While consideration must be given to differences in learning style, faculty must be careful not to make sweeping generalizations that result in stereotypes. Attention should also be given to interpersonal relations among students in the classroom as well as to culturally sensitive contact with faculty both inside and outside of the classroom.

Social work education's commitment to social justice and equity requires it to take a good look at itself and strive toward being truly inclusive. I have attempted to challenge social work educators' thinking about what it takes to be inclusive with respect to admissions and retention and hope we can begin to move in this direction.

References

Adams, M. (1992). Cultural inclusion in the American college classroom. In L. L. B. Border and N. Van Note Chism (eds.), *Teaching for diversity,* pp. 5–17. San Francisco: Jossey-Bass.

Anderson, J., and Adams, M. (1992). Acknowledging the learning styles of diverse student populations: Implications for instructional design. In L. L. B. Border and N. Van Note Chism (eds.), *Teaching for diversity,* pp. 19–33. San Francisco: Jossey-Bass.

Astin, A. (1994). Educational equity and the problem of assessment. In M. Justiz, R. Wilson, and L. G. Bjork (eds.), *Minorities in higher education,* pp. 44–63. Phoenix, AZ: American Council on Education and Oryx Press.

Atherton, C., et. al. (1993). Measuring attitudes toward poverty: A new scale. *Social Work Resesarch and Abstracts* 29 (4): 28–30.

Berger, R. (1989). Promoting minority access to the profession. *Social Work* 34:346–349.

Berger, R. (1991). Untapped sources for recruiting minority BSW students. *Journal of Social Work Education* 27:168–175.

Billingsley, A. (1970). Black students in a graduate school of social welfare. In C. A. Scott (ed.), *Ethnic minorities in social work education*, pp. 23–28. New York: Council on Social Work Education.

Carrillo, D. F., Holzhalb, C. M., and Thyer, B. A. (1993). Assessing social work students' attitudes related to cultural diversity: A review of selected measures. *Journal of Social Work Education* 29:263–268.

Clark, M. and Garza, H. (1994). Minorities in graduate education: A need to regain lost momentum. In M. Justiz, R. Wilson, and L. G. Bjork (eds.), *Minorities in higher education*, pp. 297–313. Phoenix, AZ.: American Council on Education and Oryx Press.

Cobb, N. H., and Jordan, C. (1989). Students with questionable values or threatening behavior: Precedent and policy from discipline to dismissal. *Journal of Social Work Education* 25:87–97.

Council on Social Work Education (CSWE)), Commission on Accreditation. (1988, 1991). *Handbook of accreditation standards and procedures*. Alexandria, VA: CSWE.

Council on Social Work Education (CSWE), Commission on Accreditation (1994). *Handbook of accreditation standards and procedures*. 4th ed. Alexandria, VA: CSWE.

Frans, D. J., and Moran, J. R. (1993). Social work education's impact on students' humanistic values and personal empowerment. *Aretê* 18 (1): 1–11.

Gardner, H. (1993). *Multiple intelligences: The theory in practice*. New York: Basic Books.

Gibbs, P. (1994). Screening mechanisms in BSW programs. *Journal of Social Work Education* 30:63–74.

Ginsberg, M. I. (1982). Maintaining quality education in the face of scarcity. *Journal of Education for Social Work* 18 (2): 5–11.

Goleman, D. (1995). *Emotional intelligence: Why it can matter more than I.Q.* New York: Bantam Books.

Green, M. F. (ed.). (1989). *Minorities on campus: A handbook for enhancing diversity*. Washington, D.C.: American Council on Education.

Greenberg, H. I., and Scott, C. A. (1970). Ethnic minority-group recruitment and programs for the educationally disadvantaged in schools of social work. In C. A. Scott (ed.), *Ethnic minorities in social work education,* pp. 11–22. New York: Council on Social Work Education.

Halcon, J., and de la Luz Reyes, M. (1991). "Trickle-Down" Reform: Hispanics, higher education, and the excellence movement. *The Urban Review* 23:117–135.

Hall, E. H. (1974). Increasing minority enrollment in a predominantly white university. In R. Lodge (ed.), *Black perspectives on social work education: Issues related to curriculum, faculty, and students,* pp. 26–37. New York: Council on Social Work Education.

Hepler, J. R., and Noble, J. H., Jr. (1990). Improving social work education: Taking responsibility at the door. *Social Work* 35:126–133.

Hess, D., and Williams, M. (1974). Personality characteristics and value stances of students in two areas of graduate study. *Journal of Education for Social Work* 10 (3): 42–49.

Hollins, E. (1995). Academic grading and assessment in a culturally diverse university. In B. P. Bowser, T. Jones, and G. A. Young (eds.), *Toward the multicultural university,* pp.135–143. Westport, CT: Praeger Publications.

Jones, J. M., and Jordan, A. R. (1984). Part-time education for minorities: A black and white issue. *Journal of Continuing Social Work Education* 3 (1): 53–7.

Judah, E. H. (1979). Values: The uncertain component in social work. *Journal of Education for Social Work* 15 (2): 79–86.

Justiz, M. (1994). Demographic trends and the challenges to American higher education. In M. Justiz, R. Wilson, and L. G. Bjork (eds.), *Minorities in higher education,* pp. 1–15. Phoenix, AZ.: American Council on Education and Oryx Press.

Justiz, M., and Kameen, M. (1994). Assessment in higher education and the preparation of minority teachers. In M. J. Justiz, R. Wilson, and L. G. Bjork (eds.), *Minorities in higher education,* pp. 285–296. Phoenix, AZ.: American Council on Education and Oryx Press.

Koerin, B., and Miller, J. (1995). Gatekeeping policies: Terminating students for nonacademic reasons. *Journal of Social Work Education* 31:247–260.

Kramer, P. H., and Miller, S. O. (1974). Eliminating racial barriers in schools of social work: A conceptual framework. In R. Lodge (ed.), *Black perspectives on social work education: Issues related to curriculum, faculty, and students,* pp. 38–50. New York: Council on Social Work Education.

Kuh, G. D., and Whitt, E. J. (1988). *The invisible tapestry: Culture in American colleges and universities.* Washington, D.C.: Association for the Study of Higher Education.

Lazear, D. (1991). *Seven ways of knowing: Teaching for multiple intelligences*. 2d ed. Arlington Heights, IL: IRI/Skylight Training and Publishing.

Levitt, L. (1970). Recruiting minority-group students to social work. In C. Scott (ed.), *Ethnic minorities in social work education*, pp. 7–9. New York: Council on Social Work Education.

Merdinger, J. (1982). Socialization into a profession: The case of undergraduate social work students. *Journal of Education for Social Work* 18 (2): 2–19.

Minnich, E. K. (1990). *Transforming knowledge*. Philadelphia: Temple University Press.

Moore, L. S., and Urwin, C. A. (1990). Quality control in social work: The gatekeeping role in social work education. *Journal of Teaching in Social Work* 41 (1): 113–128.

Moran, J. R., Frans, D., and Gibson, P. A. (1995). A comparison of beginning MSW and MBA students on their aptitudes for human service management. *Journal of Social Work Education* 31:95–105.

Moran, J. R. (1989). Social work education and students' humanistic attitudes. *Journal of Social Work Education* 25:13–19.

Munson, C. E. (1994). Characteristics of excellence in social work education. *Journal of Social Work Education* 30:42–53.

Oliver, J., and Brown, L. B. (1988). The development and implementation of a minority recruitment plan: Process, strategy and results. *Journal of Social Work Education* 24:175–85.

Richardson, R. C., and Skinner, E. F. (1991). *Achieving quality and diversity*. New York: Macmillan.

Robertson, M. E. (1970). Attracting minority group members to social work: Professional education's responsibility. In C. Scott (ed.), *Ethnic minorities in social work education*, pp. 1–6. New York: Council on Social Work Education.

Scott, C. A. (1971). Ethnic minorities in social work education: Issues, trends, and developments. In A. M. Pins, C. A. Scott, F. M. Loewenberg, and A. Stamms (eds.), *The current scene in social work education*, pp. 15–27. New York: Council on Social Work Education.

Smith, D. G. (1989). *The challenge of diversity: Involvement or alienation in the academy?* Washington, D.C.: ASHE-ERIC Higher Education Reports.

Thompson, B., and Tyagi, S., eds. (1993). *Beyond a dream deferred: Multicultural education and the politics of excellence*. St. Paul, Minn.: University of Minnesota Press.

Van Soest, D. (1996). Impact of social work education on student attitudes and behavior oncerning oppression. *Journal of Social Work Education* 32:191–202.

Varley, B. (1963). Socialization in social work education. *Social Work* 8:102–109.

———. (1968). Social work values: Changes in value commitments of students from admission to MSW graduation. *Journal of Education for Social Work* 4 (2): 67–76.

Vinton, L., and Harrington, P. (1994). An evaluation of the use of videotape in teaching empathy. *Journal of Teaching in Social Work* 9 (1/2): 71–84.

Wortman, J. E. (1989). Empathy and social work: The capacity of students for cognitive and emotional empathy as it relates to field instruction evaluations. Ph.D. diss., Fordham University. Abstract in *Dissertation Abstracts International* 51, 04A, p. 1392.

6

Gatekeeping in Field Education

Ginny Terry Raymond

Education for social work practice began as apprenticeships with seasoned practitioners. Eventually courses were taught to workers as in-service training in agencies, then later at colleges and universities. Summer courses evolved into a full, year-long program, then a two-year curriculum. Regardless of the amount or design of coursework, the practicum or field placement has remained central to education for social work throughout its history.

Many in the profession believe that the quality of the practicum directly affects the quality of the entire educational program and, eventually, the quality of social work practiced by graduates (Task Force 1983). Field education is the component of the curriculum that most clearly distinguishes education for professional practice from general or liberal education.

During the practicum the knowledge, values, and skills of the profession are applied in actual work with clients under the tutelage of a master. This is the *doing* component of professional education. Lodge (1975) refers to field education as both *learning by doing* and *learning for doing* and believed that other professions "looked to social work as a model in the use of the practicum" (i).

Schneck (1996) believes that the practicum "takes on a 'larger than life' significance in the professional development of our students. . . . Without a doubt, it is the primary means by which we prepare the next generation of social workers who will engage and assist people who live in a complicated, ever-changing, and problematic world" (vii). The field education experience and the field instructor, then, are central to the acculturation of students into the social work profession. It is in this positive context of acculturation (i.e., passing on information and skills and *opening* the gate) that the word *gatekeeper* is used in other disciplines such as information studies, sociology, and anthropology. Among the earliest to use this term, Lewin (1947) describes housewives who influenced the eating habits within their households as *gatekeepers*. Current investigators in information studies use the term *gatekeepers* for those who help others gain access to the information resources needed to address problems. These gatekeepers are receivers, disseminators, and interpreters of information. They expose people to new ideas and ways of behaving. They influence public opinion. They are agents of acculturation within their communities (Metoyer-Duran 1993).

By contrast, in the social work literature the term gatekeeping has taken on a negative connotation, referring to keeping the unqualified or unsuitable out of the profession—keeping the gates closed, screening out, counseling out, putting out (Cole 1991; Moore and Urwin 1991). A 1994 discussion on gatekeeping continued for weeks on one of the early social work discussion lists on the Internet. Both views of gatekeeping were expressed in this discussion; however, the focus was more often on concerns about screening out unsuitable students. Debates about gatekeeping are often most heated and intense regarding the suitability of students for practice with clients during their field practicum.

The Council on Social Work Education (CSWE) has taken the lead in gatekeeping in field education by not allowing classroom experience, life experience, or previous work experience to substitute for any portion of the 400 clock hours of field education required for a baccalaureate degree in social work (BSW) (CSWE 1994:88). Additionally, the field practicum is now the single component of a BSW program's curriculum from which students, other than candidates for the baccalaureate degree in social work, are barred according to CSWE accreditation standards (CSWE 1994:92). The CSWE requires that programs have clearly articulated criteria and processes for student admission that "reflect an appreciation for the requirements of the profession and of professional social work education" (CSWE 1994:87). These processes should lead to acceptance of those who are "best qualified to become professional social workers at the beginning level of practice" (87). However, there are no specific criteria in the CSWE's Curriculum Policy Statement or in the accreditation standards for admission to the program or to field education. Each program is required to develop these and make them known to students.

There may be some sense on a college campus that students in good academic standing (i.e., with the required minimum grade point average) have a right to take courses and proceed to the next level of coursework in the series if they have performed on exams and papers at passing levels. There is also a desire on the part of faculty to have sufficient enrollment in courses so that the program is viable. When students enter their field practicum, however, the faculty may believe it is time to look more closely at the students' suitability. Because of its proximity to professional practice, the practicum, understandably, is the component of professional education that receives the greatest attention in discussions of screening students for the profession.

Timing of Field Education

Both the nature and timing of screening students for field education are affected by the curriculum design for field education. One consideration is how soon students are allowed to enter field education after declaring social work their major. This is influenced by the structure or design of field education, that is, whether it is a concurrent, block, or partial block field placement design. A *concurrent* field placement is one in which students are enrolled in classroom courses at the same time they are in field placement. Typically students attend classes three days a week and go to their field placement two days a week, or vice versa. In a *pure block* field placement, students go daily to their field setting and do not take classroom courses at the college or university during that term. In a *partial* or *modified block* arrangement, students are typically in field education the great majority of the week, usually four days. They attend class(es) one day a week, often taking an integrative field seminar for credit hours and possibly a social work elective. In a concurrent arrangement, students usually enter field education at an earlier point in the educational program than they would in a block placement. They are often taking practice courses on campus while concurrently *practicing* in the field. Students in a block placement have usually completed the professional-level courses and can then give all of their attention to the field placement. They are putting into practice all they have learned in the classroom. There are other variations of field placement design, but some form of these three is most typical. BSW students, therefore, have usually taken some classes in the social work major prior to entering field education, although this is not always the case.

Typically, the BSW student does not begin field education, whether block or concurrent, until the junior year and, for some, not until the senior year (e.g., a 400-hour, one-semester block placement in one of the two semesters of the senior year). This kind of arrangement provides opportunity for faculty to observe both the academic performance and the behavior of the social work major for at least two or three years prior to the time that the student enters the field. The possibility of such observation is increased if the student has declared social work as a major at an earlier point and been advised by social work faculty even prior to entering the professional courses. The student has probably taken an introductory social work course and perhaps a social work elective. There might also be a social work student organization that all majors can join. These organizations often have a faculty advisor who could observe student interactions at meetings, involvement in service projects, etc.

Even in these BSW programs, however, some students transfer into social work from another major on the same campus, or they transfer from another institution with the requisite courses and hours to immediately enter the professional social work curriculum. Such students would go directly into field education if that program has concurrent field placement that begins in the first semester of the professional program. For these students, the screening process for entrance into the program also serves as screening for field education.

Screening Prior to Field Education

What are the screening mechanisms for entrance into field education? While the CSWE has no specific mandated criteria, either for entrance into the social work program or into field education,

Gibbs (1994) found in her survey of baccalaureate programs (N = 207) that 77 percent (N = 159) had a formal screening of students for admission to the program or major. *Ninety-five percent* indicated they had a screening process *for field education*. However, the criteria were typically of a *scholastic* nature for both admission to the program and to the field education, meaning grade point average (GPA) and/or prerequisite course requirements. The GPA requirement for entrance into field education varied as to which courses were used for calculating the GPA (e.g., overall GPA, in major, in certain courses). Only five of the programs asked for references or recommendations on the students for entrance into field settings. One program required NASW membership, two required malpractice insurance, and two required some measure of commitment to social work and its values as well as a concern for people. Only five used a criminal record check as part of screening for admission to field education.

The overwhelming majority (95 percent) of the programs said they gave field instructors the opportunity to reject a student from field placement at their field site, but students were then permitted to do their placement at another field site if accepted by a field instructor. In other words, a student rejected by an instructor was not automatically evaluated in a special manner, but rather immediately sent for an interview or placement with another instructor. Gibbs also found that students in these programs who were admitted to the field placement tended to complete the program successfully. Respondents stated that only five or fewer failed. Also, 82 percent said that students were given a second opportunity for field placement if they did not successfully complete their first field experience. Consequently, the overwhelming majority of students make it into and out of the program.

These data indicate that programs screen for field education largely on the basis of GPA. If field instructors are given an opportunity to screen students, they are the ones who examine suitability not just in terms of academic performance. Even then, programs tend to continue to seek another placement for students who have been rejected, and the overwhelming majority of students graduate. Students who have difficulty may just take longer to complete the degree. Some give up on pursuing the major, but rarely is anyone dismissed as unsuitable.

While Gibbs's findings indicate that few BSW programs do criminal record checks on students, at social work education conferences in the past few years faculty have reported that more and more of their field agencies are requiring this kind of check on students as part of their acceptance process. Students are screened by these agencies just as prospective employees are. What is done with the results of such checks is not known. Some anecdotal reports indicate that persons who have been convicted of a felony are not accepted by some agencies for field placement. Convicted felons are not allowed to take a social work licensing exam in some states. The question has been raised as to whether social work programs in states that do not allow persons with a felony conviction to sit for a licensing exam should be held responsible for informing prospective students that they are not eligible for a social work license in the state even if they graduate from the program. Currently, social work programs are not typically using criminal records checks as part of screening for the program or of gatekeeping for the field education, though some social work educators predict that agencies will increasingly require such checks. Because so many programs screen only by grade point average, field instructors complain that social work programs are placing more and more of the gatekeeping burden on them while the program simply calculates grade point averages. In discussions about gatekeeping at national conferences, faculty and program directors report that fear of litigation causes them to shy away from applying professionally oriented standards that are hard to define and measure and are often erroneously referred to as "nonacademic" standards, as discussed later in this chapter. Field instructors have reported that they feel discouraged by the program to use gatekeeping procedures against students because the program fears litigation (Hipple and Harrington 1995).

Many in the profession might be troubled to hear that grade point average and course requirements are most likely to be used by programs to determine a student's readiness for field education. However, a study that measured factors predicting the success of baccalaureate students in field education found that GPA is as good a measure as any. Cunningham (1982) compared faculty evaluations of student performance in the field ($N = 83$) with GPA, age, assertion inventory scores, previous organization leadership and membership roles, volunteer experience, and previous work experience. The findings indicate high grade point average to be the most important variable in predicting success in field education. Another variable, lower age, also was significantly related to good performance in the practicum. An earlier study (Dailey 1974) had examined academic admission procedures in schools of social work and found that full-time faculty showed some capacity to predict classroom success for social work students but no capacity to predict field placement success of students.

Moore and Urwin (1991), while acknowledging Cunningham's finding of high GPA as the best predictor of success in field education, call for more guarding of the field education gate. They believe that students should be assessed with regard to what Bloom (1990) refers to as "psychological equilibrium" (94), and what Cobb and Jordan (1989) consider essential to practice, that is, "ethical behavior and psychological well-being sufficient to interact positively and instructively with clients" (94). Moore and Urwin recommend a structured interview process, which they prefer to call an "evaluation conference," to reflect both the self-evaluation the student engages in and the faculty team's evaluation of the student, including scholastic areas of performance as well as professional values and behavior. They view this process as assessment of academic performance in scholastic areas, of the student's self-awareness, and of the fit of the student's values with those of the profession. The combination of these variables, they believe, more adequately represents a truly professional assessment.

Their evaluation process starts with the student's application for field education. As part of the application, students are required to describe their strengths and limitations, practice interests, previous experience with giving and/or receiving help, demographic information, and academic record. A conference with the student is then scheduled with a small group of faculty (usually three). In the conference there is discussion with the student about

> academic performance (both achievement and skills); volunteer experience and evaluation of that experience; work experience; and any extenuating circumstances that may have affected performance such as family problems, illness, job responsibilities, and behavioral patterns. Factors that impact student choice of social work as a major are discussed with emphasis on how those factors can be positive or negative. Also discussed are personal/family background, life experiences, and experiences as a client that can affect professional potential and readiness.

(11–12)

Moore and Urwin explain that faculty are evaluating the student's sense of responsibility, communication skills, adherence to social work values, and ability to handle criticism or accept feedback. After this phase of the conference, the student is excused while the faculty discuss what has taken place and also make a decision regarding the field placement. The student is then invited back in for the final phase of the evaluation conference. The faculty present their decision, feedback, and potential field site to the student if the student is approved. The student can then share reactions to the feedback and decisions. The faculty makes one of three choices for the student: approval, postponement of placement, or removal from the program. In most cases faculty approve students for field placement.

Moore and Urwin see this screening process as helpful to the student in that it is a rehearsal for the next phase in the approval process, the interview with the field instructor. For those students found not yet ready, goals and objectives are clearly stated. Most often, such students are asked to get more academic or volunteer experience and to reapply in a year. Specific referrals are made if appropriate (to writing centers, study skills classes, etc.). Although Moore and Urwin do not discuss this, some programs refer students to counseling or therapy about concerns that have arisen. Some make the therapy a condition for continuation in the programs or for reconsideration of the student's application in the future. Olkin and Gaughen (1991) caution, however, that personal therapy as a remedial plan is problematic. Goals are unclear. Are those goals set by the therapist or the program? Time lines are not clear. The question arises as to whether the student should continue in the program while in therapy or withdraw and, if so, for how long? Treatment and its progress are confidential; therefore, the program should not participate in it. Finally, according to Olkin and Gaughen, the link between therapy and the essential skills for professional practice are "shaky."

No doubt, some students whose field placement is postponed choose to change majors because of the additional time it would then take to complete the social work major. The program may consider them as having been "counseled out" of the program, though the student may view it as a voluntary withdrawal or simply a change of major.

Moore and Urwin (1991) do not state directly how often students are terminated from their program during this evaluation for field education; however, based on the few studies that have been done (Constable 1977; Dinerman 1982; Gibbs 1994), it is safe to guess that this rarely happens. Examples Moore and Urwin give of students terminated are those who demonstrate "values . . . inconsonant with the profession, inappropriate motivation for entering the profession, or behaviors that can be detrimental to both clients and students" (13).

Moore and Urwin recognize that this type of screening requires commitment of faculty time and energy and the support of the university administration since law suits might result. It is important that students are given due process; that is, they must be apprised of this procedure well in advance of its occurrence. This can be done through description of the requirements and the process in catalogues, application materials, student handbooks, and field manuals. The use of a panel of faculty, rather than one person for the interview and evaluation, is highly recommended because such evaluations inevitably involve subjective judgments. Courts have already ruled that subjective judgments, such as personal interviews of students by faculty, are not automatically arbitrary and capricious (*Arizona Board of Regents v. Wilson* 1975; *Grove v The Ohio State University College of Veterinary Medicine* 1976). The deliberation of a panel of professionals adds credibility to the procedure.

Moore and Urwin's approach to screening for the field practicum provides one alternative to the use of strictly scholastic measures such as GPA. Others philosophically counter the alarm raised by heavy reliance on GPA and other scholastic standards as measures of readiness for field education by advocating that the field practicum be approached as any other course. They believe that social work majors should be given an opportunity to succeed or fail in the field if they are successful in the courses that are prerequisite to the practicum. The idea is that students are not finished products. They go into the field to learn, to be acculturated into the practice of the profession by gatekeepers who should approach them in the positive sense of the word. Students enter the field setting with practice skills learned in the classroom (or skills they will be learning concurrently if they are in a concurrent field placement). However, these practice skills cannot possibly be finished products since they are the result of skills developed, typically, in role play with fellow students, rather than in actual practice with clients.

Unlike those who are concerned that programs are screening students for field placements based primarily or solely on scholastic achievement, some educators in social work are alarmed that faculty would attempt to screen students based on information of a more subjective nature. An Internet social work discussion group of faculty and practicing social workers, SOCWORK, had a lively interchange on this topic in 1994. The group discussed students being rejected from programs because the applicants dared to state career goal interests in private practice and/or marriage and family counseling (MSW applicants) or because they dared to state that they thought not all problems are necessarily social problems and that individuals can also be the source of problems, or they expressed some other "politically conservative" opinion (April 18, 19, 21, 1994). In the words of one person who wrote that he works in an agency and has a private practice on the side, "What is surprising, in a profession which strongly advocates for tolerance and understanding of diversity of belief, behavior, and life-style in our clients, is our near zero tolerance of dissent within our own ranks." He commented on his observations of responses in the *NASW News* when someone expresses something other than the "party line," such as an anti-abortion opinion. The response, he said, is "condemnation for heresy" and "they don't belong in the profession" and "calls for excommunication." He believes social work faculty are all too often "pure ideologues" not in touch with the realities of practice. Somebody else wrote, "I think that nowhere in social work is there more nonsense than around the admission process and the [expletive] words of those who think they know what they are looking for—especially in terms of values. We have had enough of guilty faculty projecting their fears on to student applicants" (April 21, 1994). A Canadian, who posted a message on September 28, 1994, agreed with those on the list and noted that there was no known research that supports the idea that certain personality characteristics make one a successful social worker.

These writers believe that the profession is (or should be) broad enough to accommodate a range of personality types.

Another strong argument could be made that grade point average is a good indicator of readiness for practice responsibilities in field education, especially if those grades include social work practice courses. Students' grades, particularly in practice courses, should reflect their knowledge of the values and ethics of the profession and their performance in role play involving practice skills, including ethical dilemmas and exercises for the clarification of values. Programs often include volunteer experience as part of their introductory courses and/or practice courses. Often these assignments require the student to keep a journal, which could reflect performance in practice roles as well as the student's level of self-awareness. Grading this volunteer work might also include feedback from professionals and other staff at the human services agency or organization about the student's behavior and performance. Grades earned in these courses should, therefore, reflect more than the performance on exams.

The Field Instructor's Role in Gatekeeping

As Skolnik (1985) states, "Field education provides an arena for skill development, knowledge integration, and affective learning; as such, it is a pivotal core component in the professional education process" (1). Such a view might best be expressed by the phrase: students going into the practicum should be ready *for* practice, but not necessarily ready *to* practice. According to this philosophy, the field instructor is truly a teacher and gatekeeper (one who acculturates), rather than a supervisor or monitor of the student's practice. This approach places tremendous responsibility on field instructors. Programs must take seriously the mandate from the CSWE and not only orient field instructors but also train them in their important task of preparing students for beginning professional practice. Some programs offer credentialing programs to their field instructors and require that all instructors be credentialed prior to being assigned a student for placement. Programs must not only prepare field instructors for their teaching role but also involve field instructors in development, assessment, and revision of the curriculum (CSWE 1994:92). Moreover, program faculty and/or staff must be involved in the student's field instruction through "frequent liaison visits to the agency to coordinate and monitor field learning assignments" (92).

Liaisons from the social work program worry that field instructors are busy and, therefore, do not want to be bothered with frequent contacts by the liaison. Or the liaison may simply not want to spend the time that visits and contacts involve. Recent studies (Bennett and Coe 1997; Coe 1994) have found that the field instructor's satisfaction with the academic program is, in part, related to interactions with the liaison and perception of support by the liaison. Furthermore, the field instructor's satisfaction increased when the frequency of contacts with liaisons and the perceived willingness of the liaison to consult with the field instructor increased. Bennett and Coe (1997) reported that five contacts by the liaison (i.e., on site at the placement or a combination of meetings on site, at the university, and/or by telephone) were typical of those field instructors who were highly satisfied.

Evaluation During Field Education

The CSWE accreditation standards require that programs have explicit policies regarding the assessment of students' academic and field performance, including procedures for terminating students for reasons of academic and, as they call it "nonacademic" performance (CSWE 1994:89). (See chapter 13 for a complete discussion of academic and nonacademic standards.) As with other such accreditation standards, however, the CSWE leaves it to each program to define these performance standards and present them explicitly to all parties.

Evaluation of students' practice is especially complex and problematic because of its subjective nature. Although the knowledge, values, and skills learned in the classroom are put into practice in the field, it is in practice that the art dimension of the art and science of the profession is most evident. In practice, the *use of self* is operationalized. Each social worker will develop his or her unique manner or style. Field instructors are asked to value the uniqueness of each student and the diversity among the students with whom they are entrusted, while being vigilant that all students meet, admittedly at a subjectively determined acceptable level, the requirements set forth by the program.

Social work programs must take seriously the requirement to develop policies and procedures for the evaluation of students. This requirement is in the best interest of all parties. How can our students knowingly achieve what we are asking of them if we do not make our requirements clear and linked, whenever possible, to measurable and observable criteria? In developing these criteria and policies, we must also be able to explain why these expectations are important in preparing students to be competent social workers. Field instructors who will use these criteria to evaluate students should be involved in developing them, as should those who will serve as faculty liaisons.

The instrument used for evaluating students' performance in field education should be developed from these criteria and policies, and such criteria and policies should be included in a course outline for field education as well as in a field manual. The criteria and policies must be consistent with the current CSWE Curriculum Policy Statement and with the accreditation standards for BSW programs (CSWE 1994) as well as with the unique mission and objectives of the program.

To start with, in developing a course outline for field education and the evaluation instrument for field education, a program should turn to the "Curriculum Policy Statement for Baccalaureate Degree Programs in Social Work Education," which is included in the *Handbook of Accreditation Standards and Procedures* (1994). It lists twelve objectives of what graduates of baccalaureate social work programs will be able to do (99) as well as specific requirements for practice content, including skills students must acquire (102–103). It is expected that these skills will be demonstrated and further developed in field education. Finally, the expectations about what the student should have the opportunity to do or experience in the field practicum are also listed (104).

The Evaluation Instrument

The evaluation instrument on the basis of which the students' performance in field education will be rated or graded should be reviewed with students at their entrance into field education. This activity mirrors the review of the course syllabus by the classroom instructor on the first day of class, which always includes the criteria for the evaluation of students by the instructor. This is the first step in due process; that is, students must be informed from the outset about what is expected of them and how they are to be evaluated.

The evaluation instrument (there may be one for midterm and a different one for final evaluation or one instrument used for both), is the contract that must be agreed upon by the program, the field instructor, and the student, just as a course outline is considered a contract between the student and the professor. As previously noted, the evaluation instrument(s) should be derived from the course outline for field education. Some programs or their various liaisons require that the instructor and student develop an additional contract that is more specific regarding what is to be accomplished at the agency and how. This more detailed contract may also be initiated by the field instructor or the student in the absence of such a requirement by the program.

The program's field evaluation instrument is often generic in order to accommodate the variety of settings in which students are placed. The contract states in more specific, preferably measurable and observable terms, what will be expected of the student in that particular agency setting. For example, one objective in the course outline for field education would be that students be able to do a case assessment. The evaluation instrument would list this as an expectation and have some kind of rating scale in order to indicate the student's level of performance. An additional more specific contract might state *how many* case assessments the student will conduct during the time in the placement at that particular agency.

Role of the Program Liaison

It is imperative that the faculty or staff liaison have contact very early in the field placement to review the evaluation instrument with the instructor and student so that there is clear communication and understanding among all parties about what is expected and how these expectations will be achieved.

The liaison should have the next conference no later than midterm in order to review the evaluation with the field instructor and the student. At the completion of the midterm session, it should be clear to all parties how the student has performed and what the expectations are for the student to successfully complete the field education experience. Agencies are often not able to provide the student by midterm with all experiences required for completion of the placement (e.g., the student has yet to conduct an interview, an assessment, a group session, etc.). A clear understanding must again be reached among all parties as to what each must do in the subsequent weeks so the student can accomplish, by the end of the placement, the expectations set forth in the program's field evaluation instrument and any additional contract that may be in use.

The importance of conferences with the student and all parties who will participate in the evaluation of the student cannot be overemphasized. If the student is assigned a field instructor and in turn is assigned by the instructor to another staff member for specific tasks or experiences, then that staff member—sometimes called a task supervisor—should be involved in an appropriate manner in the student's evaluation. As Nichols and Cheers (1980:55) pointed out, "Views of appropriate social work practice are often widely discrepant between agencies as well as between particular agencies and the training institution as well as between particular field instructors." The field liaison must be vigilant that all participating parties understand the expectations being placed on the student and how performance is to be evaluated. Outcomes must be specified and these must be translated into observable and measurable student behavior.

Nichols and Cheers also warn that it is important to insist on evidence from the field instructor (and anyone else who is responsible for evaluating the student) to support their evaluation of student behavior and performance. This is consistent with the faculty expectation that students give evidence to support their assessments of clients. Such an approach means that field instructors must have direct, firsthand information about the students' work on which to base their comments. This is not always easy to accomplish, but efforts should be made to directly observe the student's interaction with clients and agency staff. Outcome measures (i.e., learning contracts and evaluation tools) should be agreed upon and used. Staff with whom the student interacts should be asked about the student's performance, and client feedback should be sought whenever possible. In any case, it is imperative that those responsible for evaluation justify their assessments with concrete examples. This is most convincingly done when tied as closely as possible to behavior, preferably to more than one instance of the behavior.

Evaluation of Professional Performance

Beliefs and behaviors that are problematic or of concern with regard to professional ethics and performance are most likely to become apparent in field education, even if they have not been identified in the classroom. Some students do not speak up in the classroom setting or do not have occasion to exhibit problem behavior in that milieu. In practice courses, for example, role plays may be structured and may never elicit the particular problem behaviors or beliefs. The expectations of field education demand that students carry out workplace responsibilities and interact with clients and staff to solve problems. The student's competence in interacting with others and assuming professional roles is on display. Field instructors and program liaisons may serve as teachers, mentors, and role models–positive *gatekeepers*. However, the student must eventually perform in social work roles and tasks, as outlined in the field evaluation instrument, at an acceptable level in order to successfully complete this essential component of the curriculum.

As cited earlier, grade point average in academic coursework is the criterion that overwhelmingly determines admission to and success in professional social work programs, and very few students are unsuccessful (Dinerman 1982; Gibbs 1994; Hepler and Noble 1990; Wahlberg and Lommen 1990). If the overwhelming majority of students are admitted to and successfully complete social work programs, then perhaps the lively discussions and published articles on the topic of gatekeeping are much ado about nothing. However, it is reported in discussions at professional conferences, and in some publications, that classroom faculty and field instructors often shy away from or are discouraged from bringing problems concerning the conduct of students to the attention of others, especially in a formal manner (Cobb 1994; Hipple and Harrington 1995). One might conclude, therefore, that the number of students who are a concern to faculty and field instructors with regard to conduct and ethics is not truly reflected in the dismissal or failure statistics reported in published studies. As Cobb (1994) stated:

> Inevitably, social work faculty encounter students who violate ethical standards with clients, harass other students, or even threaten faculty members or staff. . . . Social work faculty members have conflicting perspectives on protecting the civil rights of students, faculty, staff, and current or future clients. Moreover, university attorneys and administrators are understandably reluctant to become involved in protracted legal struggles involving student dismissals.

(18)

Fear of litigation apparently persists in spite of a number of published legal cases in which universities have been justified in failing or dismissing students on academic grounds as well as on conduct that is often mistakenly referred to as *nonacademic* grounds. (See chapter 13 for a detailed discussion of academic and nonacademic standards.) These cases have been reported in social work and higher education journals (Cobb 1994; Cobb and Jordan 1989; Cole and Lewis 1993; McCarthy 1985).

Traditionally, courts have been reluctant to intervene in the academic matters of grading students, preferring to leave such judgments to faculty who are the recognized experts in their fields. Attorneys, program administrators, and faculty (including field instructors) are typically more reluctant to fail a student in field placement or to dismiss the student from the program due to conduct or performance in the field placement. This is because of the relatively subjective nature of grading or evaluating performance and the perceived difficulty of defending subjective judgments when challenged. However, courts have declared that a student's behavior or conduct can be considered an *academic* matter. Such rulings are extremely important. When the action by the institution involves a disciplinary response to *personal misconduct* and the student files suit to challenge this action, the court must examine closely the procedures followed by the academic institution in making its decision to deny the student some liberty or property (i.e., a passing grade, continuation in the degree program, graduation). When the behavior or conduct is determined to be an *academic* matter, the court recommendations for due process are much less burdensome and time-consuming.

The best known case relating to conduct in field education as an academic matter is that of the *Board of Curators of the University of Missouri v Horowitz* (1978). Horowitz was a student who had passing grades in her classroom courses, yet was dismissed from medical school because of deficiencies in her clinical performance. The decision for dismissal was based on her poor personal hygiene, poor interpersonal relationships with patients or clients, and her uncooperative style with peers. The medical school considered these personal qualities and behaviors integral to her *clinical performance*. The courts, in turn, decided that her clinical performance was an *academic* matter, most appropriately judged by the observation of experts, her clinical supervisor or instructor, in conditions of actual practice with clients or patients.

The Horowitz case clarified that inappropriate or unacceptable clinical performance in a practicum situation constitutes a violation of *academic standards* rather than *personal* conduct. This was a landmark decision for professional programs. The Horowitz decision reaffirmed cases that preceded it, and it has been upheld in subsequent cases (Cobb 1994). Social work faculty and administrators should, therefore, not shy away from enforcing standards of professional, ethical behavior on the part of students in field education. Their attention should, instead, be directed to having in place clear standards and expectations as well as procedures that ensure that students' rights are not violated in the gatekeeping process.

Courts tend to focus not on the grade or specific judgment of the faculty, but rather on whether the constitutional rights of the student have been upheld in the process. As stated earlier, courts look more closely at due process in the case of dismissals for personal misconduct than they do when the dismissal is based on academic misconduct. Nonetheless, due process concerns also must be addressed in program policies for academic performance. Unfortunately, courts that have ruled in academic cases, such as *Horowitz*, have not issued clear standards or procedures for meeting the requirements of due process, which might be useful in developing program policies for academic performance and performance review. (See appendix 4 for a sample academic performance review policy.)

In lieu of specific standards and procedures issued by the courts, academic programs would be well advised to follow general principles of due process in setting up procedures. There needs to be *proper notice* to students of *loss of liberty or property*. This would involve proper notice of the expectations for admission to the program and to field education, required standards of performance in field, codes of conduct, grading criteria and policies, and the consequences if the student does not comply, as discussed more fully in chapter 9.

Avenues for making the standards for admission to the program and field placement and the evaluation instrument known to students were discussed earlier in this chapter. With regard to the standards for ethical conduct and behavior in field education, courts expect that the academic program can show that the evaluation of the student's behavior in the field setting is "based on professionally accepted standards of behavior" (Grant 1989). The *NASW Code of Ethics* (National Association of Social Workers 1996) is clearly the most authoritative and recognized source for the standards of ethics and behavior of the profession. Therefore it is logical that a social work program can adopt and enforce the code as its required code of professional conduct in field placements, whether students are members of NASW or not. The social work program is responsible for overseeing and evaluating the student while in a field placement required by the program. Similarly, programs might also require conduct during field education that is consistent with the professional standards required by the state's social work licensing board. It is important that students understand these expectations prior to or immediately upon entering their field placement.

Academic programs should introduce the code of ethics to students in the first course majors are required to take. Most introductory social welfare and social work texts include the code of ethics, or a summary version, in an appendix. Reference is made to the code in chapters on values and ethics of the profession and in chapters on the practice of social work. According to accreditation standards, values and ethics must be taught or infused throughout the curriculum (CSWE 1994:98). With that as a given, aspects of the code should be taught in every social work course. There should be course objectives that show the code's importance to professional practice and help students to know and understand the code. There should be assignments and exam items that address the students' knowledge of the code and its use in practice situations. At the point of admission to the program, students might be required to read the entire code of ethics and write an essay on how one or more of the code's principles applies in a hypothetical practice situation. Some programs have students sign a statement that they have read the code and agree to practice in accordance with it, during their field education as well as later. (See appendix 3 for a sample contract.)

Students should be given opportunities to meet with a faculty advisor(s) or the chair of the program to discuss any aspect of the code they do not understand or that they believe they would have difficulty following in their professional practice due to their personal and/or religious beliefs. It is far better to clarify value and role conflicts prior to field placement and to resolve these than to wait until problems emerge in practice.

If the student's agreement to practice in accordance with the code of ethics has not been obtained in writing during admission to the program, then it should be obtained prior to admission to field education. It seems only logical that due process would involve that students are made aware of the expected code of conduct and are asked to agree to practice in compliance with it. Programs also might include expectations for adherence to the code of ethics in their policies on academic standards.

As discussed in chapter 9, another component of meeting due process requirements is evidence that the process for failing or dismissing the student was not arbitrary, capricious, or conducted in bad faith. It is important to point out here that the credibility of evaluations of students by faculty as experts is enhanced when more than one expert in the profession is involved in the process and both (or all) are in agreement with the evaluation of the student's performance. The earlier discussion on the importance of clear communication (and preferably frequent contact) between the liaison from the program and the field instructor (and anyone else at the agency involved in instructing and evaluating the student) is quite relevant to due process concerns.

Finally, due process includes not only proper notice but also the opportunity for all parties to express openly their concerns and disagreements with the charge and the action taken (Alexander and Alexander 1985). Students should be given an opportunity, but not be required, to respond to the charges or reasons for the action taken against them.

In sum, the evaluation of field performance includes the assessment of all facets of academic performance, and due process must be protected at all junctures.

Students with Handicapping Conditions

Most social work programs by now have addressed or begun to address the requirements of the Americans with Disabilities Act (ADA 1990) during the admissions process and in relation to accommodations in the classroom and in all facilities important to required and general student activities. Mention needs to be made here of the implications of the law for field education. The two aspects of the law that have become the focus for whether or not the program or institution complies with the law and that are still being defined and clarified on a case-by-case basis are: what are the *essential functions* that must be performed by the person and what constitutes *reasonable accommodation* by the institution, faculty, and administrators?

Agencies are subject to the ADA with clients, employees, and job applicants; therefore, most have already addressed some of the concerns that might arise when a student with a handicapping condition applies for placement at an agency. When agencies are asked to address a unique situation with a student, perhaps the BSW program can be of assistance in working out the reasonable accommodations. The agency would then be prepared to accommodate potential employees with similar handicapping conditions.

The most important point for the program is the same point made earlier regarding the evaluation of students. It is imperative that faculty define as clearly as possible what the essential requirements are for being a social work student (admission to the program) and for being a social work student *in field education—ready for practice*, even if students are still in the process of *learning to practice*. Then reasonable accommodations must be defined on a case-by-case basis. It is important to point out here that there is a difference between the classroom and the field placement as far as protecting the rights of all parties is concerned. In field education the rights of clients also have to be protected. In fact, the rights of and obligation to clients *are primary* in the agency, rather than the educational needs of the students. (Chapter 10 provides an expanded discussion of disability law.)

Special considerations of the liability of field instructor and agency with regard to students and their clients are discussed in the next section.

Supervisor's Liability

Earlier sections of this chapter alluded to the reluctance of classroom faculty, field instructors, and program administrators to fail a student or recommend dismissal from the program for poor performance due to fear of litigation by the student, particularly when the action involves a judgment that appears to be of a subjective nature. A series of articles in social work and counseling journals has emerged alerting instructors and supervisors to their responsibility and liability for the trainee's practice and behavior.

Sharwell (1979–1980) used the provocative title, "Learn 'Em Good: The Threat of Malpractice," to draw attention to field instructors' liability for their students' practice. As he stated, "The social work educator . . . engaged in the supervision of a student or other person in the practice of counseling, casework, group work, or other social work functions can be sued by the client, by his representative, or a third party for negligent or improper professional practice" (41). Lawsuits brought against social workers are relatively few; however, in the past decade there has been a dramatic increase not only in the numbers but also in the amount of damages sought. More than one third of cases filed under NASW's malpractice insurance involve what is variously referred to as the *respondeat superior doctrine, indirect liability, imputed negligence,* or *vicarious liability* (Zakutansky and Sirles 1993). Vicarious liability can involve erroneous actions or omissions by a trainee for which the instructor or supervisor can be held responsible.

Instructing supervisors must be concerned about their students, but as Davenport (1992) reminds us, the supervisor's first responsibility is to the client, both ethically and legally. The *NASW Code of Ethics* is clear about this primary responsibility. There are some specific problem areas and suggested guidelines of which all supervising instructors for students in field education should be aware.

First, clients should be informed that the person assigned to work with them is a student in training. A consent form that advises the client of this in writing should be read to the client and signed by the client. These are the kinds of documents that make up the "paper trail" attorneys like to have as supporting evidence in case a complaint is lodged. The client also should be told of the limits of confidentiality, for example, that all (or most) of the student's work will be discussed with the supervising instructor and that the student's records will be read by the instructor. Otherwise, the door is left open for civil or criminal action based on failure to properly inform and failure to get proper consent. Also, it has been recommended by at least one state grievance board in its guidelines for supervision (of employees as well as students) that clients be given the name, address, and phone number of the supervisor (Robke 1993).

Field instructors must ensure adequate supervision. Under the doctrine of *respondeat superior*, the supervising instructor and the student are viewed as *one* regarding their responsibility for the client. If the student takes an action, the assumption is that he or she is acting with the permission of and as an extension of the supervising instructor. If the student makes a serious mistake or acts incompetently, the supervising instructor can be held responsible for allowing an incompetent, unprepared student to perform and thus putting clients at risk (Kadushin 1985).

Another area of liability involves requirements for the agency's record keeping. Keeping adequate records is imperative for all social work practitioners. Field instructors must require students to keep thorough records as one way for the instructor to stay informed of student performance and interventions. As Zakutansky and Sirles (1993:341) warn, "The instructor also must be able to spot areas of potential concern before an incident happens and ensure client well-being, while also protecting the student's autonomy."

Field instructors must take seriously their responsibility and liability with regard to students and the clients students are assigned. Taking this responsibility seriously involves arranging adequate time to read student recordings and having regular supervisory sessions with the student. The instructor must at all times be aware of the status of the student's clients.

Likewise, the field instructor needs information from the student and the social work program prior to accepting the student in the placement if that information is relevant to the student's ability to perform the essential functions of that field placement. Otherwise, it would appear that the program could be held responsible for failure to inform and other negligence if a client is harmed by a student. (Chapter 17 discusses thoroughly the issue of sharing information about a student with field instructors and includes a sample policy.)

Social work programs need to take seriously the CSWE requirement, contained in the Curriculum Policy Statement (CSWE 1994:104), to provide orientation, training, and ongoing communication with and support for field instructors. Very few social workers have had courses or formal training in supervision, a role that is apparently becoming increasingly vulnerable to litigation.

Education in the field was the first form of social work education, and many in the profession today continue to view it as the most important aspect of education for professional practice. Because of its proximity to professional practice, field education is also considered by many to be the most important opportunity for gatekeeping, both in the positive and negative senses of the word.

The field instructor, in the role of mentor, and the practice experiences provided in the field placement acculturate students into the profession. The experiences give students the opportunity to put into practice with clients and further develop and integrate the knowledge, values, and skills acquired in the classroom. They also give the instructor, as well as the program liaison, an opportunity to evaluate the student in ways not otherwise possible. Classroom evaluations, typically in the form of written exams, most often assess knowledge. Professional values and skills, which are considered essential to competent professional practice, are evaluated best in practice situations with clients. Field education, then, provides a unique opportunity to close the gate or to keep students out of the profession (even those students who have performed well in the classroom situation) if they cannot satisfactorily demonstrate the knowledge, values, and skills of professional practice.

The subjective judgment that inevitably comes into play in determining a satisfactory level of professional performance often makes many field instructors and program liaisons uncomfortable.

Court decisions that have determined that field (or clinical) performance is an academic matter and that the faculty or supervising instructor is the best judge of this performance should be encouraging to those who feel vulnerable to lawsuits from students. The liability of supervisors and instructors as it relates to clients of their trainees is a more recent concern that may add to the discomfort of some; however, it could just as likely encourage closer supervision and gatekeeping.

There is general agreement in the profession on the necessity for students to demonstrate not only the knowledge of the profession but also its values and skills before they are awarded a professional degree. What those essential values and skills are is still being debated. How to evaluate students with regard to professional values and skills is also still very much open to debate.

A central theme of this chapter has been the continuing necessity for our profession and social work education programs to define the essential functions and skills of social work practice and ways to measure them. This is especially important with regard to students with handicapping conditions. We also must continue to clarify the essential values and ethics of professional practice and be able to explain to one another, and others, why it is necessary for all social workers to practice according to these ethics. The *NASW Code of Ethics* is the generally recognized and accepted code by which our profession practices; however, it is a broadly defined code that must be interpreted in relation to specific behavior and circumstances.

If we are unable to specify for students, and for courts of law, what is essential for the competent practice of social work and *why* it is essential, it will be difficult, if not impossible, to effectively implement and defend our gatekeeping practices and decisions. Many of the chapters in this book suggest actions that programs can take to ensure a clearer understanding between students and the program faculty and staff and to guarantee due process for students. These actions should begin well before and continue throughout the field experience. If social work programs are successful in this endeavor, they will be the models that other professions look to in the use of the practicum, as Lodge (1975) suggested.

References

Alexander, K., and Alexander, M. D. (1985). *American public school law*. 2d ed. New York: West Publishing.

Americans with Disabilities Act, Public Law 101–336. 42d Cong., sect. 12101. 1990.

Arizona Board of Regents v Wilson, 539 P 2d 943 (Ariz App 1975).

Bennett, L., and Coe, S. (1997). Field instructor satisfaction with university liaisons. Paper presented at the 43d Annual Program Meeting of Council on Social Work Education, Chicago, Ill.

Bloom, M. (1990). *The drama of social work*. Itasca, Ill.: Peacock.

Board of Curators of the University of Missouri v Horowitz, 435 US 78 (1978).

Cobb, N. H. (1994). Court-recommended guidelines for managing unethical students and working with university lawyers. *Journal of Social Work Education* 30:18–31.

Cobb, N. H., and Jordan, C. (1989). Students with questionable values or threatening behavior: Precedent and policy from discipline to dismissal. *Journal of Social Work Education* 25:87–97.

Coe, S. (1994). Role satisfaction of social work field instructors. Ph.D. diss., University of Illinois at Chicago.

Cole, B. S. (1991). Legal issues related to social work program admissions. *Journal of Social Work Education* 27:18–24.

Cole, B. S., and Lewis, R. G. (1993). Gatekeeping through termination of unsuitable social work students: Legal issues and guidelines. *Journal of Social Work Education* 29:150–159.

Constable, R. T. (1977). A study of admissions policies in undergraduate education. *Journal of Education for Social Work* 13 (3): 19–24.

Council on Social Work Education (CSWE), Commission on Accreditation. (1994). *Handbook of accreditation standards and procedures*. 4th ed. Alexandria, Va.: CSWE.

Cunningham, M. (1982). Admissions variables and the prediction of success in an undergraduate fieldwork program. *Journal of Social Work Education* 18:27–34.

Dailey, D. M. (1974). The validity of admissions predictions: Implications for social work education. *Journal of Education for Social Work* 10 (2): 12–19.

Davenport, D. S. (1992). Ethical and legal problems with client-centered supervision. *Counselor Education and Supervision* 31:227–231.

Dinerman, M. (1982). A study of baccalaureate and master's curricula in social work. *Journal of Education* for *Social Work* 18:84–92.

Gibbs, P. (1994). Screening mechanisms in BSW programs. *Journal of Social Work Education* 30:63–74.

Grant, A. B. (1989). Dealing with a student grievance. *Nurse Educator* 14 (6): 13–17.

Grove v The Ohio State University College of Veterinary Medicine, 424 F Supp 377 (S D Ohio 1976).

Hepler, J. B., and Noble, J. H. (1990). Improving social work education: Taking responsibility at the door. *Social Work* 35:126–133.

Hipple, L., and Harrington, I. (1995). The role of the agency-based field instructor in the gatekeeping process. Paper presented at the 13th Annual Conference of the Association of Baccalaureate Program Directors, Nashville, Tenn.

Kadushin, A. (1985). *Supervision in social work.* 2d ed. New York: Columbia University Press.

Lewin, K. (1947). Group decision and social change. In E. E. Macoby, T. M. Newcomb, and E. D. Hartley (eds.), *Readings in Social Psychology*, pp. 197–211. New York: Holt.

Lodge, R. (1975). Foreword. In *The dynamics of field instruction: Learning through doing.* New York: Council on Social Work Education.

McCarthy, M. M. (1985). Legal challenges to academic decisions in higher education. *College and University* 60 (2): 99–112.

Metoyer-Duran, C. (1993). *Gatekeepers in ethnolinguistic communities.* Norwood, N.J.: Ablex Publishing.

Moore, L. S., and Urwin, C. A. (1991). Gatekeeping: A model for screening baccalaureate students for field education. *Journal of Social Work Education* 27:8–17.

National Association of Social Workers (NASW). (1996). *NASW Code of Ethics.* Washington, D.C.: NASW.

Nichols, M., and Cheers, J. (1980). The evaluation of practicum. *Contemporary Social Work Education* 3 (1): 54–71.

Olkin, R., and Gaughen, S. (1991). Evaluation and dismissal of students in master's level clinical programs: Legal parameters and survey results. *Counselor Education and Supervision* 30:276–288.

Robke, D. O. (1993). Supervisor liability: The buck stops here. *National Federation of Societies for Clinical Social Work* 11 (1): 14–15.

Schneck, D. (1996) Foreword. In B. Thomlison, G. Rogers, D. Collins, and R. M. Grinnell, Jr. *The social work practicum: A student guide*, pp. viii–x. 2d ed. Itasca, Ill.: Peacock.

Sharwell, G. R. (1979–80). Learn 'em good: The threat of malpractice. *Journal of Social Welfare* 6 (2): 39–48.

Skolnik, L. (1985). *Final Report: Field Education Project.* Washington, D.C.: Council on Social Work Education.

Task Force on the Future Role and Structure of Graduate Social Work Education (1983). *Strategic issues in the future role and structure of graduate social work education in the United States.* National Conference of Deans and Directors of Graduate Schools of Social Work.

Wahlberg, J., and Lommen, C. (1990). An analysis of admissions and termination criteria in BSW Programs. Presentation at the 8th Annual Conference of the Association of Baccalaureate Social Work Program Directors, Minneapolis, Minn.

Zakutansky, T. J., and Sirles, E. A. (1993). Ethical and legal issues in field education: Shared responsibility and risk. *Journal of Social Work Education* 29:338–347.

7

Creating a Bridging Environment:
The Screening-in Process in BSW Programs

Robert G. Madden

Social work educators have long understood their responsibilities to ensure that graduates are competent to practice social work (Feldstein 1972; Reynolds 1942). *Gatekeeping* is the term used to describe this duty, which has included the development of assessment and evaluation strategies at various points in the students' professional development. The ultimate goals of gatekeeping are quality control, program integrity, and protection of those seeking services from graduates. Many of the discussions and articles on this topic over the last several years have focused on the need to tighten our gatekeeping, with a heavy emphasis on more rigorous admissions screening (Hepler and Noble 1990; Moore and Urwin 1991). This chapter will argue for a process that screens in students applying to a social work program. Built on a foundation of respecting student rights, valuing the diversity of the profession, and enabling human development, screening-in fulfills the responsibility of guarding the door to the profession while acting in consonance with our professional identity.

The recent debate over the admissions stage of gatekeeping has been difficult to follow due to the variety of experiences and needs of BSW programs. In some schools, the number of students seeking entry into the social work major far exceeds the number of slots available. In these programs, criteria have had to be developed to help in admissions decisions. Most of the criteria are based on a combination of number of credits, grade point average (GPA), completion of an introductory course and/or volunteer experience, written applications, letters of recommendation, and interviews (Gibbs 1994). In programs with more students than slots, these criteria help faculty to assess students against various criteria to project their fit with the profession and their likelihood of success in the program. The goal is to screen out those students who are least likely to do well in the program and to admit those students with the strongest potential. Some social work programs have enough slots for the number of students applying to the major. Elsewhere, institutional policy precludes social work programs from denying entry to the major. In both of these situations, the focus of admissions should be screening students into the social work major.

When the topic of gatekeeping arises at national conferences and in the literature, there are various perceptions as to what that concept includes. It has not always been clear that the term *gatekeeping* refers only to the responsibility, not the strategies. As a result, there has been little consensus on how and where to exercise our gatekeeping responsibilities. The manner in which undergraduate social work programs develop their gatekeeping strategies requires a well thought out analysis of the purpose and necessity of criteria at each stage of the student's career (admissions, evaluation of academic courses, field practicum entrance, evaluation of field practicum performance, and exit testing) to meet specific program needs.

One fact that seems to be lost in the discussion of admissions is that faculty are not guarding the entrance to the social work program; they are guarding the entrance to the profession. This distinction is important in the choice of screening strategies. It allows programs to admit some students about whom there are concerns, as long as the other program checkpoints are operational and effective.

Screening-In

Screening procedures are used by most programs to assess a student's needs and aptitude for the practice of social work. Screening-in is a purposeful approach to the admissions process, which uses specific strategies for assessing the students' potential and their readiness for social work. The screening-in process may include criteria similar to those previously described, such as GPA, relevant experience, an interview process, and so on, but the focus is on identifying strengths on which a student can build. The faculty's assessment of a student involves those competencies, the repertoire of values, skills, knowledge, and personal qualities that enable the student to interact effectively with the environment (White 1963) when assuming the role of social worker. But the assessment process should not stop with the evaluation of the student. Beyond the traits of the individual, competence involves the fit between the individual and the environment (Maluccio and Libassi 1984).

In social work programs, we must ask whether a student's motivation and skills are truly deficient or whether the institution and faculty are reluctant to meet all students where they are. Screening-in does not preclude a program from denying admission, counseling a student out of the major, or assigning failing grades for a student's poor performance. In fact, it relies on honest and timely evaluation of students against clear and consistent performance guidelines. However, screening-in provides students with a supportive environment that facilitates their successful achievement of performance expectations.

The Admissions Process

It has long been the practice in certain disciplines to use introductory courses as screening devices. This is generally done by "ratcheting-up" the workload and difficulty of these courses to separate out the least prepared students from the rest. The courses thus operate as a sieve, with many going in but few emerging to continue in the major. For a profession that combines art with science, the idea that we can pick the "best and brightest" by using this type of process is questionable. (For further discussion of social work's art dimension, see chapter 17.)

Admission policies that are overly reliant on such measures as test scores, GPAs, and writing samples to reject students are simplistic at best, elitist and perhaps discriminatory at worst. Rather than using procedures that act as a sieve, we should be exploring procedures that act as pumps, empowering students to succeed.

There is some common ground in screening procedures regardless of program size or agenda. There is a responsibility to screen out students whose behaviors or interaction skills are so *inappropriate* as to negatively affect other students' learning. Also, placing such students in the field practicum could be dangerous to potential clients and injurious to the school's ability to maintain quality practicum sites. These students, however, are comparatively easy to identify. We don't require elaborate measures to identify students who are "obviously unsuitable." These students' values, interpersonal interactions, and emotional or mental instability are apparent in initial interviews, observations, or introductory classes. The rigorous admissions standards, therefore (absent the need to choose a class of limited size from a large applicant pool), must be designed to select out those students who are *unready*. It is precisely this group of students that is harmed the most by deficit-oriented admissions criteria.

Reynolds, in her book *Learning and Teaching in the Practice of Social Work* (1942), described the stages students move through as they learn in social work education. In the initial stage, students behave in response to new expectations with "psychic substitutes for flight" (75). She urged teachers not to label but to recognize that those threatened by new situations revert to earlier patterns.

> Above all, it is desirable that the teacher be not in turn threatened by this behavior to the point of punishing the learner for the teacher's insecurity. The role of the teacher in this stage of learning is security-giving, helping the learner to find the solid ground of personal adequacy he already has on which to plant his feet while he struggles with the new experience.
>
> *(76)*

If our gatekeeping strategies are rigidly applied early in students' experiences in social work, we may be responding to students' coping mechanisms rather than to their potential for social work. Instead, it is often necessary to follow Reynold's teaching about "teaching" and believe in our students, sometimes before they believe in themselves.

This approach fits in well with the focus on strengths in generalist social work practice. In this strengths perspective, the social worker identifies the competencies of the client and uses them to engage in a collaborative process of working on the client's goals (Saleebey 1992; Weick et al. 1989). If students have been able to get to the point of applying to a BSW program, they possess some strengths and motivations. When we replace skepticism with acceptance and validation, students can freely explore their potential.

It is unlikely that many of us teach our students to be judgmental of clients at the initial stages of the professional relationship, thereby dissuading them from their goals (unless the client is clearly set up to fail or be harmed, the same standard we use to screen out unsuitable applicants). Yet that is what we model when we use criteria that screen out students based on where they are at admission (deficit-oriented), rather than where they might get to by the time of graduation (competence-oriented).

Another problem with using admission criteria to identify deficits is the message this conveys to students. Blake (1985) explored the deficit perspective as it is applied to historically oppressed groups (especially persons of color, but also women; persons with disabilities; homosexuals; lesbians; survivors of physical, emotional, or sexual abuse; and others). Members of these groups may carry vestiges of the oppression in the form of internalized negative feelings about the self. When faculty are searching for or expecting deficits in students, these behaviors and feelings may be isolated, leading faculty to assess the student to be unsuitable. Instead, Blake supports an approach focusing on the students' strengths, even if these strengths are not the ones typically assessed in academia. When this focus on competency is combined with high expectations and supports, students can show dramatic success in overcoming deficits.

The rigidity and judgmentalism implicit in the admissions procedures of some social work programs seem to assume the following:

- We can catch problem students before they get into the major and keep them out, thereby allowing faculty to spend less time on remediation and avoiding the messy situation of dismissing a student who is not successful.

- Students who start out as problem students will never succeed in being competent professionals.

· In order to be successful in the profession, students should believe and think what faculty believe and think.

· The faculty and program have failed if they have to dismiss or counsel out a student who is already in the program.

Each of these assumptions rests on questionable foundations, which will be explored in the remainder of this chapter.

Legitimacy of Screening

A basic question to be asked of all screening procedures is whether they can predict student performance. Very few studies have been done examining social work preadmissions criteria, especially on the baccalaureate level (Cunningham 1982). McClelland, Rindfleisch, and Bean (1991) examined faculty rating of applicants from preadmissions information and found the ratings of several faculty, when used together, were accurate. But individual faculty varied dramatically in their assessments. The study suggested that faculty placed different priorities on criteria used for judging the students' potential for success by choosing factors they individually felt were valid predictors. The authors expressed concern about their findings, which identified a capricious aspect of the admissions process.

Given that the admissions criteria most commonly in use are essentially untested and that even when a structured set of criteria is used, faculty raters may each prioritize different criteria in coming to a decision (McClelland, Rindfleisch, and Bean 1991), it can be argued that far more research and much clearer processes will need to be developed to establish any predictive validity of admissions criteria. The absence of reliable and valid means for judging students creates discomfort and uncertainty for faculty and contributes to the intensity of the current gatekeeping debate.

In addition to questions concerning the validity of preadmissions criteria for predicting success in social work, there are concerns about inherent cultural, socioeconomic, and other biases within many of the criteria. Do criteria such as GPA, writing tests, and standardized tests accurately reflect the strengths of students of color, those from low socioeconomic backgrounds, those with hidden disabilities, or those for whom English is a second language? Is it appropriate to rely on these criteria for entry into a profession that preaches inclusiveness and works disproportionately with persons who share these very characteristics?

These concerns raise the question of whether we can rely on current admissions screening criteria to accomplish what we would like. What are the characteristics of those students who are *inappropriate* for admission to a social work program? Peterman and Blake (1986:30) define the inappropriate student as "one who cannot or will not internalize the value system, understand the complexities of the knowledge base, or demonstrate skills required for beginning level social work practice." Unfortunately, this definition is limited in its applicability to the admissions debate since it describes characteristics that are difficult to assess at admissions. The very language of the definition suggests outcome criteria that may only be evaluated as students move through the program.

A second classification is needed to describe those students who are unsuitable for admission into a social work program. An *unsuitable* student is defined as one who exhibits emotional or mental instability that poses a risk of harm to the student or to potential clients or whose values are in clear and direct conflict with those of the social work profession. It is in everyone's best interests to deny admission to these students. (Chapters 2 and 12 further examine the issue of students' values and ethics in relation to gatekeeping efforts.)

With the exception of the obviously unsuitable student, there is little evidence that students who will not succeed can be identified in advance. The best we can hope for is to identify those students who might have difficulty or who will require assistance with some aspect of the program (i.e., those who are *unready*). If this is our purpose, then the focus of the screening process is to bring students into the program with adequate supports. If our purpose is to keep out students who might eventually fail, however, we are likely to exclude many who would succeed to catch the few who cannot.

Students' Rights Perspective

The analysis of the students' rights perspective includes an examination of principles of justice as well as the ethical dimensions of the choices implicit in admissions decisions. The social work profession has been committed to social justice and to safeguarding the rights of individuals since its inception. Screening-in is a strategy that protects the rights of all students who apply to social work programs. Policies to assure the fair and equal treatment of students protect individual rights. Not only is this the most sensitive and proper way to deal with students, it also becomes an institution's best protection from litigation (Madden 1993).

An understanding of the social justice issues in the admissions process can be drawn from the work of Rawls (1971). Rawls's theory of justice is built on the concept of distributive justice, the fair distribution of social benefits and burdens. The principle of equal opportunity governs the distribution of social primary goods by ensuring freedom of movement, choice of occupation, and the like. The central idea is that no structural barriers exist for any individual to obtain the means to education, employment, or other basic life tasks. A second, related principle is the difference principle. It requires that any inequities of distribution that arise should be to the advantage of the least favored (Griffin 1987). Rawls would consider institutions to be just when no arbitrary distinctions are made between persons in assigning basic rights and duties and when rules determine a proper balance between competing claims to the advantages of society.

The theory of justice focuses on fairness of opportunity as the primary element of a just system. When applied to the issue of admissions, the priority for a just policy would be equal opportunity. An open admissions policy involving no structural barriers to access for any individual or group would provide equal opportunity. The only inequalities that would be just are those necessary to benefit the least advantaged. An example of this might be when a program uses admissions criteria that focus on scholastic achievement but also allows for members of traditionally oppressed groups to be admitted into the program, even when they are below the admissions standards, in order to improve the diversity of the class.

When students come to the social work program from educational systems that have poorly prepared them for the academic rigors of college, inequities (such as "liberal" admissions policies and support services) allowing for advantages to the least favored groups, are just. On the other hand, not making allowances for the different needs of students (having "objective" admissions policies), while nominally fair (it sounds like equal treatment) may in practice contain structural barriers to admission for certain students. For example, students with learning disabilities may not test well and may be systematically excluded from a program if a minimum score on a standardized test is required for admission.

There is an ethical dimension to the screening-in process as well. The value of self-determination is important to social work and should be considered in relation to admissions. According to the concept of self-determination, individuals should be able to make decisions concerning their life (Wells and Masch 1991). As social work educators, we have a responsibility to help students explore their capabilities and limitations. Faculty may advise students that social work is not a good choice of major and may assess the student to be inappropriate for the profession (Peterman and Blake 1986). However, for the student who elects to proceed despite being informed of the faculty's concerns, the value of self-determination supports the student's right to make this choice.

It is only when the faculty assess a student to be unsuitable (harmful to self or others due to emotional or mental instability or as the result of a direct conflict with social work values) that the faculty have a clear duty to deny admission. In cases such as these, safety becomes a primary concern and rates as a higher order obligation than upholding a student's right to self-determination (Loewenberg and Dolgoff 1988). The faculty thus has the duty to guard the gate by excluding these students from the social work program.

The most challenging dilemma for social work programs involves students who are initially assessed to be inappropriate rather than unsuitable. For students who are judged inappropriate, the right to self-determination, the right to gain entry to the major, needs to be respected and supported. The admissions process should be focused on competencies and provide plans and resources for the students to work on their deficiencies. When there are clear, consistently applied standards across the curriculum, students are provided with a legitimate chance to succeed while the program maintains its obligations to be a gatekeeper for the profession. It is in the best interests of the profession to enable a broad range of students to enter the professional practice community. If some of the students we screen in are eventually not successful and are dismissed from the program, we have not failed. We have supported their right to make an informed choice to try. (For an elaboration of this perspective, see chapter 5.)

Developmental Perspective

There are two primary developmental considerations that support the use of screening-in procedures. First, if we are screening students of traditional college age, we need to be sensitive to the behaviors that can be expected at this stage of the students' development and that might be observed by faculty in the preadmissions screening process. Faculty must avoid misinterpreting behavior and emotions related to normal developmental issues and mistakenly viewing such characteristics as indications of a student's unreadiness or unsuitability for professional practice. According to Kegan (1982), college age is a time of vulnerability and high susceptibility to depression. It is a time when the student may experience the loss of balance that comes from being "cut loose" from family and supports with the expectation of becoming independent. The results of this disequilibrium often manifest in immobilizing depressions and inability to do the activities related to class work.

Kegan suggests that colleges should provide more of a "bridging environment" (186). Students struggling with developmental issues need time and support to develop psychological autonomy. It is common for students to have excellent academic skills and potential but a very low GPA. Often, students "find themselves" while experiencing professional roles during the field practicum and do well in the social work program thereafter. Admissions criteria that are "objective" may block students in these developmental crises from an appropriate opportunity to grow into their potential.

Many students, regardless of their age, enter the social work major with personal experiences as clients of the helping professions. Here too, there are developmental considerations, such as when a student is in treatment or recovery. It is not uncommon to see a junior-level student who is absorbed with personal issues having difficulty in class and field placement. With support, how-ever, many of these students gain the ability to manage their own issues, to become more focused academically, and to be empathic in interactions with clients. Like their peers, students working through personal issues also need an environment that will pro-mote their development, a nonjudgmental and supportive faculty and peer network, and (not inconsistent with these needs) clear expectations.

Screening-In Concerns

The most obvious concern faculty have about adopting a screen-ing-in admissions policy is the honesty of the commitment that can be made to a student. The first part of the concern is based on resources. With many programs facing rising numbers of stu-dents—more and more of them with poor academic preparation—and dwindling budgets for support services, it is difficult for faculty to bring a student into the program if the conditions for success are not present. If lack of necessary supports provides the rationale to rule out a screening-in approach, social work faculty have an obligation to advocate for policies and resources to change these conditions. The social work major is no more or less demanding than most other majors in most institutions. If the school is admitting underprepared students, it has an obligation to provide remedial and tutorial services, rather than fail a student who is academically unready for upper-level courses.

A second concern for faculty is the decision whether to admit a student struggling with emotional difficulties. Isaac, Johnson, Lockhart, and White (1993) suggest that some "dysfunctional" students are allowed to enter programs (and complete their degrees) because social work educators and field instructors have difficulty separating their educator role from their clinical role. Their comments are troubling for a variety of reasons. If faculty are meeting their own needs by serving as clinicians to students, their behavior is ethically insupportable. Furthermore, the charac-terization that social workers are acting as "clinicians" when they allow students to move through a social work program without meeting standards, calls up the worst stereotypes of what it is social workers do in practice. While we need to be vigilant about not confusing roles or boundaries (as Shulman [1987] puts it: maintaining the educational contract), we should not forget our mission and identity that may call for us to be understanding and supportive of students who are experiencing emotional difficulties: to create a bridging environment.

The issue of program integrity, holding students to evaluative standards throughout the program, is another area of concern. Several authors stressing the need for tight admissions policies in social work programs have argued that once admitted, social work students rarely flunk out (Hepler and Noble 1990). The decision to admit has even been described as a "tacit decision to award the degree" (Born and Carroll 1988). Although these studies focused on graduate social work programs, similar comments have been made concerning undergraduate programs (Peterman and Blake 1986). The conclusions of these studies and commentaries rest on questionable reasoning. Identifying loose admissions policies as responsible for allowing unqualified students to graduate is to put the blame in the wrong place. The blame (if the premise is correct that unqualified students are graduating) belongs to the failure of subsequent stages of the gatekeeping continuum to hold students to standards. These studies, furthermore, infer that low drop-out and flunk-out rates in social work programs combined with liberal admissions policies necessarily mean that unqualified students must be graduating. It is at least as plausible to speculate that the support and work of social work faculty with underprepared students result in these students reaching expectations by graduation.

Gatekeeping has become an increasingly important issue for BSW programs. In the process of developing objective means to assess the potential of students' to succeed in the field, social work faculty have embraced a variety of criteria. No one questions the need to perform an admissions screening to redirect students for whom the profession is not a good fit. But strategies that seek to exclude students who may be underprepared, disadvantaged, or otherwise seen as at-risk threaten to violate students' rights and keep potentially good practitioners out of the field.

Screening-in is more than a strategy. For programs not constrained by an admissions cap, it can be an approach to the admissions process that allows social work faculty to create a bridging environment between where a student is when entering the program and where the student will have grown to by the time he or she graduates. It reflects the values and philosophy of the profession and therefore models professional practice. It acknowledges that not all students who enter the program will complete the degree but accepts the right of students to prove themselves. Finally, screening-in is understood as one stage of evaluation. Gatekeeping, the responsibility to guard the entrance to the profession, involves evaluation at various points as students move through the program. If faculty accept this responsibility in academic courses, field practica, and exit evaluations, there is no need to rely on exclusionary admissions policies.

References

Blake, J. H. (1985). Approaching minority students as assets. *Academe* 71 (6): 24–28.

Born, C. E., and Carroll, D. J. (1988). Ethics in admissions. *Journal of Social Work Education* 24:79–85.

Cunningham, M. (1982). Admission variables and the prediction of success in an undergraduate field program. *Journal of Education for Social Work* 18:27–34.

Feldstein, D. (1972). *Undergraduate social work education: Today and tomorrow.* New York: Council on Social Work Education.

Gibbs, P. (1994). Screening mechanisms in BSW programs. *Journal of Social Work Education* 30:63–74.

Griffin, S. M. (1987). Reconstructing Rawls' theory of social justice: Developing a public values philosophy of the constitution. *New York University Law Review* 62:715–728.

Hepler, J. B., and Noble, J. H. (1990). Improving social work education: Taking responsibility at the door. *Social Work* 35:126–133.

Isaac, A., Johnson, R. N., Lockhart, L. L., and White, B. (1993). Gatekeeping: How well are social work educators performing this function? Presentation at 39th Annual Program Meeting of the Council on Social Work Education, New York.

Kegan, R. (1982). *The evolving self.* Cambridge, Mass.: Harvard University Press.

Loewenberg, F., and Dolgoff, R. (1988). *Ethical decisions for social work practice.* 3d ed. Itasca, Ill.: Peacock.

Madden, R. G. (1993). Protecting all parties: A legal analysis of clinical competency and student dismissals. *Journal of Law and Social Work* 4 (1): 1–13.

Maluccio, A. N., and Libassi, F. (1984). Competence clarification in social work practice. *Social Thought* 10 (spring): 51–58.

McClelland, R. W., Rindfleisch, N., and Bean, G. (1991). Rater adherence to evaluative criteria used in BSSW admissions. *Aretê* 16 (2): 10–18.

Moore, L. S., and Urwin, C. A. (1991). Gatekeeping: A model for screening baccalaureate students for field education. *Journal of Social Work Education* 27:8–17.

Peterman, P. J., and Blake, R. (1986). The inappropriate BSW student. *Aretê* 11 (1): 27–34.

Rawls, J. (1971). *A theory of justice.* Cambridge, Mass.: Harvard University Press.

Reynolds, B. C. (1942). *Learning and teaching in the practice of social work.* New York: Farrar & Rinehart.

Saleebey, D. (ed.). (1992). *The strengths perspective in social work practice.* New York: Longman.

Shulman, L. (1987). The hidden group in the classroom. *Journal of Teaching in Social Work* 1 (2): 3–33.

Weick, A., Rapp, C., Sullivan, P., and Kisthardt, W. (1989). A strengths perspective for social work practice. *Social Work* 34:350–354.

Wells, C. C., and Masch, M. K. (1991). *Social work ethics: Day to day.* Prospect Heights, Ill.: Waveland Press.

White, R. W. (1963). *Ego and reality in psychoanalytic theory.* New York: International Universities Press.

8

Screening Students Out of BSW Programs: Responding to Professional Obligations and Institutional Challenges

Patty Gibbs

Accreditation standards advanced by the Council on Social Work Education (CSWE) require programs to articulate and implement criteria and processes that select from a group of admissions applicants those who are "best qualified to become professional social workers at a beginning level of practice" (1994:87). Gatekeeping in its broadest sense requires screening students at various points throughout the professional program (Moore and Urwin 1990), for example, during introductory courses, at the point of admissions and entry to the field placement, prior to and during field experiences, and throughout the professional foundation coursework. Studies of gatekeeping at the BSW level confirm that programs are reluctant to engage in screening-out practices (Dinerman 1981; Gibbs 1994a, b; Isaac et al. 1993; Wahlberg and Lommen 1990), a phenomenon that suggests possible abandonment of gatekeeping functions and responsibilities.

Screening students into social work programs generally involves admitting all students who declare an interest in a social work career (often referred to as universal admissions), building on the innate strengths of those who enter the major, attending to those who have difficulties, establishing supports for those who need remedial work, cultivating the desirable attributes in those whose attributes need enhancement, and nurturing all students toward successful completion of their degree. In terms of gatekeeping, a commitment to consistent screening-in practices keeps the gates open, with a central goal of facilitating successful completion of a BSW degree.

Screening-out, on the other hand, selectively closes the gate in certain instances and at different junctures as students journey toward attainment of the BSW degree. Screening-out might occur at admissions or at a later point in the program. Screening students out of a program at any point occurs infrequently and usually involves the students' failure to meet screening criteria related to scholastic expectations, such as grade point average (GPA) (Gibbs 1994a). Less frequent is the practice of screening students out when their suitability for a career in social work is in question (Gibbs 1994a; Peterman and Blake 1986), in other words, when they fail to meet professional expectations. The practice of screening students out of the program because their fit with the profession is dubious is often referred to as "counseling out" rather than as screening out.

In recent years, a focus on screening students into (and all the way through) social work programs has become a luxury that many programs can ill afford due to institutional realities and demands that require more stringent screening-out practices and policies. Furthermore, program faculties must come to terms with their abandonment of traditional gatekeeping functions relative to screening out (or counseling out) unsuitable students who have, at best, a questionable capacity for alignment with what Schriver (1995:6), in the first edition of his textbook on human behavior, refers to as the "core concerns of the profession." These core concerns have grown out of social work's historic mission and purposes as well as out of the professional values and ethics that guide practice. According to Schriver, "all accredited undergraduate and graduate social work education programs are responsible for educating social workers who accept and pursue achievement of the purposes of social work and who practice in accordance with its values" (6).

The first part of this chapter examines two factors associated with the faculty's gatekeeping responsibilities: institutional challenges that no longer allow a screening-in approach to gatekeeping and professional obligations that require unsuitable students to be screened out, despite the faculty's resistance to carrying out this responsibility. Institutional challenges involve a constellation of political, demographic, and sociocultural factors spanning a period of nearly four decades. The faculty's resistance to gatekeeping in the form of screening out students who are unsuitable is a result of changes in ideological and legal positions during this same time span. These historical shifts and trends provide a backdrop for the screening-in versus screening-out debate.

The latter part of this chapter provides concrete suggestions for developing and implementing gatekeeping standards and mechanisms. It also examines the use of the *NASW Code of Ethics* (National Association of Social Workers [NASW] 1996) and the 1992 Curriculum Policy Statement (CPS) and accreditation standards (Council on Social Work Education [CSWE] 1996) in shaping gatekeeping policies. Finally, several gatekeeping mechanisms are identified and discussed.

Historical Perspectives

Gatekeeping in social work education has reflected not only the state of the art at any given time but also the systemic contexts in which it developed and flourished. Over the years, these contexts have undergone changes.

Ideological and Legal Shifts

At the present juncture in the evolution of social work and social work education, many faculty members carry the baggage of an earlier era when students' rights and civil liberties were sometimes flagrantly violated by MSW gatekeeping practices that were rooted in psychoanalytic theory. According to anecdotal reports, students were terminated from MSW programs because of—for lack of better terminology—unorthodox behavior or beliefs. From the vantage point of students who were pursuing their MSW degrees during that era, it appeared that classmates would quickly but mysteriously disappear from the program for reasons that were never made known to those who remained behind. Students who were not the targets of these ostensibly random ejections were left to speculate on the character defects or behavior flaws that led to the banishment (i.e., "counseling out") of classmates. They also were left to speculate on their own uncertain futures in the program if their personal "character flaws" were discovered.

Given today's policies in higher education, many of yesteryear's decisions to counsel students out would be judged arbitrary and capricious. Furthermore, today's legal system would have a field day with due process issues had these practices not been relinquished. But the pendulum seems to have swung too far in the other direction (Gibbs 1994a, b); earlier hypervigilant gatekeeping has given way to a near dereliction of gatekeeping responsibilities in academia today.

With bad memories of yesteryear, coupled with overblown fears of litigation and limited time to engage in the kinds of protracted counseling-out efforts required in a litigious society, social work faculty of today are inclined to surrender their gatekeeping responsibility in all but the most dramatic cases. Sometimes faculty merely turn a blind eye and a deaf ear to the problems or concerns. Ignoring or avoiding problematic behavior seems almost justifiable in the face of course objectives and outcomes that tend to address only cognitive capacities. At other times, faculty and field instructors alike lower standards and "nurse" a student through the program when such efforts are clearly contraindicated, for example, when *basic* interpersonal skills are strikingly deficient. These miscarriages of gatekeeping appear to stem from the faculty's and the field instructor's difficulty with separating their role as educator and their function as gatekeepers from their role as helpers and clinicians (Cole 1991; Isaac et al. 1993). Because faculty are reluctant, or possibly unable, to resolve the issues that would allow effective and responsible gatekeeping, instances of screening out tend to be infrequent, processes for dealing with unsuitable students tend to be ad hoc, and gatekeeping standards tend to focus on quantitative and scholastic achievements and capabilities while excluding professional capacities.

Academic standards that relate to expected professional behavior are often glaringly absent from lists of program criteria and standards, except during the field practicum (Gibbs 1994a). The faculty's reluctance to fulfill gatekeeping responsibilities by failing to either articulate or enforce criteria related to professional expectations regrettably allows some students to become social workers even though their compatibility with the profession is a major issue (Born and Carroll 1988; Cobb and Jordan 1989; Peterman and Blake 1986). If faculty are unable to screen students out when their basic compatibility with the profession is questionable, it is not likely that faculty will be able to meet the additional gatekeeping challenges arising from changes in student enrollment and institutional resources. Managing enrollment caps requires faculty to make very fine distinctions during the admissions process.

Changes in Student Enrollment and Institutional Resources

Enrollment caps are not new to some BSW programs; however, their existence today creates a gatekeeping crisis in social work education that did not exist previously. Because of mushrooming enrollments in some programs during recent years, students have been turned away at the gate despite their basic compatibility with the profession and despite their ability to meet admissions criteria. This unfortunate state of affairs stems from a new constellation of changes in enrollment and resources.

The 1960s and 1970s brought tidal waves of baby boomers into higher education (Kerr 1990), and the climate and ideology of that era brought a substantial number of those students into the field of social work. During those decades, social work programs enjoyed burgeoning growth and substantial financial resources in the form of state and federal monies (Born and Carroll 1988). Resource-rich social work programs were well equipped to accommodate all who had interest in and basic compatibility with the profession and its ideals.

In the 1980s the philosophical underpinnings of Reaganomics seemed to permeate national ideology, and it trickled down to impact enrollment trends in social work education (Moore and Urwin 1990). During that era social programs were reduced or killed by the saber of Reaganomics (Ginsberg 1982), and the market-economy mentality of the times prompted college students to turn away from humanitarian ideals (Peterman and Blake 1986) in favor of personal economic goals. Thus, the 1980s gave rise to the college-age me-generation during a decade of "glitz," greed, and narcissism. The me-generation of the 1980s wanted the "good life," which translated into power, status, and wealth. Although enrollments in higher education remained stable (Kerr 1990), enrollment in social work programs went into a downward spiral (Frost, Anderson, and Sublette 1987; Peterman and Blake 1986) as students thronged to the high-paying fields of business, engineering, medicine, and the like. Consequently, social work programs and their faculty tended to shrink during this period.

At the same time, other external factors produced additional headaches for American higher education as it came under the gun from various constituents. Pressures for accountability increased and budgets simultaneously decreased (Mortimer and Edwards 1990; Pratt 1993). This legacy of economic austerity coupled with increased demands on higher education has continued into the 1990s (Wilson 1990).

> Stretching resources has finite limits, and many institutions are up against them. . . . In 1992, *U.S. News and World Report* found that 70 percent of the colleges and universities surveyed plan this year to increase class size while simultaneously reducing the number of faculty and increasing their teaching loads (47 percent).
>
> *(Pratt 1993:8)*

Although enrollment trends in higher education currently show some decline, many college students have rediscovered a humanitarian ethos (Wilkerson 1987), and national projections show social work as a high-growth field during the 1990s ("Hot Tracks," Oct. 31 and Nov. 1, 1993). Unfortunately, in the absence of resource-rich programs to accommodate the growing demand for social work education (Munson 1994), social work faculty are forced to make tough decisions: how to manage mushrooming enrollments in the program during an era of tenuous financial support for higher education and increased demands on faculty time.

Shifts in Faculty Demographics and in Workload Expectations

Three additional realities that affect the ability to manage growing enrollments in social work education include the dramatic changes over the years in faculty demographics (Jacobs 1990; Wilson 1990), in faculty workload expectations (Pratt 1993), and in requirements for promotion and tenure (Gibbs and Locke 1989). Recent years have witnessed numerous retirements within the professoriat (Wilson 1990). Massive increases in instructional staff during the 1960s account for a currently aging cohort, many of whom have already reached retirement (Jacobs 1990). Large numbers of retirements have created many faculty vacancies, for which there seems to be an inadequate supply of qualified new recruits—

and *qualified* is the operative word here, given changes in criteria for hiring and tenuring faculty.

When the faculty cohort of the 1960s came to higher education, very few published or held doctorates (Wilson 1990), particularly in social work, because faculty were recruited based on rich practice backgrounds rather than on advanced academic credentials. Now, however, a doctorate is generally required for hiring at most institutions, with retention resting primarily on substantial expectations for scholarship (Gibbs and Locke 1989). Some faculty fail to meet these increased expectations for promotion and tenure, which creates additional vacancies. Conducting national searches to fill all of these vacancies takes incredible amounts of faculty time and energy. Further, when new faculty are brought on board, they must invest inordinate amounts of time not only in preparing to teach a heavy course load and acclimating themselves to the world of higher education but also in meeting the elevated criteria for promotion and tenure in a relatively brief period of time (Jacobs 1990). In some programs with a sizable number of newly hired faculty members, the problem of juggling too many tasks and responsibilities is exacerbated.

Other realities that have increased faculty workloads considerably include the movement in higher education for increased accountability for achieving and measuring outcomes (Mortimer and Edwards 1990) as well as a noteworthy expansion of accreditation standards and processes over the past twenty years.

In sum, all of these forces, trends, and demands leave faculty, as well as the institution itself, in the unfortunate position of having limited time and resources to provide the help that may be necessary to bring students "up to speed" if a large amount of extra attention, nurturing, and supportive services is required to do so. The lack of time and the dwindling resources do not allow it.

> Public four-year institutions, faced with the funding crisis, have had to resort to larger classes, fewer faculty members, fewer course offerings, and cutbacks in library holdings and academic support programs like advising and counseling.
>
> *(Pratt 1993:8)*

As a result of these unwelcome realities, screening students out of programs takes on increased significance.

Screening Out: Identifying the Difficult Issues

As noted previously, screening students out of the program occurs not only when enrollment limits are reached but also when students are not well suited to the profession. In both situations the issues relative to establishing clear and specific performance standards and screening processes are inextricably intertwined, yet these two situations also involve very different issues. One critical difference is that inappropriate students may be screened out at any point in the program when their unsuitability becomes clear, but enrollment caps require students to be screened out at the "front door," during admissions.

Unfortunately for applying students, admissions criteria are relative; that is, they are heavily influenced by the operative pressures and forces during any given admissions cycle (Born and Carroll 1988). When the number of applicants is small and the resources of the program are sufficient, if not generous, faculty tend to overlook students' deficiencies and problems, which leads to variations in admissions policy and to what is often called universality of admissions (Born and Carroll 1988) or "open admissions." Open admissions occurs when there are abundant resources to provide the supports necessary for nurturing most, if not all, students through the program after they are admitted. Conversely, when there is a large number of applicants and resources are limited, if not scarce, screening out becomes a necessity (Moore and Urwin 1990).

Because strained and impoverished resources disallow a large array of critical supportive services, and large numbers of students cannot be easily absorbed into systems whose resources are already stretched thin, some students must be turned away at the point of admission to the program. During the lean times admissions criteria are not only more closely adhered to but are also frequently elevated (Cobb and Jordan 1989). As a result, some applicants fail to gain entry to social work programs due to time and circumstance—in the form of enrollment caps—rather because they fail to meet admissions criteria. At a different time or in a different program without a cap, these same students might have been allowed to pass through the admissions gate.

Another critical difference between screening out the unsuitable student and screening out because of enrollment caps is that enrollment-cap screening bars some applicants from the program even though they meet all of its performance standards, which is not the case when a student is screened out because of unsuitability. Screening out students who meet all admissions criteria presents a special set of challenges for faculty.

Enrollment Cap Issues

Enrollment caps force admission cutoffs. When there are more qualified applicants than there are available slots, the number of students who exceed the cap must be rejected even when they meet all specified criteria. Under these circumstances, determining who passes through the admissions gate and who does not is a painful task for faculty because it requires rejecting applicants who meet at least the minimum standards for entry into the program. Due to the sensitive nature of turning away applicants who have the potential for becoming effective social workers, but may be denied that opportunity because of enrollment caps, faculty must judiciously develop criteria and processes that not only ensure fair decisions but also take into account the full range of qualities that would indicate a student's potential for effective practice (Cobb and Jordan 1989).

However, formulating criteria that will facilitate making fine distinctions among applicants who meet all of the basic criteria is a formidable task for the faculty assigned that responsibility. In essence, the challenge lies in developing criteria or standards that would separate the potentially good candidate from the potentially better one, which is a staggering charge at best. Anecdotal information as well as recent research (Isaac et al. 1993) suggest that the vast majority of programs have not yet effectively addressed the problem of screening out unsuitable students; consequently, developing criteria and processes for use in screening out suitable candidates for admission is an ostensibly insurmountable task for faculty who are already apprehensive and reluctant gatekeepers (Moore and Urwin 1990).

Given the current state of gatekeeping efforts, developing effective and fair admission criteria to manage enrollment caps presents a dual challenge: criteria must reflect scholastic as well as professional standards and they must also lend themselves to making subtle distinctions among applicants.

As previously noted, faculty currently tend to rely on academic and scholastic criteria during screening processes because of the difficulty in articulating criteria and standards that reflect the professional qualities expected of social workers (Cobb and Jordan 1989; Gibbs 1994a, b). Furthermore, faculty often resort to the use of a single admission criterion, usually GPA, as the primary, if not exclusive, definer of capability and potential (Gibbs 1994a; Wahlberg and Lommen 1990). Using GPA as a default solution for managing enrollment caps is frequently viewed by many faculty gatekeepers as a palatable tack for several reasons: (a) given the analytic tasks required of social workers, many educators and practitioners believe in a link between academic success (GPA) and the ability to practice effectively; (b) students themselves accept the GPA as the primary evidence of their ability and therefore are disinclined to challenge decisions made on the basis of the GPA; (c) the GPA criterion is quantitative, which aligns with the desire for measures that are ostensibly more "scientific"; and (d) the GPA is a scholastic criterion, which allows faculty to avoid the hard question of assessing professional capacities. In sum, faculty often rely on the GPA as the gatekeeping path of least resistance.

When the GPA is used as the primary definer of students' potential for success in the program as well as in future practice, admissions committees need only go down the list of students whose GPAs have been arrayed in descending order and then draw the line, thereby "screening out" all of the students whose names fall below the magic line of the enrollment cap. Although this solution seems to greatly simplify the task at hand, it raises at least as many pressing questions and issues as it answers.

One such issue is that not all students with high GPAs are well-suited to the profession. Furthermore, some students with lower GPAs provide, in the eyes of faculty, a compelling argument for admission to the program despite the fact that they fall below the magic cutoff line during admissions when GPA is the primary, if not sole, definer. The compelling argument generally rests on a given student's demonstrated or projected "good fit" with the profession. Good fit usually refers to those elusive but nonetheless highly valued qualities and characteristics believed to characterize an effective, if not ideal, professional social worker. It is at this juncture that things get rather complicated because the issues have come full circle; the professional expectations must be identified.

General Gatekeeping Issues

What *are* the elusive professional qualities that faculty must artic-ulate in the form of admissions criteria and performance stan-dards? This is the first critical question to which faculty must respond, whether they are screening students to manage enroll-ment caps, to address more global gatekeeping responsibilities, or to meet the dictates of CSWE accreditation standards. Assuming successful resolution of this problem, faculty must then determine the relative importance of each standard or criterion, particularly when the context for gatekeeping is at the point of admission. The overwhelming challenge of weighting standards or criteria becomes clearer when it is juxtaposed with the heretofore unmet challenge of identifying and committing to writing what are deemed adequate gatekeeping standards.

Another gatekeeping issue is to what degree students must pos-sess these capacities or qualities when they come into the program. Those who believe that students must be able to demonstrate these capacities at entry to the program must ask themselves why social work education is needed at all if students are expected to come into the program already fully qualified, skilled, and profession-ally socialized. If one of the purposes of social work education is to develop, shape, and mold some of the critical professional qual-ities, it is fallacious to require outcome performance at entry. However, it is not unrealistic to expect students *to show potential* for developing the qualities that are expected of professional prac-titioners.

Another issue is particularly troublesome. As social justice advocates who are ethically committed to preventing discrimina-tory practices, faculty must guard against inadvertent cultural and socioeconomic bias in the standards they develop and the meas-ures they choose. Although the debate is far from being settled, there is some agreement that certain standards, such as GPA and its correlates (writing skills tests, standardized tests, and the like), may disadvantage some minority groups, nontraditional students, low income students, and others who may have experienced envi-ronmental barriers and limited opportunities (see, for example, Dawes 1993; Humphreys 1993). While it is impossible to rule out every standard that carries potential for some type of bias because that would seriously undercut the ability to fulfill gatekeeping responsibilities, heavy weighting of or exclusive reliance on a single standard must be avoided. By balancing several scholastic academic standards with a range of other academic standards of a professional nature, no group of students will be categorically disadvantaged by gatekeeping efforts. (See chapter 5 for an elaboration of how gatekeeping standards and processes can enhance enrollment of rather than disadvantage special populations.)

In sum, the questions and issues raised thus far in this chapter form some of the disconcerting wrinkles in the tapestry of gatekeeping. In response to the issues, several guiding principles for developing screening criteria and performance standards are noteworthy. Of central importance in any discussion about gatekeeping is the fact that *all* standards must be framed as academic standards (Cobb 1994; Cole 1991; Moore and Urwin 1990), whether they relate to scholastic or to professional performance expectations. (See chapter 13 for further information on this issue.) Additionally, students' rights must be a significant factor in the gatekeeping equation (Cobb and Jordan, 1989; Cole 1991; Cole and Lewis 1993; Madden 1993, 1994a, b). (Chapter 7 and all chapters in Part 2, "Legal Perspectives," explore this topic fully.) Furthermore, faculty must be judicious in developing admissions criteria and performance standards that do not systematically exclude applicants representing disadvantaged groups or protected classes, and the program must have multiple gatekeeping points (Moore and Urwin 1990). (Chapter 5 elaborates issues associated with achieving diversity.) Finally, criteria and standards must relate to the students' potential to accept and pursue achievement of the core concerns of social work, as discussed earlier.

Gatekeeping Strategies

Even when a program's overarching approach to gatekeeping is screening in, academic standards and mechanisms for implementing them must be in place, not only to meet accreditation standards but also to deal with the occasional student who cannot be successfully nurtured into the profession because of basic incompatibility with the core concerns of social work. Furthermore, when enrollment caps force faculty to turn applicants away from the program despite basic suitability, resolving the gatekeeping issues that will allow faculty to differentiate between the good applicant and the better one is critically important.

Framing Effective Academic Standards

Because faculty tend to have difficulty articulating effective academic standards in general, and academic standards that relate to expected professional behaviors in particular, this section will provide some guidance and identify some possibilities. Rather than labor over reinventing the wheel, two sets of preexisting standards can be used to inform a program's academic standards and other screening criteria: The *NASW Code of Ethics* (NASW 1996) and the standards advanced in the fourth edition of CSWE's *Handbook of Accreditation Standards and Procedures* (1994), particularly those identified in the section of the handbook that contains the 1992 Curriculum Policy Statement (CPS).

The professional expectations set forth in the *NASW Code of Ethics* serve as an excellent resource for framing academic standards because the professional expectations are both comprehensive and nationally accepted. This resource's value to social work faculty for framing academic standards lies in the fact that the code addresses standards for practice performance as well as expectations for personal conduct and comportment as a social worker. For instance, the code addresses the issue of personal impairments and sets the expectation that such impairments must be addressed when they interfere with professional performance. According to the NASW, impairments include personal problems, psychosocial distress, legal problems, substance abuse, or mental health difficulties that interfere with professional judgment and performance or that jeopardize the bests interests of the people for whom a social worker has a professional responsibility (1996:23). These types of impairments that render some social work students dysfunctional have presented ongoing concerns to many faculty over the years. For purposes of gatekeeping, the expectations in the code easily translate into an academic standard addressing impairments that obstruct the student's ability to meet the standards of the program. (See chapter 10 for information on framing standards that are in line with the Americans with Disabilities Act.)

Faculty tend to agree that awareness of one's self as a helper, which includes reconciling values that are inconsistent with professional practice, is an important performance standard, and both the NASW code and CSWE's CPS address this expectation. According to the CPS, students must be assisted to develop an awareness of their personal values and to clarify conflicting values and ethical dilemmas (CSWE 1994:100). In this same vein, one of the BSW program objectives states that students must "demonstrate the professional use of self" (99). The CPS also requires that the practicum provide opportunities for students to develop "an awareness of self in the process of intervention" (104).

Guidelines for interpersonal interactions with colleagues are provided in the code of ethics (NASW 1996:15–18). For the purpose of setting academic standards, the NASW guidelines can be generalized to include expectations for positive relationships with classmates and also with agency personnel during field practica. According to the code, collegial interactions must be characterized by respect (15). In a related standard that can be derived from CSWE's CPS, "social workers' professional relationships are built upon regard for individual worth and dignity, and advance[d] by mutual participation, acceptance, confidentiality, honesty, and responsible handling of conflict" (CSWE 1994:100).

Critical thinking skills are central to practice activities, and faculty generally agree that students must be able to demonstrate these skills prior to graduation. CSWE's CPS addresses critical thinking skills as one of the program objectives. According to the CPS, graduates of the program must "apply critical thinking skills within the context of professional social work practice" (CSWE 1994:99).

The CPS identifies other important expectations that easily translate into academic standards, such as receptivity to constructive, corrective feedback; appropriate use of supervision; and expectations for critical self-evaluation, all of which are found in the section on learning opportunities that must be provided for students (1994:99, 104). A standard regarding the need for effective interpersonal communication skills that would allow for rapport-building and purposive, productive relationships is found in the BSW program section on objectives (99).

Program concerns about discriminatory behaviors and respect for diversity are reflected in the NASW standards for ethical responsibilities to clients, to society, and to the profession (1996:9, 26–27, and 22–23 respectively). For example, according to the code, social workers

> should not practice, condone, facilitate, or collaborate with any form of discrimination on the basis of race, ethnicity, national origin, color, sex, sexual orientation, age, marital status, political belief, religion, or mental or physical disability.
>
> *(22–23)*

The NASW code sets expectations that social workers not only *avoid* engaging in any form of discriminatory practices (22) but *act to prevent and eliminate* practices that are inhumane or discriminatory (27).

Diversity concerns are further supported in CSWE's CPS (1994). Implied in the nine BSW curriculum content areas of the CPS are statements that can be framed as academic standards. For example, as one of the values and principles that must be infused into the curriculum as a whole, social workers must "demonstrate respect for and acceptance of the unique characteristics of diverse populations" (101) as well as understand and respect the positive value of diversity (99).

Also implied in the CPS is respect for the clients' rights to make independent decisions (1994:100), which addresses faculty concerns about students who impose their own values and paradigms onto clients rather than facilitating the client's self-determination. The NASW code reinforces this position by stating that social workers should "respect and promote the right of clients to self-determination and assist clients in their efforts to identify and clarify their goals" (1996:7).

Although the standards contained in the NASW code and the CSWE CPS are not meant to be exhaustive, it is clear that these two resources address the vast majority of concerns faculty raise about any given student whose value system does not seem compatible with professional ideals. Even concerns about plagiarism are covered in the code via the principle that research and scholarship be guided by the conventions of scholarly inquiry.

In sum, the academic standards that faculty seem to have the most difficulty coming to terms with and committing to writing as part of program materials have been hammered out already by our professional reference groups. Social work educators need only draw on these and tailor them to their respective programs. In so doing, the program will have academic standards that address professional capacities, which will facilitate decision making during admissions screening when enrollment caps force faculty to distinguish between the good applicant and the better applicant or when a student's compatibility with the profession is in question.

Establishing Effective Gatekeeping Mechanisms

Developing effective standards is only half the battle. Faculty also must establish the processes and mechanisms for implementing the standards. Often, multiple gatekeeping points are necessary for effective gatekeeping. The first gatekeeping point generally occurs prior to the time students undergo the admission review.

Before students are admitted into the social work major, they are generally required to take introductory courses in social work (Gibbs 1994a; Wahlberg and Lommen 1990). The use of reference letters from these course instructors, designed to address scholastic and professional compatibility concerns, provides one of the first opportunities to implement gatekeeping. Of course, the enrollment in these courses must be limited to a manageable size that would allow the faculty member to assess each student effectively. When resource constraints prevent smaller course enrollments, short interviews with each student by the instructor at the conclusion of the semester, although time-consuming, provide an additional opportunity for assessment.

Many programs require the completion of some form of human service activity as part of admission requirements (Gibbs 1994a; Wahlberg and Lommen 1990). Because students may demonstrate different sets of behaviors in field settings than are evident in classroom situations, simple assessment tools can be developed for use by the supervisors of these service activities, and these assessments can become part of the application for admission.

During the admissions process, programs tend to use several kinds of supportive materials, or "admissions accouterments," for making assessments. The most commonly used accouterment is a written essay that addresses the reasons why students want to pursue a career in social work, social problems of interest to them, self-assessment, and other relevant topics. Regardless of the kinds of materials that are required in admissions applications, a tool that serves to free the process of inherent bias against disadvantaged groups is an admissions rating sheet. A well-conceived rating sheet allows for a balance to be struck between academic standards that are scholastic in nature and those that reflect professional potential rather than putting undue emphasis on scholastic achievement and potential. (Appendix 2 contains a sample rating sheet.)

Successful completion of the coursework itself provides additional points in the gatekeeping continuum after students have entered the major. Skills labs are particularly useful because students have opportunities to demonstrate their abilities to adhere to academic standards of a professional nature as well as their ability to utilize knowledge to guide interventive efforts. In addition, classroom assignments can be designed to reflect professional capacities rather than focus strictly on analytic abilities that reflect only scholastic aptitude.

Toward the latter part of the curriculum, passage into the practicum offers another gatekeeping point. Capstone gatekeeping occurs during the field practicum experience. The importance of strong assessment instruments and committed field instructors cannot be stressed enough. However, the practicum should be viewed as only one of many points along the gatekeeping continuum, contrary to current practices that place undue reliance on field instructors for counseling out students who are identified earlier in the program as unsuitable candidates for a career in the profession (Gibbs 1994b).

Accreditation standards require the development of program policies and procedures for accepting from a group of applicants "those who, in accordance with the program's educational goals, are best qualified to become professional social workers at a beginning level of practice" (CSWE 1994:87). When individualized attention is necessary to ensure that students complete the professional curriculum, some programs are able to provide the time and resources that enable a student who needs extra nurturing to meet, at least minimally, the program's requirements. However, many programs no longer have the luxury of a screening-in approach because of institutionally enforced enrollment caps.

Enrollment caps, as well as other current realities in higher education, raise troubling issues in relation to gatekeeping responsibilities. They make it difficult to consider bringing an applicant into the program who is minimally qualified if there are sufficient numbers of applicants who are more qualified. The lack of institutional supports for the weak or needful student coupled with the increased demands on faculty, whose plates are already full, creates a painfully difficult state of affairs in social work education today.

Although it may be difficult to accept, the pressures of enrollment caps and the requirements for traditional gatekeeping will not go away. Gnashing of teeth will neither magically nor painlessly transform an overly large group of suitable, basically qualified admissions applicants into the enrollment-cap number established in accordance with the program's or the institution's mandates. Furthermore, neglecting traditional gatekeeping functions will not keep away students whose behavior is incompatible with professional standards. Therefore, a central challenge for faculty is in both framing and weighting fair, valid, and reliable criteria that can select, from any group of students, those who demonstrate the greatest potential to become professional social workers. A second challenge is in establishing effective and fair mechanisms and processes for carrying out gatekeeping functions. The overarching challenge is in protecting students' rights during admissions as well as at all other points along the gatekeeping continuum.

The bottom line is that the issues raised in this chapter must be satisfactorily resolved because the reality of enrollment caps is not expected to vanish in the near future, and students who display tenuous compatibility with the core concerns of social work will continue to inappropriately select the social work major as their career of choice. In response to these realities, faculty carry a responsibility for judiciously attending to gatekeeping functions not only to comply with accreditation standards but also to protect future recipients of social work services.

References

Born, C. E., and Carroll, D. J. (1988). Ethics in admissions. *Journal of Social Work Education* 24:79–85.

Cobb, N. H., and Jordan, C. (1989). Students with questionable values or threatening behavior: Precedent and policy from discipline to dismissal. *Journal of Social Work Education* 25:87–97.

Cole, B. S. (1991). Legal issues related to social work program admissions. *Journal of Social Work Education* 27:18–24.

Cole, B. S., and Lewis, R. G. (1993). Gatekeeping through termination of unsuitable social work students: Legal issues and guidelines. *Journal of Social Work Education* 29:150–159.

Council on Social Work Education (CSWE), Commission on Accreditation. (1994). *Handbook of accreditation standards and procedures.* 4th ed. Alexandria, Va.: CSWE.

Dawes, R. M. (1993). Racial norming: A debate (Part 1). *Academe* 79 (3): 31–34.

Dinerman, M. (1981). *Social work curriculum at the baccalaureate and masters levels.* New York: The Lois and Samuel Silberman Fund.

Frost, C. H., Anderson, M. F., and Sublette, S. (1987). How to increase enrollment in undergraduate and graduate schools of social work. *Journal of Social Work Education* 23:75–82.

Gibbs, P. (1994a). Screening mechanisms in BSW programs. *Journal of Social Work Education* 30:63–74.

———. (1994b). Gatekeeping issues in BSW programs. *Aretê* 19 (2): 15–27.

Gibbs, P., and Locke, B. (1989). Tenure and promotion in accredited graduate social work programs. *Journal of Social Work Education* 25:126–133.

Ginsberg, M. I. (1982). Maintaining quality education in the face of scarcity. *Journal of Education for Social Work* 18 (2): 5–11.

Hot tracks in 20 professions. (1995, November 1). *U.S. News & World Report.*

Hot tracks in 20 professions. (1995, October 31). *U.S. News & World Report.*

Humphreys, L. G. (1993). Racial norming: A debate (Part 2). *Academe* 79 (3): 35–37.

Isaac, A., Johnson, R. N., Lockhart, L. L., and White, B. (1993). Gatekeeping: How well are social work educators performing this function? Presentation at the 39th Annual Program Meeting of the Council on Social Work Education, New York, N.Y.

Jacobs, F. (1990). Expectations of and by faculty: An overview for the 1990s. *New Directions for Higher Education* 70:67–72.

Kerr, C. (1990). Higher education cannot escape history: The 1990s. *New Directions for Higher Education* 70:67–72.

Madden, R. G. (1993). Protecting all parties: A legal analysis of clinical competency and student dismissals. Paper presented at the 39th Annual Program Meeting of the Council on Social Work Education, New York, N.Y.

———. (1994a). Creating a bridging environment: The screening-in process in BSW programs. Paper presented at the 12th Annual Conference of the Association of Baccalaureate Social Work Program Directors, San Francisco, Ca.

——. (1994b). Disability law and undergraduate social work education: Practicing what we preach. Paper presented at the 12th Annual Conference of the Association of Baccalaureate Social Work Program Directors, San Francisco, Ca.

Moore, L. S., and Urwin, C. A. (1990). Quality control in social work: The gatekeeping role in social work education. *Journal of Teaching in Social Work* 4:113–128.

Mortimer, K. P., and Edwards, S. R. (1990). A president's view of the 1990s. *New Directions for Higher Education* 70:67–72.

Munson, C. E. (1994). Characteristics of excellence in social work education. *Journal of Social Work Education* 30:42–53.

National Association of Social Workers (NASW). (1996). *NASW code of ethics*. Washington, D.C.: NASW.

Peterman, P. J., and Blake, R. (1986). The inappropriate BSW student. *Aretê* 11 (1): 27–34.

Pratt, L. R. (1993). Quality or access? *Academe* 78 (7): 8–9.

Schriver, J. M. (1995). *Human behavior and the social environment: Shifting paradigms in essential knowledge for social work practice.* Boston: Allyn and Bacon.

Wahlberg, J., and Lommen, C. (1990). An analysis of admissions and termination criteria in BSW Programs. Presentation at the 8th Annual Conference of the Association of Baccalaureate Social Work Program Directors, Minneapolis, Minn.

Wilkerson, I. (1987, November 9). Schools swamped by applicants. *New York Times,* p. A18.

Wilson, J. (1990). Moving in and moving up: Women in higher education in the 1990s. *New Directions for Higher Education* 70:67–72.

PART TWO

Legal Perspectives

9

Legal Issues Facing Social Work Academia

Robert G. Madden and Norman H. Cobb

Prior to the early 1960s, administrators, faculty, and staff exercised considerable "parental authority" (*locus parentis*) over students enrolled in colleges and universities. Kaplin (1985) identifies several reasons for this degree of authority given to faculty and administration. The university held a unique place in society. Faculty were seen as having a special mission to be "guardians of knowledge," which required considerable expertise and intelligence. This resulted in a high level of status and respect accorded to faculty and administrators. In this atmosphere, it was considered inappropriate for an outsider to presume to tell an institution of higher education how to do its business. This was particularly true of lawyers and judges, most of whom were not products of the university, having been trained instead in the apprenticeship model ("reading law"), studying, and working in a practitioner's office.

Historically, attendance at a university was considered a privilege rather than a right. Faculty and administrators chose students and granted degrees according to their judgment of each student. As a result, students entering a university were under the near complete authority of school personnel. Their physical care and custody were controlled by the student-life/student-services staff. Students' moral behavior was controlled by honor

Sections of this chapter include revised material from the following article, used with permission of the publisher: Madden, R. G. (1993). Protecting all parties: A legal analysis of clinical competency and student dismissals. *Journal of Law and Social Work* 3 (1): 1–13.

codes, strict rules of personal conduct, parietals, and curfews. The educational life of a student was completely controlled by faculty through restrictive admissions policies, curriculum design, assignment policies, evaluation criteria, graduation requirements, and dismissal decisions.

The landmark case, *Dixon v Alabama State Board of Education* (1961) presaged a gradual increase in judicial involvement with student-university relationships and a winnowing away of the absolute discretion institutions and faculty once enjoyed. In *Dixon,* the college dismissed five students who had been involved in a civil rights demonstration. The court overturned the dismissals, finding that the public institution was required to have adequate procedures to protect the rights of the students. Since *Dixon,* courts have continued to recognize and extend due process safeguards to students in disciplinary cases.

In much the same way as the general population has increasingly sued product manufacturers, businesses, contractors, and others, students have turned to the legal system for resolution of complex educational problems. A series of cases since *Dixon,* in which students have challenged the actions of universities and faculty, has resulted in the development of legal standards. These standards define some of the rights of students and clarify the responsibilities of the faculty. Despite these important cases, many areas of student-faculty interactions remain difficult to manage since each situation involves unique circumstances. In social work education, these situations are particularly complex because in addition to traditional disciplinary and academic dismissals programs must contend with such concerns as clinical competency and ethics violations. Faculty also must be concerned with their responsibility for credentialing students, in particular, for withholding credentials from those who are not suitable or prepared for professional practice.

Faculty may be uncertain about their legal standing to evaluate students' technical and interpersonal skills as well as their professional character and behavior. However, the United States Supreme Court has repeatedly upheld an institution's right to establish noncognitive academic requirements for graduation and has consistently deferred to faculties' professional judgment of clinical competency (*Regents of the University of Michigan v Ewing,* 1985). For example, in the influential 1978 case *Board of*

Curators, University of Missouri v Horowitz (hereafter *Horowitz*) a medical student sued a college as a result of her dismissal. A student in the third year, she was given a negative evaluation for displaying a lack of patient rapport, erratic attendance, and poor personal hygiene, all of which suggested a lack of clinical competency. When the student failed to demonstrate improved performance, she was dismissed.

The United States Supreme Court, in upholding her dismissal, found that the faculty was making an academic judgment of her clinical abilities. The court declined to intrude into the student-faculty relationship. The rationale in this decision was based on acceptance of the premise that it requires someone with a high level of expertise in a field to evaluate a student's performance. Therefore, judges are ill equipped to second-guess an academic decision. *Horowitz* has been cited in many cases related to academic dismissals and has clearly established that courts will adopt a hands-off policy regarding review of academic decisions. However, nonacademic issues (such as personal misconduct or disciplinary actions) do not receive the same deferential treatment by the courts. Faculty may be required to defend their actions in court more frequently in nonacademic cases.

In academia, legal issues are continuously evolving and becoming more complex, and yet faculty remain fairly uninformed of their impact on course management and other academic duties. For example, social work faculty and administrators must attend to the constitutional requirement of due process in resolving student concerns. Gone are the days when benevolent administrators or faculty members single-handedly passed judgment on students and sent them home (or perhaps to other academic departments). Unfortunately, however, unethical, inappropriate, or academically deficient students are occasionally identified, and evaluations and procedures that satisfy legal due process requirements must be in place if the faculty is to carry out its gatekeeping functions.

Similarly, social work faculty must become well informed about the evolving legal parameters of the contractual relationship between themselves and their students. For example, while college catalogues are written to disclaim contractual expectations, course syllabi are increasingly seen as educational agreements. Laws protecting persons with disabilities require reasonable accommodations for students with disabilities who must take written exams, write papers, view videotapes, and attend field trips or class sessions in buildings that are not easily accessible.

Faculty may be surprised by the potential consequences of failing to provide reasonable accommodations to students with documented disabilities, overlooking contractual expectations, or violating the students' due process rights. Regardless of whether lawsuits are filed or merely threatened, the repercussions may include enormous legal fees, the school's tarnished reputation, diminished alumni support, and tremendous demands on the faculty's and administrators' time.

This chapter provides an overview of the legal issues faced by social work educators. Students who are aggrieved by the actions of faculty or administration may file a lawsuit against the faculty and the institution. These lawsuits can take many forms but are generally based on one or more legal theories, including constitutional law, contract law, claimed violations of statutory law, or tort law. These legal theories are illustrated by a review of cases brought by students. Based on an analysis of case law, specific policy and procedural guidelines are suggested for dealing with unethical, inappropriate, or academically deficient social work students.

Constitutional Law: Abiding by Due Process

Public colleges and universities often face claims by students that their constitutional rights have been violated. Although some cases rest on discriminatory acts prohibited by law or the restriction of free speech, most cases involve the violation of due process.

Due process encompasses a complex array of factors that can be classified as substantive due process or procedural due process. The federal constitution, by virtue of the Fourteenth Amendment (Section 1) asserts that no state may abridge the privileges of any citizen (substantive due process). In essence, the state and its agents (e.g., public education facilities and faculty) may only withhold a government benefit or service if the reason is legitimate. In practice, courts usually defer to the judgment of the public authority unless the original denial was based on arbitrary or capricious reasons (*Schware v Board of Bar Examiners of New Mexico* 1957).

In academia, the legal standard for proving an arbitrary denial of a benefit requires a high degree of evidence, because institutions can almost always assert some rational basis for their dismissal actions. Even in these cases, however, procedural due process remains a basic protection. Section 1 of the Fourteenth Amendment includes the phrase "nor shall any state deprive any person of life, liberty, or property without due process of law." Procedural due process requires some level of notice and an opportunity to be heard. Dismissing a student for personal misconduct (a disciplinary dismissal) involves more cumbersome procedures than does a dismissal on academic grounds (an academic dismissal). Most student problems in social work programs may be conceived of as academic violations and, therefore, require minimal due process standards (Cobb and Jordan 1989; Cobb 1994).

Since adequate procedure is the basis of most court analyses, the extent of procedure is an important issue. For the notice requirement, most authors have argued for sufficient time for the student to be made aware of the faculty's dissatisfaction with academic performance and the possibility of failure or expulsion while the student still has time to remediate deficient areas (Golden 1981; Marx 1984). In developing procedures, faculty have struggled with the question of how much time to allow for students to remediate difficulties. If too much time is given, students are closer to graduation and have more invested in the degree. If not enough time is given, the students' due process rights may be violated. Courts, however, have not provided any useful guidance on this issue as they have generally found timelines to be an academic question and have deferred to the judgment of the faculty.

The requirement for a hearing is even less strict. While the courts state that every student should be entitled to a hearing prior to academic dismissal, virtually any form for the hearing is sufficient (*Sofair v State University of New York* 1978). The courts have found that academic decisions are not readily adapted to the procedural tools of judicial or administrative decision making and, in fact, these procedures are antithetical to the "continuing relationship between faculty and students" (*Horowitz* 1978:90). The only clear message from the case law concerning academic due process is that it is important for the program to develop clear and objective requirements and procedures and to make these known to the students.

The one area of procedural rights that the courts may examine is whether the process offered to a student differed significantly from the institution's established procedures. In academic dismissals, the analysis of a hearing process is not focused on the paucity of the procedures but rather on the evidence of arbitrary and capricious behavior on the part of the institution. Students are required to show some evidence of arbitrary or capricious behavior to avoid dismissal of their claims prior to the trial stage. The court examines the records and will refuse motions to dismiss cases if students are able to show that institutions have not followed basic procedures, have acted in bad faith, or have illegally discriminated (Milam and Marshall 1987). The courts require students to provide "substantial evidence" in records to test whether actions were arbitrary (*Slaughter v Brigham Young University* 1975).

In the two cases that follow, students believed they had been harmed sufficiently to bring court actions. Both situations illustrate the types of cases that can proceed to the trial stage, that is, where the students' claims that their constitutional rights were violated had merit.

In *Regents of University of Michigan v Ewing* (1985), a student was enrolled in a six-year undergraduate medical degree program. He took six years to complete the academic part of the program (normally completed in four years). He then failed five of seven subject areas of a required national examination. The executive committee of the medical school voted to dismiss him from the program and did not allow him to retake the exam, although all other students who failed were allowed a chance to retake it.

The student responded to what he considered to be unfair treatment and inconsistent procedures. The court upheld the right of the faculty to make this academic judgment, after determining that the decision involved conscientious and careful deliberation of the entirety of the student's academic career. The court held that a genuine academic decision could not be overridden by judicial review unless the judgment was such a substantial departure from accepted academic norms that the person or committee responsible did not actually exercise professional judgment.

In *Wilkenfield v Powell* (1983), a student was enrolled in a graduate program in psychology. The catalogue stated that a student was bound only by the requirements in force at the time of admission. Partway through his program, the school established written procedures replacing informal ones that had previously been operating. One of these written procedures was for a student to be working toward the degree by passing oral examinations within specific deadlines. This student failed to do so and experienced various academic and clinical difficulties. He argued that personal problems interfered with his ability to meet the deadlines and that the faculty was dismissing him because of his problems. The student believed the time requirements, established after he had entered the program, were merely a pretense.

The court found that the university had been quite fair in providing opportunities for reasonable completion of the requirements and had provided extensive appeals and reviews of faculty decisions. The difficulty in this case arose due to policies the student felt were unfairly applied to him since they were not written or clearly expressed in either the catalogue or in departmental materials upon his matriculation. However, according to the facts, it seems the real problem was the faculty's unwillingness to base the dismissal on their evaluation of deficiencies. They chose instead to rely on the technicality of a missed deadline. Even in this case where the rationale for dismissal was suspect, the courts found enough of a reasonable basis (deferral to academic decisions) and enough procedural due process (notice and hearing) to uphold the university's decision to dismiss the student.

From the court's perspective, due process is the central theme in dismissals on both academic and nonacademic grounds. The courts, however, are most likely to leave faculty and administrators in the role of decision makers in academic cases. As discussed by Cobb (1994:20), "if the courts hold to *Horowitz* (1976), as was the case in *Lipsett v University of Puerto Rico* (1986) and *Harris v Blake* (1986; cited in Dutile, 1987), and allow social work to interpret violations of ethics as breaches of academic standards, academic dismissals will largely avoid protracted court involvement." As Kaplin (1985:312) predicted:

> Overall, two trends are emerging from the reported decisions in the wake of *Horowitz*. First, extensive appellate litigation challenging academic dismissals is not occurring, and the cases that have been reported have been decided in favor of the institutions. Apparently *Horowitz*, with its strong support for institutional discretion in devising academic dismissal procedures, has depressed the market

for such litigation. Second, courts have read *Horowitz* as a case whose message has meaning well beyond the context of constitutional due process and academic dismissal. Thus, *Horowitz* also supports the broader concept of "academic deference," or judicial deference to the full range of an academic institution's academic decisions. Both trends help insulate post-secondary institutions from judicial intrusion into their dealings with students.

Since *Horowitz* (1976) established the legitimacy of terminating students with unacceptable behavior on academic grounds, social work programs have increased power and influence over troublesome situations. It is only when faculty actions are determined to be unreasonable that students can successfully argue that they have been unconstitutionally deprived of their educational benefits.

In summary, constitutional claims primarily focus on due process and are brought by students when they believe the state has denied them a full and fair assessment of their concerns. Social work programs, as part of their gatekeeping responsibility, must provide students with adequate notice and an opportunity to be heard, and the courts have found that almost any due process is sufficient in cases of academic dismissal.

Contract Law: Students' Purchase of Education

Students at both public and private institutions attempt to challenge academic dismissals on the basis of contract law. Some courts have viewed the relationship between a university and student as contractual and have construed the nature and terms of the contract from the student handbook, college catalogue, and other statements of university policy (*Ikpeazu v University of Nebraska* 1985). In cases that are based on breach of contract, students have experienced the most success when the college has failed to comply with a specific commitment made to the student (Jennings 1981:221). In response, most colleges and universities include disclaimers in an attempt to limit the contractual nature of college catalogues and other publications.

Educational contracts are considered to be unique and are construed in a manner that "leaves the school sufficient discretion to properly exercise its educational responsibility" (*Mahavongsanan v Hall,* 1976:449–50). The decisions on educational contracts have been based on the court's determination of whether the action to dismiss a student was arbitrary or capricious. As with constitutionally based claims, courts have upheld the institution's decisions, with few exceptions.

In one case, however, a federal court recognized an unusual application of contract law. *Russell v Salve Regina* (1986/1989) involved a nursing student who was extremely overweight. She was given a failing grade in the clinical course in her junior year, in part due to her weight. She received passing grades in all other academic courses. Russell signed a contract in lieu of dismissal (the usual result of a failed clinical course in nursing), promising to seek help for the weight problem and to lose two pounds each week. After failing to lose weight, she was asked to withdraw from the nursing program. Both sides characterized the relationship between student and college as contractual in nature. The question in this case was the treatment of the "subsequent agreement" between the student and college regarding weight reduction.

Following the influential *Horowitz* decision in 1978, courts have used a "reasonable expectation" standard of review to determine if one side has breached an academic contract. The test concentrates on what each side reasonably should have expected from the other when the party entered into the contract and whether these expectations have been breached. As noted, the courts have given faculty wide discretion as to what constitutes reasonable academic judgment, in essence saying that a student should reasonably expect to be evaluated according to standards set by faculty.

The trial court in *Russell,* however, deviated from the "reasonable expectations" standard of contract review. The court looked at the whole of the contract between the student and college, including paying fees, following regulations, maintaining a satisfactory GPA, and establishing the weight reduction agreement. The court instructed the jury to find for the student if it found she had "substantially performed" her side of the bargain.

In the commercial arena, the "substantial performance" standard has merit. If a builder puts up a house and completes the job except for some minor elements, the purchaser cannot void the whole deal by claiming the strict letter of the contract was not followed. Instead, the purchaser may deduct an amount equal to the uncompleted part of the "substantially performed" contract. In an educational setting, this rationale does not apply. To extend the rationale to its natural limits, a court could find a student eligible for a diploma despite not completing all degree requirements. Competence is not a piecemeal proposition, and real harm may come to an institution that is forced to grant a degree to a student who merely "substantially performed."

The *Russell* case is not likely to be followed by other courts in its contract analysis except under exceptional circumstances. The student won her case because the jury was sympathetic to the insensitive treatment Russell received from the nursing program. Also, the judge appeared willing to use the substantial performance doctrine due to the tenuous connection between weight and academic standards. A contract to improve a student's deficiencies, therefore, must be academically relevant or it may be relegated to an incidental factor if a student has otherwise satisfied his or her side of the bargain.

In *Connally v University of Vermont* (1975) a student was in his third year of medical school but received a failing grade in two clinical rotations. Despite receiving scores of 82 and 86 (out of 100) on exams and making up lost clinical time, the student's failing grade remained in effect, and his petition to repeat his third year was denied by the school.

Although the court upheld the faculty's decision, a clear rationale exists for why the student believed he was aggrieved sufficiently to pursue litigation. From his vantage point, the primary issue was his dismissal despite completing remedial work as directed by the school. Accordingly, faculty must be certain to develop contracts for remedial work that will satisfy the alleged deficiencies of the student if the work is successfully completed.

Even when a contract claim is based on the institution's breach of a specific commitment, the length of the contract may be a factor in the remedy. A student who registers for courses and pays fees each semester has been seen by at least one author as having a strong contractual claim only for that semester (Marx 1984). The action would have less validity if it claimed a contractual right to continue into the next semester and less still if it claimed a contractual right to graduate. Once again, however, this argument suffers from an eagerness to provide the institution with near absolute discretion. Unless the institution can point to specific failures on the part of the student (i.e., grade point average, failure of core courses, etc.) and continuing lack of satisfactory performance during the obligatory probationary period, the student does have a contractual expectation to continue in a program and to graduate.

Public and Private Institutions: Standards of Review

As a practical matter, the standard of review for faculty decisions in public and private institutions is virtually identical. As previously noted, public institutions and their agents (faculty, administration, and staff) are subject to the constraints of the federal Constitution as applied to the states by the Fourteenth Amendment. Since the Constitution was designed only to limit the exercise of government power, it is not applicable to private individuals or institutions (Kaplin 1985). The requirement for due process protects the rights of students from government actions to deny them benefits.

The courts have generally held that the case law imposes requirements on private universities that parallel those of the Constitutional due process clause (Fox 1988:7). The lead case illustrating the court's roughly similar treatment of public and private institutions in academic dismissal cases is *Slaughter v Brigham Young University* (1975). An appeals court set aside a trial court's decision awarding damages to a student dismissed for violating the honesty provision of the student code. The court tested whether the university's action was arbitrary by examining the adequacy of the procedure and the weight of the evidence supporting the university's decision. The court used constitutional due process as a guide, holding that "the proceeding met the requirements of the constitutional procedural due process doctrine as it is presently applied to public universities" (625). Further, the court found it "unnecessary to draw any distinction, if there be any, between the requirements for the public and private institutions" (625).

Whatever the theoretical underpinnings, the "arbitrary and capricious" standard is undoubtedly being used to judge academic dismissal in both public and private institutions. Therefore, it may be prudent for private institutions to use constitutional due process principles in developing dismissal procedures (Kaplin 1985:314).

Disability Law: Reasonable Accommodations

One of the most compelling advances in civil rights law has been the enactment of the 1990 *Americans with Disabilities Act* (ADA). The ADA seeks to ensure access to public facilities to equalize opportunities. The scope of the law is broad, specifically noting that any "undergraduate, or postgraduate private school, or other place of education" is included in public accommodations subject to ADA regulations (Sec. 301[7][J]).

Although the parameters of the law have yet to be fully litigated, colleges and universities clearly must go beyond improving the physical accessibility of buildings and facilities. Institutions are required to make reasonable accommodations to the known physical and mental limitations of a student that impact academic performance. The legal question in these cases is the determination of what is reasonable. The basic elements of the analysis include: (a) whether a student is "otherwise qualified" to be a student in the program; (b) the nature and extent of the accommodations being requested; (c) whether the accommodation would fundamentally alter the nature of the service (education) being provided.

Students have challenged denials of admission, grading, clinical evaluations, and terminations on the basis of a violation of their rights under the ADA. The law requires programs to respond to the needs identified by students with documented disabilities. However, programs are only responsible to accommodate when students document a disability and request accommodations. The refusal or inability to provide timely and relevant accommodations is one basis of legal challenges brought by students with disabilities.

The more difficult cases involve students who perform poorly, then inform faculty members about their disabilities. Faculty must then decide whether to allow a student to retake courses and/or to stay in the program. The primary question is whether the poor performance would have occurred even with accommodations (such that a student would not be otherwise qualified). Essentially, the argument is "but for" the failure to accommodate, the student would have been able to succeed in the academic program.

The ADA has broadened the scope of protections available to persons with disabilities, and at the same time it has greatly enhanced the awareness of individuals and institutions. A variety of reasons explain why a proportionately large number of these cases are appealed to courts and administrative agencies. One reason is that the educational institution has an affirmative duty to respond to a legitimate student request. Also, the system of grievances is well established and not extremely costly to access. Complaints against postsecondary educational institutions are lodged with the Department of Education's Office of Civil Rights (OCR). This administrative remedy spares the expense of a trial and can often be completed in a timely manner. Civil lawsuits are also brought to enforce the ADA, and in some cases both judicial and administrative complaints are filed. While this proves to be anxiety-producing and costly for the schools, the mechanism helps to force social change and equalize access to educational opportunities.

The ADA has generated increased attention on the duty of academic programs to make reasonable accommodations to the needs of students with disabilities. The ramifications of this duty are relevant to the gatekeeping strategies of social work programs. Programs must examine entry requirements to ensure they are not keeping out students with disabilities. For example, relying too much on a writing sample could eliminate the opportunity for a student with a learning disability to pursue a social work degree. Also, students' requests for accommodations must be evaluated objectively, and appropriate accommodations must be made, such as increasing time for taking a test or completing a program, giving alternative assignments, providing auxiliary aids, and so forth. Programs and faculty who assume a flexible stance while holding to standards and program integrity not only will be abiding by the law but will also be modeling social work's time-honored principle of empowerment and inclusiveness.

While the law prohibits eligibility tests or criteria that tend to screen out persons with disabilities, students should be encouraged to report their disabilities so that accommodations can be made by the program. This includes making reasonable accommodations for students to have access to field placement sites (Reeser 1992). For a more comprehensive treatment of disability law, see chapter 10.

Tort Law: The Violation of Duty

Another basis on which students might contest a dismissal is a tort claim. Under these actions, the dismissal itself is not the primary issue but rather the conduct of the faculty and administration is the subject of the complaint. In tort actions, plaintiffs allege that they have been injured by wrongful actions of the defendants and seek monetary damages from them. Not all wrongful acts give rise to tort actions. The person filing a lawsuit must establish (a) a legal duty: an obligation to do (or to refrain from doing) some action; (b) a breach of that duty; (c) an injury to the plaintiff; and (d) a reasonably foreseeable, causal relationship between the breach of duty and the injury (Saltzman and Proch 1990:412).

Duty is a legal term that represents how one person should act toward another. The duty owed by faculty to students has both objective and subjective components. Objective elements are defined by a standard of care that is either generally accepted for a profession or written in policies. For example, a faculty member who sexually harassed a student would be violating an objective standard of care since most colleges have specific policies forbidding this behavior.

The subjective elements of duty are more difficult to analyze. The judge and jury are responsible for evaluating whether a particular behavior that is the subject of the complaint falls outside of "reasonable faculty behavior" given the circumstances. These situations typically involve no violations of specific policies. The behaviors are judged to violate the standard of care expected of faculty due to the degree of negligence or intent to injure. For example, if a student shares sensitive, personal information with a faculty member expecting him or her to keep it confidential, but the faculty member publicly announces this information to a group of students, this violation of confidentiality (the tort "invasion of privacy") could be the basis of a lawsuit. If a professor writes untrue statements on a student's recommendation causing the student not to get a job, the faculty member might be sued for libel (or slander if the untrue information was conveyed orally). In these cases, a jury might conclude that the educator owed a duty to the injured student but failed to exercise due care. The jury would have to decide whether the faculty member's behavior violated the standard of care, whether the student was injured as a direct result, and how much should be awarded to compensate the student for damages.

One case that analyzed tort liability was the previously discussed *Russell v Salve Regina* (1986/1989). In this case (involving the nursing student and weight reduction) the student attempted to prove that the faculty had mistreated her. One of Russell's claims was that the faculty violated their duty to refrain from actions that would cause harm to her. The district court indicated that Rhode Island law would extend the parameters of the "intentional infliction of emotional distress" tort to the student-university relationship. The court went on to say that "although wide discretion must be given to a private college in enforcing its scholastic standards, there is no justification for debasement, harassment or humiliation" (1986: 404). After analyzing the facts, the court did not find the conduct "extreme and outrageous" enough to reach the level of a tort.

The appellate court, while upholding the district court's determination, noted that the question was "close" (1989:488) especially given the context of the relationship between faculty and student. These courts seemed to be inferring that there is a power disparity in faculty-student relationships. As part of the expected standard of care, faculty should not abuse the power their role affords them. While in *Russell* the court did not find the behavior reached the level of a tort, another court deciding on these same facts might reach a different conclusion.

Few cases to date have relied on tort law, and most tort claims against colleges involve negligence in maintaining a safe environment. For example, a student who was assaulted after an evening class may sue a college for failing to provide adequate lighting in a parking area. If a cafeteria on campus served tainted food that resulted in serious injury to a student, the college may be sued for damages. While there have been relatively few tort claims against faculty, social work faculty should be cognizant of the duty to treat students reasonably and to refrain from behavior that negligently or intentionally causes harm.

Supervisors' Liability

Field instructors and faculty should be cognizant of a growing trend in mental health law to hold supervisors legally liable for the practice of those they supervise (Reamer 1989). When a field instructor agrees to a student placement, there is an implied or explicit agreement (depending on whether the program uses formal contracts with field agencies) to assume responsibilities that include:

- assigning cases appropriate to the experience and level of the student,
- providing opportunities for the student to gain necessary knowledge and skills,
- monitoring the student's performance, including assessments and intervention plans,
- ensuring that students are practicing in accordance with the *NASW Code of Ethics* (1996).

Social service agencies have experienced staff reductions and budget cuts over the last ten years. This has increased the pressure on supervisors to do more with fewer resources. Often it is supervision time that is eliminated in the process. Further, social work students may be assigned more complex cases that previously might have been handled by professional staff. As a result, supervisors may be at risk for being brought into a legal action to answer for the practice of the students they supervise. More important, there are serious ethical concerns about putting clients and students at risk through inappropriate supervision.

One legal theory relied on for supervisors' liability is *respondeat superior,* "let the master respond" (*Blacks Law Dictionary* 1983). This is a contract-based theory that holds supervisors and agencies responsible for the actions of workers that occur within the scope of their job responsibilities. The rationale is to ensure that the legal entity not be able to avoid responsibility for actions done by employees by claiming that the individual was at fault. A second legal theory supporting a claim of supervisor liability is vicarious liability, which is based on negligence. In these cases, the supervisor and agency are charged with negligent hiring or failure to adequately supervise. In most cases, the worker, supervisor, and agency are all named as parties to the lawsuit and all would be jointly liable for the damages.

Reamer (1995) examined malpractice claims against social workers from 1969 to 1990. Although he found less than 2 percent of the claims were related to supervisor liability, the data raise concerns about potential lawsuits in this area. Most of the claims against social workers involved issues such as incorrect diagnosis and treatment, violation of confidentiality, and sexual impropriety. In theory, responsible supervision should identify and correct many of these problems in practice. Regularly scheduled meetings may not be sufficient to defeat a claim of supervisor liability. The supervisor is expected to stay informed about each case and to provide closer monitoring in difficult cases and for inexperienced workers (Reamer 1989).

Students are clearly susceptible to legal actions given their inexperience. In most cases, the liability will be imputed to the supervisor who has ultimate responsibility for the cases assigned to the student. Faculty and BSW programs may also be implicated if the student has been placed inappropriately or if information about the student's misconduct or impairment has been withheld. Zakutansky and Sirles (1993) looked at the relationships among clients, students, field instructors, and faculty liaisons and identified areas of potential liability. They recommended close working relationships among all parties to reduce the chance of mistakes that might lead to liability. Field instructors and faculty must be aware that supervision is a relationship with legal implications and must act to ensure appropriate practice by students.

Guidelines for Developing Policies and Procedures

Social work programs must develop specific policies and procedures to process claims against students. The policies and procedures are necessary to demonstrate an institution's careful consideration and respect for all parties.

The procedures focus on students who are not appropriate for the degree that is awarded by the academic unit. In most cases *inappropriate* has been defined as students' poor academic performances and resulting low grades. In social work and other professional programs, however, *appropriate* is defined as not only being capable of learning the required knowledge but also possessing the needed interpersonal skills and ethical standards. Both knowledge and skills are required of professionals who must safeguard the trust of vulnerable persons. Unfortunately, a small portion of social work students are themselves vulnerable persons and may pose risks for future clients.

Students' backgrounds or current lives may involve criminal activity, substance abuse, abuse of children, and other behavior that would be considered unethical or professionally unacceptable. They may create a potential threat to other students in the program and to future clients. Consequently, an enormous burden falls on faculty members who must evaluate them and, in most cases, recommend corrective actions. The burden of judging students' appropriateness is intensified by the double bind that results, on the one hand, from the faculty's commitment to the profession's nonjudgmental acceptance of diverse persons and from the faculty's responsibility for academic gatekeeping to protect clients and the profession on the other.

Previous court cases such as *Board of Curators of the University of Missouri v Horowitz* have given faculty members the legal support to evaluate students' behavior on academic grounds (Cobb 1994) rather than on the more traditional personal misconduct grounds, the latter of which involve time-consuming disciplinary procedures (Cobb and Jordan 1989). Program policies should define behavior as academic criteria in much the same way as grades, attendance, and other more widely accepted academic expectations are defined. The policies should avoid legal jargon and requirements associated with civil or criminal law. The central themes in policy development, therefore, are attention to due process, articulation of professional standards for behavior, and identification of all performance expectations as *academic* standards and criteria.

The policies must outline a protocol for notice and hearings that allows interested parties to make claims against troublesome students. It is important to remember that during implementation the policy's purpose and the requirement of due process are most likely legally fulfilled, even if the actual sequence of procedures is slightly altered or inadvertently changed.

Criteria for behavior must be defined and based on acceptable practices, such as behavior outlined in the *NASW Code of Ethics* (1996).

The courts have recommended that behavioral criteria meet general rules rather than contain long lists of specific behaviors. For example, a list of inappropriate behavior should also contain the message that the list is not exhaustive but merely exemplary. The courts have recommended that the source or authorship of the criteria should be appropriate to the profession. The criteria, therefore, must have traditional relevance for students and the profession. The provisions of the *NASW Code of Ethics* are the most time-honored and professionally-based set of criteria available, and they are widely printed in social work texts. All students should study the code in their courses.

A social work program may specify that the standards for professional behavior apply to relationships with current and future clients, coworkers, or others. The criteria may be applied to behavior on campus or off campus, or even to previous behavior, as long as the likely recurrence of the behavior can bring potential harm to present or future clients. For example, a person who prior to enrollment in the social work program had a history of indecency with children may well be evaluated as unsuitable for the program and the profession.

In assisting students and faculty to make claims about a student's suitability for a career in social work, reasonable procedures and guidelines should include a sequence of steps for resolving the situation. For example, anyone making a claim should attempt to resolve the issue directly with the student in question. If the issue cannot be resolved, the person who is making a claim against a student should contact an administrator, such as the BSW program director. If the administrator is unable to resolve the issue, a hearing committee may be necessary. To facilitate an orderly process, time limits should be established for resolving disputes, notifying students, holding meetings, and making final judgments.

Such procedures are designed not only to protect due process rights but also to clarify everyone's roles and responsibilities. For example, persons making claims are required to put their concerns in writing, and they may be asked to present them to the faculty committee. In academic questions, accused students do not have a constitutional right to face-to-face meetings with their accusers. Hearing committees composed of faculty members meet with all parties, evaluate the validity of evidence, and make decisions. Since the students' futures are determined on academic grounds, all proceedings are held in confidence, even from other academic programs, because students maintain property rights to their academic reputations. Chairs of committees insure that their committees follow the procedures for due process as closely as possible. The committee maintains the standards for an academic meeting rather than for a court of law. For example, meetings are informal and directed toward the primary purpose of gathering information, and accused students do not attend meetings when accusers are presenting their claims.

College and University Attorneys

Most faculty in social work programs have limited experience with their institution's legal counsel. Moreover, few attorneys understand the peculiarities of professional education (Cobb 1994). Therefore, with the prospect that social work faculty and administrators may need legal counsel in the future, a realistic perspective on the role of the institution's attorneys may be helpful.

Attorneys are trained and hired to keep their clients (i.e., their universities or colleges) out of court. They carefully examine all contracts (including field agency contracts), institutional policies, hiring practices, and the like to protect the institution from lawsuits. They are understandably reluctant, therefore, to pursue terminations of students, grade grievances, or other student-faculty problems because these actions may move their client directly into court. They know how expensive and time-consuming such proceedings can be. In fact, a note circulated among deans on some campuses emphasized the benefits of avoiding student-related litigation. It explained that the graduation of one troublesome student was not worth the cost and time of a lawsuit!

Attorneys who are uninformed about professional education may not appreciate the risk factors associated with allowing inappropriate or unethical social work students to continue in the program. In the area of field placements, lawyers readily examine contracts with agencies, and they may recommend liability insurance for students; however, they remain largely uninformed about social work clients who are at risk and vulnerable and about the role of our students in providing services to them.

The attorneys' lack of knowledge is largely related to their training and their field of interest, which may not prepare them for differentiating between actions that pose little legal and financial risks to the institution (e.g., dismissals based on academic standards) and actions that may pose greater risks (e.g., disciplinary dismissals that stem from personal misconduct). In cases of academic dismissals, attorneys may incorrectly subscribe to a view of liability based upon the legal doctrine of *respondeat superior,* which implies the institution's liability for the students' conduct with clients and staff (Gelman and Wardell, 1988). For example, while Gelman and Wardell reported only a handful of lawsuits concerning the conduct of students in field agencies, lawyers may see the institution's liability in this situation as a legal threat, although it is an academic issue rather than a disciplinary matter.

The institution's legal staff may benefit from a brief review of social work's mission, purpose, and clientele. Many attorneys are surprisingly sympathetic to social work values. Their interest will be heightened when faculty and administrators ask them for legal suggestions on ethical dilemmas facing social work programs. For example, what is the potential harm to clients (and the social work program) when a particular student is in recovery for a "sexual addiction" involving children? What are the concerns related to graduating a student who is on probation for a vicious attack on his girlfriend or the rape of a woman in his apartment? If a former drug dealer (current student) has "paid her debt to society" in federal prison, is she safe to serve in a field placement in her newly chosen field of medical social work? In summary, information sessions with university attorneys, get-to-know-you lunches, and requests for advice are helpful tools to build supportive relationships and may pay off when the need for their assistance arises.

Legal issues are an increasing concern for social work programs. Students will inevitably question the limits of judgment and fairness as we carry out our gatekeeping functions. In fact, social work has a long history of affirming people's right to stand up for what they believe to be fair, moral, ethical, and correct.

Careful planning of policies and procedures can decrease future complaints and prevent perceptions of unfair treatment. Demonstrating respect for students in the planning and management of courses reinforces social work values and communicates a caring and concerned public image. These efforts are likely to ward off claims of unreasonable, unfair, arbitrary, or capricious behavior.

Faculty members must always be willing to set the limits on what is ethical and acceptable. The relative nature of right and wrong need not be a burden when we understand the profession in the context of social responsibility and education. Students, faculty, and administrators are judged by their behavior and not by their good intentions or ethical beliefs. Due process, contracts, torts, disabilities, and ethical standards are not offensive or restrictive to academia or the profession. Instead, the lack of attention to ethical responsibilities and the lack of application of legal principles create the real burden. Ultimately, social work programs need to assert to students and professors that the program is committed to supporting the overall mission of social work and defending, in or out of court, the faculty's judgments and actions.

References

Americans with Disabilities Act of 1990. 42 USCA sect 12101 *et seq.* (West 1993).

Blacks Law Dictionary. (1983). Abridged 5th ed. St. Paul, Minn.: West Publishing.

Board of Curators of the University of Missouri v Horowitz. 435 US 78 (1978).

Cobb, N. H. (1994). Court-recommended guidelines for managing unethical students and working with university lawyers. *Journal of Social Work Education* 30:18–31.

Cobb, N. H., and Jordan, C. (1989). Students with questionable values or threatening behavior: Precedent and policy from discipline to dismissal. *Journal of Social Work Education* 25:87–97.

Connally v University of Vermont. 244 F Supp 156 (DC Vt. 1975).

Dixon v Alabama State of Board of Education. 2294 F2d 150 (5th Cir 1961).

Doherty v Southern College of Optometry. 862 F2d 570 (6th Cir 1988).

Dutile, F. N. (1987). The law of higher education and the courts: 1986. *Journal of College and University Law* 14:303–357.

Fox, K. H. (1988). Due process and student misconduct. *American Business Law Journal* 25:697–700.

Gelman, S. R., and Wardell, P. J. (1988). Who's responsible?: The field liability dilemma. *Journal of Social Work Education* 24:70–78.

Golden, E. J. (1981). College student dismissals and the Eldridge factors: What process is due? *Journal of College and University Law* 8:495–509.

Ikpeazu v University of Nebraska. 775 F2d (8th Cir. 1985).

Jennings, L. (1981). Breach of contract suits by students against post-secondary institutions: Can they succeed? *Journal of College and University Law* 7:204–217.

Kaplin, W. A. (1985). *The law of higher education.* San Francisco: Jossey-Bass.

Lipsett v University of Puerto Rico. 637 F Supp 798 (DPR 1986).

Mahavongsanan v Hall. 529 F 2d 448 (5th Cir 1976).

Marx, C. A. (1984). Horowitz: A defense point of view. *Journal of Law and Education* 13:51–58.

Milam, S. J., and Marshall, R. D. (1987). Impact of regents of University of Michigan v. Ewing on academic dismissals from graduate and professional schools. *Journal of College and University* 13 (4): 335–352.

National Association of Social Workers (NASW). (1996). *NASW code of ethics.* Washington, D.C.: NASW.

Reamer, F. G. (1995). Malpractice claims against social workers: First factors. *Social Work* 40:595–601.

Reamer, F. G. (1989). Liability issues in social work supervision. *Social Work* 34:445–448.

Reeser, L. C. (1992). Students with disabilities in practicum: What is reasonable accommodation? *Journal of Social Work Education* 28:98–109.

Rehabilitation Act of 1973. 29 USC Section 701 *et. seq.* (1988).

Regents of the University of Michigan v Ewing. 474 US 214 (1985).

Russell v Salve Regina College. 649 F Supp 391 (DC RI 1986); *aff'd.* 890 F2d 484 (1st Cir 1989).

Saltzman, A., and Proch, K. (1990). *Law and social work practice.* Chicago: Nelson-Hall.

Schware v Board of Bar Examiners of New Mexico. 353 US 232 (1957).

Slaughter v Brigham Young University. 514 F2d 622 (10th Cir 1975).

Sofair v State University of New York. 44 NY 2d 475 (1978).

Wilkenfield v Powell. 577 F Supp 579 (1983).

Wynne v Tufts University School of Medicine. 932 F2d 570 (1st Cir 1991).

Zakutansky, T. J., and Sirles, E. A. (1993). Ethical and legal issues in field education: Shared responsibility and risk. *Journal of Social Work Education* 29:338–347.

10

Disability Law and Undergraduate Social Work Education: Practicing What We Preach

Robert G. Madden

A student who has been doing poorly in her academics and is about to be dismissed from the social work program announces to the faculty that she has a learning disability. She asks to be allowed to retake a course, and to have the college pay for a tutor to assist her in writing her papers.

A student who is visually impaired requests that all assignments be done on tape. Faculty are concerned about assessment and integration of theory. Also the student's request to have a math requirement waived has been rejected by the college.

A student is denied admission to a baccalaureate social work program that has a competitive admissions process. He performed poorly on a writing sample required of all applicants. The student claims to have a learning disability but has not provided documentation to the social work program.

A student with a traumatic brain injury seeks course modifications including open-book multiple choice examinations, "time and a half" to take tests, tutoring, and a note taker for all courses.

This article was originally published by the Association of Baccalaureate Social Work Program Directors in the premier issue of *The Journal of Baccalaureate Social Work* 1 (1), October, 1995. Copyright © 1995, National Association of Baccalaureate Social Work Program Directors. It is reprinted with permission of the publishers. An earlier version of this article was presented at the 1994 Baccalaureate Program Directors Conference in San Francisco, California.

Social work educators have confronted increasing numbers of cases similar to these in recent years. How social work programs respond is important on several levels. First, we have a moral obligation to treat individuals fairly and not to discriminate on the basis of a disability. Also, as a social work program, we model the values of the profession. Lastly, not to act in a fair manner means we may be putting our program and institution in legal jeopardy.

One of the major items on the political agenda of the 1980s was the development of specific protections for persons with disabilities. The most prominent of these developments was the passage of the *Americans with Disabilities Act* (P. L. 101–336, 1990; [hereafter, ADA]), which strengthened existing disability laws (particularly sec. 504 of the *Rehabilitation Act* of 1973). The ADA provides civil rights protections for persons with disabilities in employment and requires improved access to public accommodations (including educational institutions).

As we consider the political agenda for social work education in the remainder of the 1990s, we would be well served to begin by examining how undergraduate social work programs can respond to students with disabilities. With a rich tradition of support for those with special needs, social workers are at the forefront of advocacy movements (Lynch and Mitchell 1995). Social work education should likewise be a leader in ensuring true access to the profession for persons with disabilities.

This paper will summarize the laws governing higher education's treatment of individuals with disabilities. A case study method is used to analyze the legal bases for complaints, discuss university responses, and make recommendations as to how Social Work Programs can support individuals with disabilities to successfully meet degree requirements.

Recently there has been increased attention to gatekeeping in social work programs (Gibbs 1994; Cole and Lewis 1993; Moore and Urwin 1990). This discussion raises serious concerns that programs may unintentionally erect barriers to persons with disabilities. The rhetoric of program integrity may cloud the determination of whether a student might be provided the supports or adjustments needed to successfully meet requirements. Also, the field practice component complicates social work programs' consideration of a student's suitability for the profession (Reeser 1992).

Social work has long viewed itself as an inclusive profession and one that speaks out on matters of public policy. Despite this, social work education has given little attention to persons with disabilities (Reeser 1992). Recently, the social work profession has been experiencing a rededication to making society more accepting and supportive of all its members (Specht and Courtney 1994). One place to begin to practice what we preach is to improve our own efforts at acceptance and support for students with disabilities. Students' rights can be protected while maintaining standards and program integrity if faculty can respond flexibly to the varied needs of students with disabilities (Madden 1993).

Defining Disability Discrimination

Blacks Law Dictionary defines discrimination as a failure to treat all persons equally where no reasonable distinction can be found between those favored and those not favored (1983). This definition gets to the critical elements of the laws providing protection from disability discrimination. The law's primary aim is the equalization of opportunity and the intolerance for limiting assumptions about persons with disabilities. In the same way society will not allow an employer to refuse to hire someone solely on the basis of race, no one can be refused opportunities solely on the basis of a physical or mental impairment. Decisions made about exclusions must be made individually and have a reasonable basis. Although this sounds logical and just, the mechanics for its operation are subject to wide interpretation.

The definition of disability in the ADA is similar to the approach used in the Rehabilitation Act. In order to qualify for protection under either statute, a person must (a) have a physical or mental impairment that substantially limits a major life activity, (b) have a record of such an impairment, or (c) be regarded as having such an impairment (34 CFR sec. 104.3 [j] and 28 CFR sec. 35.104). The first part of the definition involves the classification of physical and mental impairments. Rather than listing each condition or diagnosis, the law is purposefully vague and inclusive in its language. This is due to the indeterminable number of impairments that could result in a person experiencing discrimination. Appropriate documentation from a physician may be required to support a claim, especially where diagnosis is not visible or obvious such as a learning disability or a mental impairment (Castellano and Chapman 1993).

The second part of the definition requires an examination of the effect the impairment has on the life of an individual. This determination assesses the nature and severity of the impairment and its effect on one or more basic life activities (Castellano and Chapman 1993). For an individual to qualify as a person with a disability entitled to protection, a substantial limitation must be shown. Having a diagnosis of a disability is not technically sufficient to trigger protection mechanisms. In practice, however, even without a substantial limitation, a person may still be legally "regarded as having" a disability such that the protection from discrimination is ensured.

Congress specifically excluded some impairments that could otherwise have been argued to require protections. One of these, in particular, is relevant to social work programs. A person currently using illegal drugs is *not* considered to be an individual with a disability; however, someone who has been addicted in the past may be protected under these laws.

The important consideration for social work programs is to understand that finding a student or applicant has a disability and the disability substantially limits a major life activity, is only the threshold standard. A student protected from discrimination by law is not being granted any rights other than the right to be given equal access to programs and activities. The deeper question for a program to be concerned with is whether the student who has a disability is being fairly accommodated and is not being evaluated in a manner that is reflecting the disability rather than the capabilities of the student.

Enforcement Mechanisms

The attorney general is given responsibility to enforce the nondiscrimination and accessibility requirements for public accommodations covered by Title III of the ADA. When postsecondary educational institutions are involved, this is carried out through the Department of Education's Office of Civil Rights (OCR). OCR conducts investigations of complaints against colleges and universities to determine whether they are in compliance with the regulations. Either the attorney general's office or a private individual may pursue civil actions to enforce Title III (Bleyer 1992). It is not necessary for an individual to exhaust all administrative remedies before filing a private lawsuit for violations of the ADA or Rehabilitation Act (*Pushkin* 1981). Courts may grant injunctive relief or may award monetary damages to the student and impose civil penalties on the institution. Attorney fees may also be awarded to the prevailing party in these actions (sec. 505, 42 USC sec. 12205).

Disability Laws and Higher Education

Most colleges and universities have been required to comply with the Rehabilitation Act since its inception. Originally they were brought under the federal law by virtue of receiving federal funds (financial aid, grants, etc.). With the passage of the ADA, which broadened the scope of protections, "public accommodations" became subject to the regulations. "Undergraduate, or postgraduate private schools or other place of education" are specifically included in the list of public accommodations subject to the ADA (sec. 301[7] [J]).

There are several regulations detailing the college's responsibility not to discriminate on the basis of a disability. As 34 CFR sec. 104.43(a) states, "no qualified individual with a disability shall, on the basis of disability, be excluded from participation in, be denied the benefits of, or otherwise be subjected to discrimination under any academic, or other postsecondary education program or activity." In order to avoid discriminating, the law requires educational institutions to make reasonable modifications to accommodate student needs. The regulations specify the type of accommodations intended.

According to 34 CFR sec. 104.44(a), a college is required to make such modifications to its academic requirements as are necessary to ensure nondiscrimination. Academic requirements that the college can demonstrate are essential to the program of instruction being pursued by such student, or to any directly related licensing requirement, are not regarded as discriminatory within the meaning of this section. Modifications may include changes in the length of time permitted for the completion of degree requirements, substitution of specific course requirements, and adaptation of the manner in which specific courses are conducted.

The regulations attempt to describe a balancing of interests. The accommodation has to be able to satisfy the legitimate interests of both the student and the school. Just as a school cannot have a single teaching or evaluative procedure and refuse to adjust to the needs of a student with a disability, the student cannot require a school to diminish standards to allow for successful completion of an academic course or program. The latter issue is termed by the law "otherwise qualified" (although the newer language in the ADA has dropped the word "otherwise"). The balance between "otherwise qualified" and "reasonable accommodation" is the primary subject of most legal challenges raised by students with disabilities. However, other specific categories of cases have been brought by students including: Whether a program may make preadmission inquiries; the extent of the duty to adjust academic requirements, provide auxiliary aids, or allow alternative evaluation measures to be used and the adequacy of due process procedures. The legal principles in each will be illustrated by representative cases. Specific implications for baccalaureate social work programs will be discussed.

Preadmission Inquiries

The goal of the Rehabilitation Act and the ADA is to eliminate discrimination against persons with disabilities. The laws and their subsequent regulations create a structure in which discrimination is less likely to be involved in a decision about a person with a disability. The regulations specifically provide that a college or university may not make preadmission inquiries as to whether an applicant for admissions is disabled (34 CFR sec. 104.42[b] [4] [1989]). Each applicant should be judged on the same criteria unless these criteria have an adverse effect on disabled applicants (such as standardized tests).

This information is generally known to colleges and does not directly impact undergraduate social work programs, which typically don't see a student until after admission to the college. The regulations, however, raise some issues for a department's admissions process. Since a student has already been admitted to the college, a social work program is allowed to confidentially inquire about disabilities that may require accommodation. It must be made clear that the information is voluntary and for the purposes of assisting the student with special needs. If a student chooses not to identify and document a disability, the program is under no obligation to provide accommodations.

Admissions and Retention

A case illustrating the determination of whether a student is a "qualified" applicant is *Pushkin v Regents of University of Colorado* (1981). In this case, a student sought admission to a psychiatric residency program. Pushkin had multiple sclerosis and was confined to a wheelchair. He was disabled in his abilities to walk and write. During the admissions process, Pushkin was interviewed several times by an admissions committee, which found him to be "far below the level of any other persons accepted into the program" (at 1386). However, the court examined the reasons for the poor evaluation and found they were related to his disability. The admissions committee felt (mistakenly) that the effects of multiple sclerosis made him a poor candidate to handle the stress of the residency program. Further, they also claimed his multiple sclerosis and wheelchair would have detrimental psychological effects on patients. The court examined the characteristics of the incoming class, which indicated Pushkin was qualified for admission. It found the reasons articulated by the university showed "unjustified consideration of the handicap itself" (at 138). The committee presumed that Pushkin was unqualified rather than relying on actual evidence of his aptitudes.

The university tried to argue that its considerations were evenhanded (i.e., that Pushkin was given equal treatment). This argument is the one used in other discrimination cases and involves an analysis of intent. The university sought to show it had not violated its duty to ensure the equal protection of all students. The court rejected their position, finding the proper standard requires the student initially to show she/he is qualified. Then the burden switches to the school to demonstrate how the denial of admission was based on legitimate, nondiscriminatory reasons. For disability cases, the court must determine whether the university rejected the student because he was not qualified or whether its decision was based on incorrect assumptions about the disability. Equal treatment is not the same as equal opportunity.

Students entering a social work program may similarly present with disabilities giving rise to faculty doubts about potential success in the field. In social work, students with communication difficulties are especially prone to this scrutiny. Faculty may justify a denial of admission by not wanting to place students in a situation of having to meet expectations beyond their capabilities (in the vernacular, not setting the student up to fail). *Pushkin* illustrates the requirement that admissions decisions must be based on more objective criteria than assumptions and the desire to protect the applicant.

In *Halasz v University of New England* (1993), a student with learning disabilities and Tourette's Syndrome participated in a program at a private college designed for those with learning disabilities. He performed poorly, receiving low grades (despite accommodations and support services) and was not admitted to the college as a transfer student. The court analyzed the facts and found he was not academically qualified for admission, therefore the college had not discriminated. It based its reasoning on whether the person with a disability was provided meaningful access to the educational program. In this case, the college had offered accommodations and supports, but when the student was still not able to meet standards, the college's affirmative duty was met.

Halasz is relevant to BSW programs, which regularly admit transfers who have taken courses as nonmatriculated students. These transfer applicants who do poorly and are not accepted into the college may have unmet needs. If these students have requested accommodations and supports for a documented disability, the college has an affirmative duty to provide these. The social work program must have procedures for tracking and providing accommodations to nonmatriculated students taking introductory social work courses. A failure to respond with appropriate accommodations effectively precludes meaningful access and would be in violation of the ADA and the Rehabilitation Act.

Academic Adjustments

Students with disabilities frequently require academic adjustments and/or auxiliary aids to enable them to have access to the educational program. These adjustments may include requests for alternative testing procedures, provision of tutors or note takers, substitutions for some requirements, availability of tape-recorded lectures, recorded texts and the opportunity to complete the course or program at a slower pace.

These cases usually are pursued by students in relation to either admissions or retention. Students may claim that with proper adjustments, they would be able to succeed in a program and are being denied admission based on a judgment of their qualifications without the accommodations. The argument is that the admissions criteria may reflect particular skills impaired by the disabling condition rather than actually measuring the applicant's aptitude. In retention cases, students generally claim "but for" the school's failure to provide adjustments, they would have been able to succeed.

The regulations state that schools are not responsible for providing attendants, individually prescribed devices, readers for personal use or study, or other devices or services of a personal nature (34 CFR sec. 104.44 [2] [2] [1989]). In most cases, courts and administrative agencies have found a "good faith" effort on the part of the college to provide accommodations to be sufficient. The response, however, must be timely, to ensure the student has the supports in place to be successful in a class (*Oregon State University* 1993). Also, the cases affirm the responsibility for requesting needed adjustments belongs with the student (*Massachusetts College of Pharmacy* 1993).

There are some cases, however, where colleges have been found in violation of the Rehabilitation Act for failure to provide accommodations. OCR found San Francisco Community College had not provided adequate assurances that a student would have a test proctor available as required to accommodate her disability (1990). In another case, St. Charles Community College (MO) was found to be in violation of Section 504 for failing to have a procedure in place for providing a visually-impaired student with books on tape (1991). A parent successfully charged Tuskegee University with a Section 504 violation for failure to provide timely evaluation of his son's learning disabilities such that academic adjustments did not occur when needed (1990). The common problem for these schools was the lack of a clear process to provide students with necessary adjustments.

One other area of controversy evident in the case analysis was the problem of who is to pay for accommodations. The most frequently litigated question has been payment for interpreters and note takers for hearing-impaired students (Tucker and Goldstein, Supp. 5, 1994). In *Camenisch v University of Texas*, a federal appeals court upheld a lower court ruling ordering the university to procure and compensate an interpreter and note taker for a hearing-impaired student. Similarly, in *Prince v Rutgers*, a deaf student succeeded in having the court issue an order barring the school from holding classes in two courses until they had recorded the lectures and provided next day transcripts to the student. Despite these cases, the issue of payment for accommodations and aids is not clear. The laws only require institutions to "take such steps as are necessary to ensure that no handicapped student is denied the benefits of, excluded from participation in, or otherwise subject to discrimination under the education program" (45 CFR sec. 84.44 [d] [1]). Many institutions have interpreted this duty to include paying for educational evaluations where there is suspicion that a student has a learning disability. It is unclear whether these efforts have arisen from a commitment to students or from an emphasis on retention, but the effect has been positive.

Modifications to Methods of Evaluation

One other accommodation frequently sought by students with disabilities is a modification in methods of evaluating performance (primarily examinations). The leading case on this subject is *Wynne v Tufts University School of Medicine* (1991). The case was brought by a student who suffered from dyslexia and experienced particular difficulty on multiple-choice exams. After failing several first-year courses, he was allowed to retake them but still failed one required course. The school voted to dismiss him from the program. The student's complaint under Section 504 was the school's failure to offer an alternative to written multiple-choice examinations. The school submitted evidence that it had evaluated alternatives to its testing format and concluded that a change was not practicable. Although the faculty's rationale was not convincing, the court upheld its position. Other cases in which students request extra time for completion of exams and assignments, or opportunities to submit oral/taped assignments in lieu of written ones, are likely to be considered "de minimis," and academic institutions should provide this type of accommodation in a timely manner.

Clinical Competence

One aspect of the "otherwise qualified" standard important to social work educators is the question of whether a student is qualified to do the clinical aspects of the program. The regulations specifically address this issue by stating a qualified handicapped person (sic) is one who meets academic and *technical* standards prerequisite to admissions or participation in the school's education program (45 CFR sec. 84.3 [k] [3] [1978]). An explanatory note to the regulations identifies technical standards as "all nonacademic admissions criteria that are essential to participation in the program" (45 CFR pt. 84, App. A, [1998]) (as cited in *Southern Community College v Davis* 1979).

This issue has been litigated on several occasions and each time the courts have upheld the right of the college to decide on the basic clinical competencies necessary for the degree. If a student's disability precludes the attainment of these nonacademic, technical skills, regardless of available accommodations, the individual is not considered qualified for admission or retention. In *Southeastern Community College v Davis* (1979), a student who had a serious hearing disability applied for admission to a nursing program. The school denied admission, citing the need to provide the student with full-time supervision whenever she interacted with patients. The court agreed with the college that reasonable physical qualifications for admission into a clinical training program were justifiable, and that the modification of full-time supervision would amount to lowered standards.

Similarly in *Doe v New York University* (1981) a medical school applicant with a history of psychiatric problems was denied readmission to the program after taking a leave of absence. The school found her unable to meet the technical aspects of the program. Because her disorder was long-standing and had been triggered by stress in the past, the school felt she would be unable to complete the clinical portions of the program. The court gave some guidance in a note stating that schools should exercise care not to permit prior mental illness to be routinely regarded as a disqualification. It distinguished the facts in this case, particularly the severity of the disorder, and the student's lack of commitment to treatment.

In a related case, a nursing student whose behavior with patients in a clinical setting was inappropriate, was failed in that course. The program refused to allow her to retake the clinical until she provided additional information concerning her mental health disability. OCR found this to be an issue of clinical competency within the purview of the faculty and refused to find the school had violated the student's rights.

These cases illustrate the deference given to faculty to determine the essential clinical skills necessary for a professional degree. Disability law repeatedly uses the concept of "essential functions" to balance the rights of the individual to be accommodated with the rights of the institution to maintain its standards (Tucker and Goldstein 1994). Based on disability case law, it is clear that clinical knowledge, skills, and values, including ethical violations, should be articulated by social work programs as being academic (i.e., theory based, teachable and subject to evaluation). This designation allows a program to identify those areas considered to be "essential functions" of social work practice.

Social work programs may determine that a disability prevents a student from meeting essential clinical standards, but the determination must not be based on beliefs about the disability and must consider whether a student could meet the requirements with reasonable accommodations. For example, if a student is unable to communicate in writing, a program may arrange for an agency to provide alternative means of meeting requirements for documentation. If a student is unable to tolerate the emotional demands of a professional social work relationship, the faculty may deem this to be an essential function of practice and deny admission if no adequate accommodation can be determined.

The Council on Social Work Education's revised standards require baccalaureate programs to have procedures in place for terminating a student's enrollment for reasons of academic and nonacademic performance (CSWE, sec. 5.8, p. 89, 1994). This standard has caused some confusion as to what constitutes a nonacademic issue and is relevant to the treatment of students with disabilities. A recent survey of MSW programs found that faculty and administrators had a fairly consistent view of what constituted nonacademic issues. They included unethical behaviors, mental or emotional problems, criminal activities, and inappropriate field and classroom behavior (Koerin and Miller 1995). Social work programs should use academic criteria for these behaviors that occur within the educational setting, including the field practicum (Cobb 1994).

By using the term *nonacademic,* CSWE standards unwittingly put BSW programs at risk. When nonacademic cases are analyzed, a student's lawyer has a convenient argument. Since the denial of admissions or dismissal was based on nonacademic reasons, faculty should not be granted the historic deference they receive in academic decisions. Further, the standards for nonacademic dismissals are more difficult to clearly articulate and courts are likely to refuse a motion to dismiss before trial, allowing a jury to determine if there was any arbitrary or capricious action by the faculty.

Undue Hardship

Institutions may not be responsible for providing accommodations or aids that constitute "undue hardship" to the school. The hardship relates to both the difficulty and expense. This issue has been examined more fully in Title I of the ADA regulating employment. The legislative history of this section describes undue hardship as an action that is unduly costly, extensive, substantial, disruptive, or that will fundamentally alter the nature of the program (Parry 1992:529). Although it is not explicit in the regulations specific to education, the same standards seem to apply to administrative and court analyses of how much the school should do to accommodate the student. The concept of undue hardship is intended to provide some balance to the requirements of the act.

One case in the educational arena where undue hardship was evaluated was *Wynne* (1991). In examining the institution's obligation to provide an accommodation, the court determined that if a school evaluated feasibility, cost and effect on the academic program, and came to a rationally justifiable conclusion that the alternatives would result in lowering academic standards or requiring substantial program alterations, then it had met its duty (at 26). When this is combined with the court's historical deference to academic decisions (Madden 1993), the student carries a heavy burden to prove discriminatory treatment if the school has policies and procedures in place, and leaves a paper trail of reasonable attempts to accommodate.

Recommendations

In the past twenty years, protections have been developed for people with disabilities with the goal of eliminating barriers to full participation in education and related services. Increasing numbers of students with disabilities are entering institutions of higher education and they are aware of their rights to receive accommodations (Cole, Christ, and Light 1995). A review of the cases brought by students against colleges and universities reveals some useful parameters for baccalaureate social work programs.

1. The social work program director and interested faculty should arrange a meeting with the office or person designated by the institution as being responsible for coordinating services to students with disabilities. At this meeting, the program can learn more about the services offered by the school. Also, they [the social work faculty] can educate the support staff about the requirements of the social work degree, especially the practicum requirements.

2. The program should designate a departmental coordinator whose duties would include: educating all faculty members about concerning their responsibility to provide reasonable accommodations, monitoring the timeliness and adequacy of accommodations, and ensuring consistency.

3. The social work program should develop a plan to expand opportunities for students with disabilities. This plan may arise out of an assessment of current barriers to access, including structural impediments, admissions policies, and the institutional climate.

4. Faculty should encourage students to confidentially report their disabilities in order to receive support and accommodations. Including a statement on all syllabi and verbally inviting students to share their special needs can set the climate of acceptance necessary for many students to come forward.

5. The social work program should routinely educate field practicum agencies concerning the needs of students with disabilities. The field practicum coordinator should maintain a list of agencies that are not accessible and advocate for agencies to meet the special needs of students. Students are responsible for sharing information about disabilities with their practicum instructor. Program faculty should respect the rights of the student to determine what information will be shared with the agency.

6. The social work program should review admissions policies to determine if the measures are unintentionally screening out students with disabilities.

BSW programs should be leaders in ensuring access to educational benefits for individuals with disabilities. Because of the nature of social work, we should attempt to recruit and retain students with diverse backgrounds, including those with disabilities. To effectively accomplish this goal, programs must make a commitment to actively and creatively pursue accommodations. We must not be caught up in a false sense of allegiance to the teaching and evaluation methods we have always used. There is a legitimate concern to guard the integrity of the profession by not lowering standards. Administrative and court decisions are clear that this is not what is required by the regulations. What is required is for programs to create an environment in which students feel safe to self-report disabilities and encourage an open dialogue about how to both accommodate to the needs of the student and ensure that the student graduates with the same knowledge and skills as any other graduate.

Discrimination is not always an overt act. Often barriers to institutions are produced by an omission or an insensitivity that creates an unwelcoming environment having the effect of excluding. Social work programs that are committed to develop opportunities for all students model the type of inclusiveness and support that is the very essence of the profession. We have a responsibility to do our part to see that there is a goodness of fit between each student and the educational system.

References

Americans with Disabilities Act of 1990. Public Law 101 Stat. 327 (codified at 42 USCA 12101 *et seq.* [West Supp. 1991]).

Blacks Law Dictionary. (1983). Abridged 5th ed. St. Paul, Minn.: West Publishing.

Bleyer, K. (1992). *The Americans with Disabilities Act: Enforcement Mechanisms.* MPDLR 16 (May–June): 347–350.

Camenisch v University of Texas. 616 F2d 127 (5th Cir 1980).

Castellano, L. A., and Chapman, R. (1993). *The Prentice Hall ADA Compliance Advisor.* Englewood Cliffs, N.J.: Prentice Hall.

Cobb, N. H. (1994). Court recommended guidelines for managing unethical students and working with university lawyers. *Journal of Social Work Education* 30:18–31.

Cole, B. S., Christ, C. C., and Light, T. R. (1995). Social work education and students with disabilities: Implications of Section 504 and the ADA. *Journal of Social Work Education* 31:261–268.

Cole, B. S., and Lewis, R. G. (1993). Gatekeeping through termination of unsuitable social work students: Legal issues and guidelines. *Journal of Social Work Education* 29:150–159.

Council on Social Work Education, Commission on Accreditation. (1994). *Handbook of Accreditation Standards and Procedures.* 4th ed. Alexandria, Va.: CSWE.

Doe v New York University. 666 F2d 791 (1st Cir 1992).

Fair Housing Amendments Act of 1988. 42 USC 3601 *et seq.*

Gibbs, P. (1994). Screening mechanisms in BSW programs. *Journal of Social Work Education* 30:63–74.

Halasz v University of New England. 816 F Supp 37 (D. Me. 1993).

Koerin, B., and Miller, J. (1995). Gatekeeping policies: Terminating students for nonacademic reasons. *Journal of Social Work Education* 31:247–260.

Lynch, R. S., and Mitchell, J. (1995). Justice system advocacy: A must for NASW and the social work community. *Social Work* 40:9–12.

Madden, R. G. (1993). Protecting all parties: A legal analysis of clinical competency and student dismissals. *Journal of Law and Social Work* 4 (1): 1–13.

Massachusetts College of Pharmacy. NDLR 1 (19) 1993.

Moore, L. S., and Urwin, C. A. (1990). Quality control in social work: The gatekeeping role in social work education. *Journal of Teaching in Social Work* 4:113–128.

Oregon State University. 5 NDLR 19, 1993.

Parry, J. W. (1991). Employment under the ADA: A national perspective. MPDLR 15 (Sept–Oct.): 525–534.

Prince v Rutgers Civ Act. 89–4740 (SSB) (D.N.J., complaint filed Nov. 14, 1989).

Pushkin v Regents of University of Colorado. 658 F2d 1372 (1981).

Reeser, L. C. (1992). Students with disabilities in practicum: What is reasonable accommodation? *Journal of Social Work Education* 28:98–109.

Rehabilitation Act of 1973. 29 USC sec. 701 *et seq.* (1988).

San Francisco Community College (CA) NDLR 1 (162) 1990.

Southeastern Community College v. Davis. 442 US 397 (1979).

Specht, H., and Courtney, M. (1994). *Unfaithful angels: How social work has abandoned its mission.* New York: Free Press.

St. Charles County Community College (MO). NDLR 1 (347) 1991.

Tucker, B. P., and Goldstein, B. A. (Supp. 5) (1994). Legal rights of persons with disabilities: An analysis of federal law. Horsham, PA: LRP Publ. 6:35–47.

Tuskegee University (AL). 1 NDLR 226, 1990.

Wynne v. Tufts University School of Medicine. 932 F2d 19 (1st Cir 1991). Reheard: 976 F2d 791 (1st Cir 1992). On remand to trial court, No. 88–1105–Z (D. Mass. Mar. 2, 1992).

11

Court Cases and Judicial Opinions Related to Gatekeeping in Colleges, Universities, and Professional Schools

Bettie S. Cole and Robert G. Lewis

The Council on Social Work Education (CSWE) requires programs to be responsible for establishing procedures to determine the "suitability" of the students it graduates. Suitability must be determined both at admission and throughout the time a student is in the social work education program (CSWE 1994:87, Evaluative Standard 5). Making suitability decisions is a difficult task and requires a working knowledge of the legal parameters within which such decisions may be made.

This chapter presents an annotated list of court cases and federal statutes and regulations related to academic and disciplinary decisions affecting student admissions and retention in professional programs. Decisions affecting admissions and termination policies and practices have dealt with four major areas of law and legal theory: constitutionally guaranteed procedural due process, arbitrary and capricious decisions, discrimination, and contract theory. The body of court cases and federal statutes and regulations presented in this chapter is intended to provide a foundation for programs to develop policies to guide their decisions to admit, to screen out, or to terminate students found to be unsuitable. Factors related to gatekeeping efforts that are addressed in the court cases include academic requirements, clinical skills, aptitude, behavioral and ethical conduct, and disability concerns.

One of the first steps a program must take in carrying out its task to determine the suitability of students is developing and validating standards and criteria both for admission and continuation in the program. The *NASW Code of Ethics* (National Association of Social Workers 1996) is useful in developing professional standards of conduct for students. Some standards and criteria, such as those more subjective judgments made in interviews, must be subjected to peer review and testing in order to assure equal access and due process to applicants. "There should be some evidence, for example, that there is a relationship between admission standards, likely program success, and ethical and responsible conduct as a professional" (Cole 1991:23). According to Carnegie (1979:42), the criteria should be reliable in "measur[ing] qualities relevant to legitimate educational objectives of the . . . professional program." There should also be provisions for an applicant to challenge the appropriateness of criteria. Although the courts allow for a degree of subjectivity, the program must guard against allegations of arbitrariness and capriciousness in its decisions. If interviews are conducted as a part of the screening process for "suitability," it must be made clear that the criteria used in the interviews are uniformly applied.

Admission and continuation criteria must be clearly articulated, published, and disseminated to all prospective applicants and must include explanations of the consequences for misconduct. Two sources for such publications are the college's or university's catalog and the student handbook. A clear distinction should be made by the program about which criteria it uses for admission of qualified candidates. For example, criteria that address academic competence or scholastic ability (e.g., GPA, grade of B or better in introductory courses) may be used to determine admissibility (applicant is minimally qualified to do the job). A second set of criteria may then be used to evaluate other characteristics, such as personal attributes, life experience, and other traits that represent a broad array of qualities found to be relevant for consideration in the selection process (Carnegie 1979). Upon request, an applicant not admitted to a program must be given a reason for the rejection.

Criteria for the evaluation of the students' performance in classroom and field placement, including such requirements as attendance, should be discussed with students and clearly identified as academic expectations in course syllabi, field instruction manuals, and institutional catalogs. The court decisions summarized in this chapter show that courts have taken the position of noninterference in academic matters, leaving to educators the responsibility of outlining the parameters of "academic decision making." Other cases support the fact that professional behavior, especially in clinical and practice settings, is an *academic requirement* and therefore an educational component of professional preparation.

Academic decisions include expectations of practice competencies that are evaluated in performance appraisals in field education and must be made in good faith, not arbitrarily or capriciously. As these appraisals are largely subjective, there must be documentation showing that the rating was a rational exercise of discretion. This can be accomplished, in part, by establishing measurable performance criteria that clearly delineate outcome measurements. Cole and Lewis (1993) suggested that decisions of clinical insufficiency, incompetence, or misconduct might best be made by a panel or committee to promote uniformity, add credibility, and further document the rational nature of the decision-making process.

When deficient class or field performance contraindicates a student's continuance in the program, constitutionally protected due process rights mandate that the student be advised of his or her poor performance prior to dismissal from the program or any other disciplinary action. To protect the student's rights to challenge academic decisions, programs must have an academic appeals process in place that allows for review and reevaluation of those decisions. While private institutions are not held to the same due process constraints as public institutions, they are nonetheless bound by contracts made with students (Cole and Lewis 1993).

The program must make sure that any standards, tests, or criteria it establishes do not have a disproportionate, adverse effect on persons with disabilities. Students must be qualified *in spite of* their disabilities and must meet both technical and academic standards for participation in the program. Section 504 of the *Rehabilitation Act of 1973* (29 USC 794 [1994]) and the *Americans With Disabilities Act* (42 USC 12101 *et. seq.* [1990]) do not require programs to lower or to effect substantial modifications of standards to accommodate persons with disabilities, but they do stress equal opportunity.

The remainder of this chapter provides brief summaries of legal decisions found relevant to social work education and gatekeeping responsibilities. This review is intended to provide legal guidelines for faculty as they develop gatekeeping policies related to academic deficiencies, misconduct, academic requirement changes, and policies that may have a detrimental impact on students with disabilities. Because the institution's attorneys and legal staff may be unaware of the case law concerning gatekeeping efforts, these cases should be shared with them, particularly if gatekeeping policies need approval by their office. In fact, based on the review of court cases and federal statutes and regulations relating to conduct decisions, the strongest guideline that can be offered is for faculty to seek the advice of the university's legal counsel while developing rules of conduct and *before* any action is taken that adversely affects a student.

Admissions

Contract Theory

Eden v Board of Trustees of State University, 374 NYS 2d 686 (NY App Div 1975). Students who had been admitted to a new school of podiatry, which was to open in 1975, sued when the school did not open for what the state cited as financial reasons. The court ordered the state to enroll the students, stating that the institution's acceptance of the petitioners' applications was sufficient to satisfy the classic requirements of a contract. The prospective student has a contract with the institution once the institution accepts the student's admission application.

Steinberg v The Chicago Medical School, 354 NE2d 586 (Ill App Div 1976). If the institution deviates from the admissions criteria outlined in its catalog, an applicant can sue for breach of contract. The published standards must be used in judging an applicant's qualifications unless the institution has specifically reserved the right to alter those standards. Programs should provide a reasonable period of time for applicants to comply with new standards.

Mahavongsanan v Hall, 529 F2d 448 (5th Cir 1976). A graduate student in education was denied a degree because of her inability to pass a comprehensive examination, a requirement instituted after she was well into the program. The student was allowed to take the exam twice and failed it both times. The university then afforded her a further reasonable opportunity to complete additional coursework in lieu of the comprehensive exam. She rejected that option and brought suit in a U. S. District Court (N.D. Ga.), which held that the university was required to grant the degree. The U. S. Court of Appeals for the Fifth Circuit overturned the district court decision for the following reason: Implicit in her contract with the university upon matriculation was her agreement to comply with the university's rules and regulations, and the university was entitled to modify these so as to properly exercise its educational responsibility. The student's claim of a binding, absolute contract was denied, and the Fifth Circuit Court held that she was denied neither procedural nor substantive due process by denial of a master's degree in education.

Prusack v State, 498 NYS 2d 455 (NY App Div 1986). The university bulletin's statements of rights and duties become part of a contract between the student and the institution.

Due Process

Grove v The Ohio State Univ. College of Veterinary Medicine, 424 F Supp 377 (SD Ohio 1976). The court reasoned that a certain degree of subjectivity in personal interviews in the admissions process did not constitute arbitrary action.

Chance v Board of Examiners, 330 F Supp 203, 222–23 (SD NY 1971). Although the institution's right to hold interviews with candidates has been upheld, the court held that interviews must be uniform and limited to specific criteria. The applicant has a constitutional right to protection against arbitrary and capricious action.

Arizona Board of Regents v Wilson, 539 P 2d 943 (Ariz 1975). A female student was denied admission to the graduate school of art because the faculty did not consider her artwork to be of sufficiently high quality. The court held in favor of the university, stating that this was a prime example of when a court should not interfere in the academic program of a university. The court maintained that it should not substitute its own opinions as to the merits of the appellee's work for that of the faculty committee.

Published admission criteria and standards constitute a contract between the student and the social work program. Whenever a program exercises its right to alter admission requirements, students must be afforded the opportunity and adequate time to comply with the new requirements. The courts have supported the use of interviews and faculty subjective reviews of student qualifications; however, all admission decisions are to be made fairly, not arbitrarily or capriciously. This calls for careful articulation of the criteria that are applied in assuring uniformity in the interview and review process.

Academic Dismissals

This section includes issues of contract, grades, attendance, behavior, and clinical skills.

Greenhill v Bailey, 519 F2d 5 (8th Cir 1975). The court held that the student must be accorded an opportunity to appear personally to contest the allegations of academic deficiency. This ruling is not to be interpreted as requiring full trial-type procedures, however. "A graduate or professional school is, after all, the best judge of its students' academic performance and their ability to master the required curriculum" (*Id.* at 9).

The court further stated the hearing should consist of an informal give-and-take between student and the dismissing agent that would give the student the opportunity to characterize his or her conduct in what he or she deems to be the proper context. See *Goss v Lopez,* 419 US 565 (1975); *Depperman v University of Kentucky,* 371 F Supp 73 (ED Ky 1974); *Connelly v University of Vermont and State Agricultural College,* 244 F Supp 156 (DC Vt 1965).

Board of Curators of The University of Missouri v Horowitz, 435 US 78 (1978). Citing *Mahavongsanan v Hall* (529 F2d at 449), the court stated that academic dismissals from state institutions can be enjoined if shown to be clearly arbitrary and capricious. The due process rights to notice and a hearing, however, are limited to disciplinary decisions. The *Mahavongsanan* court elaborated that there is "no case which holds that colleges and universities are subject to supervision or review of the courts in the uniform application of their academic standards" (*Id.* at 450).

Horowitz was dismissed from medical school when she was determined deficient in her clinical work. The court noted that evaluation of her clinical work "is no less an 'academic' judgment because it involves observation of her skills and techniques in actual conditions of practice, rather than [simply] assigning a grade to her written answers on an essay question" (435 US at 95). The court declined "to further enlarge the judicial presence in the academic community and thereby risk deterioration of many beneficial aspects of the faculty-student relationship"(*Id.* at 90).

Regents of University of Michigan v Ewing, 106 S Ct 507 (1985). The U. S. Supreme Court held that Ewing's dismissal, when he failed an examination required to complete the final two years of the program, did not constitute a due process violation. It found that the decision to dismiss was reached in a fair and impartial manner, not based on bad faith, ill will, or other impermissible ulterior motives (*Id.* at 510). The Sixth Circuit Court had ruled the action to be arbitrary since Ewing was the only student denied the opportunity to retest after failing the examination.

The Supreme Court found the "faculty's decision to have been made conscientiously and with careful deliberation, based on an evaluation of the entirety of Ewing's academic career" (*Id.* at 513). It further affirmed that judges should show great respect for faculties' professional judgment when being asked to review the substance of a genuinely academic decision. The court added that judges may not override academic decisions unless there is "such a substantial departure from accepted academic norms as to demonstrate that the person or committee responsible did not actually exercise professional judgment"(*Id.* at 513).

Contract Theory

Slaughter v Brigham Young University, 514 F2d (10th Cir 1975). As was noted earlier in this chapter's section on admissions issues, students have a contractual agreement with the university once an application is accepted. The *Slaughter* case stipulated, however, that commercial contract doctrine must not be rigidly applied.

Carr v St. John's University, New York, 231 NYS 2d 410 (NY App Div 1962) *aff'd* 187 NE 2d 18 (NY 1961). The court upheld the dismissal of four students who had participated in a civil marriage ceremony, which was against university rules as set by Catholic doctrine. The court held that "when a student is duly admitted by a private university, secular or religious, there is an implied contract between the student and the university that, if he complies with the terms prescribed by the university, he will obtain the degree which he sought" (*Id.* at 411).

Healy v Larsson, 323 NYS 2d 625, *aff'd* 318 NE 2d 608 (NY 1971). The court ruled that the *Carr* principle should apply equally to a public university or a community college. The student was denied a degree at a community college, but the court held that the student had satisfactorily completed all requirements prescribed by authorized representatives of the college.

Corso v Creighton University, 731 F2d 529 (8th Cir 1983). The university appealed an earlier court injunction against expelling a student from medical school. The student had been charged with cheating on an exam and lying about it, which the student handbook specifically regarded as a serious offense calling for a serious penalty. The student had been expelled without a hearing.

The court ruled that the student-university relationship was contractual in nature. Since the student's actions resulted in expulsion, regarded as a serious penalty, the student had a right to a hearing before disciplinary action was taken. The ruling did not specifically deal with the lying or cheating, but focused on whether or not the university complied with the provisions provided for in the handbook or contract between the parties. The provision of a right to a hearing was contained in the student handbook.

Hammond v Auburn University, 669 F Supp 1555 (MD Ala 1987). Hammond brought a civil rights action against university officials after being informed that he would no longer be allowed to enroll in any electrical engineering classes due to his failure to comply with new graduation requirements. The student had been given notice of the change in graduation requirements and had been given a reasonable and generous amount of time in which to become eligible for a degree under the old requirements.

The court held that: (a) action by the board of trustees in adopting the bulletin containing the change of graduation requirements was a reasonable exercise of its educational responsibilities; (b) the student had not been denied substantive due process; (c) the change in degree requirements did not amount to a breach of contract contained in the bulletin in effect at the time the student enrolled at the university; and (d) the student had not been denied equal protection.

The courts have consistently recognized educators as being the best judges of students' performance. Courts have further held that performance in clinical work is in the academic realm. As long as academic decisions are made in good faith, neither arbitrary nor capricious, students' due process rights are not violated. Students enrolling in both public and private institutions have a contractual relationship with the institution and have the right to expect higher education institutions to abide by the terms of the contract as outlined in catalogs and bulletins, although rigid commercial contract doctrine does not apply.

Conduct and Rules Dismissals: Due Process

Dixon v Alabama State Board of Education, 294 F2d 150 (5th Cir 1961). This is one of the leading cases on misconduct dismissals. The appellate court ruled that due process required notice and some opportunity for a hearing *before* any student at a tax-supported college could be expelled for misconduct. "Whenever a governmental body acts so as to injure an individual, the Constitution requires that the act be consonant with due process of law" (*Id.* at 155).

The court outlined the standards that should be followed in providing due process. There must be notice and an opportunity for a hearing before a student is expelled for misconduct. The specific charges and grounds justifying expulsion should be included in the notice. The hearing should provide ample opportunity to hear both sides of the issue, thus protecting the rights of all involved. The circumstances of the particular case should determine the nature of the hearing.

In this case student witnesses were not present during the hearing. Therefore, the court ruled that the names of the witnesses against the student and a report on the facts to which each witness testified were to be provided to the student. *See Nash v Auburn University,* 812 F2d 655 (11th Cir 1987), which provides further clarification of this standard.

The student should be given the opportunity to present his or her own defense against the charges, including testimony or written affidavits of witnesses. The results of the hearing (if not before the Board of Education or administrative authorities) and findings of the hearing should be presented in a report that the student has the opportunity to review (294 F2d at 158, 159).

Paine v Board of Regents of the University of Texas System, 355 F Supp 199 (WD Tex 1972), *aff'd per curiam,* 474 F2d 1397 (5th Cir 1973). Students who had been convicted and placed on probation for marijuana offenses off-campus were expelled from the university without a hearing. The university rules called for automatic expulsion for two years. The court found that the students had been denied equal protection under the law, in that students convicted of other than drug-related offenses were accorded a full hearing before suspension.

Brookins v Bonnell, 362 F Supp 379 (ED Pa 1973). Brookins, a college nursing student, was expelled "for alleged failure to submit physical examination report, failure to report prior attendance at hospital school of nursing and to submit transcript, and failure to attend class regularly"(*Id.* at 383). The court determined that the student was not dismissed solely because of academic reasons and held that he was entitled to a fair and impartial due process hearing by the college.

Depperman v University of Kentucky, 371 F Supp 73 (ED Ky 1974). Depperman, a medical student, was on probation for behavior unbecoming a potential physician. The College of Medicine had "cited an inability to function effectively with other people"(*Id.* at 74). Anticipating expulsion, the student withdrew from school and sued, claiming denial of due process. The court held that he could not claim a constitutional abridgment, since available administrative remedies had been ignored.

Goss v Lopez, 419 US 565 (1975). The due process clause of the Fourteenth Amendment requires a public school to give oral or written notice of charges against a student *before* suspension for disciplinary reasons, if the student denies the allegations.

Sofair v State University of New York, 388 NYS 2d 453, 457 (NY App Div 1976). A dismissed medical student brought suit, seeking to compel the state university medical college to reinstate him as a student in good standing. The court ruled in favor of the university but ordered a new hearing by the grades committee based on the fact that the student, having been notified on the day the hearing was scheduled that his clinical skills were insufficient, did not have adequate time to prepare a rebuttal.

The *Sofair* case also provides an important guideline in relation to professional judgment in grading. The court recognized "that course grades alone cannot realistically measure professional skill and that review by a panel helps promote uniformity in those evaluations that call for subjective professional judgment"(*Id.* at 456).

Joseph E. Hill v Trustees of Indiana University, 537 F2d 248 (7th Cir 1976). The student brought action against the university, its trustees, and the professor who had given him failing grades in two classes upon discovering that the student had committed plagiarism. The district court dismissed the case, and the student appealed. The court ruled that the student had failed to exhaust administrative remedies within the university and thus was not entitled to have his grades "corrected."

Stoller v College of Medicine, 562 F Supp 403 (MD Pa 1983). A medical student dismissed from school for academic reasons brought a civil rights action against medical school officials contesting his dismissal. The court found that the school's action was not arbitrary or capricious and that the student had an opportunity to present any reasons for his poor academic performance and to provide information that might have permitted the committee and dean to conclude that, despite his past record, his performance in the future would be satisfactory.

Woodruff v Georgia State University, 304 SE 2d 697, 699 (Ga 1983). This case is an example of judicial restraint in reviewing academic decisions. The court expressed confidence in school authorities discharging their academic duties fairly and with competence.

Stone By Stone v Cornell University, 510 NYS 2d 315 (NY App Div 1987). See *Galiani v Hofstra Univ.,* 499 NYS 2d 182 (NY App Div 1986). Since this was a private university, the student was not protected by constitutional due process.

Clements v Nassau County, 835 F 2d 1000 (2d Cir 1987). A former nursing student brought action against the college, asserting that the faculty member's grading in bad faith and evaluation of her clinical performance resulted in her inability to graduate. The court granted the college's motion for summary judgment, and the student appealed. The circuit judge ruled that the teacher's procedure did not depart from accepted academic procedures and that the student's equal protection rights were not violated.

Susan M. v New York Law School, 544 NYS 2d 829 (NY App Div 1989). Susan M. was dismissed from law school for failure to maintain a C average. She alleged that an essay question on the final exam, which contributed 30 percent of the exam grade and on which she received a grade of zero, was graded unfairly and resulted in her receiving a D for the course. The court neither agreed nor disagreed on the grade, stating, "absent some concrete allegation of improper conduct, [a professor's] grading of [a student's] paper is purely a matter of professional discretion"(*Id.* at 830). It added, however, that an irrational reading of the petitioner's essay on the exam is a possibility that cannot be ruled out. The court remanded the case for further consideration of the petitioner's grade in order to assure that the zero given her on the essay in question was a rational exercise of discretion by the grader. The court was not convinced the student's objection to the grade had been reviewed by the school's Academic Status Committee, which was a right guaranteed by the law school's published rules.

Kalinsky v State University of New York at Binghamton, 557 NYS 2d 577 (NY App Div 1990). The court cited *Dixon v State Board of Education* in finding that the petitioner's entitlement to a statement detailing the factual findings and the evidence relied upon by decision makers in reaching a determination of guilt are "rudimentary elements of fair play."

When the institution is contemplating taking action that could result in expulsion of a student for violating rules or engaging in inappropriate behavior, the courts have ruled that the student must be afforded due process. This requires a hearing *before* such action is taken. The standards for this due process procedure have been outlined in *Dixon* and expanded upon by several other court cases summarized in this chapter. The due process clause of the Fourteenth Amendment requires oral or written notice before adverse action is taken if the student denies the charges.

Discrimination in Admissions and Dismissals: General

Keys v Sawyer, 353 F Supp 936 (SD Tex 1973). A Texas law school student who was dismissed from the program sued on grounds that he was denied a public education. The court upheld the dismissal and cited, among other reasons, that only the right to equal opportunity existed, not a constitutional right to education.

Defunis v Odegard, Washington, 529 P2d 438 (1974). Action was brought by an unsuccessful applicant to the state university's law school challenging a denial of admission on the grounds that the admissions policy led to an unconstitutional denial of his application. The Supreme Court ruled that two sets of criteria based upon race could not be used in screening applicants. Apparently, the school had denied this applicant in an effort to achieve a racial balance among students.

Phelps v Washburn University of Topeka, 634 F Supp 556 (D Kan 1986). Three applicants who were denied admission to law school filed action for discrimination because of their association with civil rights causes. The court held for the university on the basis that petitioners simply were not qualified for admission to law school. The court also enumerated the principle held in several previous cases that professional school admission is not a constitutional or property right, with the exception that the rules and regulations for admission must not be discriminatory, arbitrary, or unreasonable.

45 Federal Rules Decision, 133–148, (WD Mo 1969). The federal court, having reviewed many college and university dismissal and disciplinary cases, ruled that there should not be judicial intervention unless one of the following conditions was met: an individual was deprived of due process; there was discrimination, for example, on account of race or religion; the student was denied federal rights, constitutional or statutory, that are protected in the academic community; or the action was unreasonable, arbitrary, or capricious (*Id.* at 143).

The courts have ruled that students do not have a constitutional right to an education, but they do have a right to equal opportunity. Institutions cannot use different criteria for admissions based on race in their efforts to bring about racial balance. Decisions regarding admissions and dismissals must be made fairly and within concepts of fair play. At all times, students must be afforded due process.

Discrimination Against Persons with Disabilities

The following material contains excerpts from both the Department of Health and Human Service's regulations applying to the Rehabilitation Act of 1973, 29 USC 701 *et seq.* as amended by the Rehabilitation Act Amendments of 1974, 29 USC 706, 794, and the Americans with Disabilities Act of 1990, 42 USC 12101 *et seq.*

Rehabilitation Act Regulations 45 CFR 84.3 Subtitle A 504 (1995)

The Rehabilitation Act of 1973 and the regulations promulgated thereunder define a handicapped persons as one who (i) has "a physical or mental impairment which substantially limits one or more major life activities, (ii) has a record of such an impairment, or (iii) is regarded as having such impairment." Impairments include both physical and psychological disorders and conditions.

Individuals with mental illness, mental retardation, learning disabilities, and organic brain syndrome are specifically included in the protected category.

An otherwise qualified person with handicaps is defined as one who "meets the academic and technical standards requisite to admission or participation in the recipient's education program or activity" (45 CFR 84.3 [k] [3]).

A person who is otherwise qualified shall not be deprived of participation in or receiving the benefits of, or subjected to any discrimination under any program or activity receiving federal funding, solely by reason of her or his handicap (84.4, [a]). Any public educational institution, including colleges, universities, or other postsecondary institutions, are included in the term *program* as defined by this statute (84.3, [f]).

Institutions may not use any test or criterion for admission that has a disproportionate, adverse effect on handicapped persons. If the test or criterion has been validated as a predictor of success in the education program or activity in question, it may be used but only if it can be shown that no alternate tests or criteria that have less disproportionate adverse effect are available (84.42 [2]). The program must demonstrate that academic requirements are essential and will thereby not be regarded as discriminatory (84.44).

Americans with Disabilities Act Handbook (Equal Employment Opportunity Commission and U.S. Department of Justice 1991)

The following is a brief overview of the *Handbook's* coverage of the Americans with Disabilities Act of 1990 (ADA) 42 USC 12101 *et seq.,* and federal regulations for Title II, the portion of the act relating to nondiscrimination in state and local government services. Title II extends the prohibition of discrimination of Section 504 of the Rehabilitation Act of 1973, 29 USC 794, to include all services, programs, and activities provided by state and local governments regardless of the receipt of federal funding. The ADA does not replace the Rehabilitation Act; it expands its coverage.

Title II also incorporates the provisions of Title I of the ADA, which pertain to equal employment opportunities for persons with disabilities, and Title III, which applies nondiscrimination requirements to all public accommodations and commercial facilities. Title I prohibits preemployment medical examinations or inquiries. This would apply to education programs, as it prohibits such inquiries or examinations in the admission process (CFR 28 35.103). However, the program could ask an applicant questions related to his or her ability to perform essential activities in the program.

All physical and mental impairments that substantially affect major life activities are covered under the act. These include, but are not limited to, neurological, musculoskeletal losses, speech and hearing impairments, mental retardation and mental illness, brain injury, drug addiction, and alcoholism. The act and subsequent regulations do not prohibit discrimination against a person who is currently using illegal drugs. The protections of the law apply to addicts who are not current users; therefore, an individual participating in or having completed a rehabilitation program is protected under the ADA. Alcohol is not a controlled substance, so the use of alcohol is not addressed by the ADA and its regulations. However, alcoholics are individuals with disabilities subject to protection (35.131, II–47, 1991).

A qualified individual with a disability is one who, "with or without reasonable modifications to rules, policies, or practices . . . or the provision of auxiliary aids and services, meets the essential eligibility requirements for receipt of services or the participation in programs . . . provided by a public entity" (35–104, II–26).

Discrimination exists if an institution fails to make reasonable modifications to enable persons with disabilities to have access to its programs and services. Accommodations include a wide range of auxiliary aids, devices, and services. The institution must demonstrate that to make the modifications or accommodations would fundamentally alter the program in question (36.302, III–74).

Court Cases Addressing Section 504 of the Rehabilitation Act of 1973 and the Americans with Disabilities Act of 1990

Southeastern Community College v Davis, 442 US 397 (1979). This is the U. S. Supreme Court's first interpretation of Section

504 and is a precedent-setting case. "Section 504. . . does not compel educational institutions to disregard the disabilities of handicapped individuals or to make substantial modifications in their programs to allow disabled persons to participate" (*Id.* at 405). The court upheld the institution's decision (of not allowing a deaf student to be admitted to the nursing program) on the basis that "an otherwise qualified person is one who is able to meet all of a program's requirements in *spite* of his handicap" (*Id.* at 406).

The court cited specific sections of Department of Health, Education, and Welfare regulations supporting this interpretation, which stated that the "otherwise qualified" person had to meet both technical and academic standards for admission and participation in the program. It elaborated further by giving the following example: "The term 'technical standards' refers to all nonacademic admissions criteria that are essential to participation in the program in question" (*Id.* at 406).

E. E. Black v Marshall, 497 F Supp 1088 (D Haw 1980). The court found individuals were protected from discrimination even if they did not have the condition that others perceived them as having. Also protected are those who have a mental or physical condition that does not substantially limit their life activities but who are discriminated against because they are regarded as disabled. If an assumption is made that a person has a disability, even though in reality he or she does not have one, the protections of sections 503 and 504 are applied (*Id.* at 1097).

A person is substantially limited in one of his major life activities if disqualified from employment in a chosen field and therefore the person has a substantial handicap to employment. The definitions of persons with handicaps require individual evaluation. "It is the individual that must be examined, and not just the impairment in the abstract" (*Id.* at 1099).

Pushkin v The Regents of the University of Colorado, 6685 F2d 1372 (10th Cir 1981). Pushkin, who suffers from multiple sclerosis, is confined to a wheelchair, and is disabled in his abilities to walk and to write, was denied admission to a psychiatric residency program. The court found that the university had discriminated against him solely on the basis of his handicap. In the absence of physical qualifications essential to program participation, an otherwise qualified handicapped individual may not be denied admission solely on the basis of handicap.

Doe v New York University, 666 F2d 761 (2d Cir 1981). Doe had been asked to leave medical school after failing to secure needed psychiatric treatment. She had a long history of psychiatric problems (a personality disorder that involved self-destructive and antisocial behavior). There was evidence of a significant risk of recurrence of her disorder with resulting danger to herself and others.

Although the court found her to be disabled, it also determined that she had not established that she was "otherwise qualified," finding that she would not be qualified if there was a significant risk of recurrence. In the ruling the court stated, "It would be unreasonable to infer that Congress intended to force institutions to accept or readmit persons who pose a significant risk of harm to themselves or others, even if the chances of harm were less than 50%"(*Id.* at 777).

Doe v The Region 13 Mental Health-Mental Retardation Commission, 704 F2d 1402 (5th Cir 1983). Doe was a Mental Health Associate with the Child Youth Services program. She had exhibited serious suicidal tendencies over an extended period of time. The court ruled there was evidence

> that her psychiatric problems would affect her ability to work with her patients in the future, that her tendency toward suicide might convey a bias in favor of suicide to her clients, and that her suicide would have an adverse effect on her patients [which] sustained finding that she was not 'otherwise qualified' for her position notwithstanding her mental handicap so that her discharge did not violate the Rehabilitation Act.
>
> *(Id. at 1403)*

Cook v United States, 36 FEP Cas 1260 (D Colo 1984). Cook was required to obtain a certificate of "mental restoration" to determine if he was "otherwise qualified" for federal employment since he had a history of mental illness. The court found this requirement in violation of 29 USC 794 and 29 CFR 1613.

Cook should have been required only to submit medical evidence that his condition posed no danger to himself or others. He had been required, however, to document that he had recovered from a past mental illness (36 FEP at 1262). If the policy had been applied on an individual basis to determine if Cook was able to perform the duties of the job and did not pose a risk to health or safety, it might not have been found to be discriminatory.

Cook had been told by a psychiatrist that no patient who had a psychiatric condition would get a letter stating that he or she was "restored." "Thus, he was presented with the impossible burden of participating in a program designed to assist the handicapped by proving that he was not handicapped" (*Id.* at 1263).

Alexander v Choate, 105 S Ct 712 (1985). The court cited the *Davis* (1979) case, stating that the decision struck a balance between the statutory rights of the person with a handicap to be integrated into society and the legitimate interests of those receiving federal funds to preserve program integrity. It held that those receiving federal funds are not required to make fundamental or substantial modifications to accommodate the handicapped, as was determined in *Davis*. Programs are required to make reasonable modifications to provide meaningful access to their services for persons with handicaps (*Id.* at 720).

Jasony v United States Postal Service, 755 F2d 1244 (6th Cir 1985). The court ruled that the individual with the disability had the responsibility of establishing the existence of the disability. Individuals must establish that they belong to a protected class and that they are otherwise qualified.

Blackwell v United States Department of the Treasury, 639 F Supp 289 (DDC 1986). Defining an individual with a disability includes persons *regarded* as having such an impairment. The plaintiff was a transvestite and because of this was refused a job. The employer had acknowledged that transvestitism was recognized by the American Psychiatric Association as a mental disorder. Because of the perception that Blackwell had an impairment, he was protected by the Rehabilitation Act. The "Rehabilitation Act provides remedies not only for those who have physical or mental conditions that limit their major life activities, but also provides remedies against perceived handicaps" (*Id.* at 289).

School Board of Nassau County, Florida v Arline, 107 S Ct 1123 (1987). When deciding whether a person with a contagious disease is an otherwise qualified person with a handicap, as defined under the Rehabilitation Act of 1973, there are basic factors that must be considered. These are the "nature of risk, duration of risk, severity of risk, and probability [that the] disease will be transmitted and will cause varying degrees of harm" (*Id.* at 1123).

Arline, a school teacher who had been fired from her job because of her susceptibility to tuberculosis, was found by the Supreme Court to be a handicapped individual protected against discrimination by the Rehabilitation Act. "Congress acknowledged that society's accumulated myths and fears about disability and disease are as handicapping as are the physical limitations that flow from actual impairment. The act is carefully structured to replace such reflexive reactions to actual or perceived handicaps with actions based on reasoned and medically sound judgments" (*Id.* at 1129).

Anderson v University of Wisconsin, 841 F2d 737 (7th Cir 1988). "The Rehabilitation Act forbids discrimination based on stereotypes about a handicap, but does not forbid decisions based on the actual attributes of the handicap" (*Id.* at 740). Anderson, an admitted alcoholic, was allowed to reenter the law school program twice. After failing to maintain sobriety and doing poorly in academic work, he was informed that he would not be allowed to continue. "Nothing in the record suggests that the university's decision was based on stereotypes about alcoholism as opposed to honest judgments about how Anderson had performed in fact and could be expected to perform" (*Id.* at 741).

Chalk v United States District Court, 840 F2d 701 (9th Cir 1988). The court ruled in favor of a school teacher with AIDS, stating "there is no evidence of any significant risk to children or others at the school. To allow the court to base its decision on the fear and apprehension of others would frustrate the goals of Section 504" (*Id.* at 711).

Doherty v Southern College of Optometry, 862 F2d 570 (6th Cir 1988). The court ruled that educational institutions were not limited in their freedom to require reasonable physical qualifications for admission to a clinical training program. An educational institution is not required to accommodate a handicapped individual by eliminating a course requirement that is reasonably necessary to proper use of the degree conferred at the end of the course of study. Waiver of a necessary requirement would have been a substantial accommodation (*Id.* at 575).

Fields v Lying, 705 F Supp 1134 (D Md 1988). The court refrained from addressing the issues of defining Fields as a handicapped individual (the EEOC having already declared him to be, based on borderline personality with obsessive compulsive features, including kleptomania). It did, however, rule on the "reasonable accommodation" claim.

> If Fields is . . . incapable of performing his essential duties because he cannot travel safely or be trusted as a negotiator, then he is not an otherwise qualified handicapped person in spite of his handicap. He would only be qualified but for his handicap, and as such, he is not entitled to reasonable accommodation.
>
> *(Id. at 1137)*

Franklin v U.S. Postal Service, 46 FEP 1734 (SD Ohio 1988). A former U.S. Postal Service employee, who was paranoid schizophrenic and had twice been reinstated after violent episodes, was discharged after the third episode. The court ruled that a person suffering from paranoid schizophrenia that is controllable through medication who refuses to take such medication is not an "otherwise qualified handicapped person" under Section 504 of the Rehabilitation Act. There is no cause for action if the person has not demonstrated that he or she is otherwise qualified.

The court further stated that Franklin's handicap was a created one since she elected not to take her medication. The incidents of arrest, violence, and violations of law were caused by her failure to take the medication. Since this was her choice, her employer's actions were not discriminatory (*Id.* at 1737).

Pandazides v Virginia Board of Education, 752 F Supp 696 (ED Va 1991). The Virginia Board of Education did not violate Section 504 by refusing to alter the teaching certification exam. Since the individual could not pass a part of the National Teacher's Examination, she was not otherwise qualified. To have waived the communications skills test, given unlimited time in which to complete it, or given the exam orally was deemed to be a substantial modification not required by the Rehabilitation Act.

"An inability to perform at the required standard makes an individual *not* otherwise qualified" (*Id.* at 697).

Wynne v Tufts University School of Medicine, 932 F2d 19 (1st Cir 1991). The academic institution must document that it has made every effort to find appropriate means to reasonably accommodate a handicapped person.

> If the institution submits undisputed facts demonstrating that the relevant officials within the institution considered alternative means (of testing), their feasibility, cost and effect on the academic program, and came to a rational, justifiable conclusion that the available alternatives would result in lowering academic standards or requiring substantial alteration of the program, the court could rule as a matter of law that the institution had met its duty of seeking reasonable accommodation.
>
> *(Id. at 26)*

In its ruling, the court cited the *Arline* decision stating that it was the court's responsibility to determine if the facts supported the institution's professional, academic judgment that reasonable accommodation was not available. In this case, the court found no reference to any consideration of possible alternatives, nor reference to any professional opinion supporting the need for using only multiple-choice examinations.

The institution did not indicate who had taken part in the decision nor when the decision was made. There must be a procedure that would permit the necessary judicial review.

> Were the simple conclusory averment of the head of an institution to suffice, there would be no way to ascertain whether the institution had made a professional effort to evaluate possible ways of accommodating a handicapped student or had simply embraced what was most convenient for the faculty and administration.
>
> *(Id. at 28)*

Wolsky v Medical College of Hampton Roads, 1 F3d 222 (4th Cir 1993). Wolsky, a student with a panic disorder, was dismissed from medical school. He had filed a discrimination suit under Section 504, but his suit was not filed until more than a year after the last denial of readmission. The Rehabilitation Act does not have a statute of limitations; therefore, the court must turn to the state for an appropriate statute. "In the event of such an omission, 42

USC 1988 (a) provides for the selection of an appropriate common-law statute of limitations, which is most applicable to the federal action" (*Id.* at 223).

Students applying for admission and remaining in social work programs must be able to meet the program's requirements in spite of disabilities. It is the responsibility of the student with the disability to establish that it exists and to document that it substantially limits a major life activity. Programs cannot he held responsible for not accommodating a student if the disability was not made known. It is advisable that social work educators work closely with the person or persons on campus designated to coordinate matters pertaining to students with disabilities.

Social work educators may not make preadmission inquiries regarding a student's health (mental or physical) but are encouraged to set a proactive atmosphere that is inviting for students to disclose their handicaps on their own. Announcing in the first class session that the faculty member is available to assist all students who might express difficulty completing course requirements and including such a statement in the course syllabus can be helpful to both students and faculty members.

The program must clearly articulate its essential components, which need not be modified to accommodate the student with a disability. Neither the Rehabilitation Act of 1973 nor the ADA requires programs to lower standards or to effect substantial modification of standards to accommodate persons with disabilities. Careful deliberation with the student, faculty, and other appropriate institution officials can "help determine the accommodation that best suits not only the qualified student but also the educational program" (Cole, Christ, and Light 1995). For example, there are guidelines that can assist in determining the amount of time appropriate for a student with a specific disability to complete an examination.

References

Carnegie Council on Policy Studies in Higher Education (1979). *Fair practices in higher education: Rights and responsibilities of students and their colleges in a period of intensified competition for enrollments.* San Francisco: Jossey-Bass.

Cole, B. S. (1991). Legal issues related to social work program admissions. *Journal of Social Work Education* 27:18–24.

Cole, B. S., and Lewis, R. G. (1993). Gatekeeping through termination of unsuitable social work students: Legal issues and guidelines. *Journal of Social Work Education* 29:150–159.

Cole, B. S., Christ, C. C., and Light, T. R. (1995). Social work education and students with disabilities: Implications of Section 504 and the ADA. *Journal of Social Work Education* 31:261–268.

Council on Social Work Education (CSWE). (1994). *Handbook of accreditation standards*. 4th ed. Alexandria, Va.: CSWE.

National Association of Social Workers (NASW). (1996). *NASW code of ethics*. Washington, D.C.: NASW.

12

Ethics Charges Against BSW Students: Principles and Case Examples

Norman H. Cobb, Penny Smith Ramsdell, and Ski Hunter

For more than two years, the social work program at the University of Texas at Arlington (UTA), a state-supported university, has been implementing specific guidelines for evaluating students whose behavior or ethics seemed inappropriate for the social work profession. Before the guidelines were implemented, the social work faculty had grown pessimistic and cynical about the successful management of troublesome students. For example, when someone questioned the ethical nature of a student's behavior, the faculty and administration differed over various procedural and constitutional questions: What constitutes a fair hearing? What types of evidence are fair and required by law? How much due process is required to protect the rights of the student, the victim, and the faculty? What happens when the student in question threatens to sue? Who pays the legal fees?

After the school adopted a set of guidelines and procedures, three cases involving BSW students were evaluated and processed. Additionally, the legal staff of the university reversed earlier positions and came to the support of the social work program. As a result, the faculty was empowered to deal with troublesome students and regain their gatekeeping function. Following the two-year experience, the procedures were refined. They are summarized below, and the three cases involving BSW students are reported.

Development of the Guidelines

The basic approach and guidelines for evaluating students who allegedly violated ethical standards were developed on the basis of previous court cases (Cobb 1994). A classic case, *Board of Curators of the University of Missouri v Horowitz,* empowered professional programs to avoid the long and complex procedures of university disciplinary rules and evaluate troublesome students on the basis of academic criteria and procedures (Cobb and Jordan 1989). In essence, a student's behavior and its concurrence with ethical standards is an academic issue, and therefore, academic procedures, which require less stringent legal principles than typical university disciplinary procedures, enable faculty members to make viable judgments about the appropriateness of students for the profession.

Basic Principles

The central theme in the following summary of principles for reviewing alleged student ethics violations is *due process* as guaranteed by the U.S. Constitution. If one or more of the following principles is inadvertently omitted, students may still have received due process if they are afforded an orderly process and fair assessment of their behavior:

Criteria for Evaluating Student Behavior. The criteria for assessing students' behavior are the standards from the National Association of Social Work's (NASW) *Code of Ethics* (NASW 1994 and 1996) and the standards created by the state licensing board for professional social workers. Because the 1994 version of the code was in effect when the student reviews that are discussed later in this chapter were conducted, references to particular sections of the code that were used in the decision-making process reflect the ethical principles of the 1994 code.

Critical Distinction. Students' behavior is evaluated on the *actual harm* to current clients, students, faculty, and staff and/or the *potential threat* to future clients, coworkers, and so forth. Students' actions are open to evaluation whether they occur in field placements, in off-campus settings and settings outside of social work, or prior to enrollment in the social work program. The underlying theme is potential harm to present or future clients and the consequent breach of the *NASW Code of Ethics* or the state licensing standards.

Freedom of Speech. Students maintain their freedom of speech and dissent. Such behavior must not be abridged in classes or academic disciplinary actions (*Doe v University of Michigan* 1989, cited in Stoner and Cerminara 1989).

Notice to Students. In the catalog, student handbook, or other university literature, students should be reminded that violations of the *NASW Code of Ethics* or state licensing standards may result in an evaluation of their suitability for the profession (Kaplin 1985).

Review Process. The BSW, MSW, and Ph.D. program directors initially review problematic situations concerning students. They gather relevant information, determine if the behavior potentially violates professional ethics or academic standards, and try to resolve the situations. For example, they may put a field student on notice that in order to successfully complete the field practicum a particular problem must be resolved to the satisfaction of the field supervisor. On the other hand, they may help students leave social work programs and redirect their talents to other areas of study. If the situations are not resolved at that level, they refer cases to the faculty ethics committee. The following section briefly describes the structure and components of one such committee, the Academic and Professional Standards Committee, at UTA's School of Social Work.

The Academic and Professional Standards Committee: Policies and Procedures

The UTA's School of Social Work developed the following policies to guide the composition, nature, processes, and function of its faculty ethics committee. The committee was established to review allegations of ethical violations by students, and the committee's decisions are based on the program's academic standards, which were drawn from the ethical principles contained in the 1994 version of the *NASW Code of Ethics*.

Three members of the faculty and one alternate are elected to the committee. If committee members are directly involved in a particular student's situation, the alternate serves, or the dean selects another faculty member. The chair, elected by members of the committee, ensures that procedures of due process are followed. The chair safeguards all confidential documents and manages all communication with students, involved parties, and committee members.

The chair sends a notice to the student(s) in question (see *Notice* section) and asks for written responses to specific charges. The chair may ask students for written permission to contact persons who have information about their suitability for the profession. The chair provides accused students with copies of all documents reviewed by the committee unless particular documents are classified "confidential" to ensure safety for the parties involved. It should be noted that classification of information as confidential has not been a frequent occurrence at UTA. Information was classified as confidential just once, and this occurred at the request of a relevant party who agreed to provide information only if the committee would keep it confidential. The request was based on fear for personal safety if the information were released to the accused student.

The committee meets with students and all relevant parties. Accused students have a right to know who made charges and to respond to claims about their behavior (*Esteban v Central Missouri State College* 1967); however, they *do not* have a constitutional right to face-to-face encounters with those who have made charges (see *Gasper v Bruton* 1975) because the ethics committee review is an academic review rather than a disciplinary hearing. Thus, relevant parties meet with the committee, and the student is not present when these individuals make their presentations to the committee. After the committee hears from all interested parties and weighs the evidence, it makes its decisions.

The chair communicates the committee's actions, decisions, and recommendations to the dean. The dean reviews all relevant documents. If the dean supports the committee's recommendations, proceedings are ended and students are notified. The Board of Regents of UTA restricts appeals beyond the dean of each academic unit. If the dean does not support the committee, the dean makes specific suggestions to the committee, and the committee holds new meetings and reconsiders its decisions. If the committee conducts second inquiries, decisions of the committee are final.

Governing Policies

The following policies govern the UTA ethics committee review process and procedure. The policies were developed based on previous court decisions and on the experiences of the UTA committee over the past two years.

Student Status. Until students' situations are resolved, students may attend classes unless their presence poses a threat to others.

Notice of Formal Meeting with Students. Students shall receive written notices of times and places for formal meetings. The notice includes specific charges and the committee's options for recommendations, such as dismissal of all allegations, termination from the university, suspension, and so forth.

Timing. Formal committee meetings with students are held between five and fifteen days following the dates of notices to accused students. The chair may alter the fifteen-day time period if such action is necessary to safeguard students' rights to due process.

Management of Formal Meetings. The chair, with the support of the committee, exercises complete control over the conduct of formal meetings. People may attend if they receive permission from the chair and committee. Written notes may be taken, but video or audio recordings are not allowed. The purpose of formal meetings is for the committee to gather information and make its judgments. The chair may end meetings when the committee's purpose is ended or when participants' behavior interferes with the committee's purpose and function.

Right to Legal Counsel. In academic disciplinary situations students do not have constitutional rights to legal counsel. If students wish to have attorneys present, the committee may permit such requests, but the professional capacity of the students' attorneys is strictly advisory. They may not participate unless the committee gives permission.

Standards of Evidence. Witnesses or offended parties are not required to be present at formal meetings unless the committee so requests. They may submit written statements of their charges. The committee shall neither act on nor consider anonymous letters. Witnesses or offended parties shall be assured of reasonable protection from reprisal or retaliation by accused students. Student dismissal meetings and procedures are not required to follow strict guidelines of criminal hearings. For example, to underscore the academic nature of the proceedings, legal jargon is avoided. The committee holds "meetings" with involved students rather than "hearings." Also, as a departure from legal formality and requirements, the committee weighs all evidence and bases its decision on the group's best judgment of whether the accused students were more likely than not to have committed the acts in question.

In essence, judgment in academic cases is based on majority rule because the most serious consequence of academic judgments is a denial to participate in an academic program of higher learning. In criminal or civil cases, however, where judicial decree can deprive a person of real property (money for fines, for example) or personal freedom (incarceration), higher standards of judgment, evidence, and so forth are required. Fundamentally, the extent of due process requirements is directly related to the relative value of the potential loss.

Validity of the Committee's Role. Each student who comes to the attention of the Academic and Professional Standards Committee is reminded by the committee chair of the NASW code's empowerment of professionals, according to the 1994 version of the code's fifth section, M, which sets standards for maintaining the integrity of the profession.

> The social worker should uphold and advance the values, ethics, knowledge, and mission of the profession.
>
> 1. The social worker should protect and enhance the dignity and integrity of the profession . . .
> 2. The social worker should take action through appropriate channels against unethical conduct by any other member of the profession.

(1994:9)

This reminder to the student by the committee asserts the committee's role and professional responsibility.

Publicity Related to the Committee. In academic proceedings, students retain property rights to their academic reputations. The social work program, therefore, refrains from imposing stigma or disrepute on students evaluated by the committee. Records and discussions are considered confidential, and all documents are sealed from future disclosure and kept in a confidential location. The records may be opened again under two specific circumstances. The first is litigation by the student as a result of a negative decision. The second is if an accused student continues in the program but is later referred to the ethics committee for another violation.

Three Cases of Academic Discipline

The following are three examples that illustrate many of the dilemmas facing ethics and standards committees in social work programs. Student behavior varies in type and intensity; therefore, each case presents considerable problems in processing information and making judgments. Identifying data in the following examples have been disguised to protect the students' rights.

In the first case, inappropriate behavior occurred prior to and following admission to the university. In the case of the second student, however, the unethical behavior occurred prior to enrollment in the university. The nature of his previous offenses was deemed to pose a risk for future clients. The last case demonstrates how behavior in a field placement may necessitate a critical review of behavior both in the field and outside it.

Student #1

Student History. Student #1 was in his thirties and had excellent verbal and cognitive skills. He was tall, handsome, and personally engaging. He had been a football star in college. Before enrolling in the BSW program, he paradoxically had been employed as a clinician at the master's level. For three years he was a program director in three different psychiatric hospitals. For two years he directed professional staff development in two psychiatric hospitals and a woman's shelter. He also had been a marketing director for a psychiatric hospital. In addition, he was a caseworker, supervisor, and program manager for juvenile probation for ten years.

His return to college reflected his desire to make a significant contribution to the field of social work. In the classroom, his grades and contributions were excellent.

The Turning Point. He first came to the attention of the BSW program director when the director witnessed the student's arrest by local police. When the director asked him about the situation, the student attributed his arrest to a false accusation of nonpayment of child support. He described the situation as a misunderstanding on the part of judicial representatives. The student explained that his ex-wife had conjured up the charge as a way to embarrass him at the university.

At his first field placement the following semester, he experienced another embarrassing moment. His supervisor, perhaps confused by his age and experience, incorrectly introduced him at an agency meeting as an MSW student. The student did not correct this information at the time and later reported not wanting to "embarrass her in the meeting." He did not correct her statement until the following week when they met to finalize his field contract. The student's supervisor was irritated by the delay in correcting her earlier announcement. She stated that his field arrangements were based on the expectation that he possessed graduate-level skills. She referred him to her program director to work out changes in the field contract.

In the subsequent conversation with the program director, the student asserted his willingness to continue with the previous arrangements for him as a presumed MSW student. He used his prior professional experience as a justification for more extensive responsibilities. After examining the student's employment record, the director asked how he was able to be employed at such high-level professional positions and yet be enrolled currently as an undergraduate student. The student admitted that he had presented himself to previous employers as having a master's degree in psychology. The student asserted that his effort to earn a BSW degree was his way of making amends and correcting for fifteen years of misrepresentations. The supervisor abruptly terminated his field placement and included all information in a letter to the school's director of the field program.

The Committee Process. The student was evaluated by the BSW program director and referred to the Academic and Professional Standards Committee for further assessment. During the committee's evaluation many aspects of the student's past came into question.

The student's official records affirmed that, despite an extensive college football career and fifteen years of professional experience, he had not received a college degree. His previous employment was in fact based on a history of considerable misrepresentation. In the formal meeting with the committee, the student explained that his early marriage and the birth of his children created serious financial hardships. He based the misrepresentation on the necessity to take care of his family.

He asserted that the misrepresentation did not violate the 1994 *NASW Code of Ethics* because he claimed a master's degree in psychology rather than a graduate degree in social work and, further, that these misrepresentations predated his enrollment in social work. He also contended that his return to college was his effort to "set the record straight."

In exploring the field agency's ostensible misunderstanding about whether he was a BSW or MSW student, the committee compared the copy of his field application that he had given to the campus field coordinator with the copy he had given to his field supervisor. On the agency copy of the application, the student left blank the section that would have distinguished him as an undergraduate rather than as a graduate field student.

In isolation, this minor "oversight" would have led to little or no concern over the student's credibility. He lost more credibility, however, when the committee discovered that he had willingly lied to the BSW program director about his arrest. To provide some background, it must be pointed out that Texas, like some other states, has legislation that makes certain records open to the public. In regard to this student's case, the police face sheets on previous arrests over a certain number of months were a matter of public information, and a member of the Academic and Professional Standards Committee secured a face sheet that listed the local arrests. The arrest sheet on this particular student was quite illuminating.

His campus arrest was actually for physically assaulting his date in the parking lot of a local shopping center. He described the episode as a "psychotic break" and actions taken "in the heat of the moment" because he and his date had had "too much to drink." He referred to the assault as "some questionable decisions made in the heat of trauma." Apparently, the case had gone to court and the student received a ten-year probated sentence. Additionally, the severity of the assault moved the court to amend the charge with the qualifier: with serious bodily injury. A spokesperson for the court explained that this addition was reserved for more serious physical assaults where the victim experienced acute physical harm. As a result of the assault, the woman required hospitalization.

The student claimed that he lied to the BSW program director about the arrest because the offense did not occur on campus and did not involve a student or client. He also stated that he did not know why the school would need to know about the assault and did not see the need for the social work program or the committee to be involved.

Committee's Rationale and Decision. The committee recognized the potential abuse of clients and the human service system that may be perpetrated by people who willingly place their own financial stability above the welfare of troubled and "at risk" human beings. Therefore, the committee viewed the misrepresentation as a serious violation of two standards in the *NASW Code of Ethics* (1994): the first section, A1, and the fifth section, M4:

> The social worker should not participate in, condone, or be associated with dishonesty, fraud, deceit, or misrepresentation.
>
> *(I, A1, p. 3)*

> The social worker should make no misrepresentation in advertising as to qualifications, competence, service, or results to be achieved.
>
> *(V, M4, p. 9)*

The concern regarding the physical abuse spawned extensive deliberation by the committee because the abuse occurred off-campus and the victim was not a client, faculty member, or other student. Basically, separation of public and private life from professional life was at issue within the context of academic standards based on expectations of ethical behavior. At the core of the issue was the assessment of the potential threat to future clients whether or not the behavior occurred off-campus and as part of a nonprofessional relationship. Ultimately, the committee affirmed as part of its decision making that professional social workers do not tolerate any physical abuse of others, even when such abuse occurs in the public or private rather than the professional sphere of life. Furthermore, the committee affirmed the seriousness of the physical abuse and the unacceptable explanations of psychosis or "heat of the moment" decisions. In summary, the assault, the ten years probation, and the explanations for the incidents were not acceptable from a student who three months following the assault was scheduled for a field placement with clients who might exhibit, or be the victims of, those same cognitive and behavioral "errors" manifested by the student.

The committee ruled that either the extensive misrepresentations or the assault would have been sufficient to consider termination; however, the combination negated any other options. The student was terminated from the program.

As a follow-up note, the student transferred to another social work program. When his new university asked for a reference, our program at UTA could not comment on the student's termination. Our response to the other program's inquiry was simply, "The School of Social Work is unable legally to comment on the decision that led to his termination from the social work program." UTA's reserved response was appropriate because the proceedings were based on academic issues. On the other hand, if UTA had followed the more involved and cumbersome procedures for disciplinary terminations, the committee chair could have commented more extensively on the decision.

The additional requirements for disciplinary terminations (versus academic termination) vary from one institution to another; however, locally they include higher requirements for evidence, more extensive documentation of harm to the abused, more stringent time restraints, and so forth. This situation reemphasizes the relationship between due process and potential loss.

Student #2

Student History. The second BSW student was a charming, articulate man in his forties who lived with a warm, supportive woman. Prior to his enrollment in the university, he had been a speaker in classes on human sexuality to discuss his history and recovery as a sex addict. He was receiving treatment in a well-established recovery program that specialized in sexual addictions. His career goal was to work with perpetrators of incest, rape, and indecency with children. He attributed his commitment to social work clients as a therapeutic response to his previous behavior.

The Turning Point. Early in his social work courses, he made known to an instructor that he was a recovering sex addict. He clearly stated that he was in recovery and that sexual addiction required him to make a life-long struggle to control his behavior. He, therefore, proclaimed that he must not work with women and children, yet he could work effectively with male perpetrators. The faculty member notified the director of the program and provided him with a recent newspaper article covering both sexual addiction and assault. As part of the article on sexual addiction, our student's name, prior behavior, and his victims were described.

Although the director was influenced by the public attention to the student, of greater concern were the student's own statements about the difficulty of recovery and the need to limit his exposure to clients. Consequently, the director referred the situation to the committee.

The Committee Process. The committee chair was struck by how this case exemplified the tension between rehabilitation and potential risk to future clients. The student's commitment to social work was offset by the poor recovery history for sexual addictions as reported in the professional literature. Ironically, the student asserted that he would not be able to recover or be responsible unless he admitted that controlling his sexual propensities would be a life-long struggle. Similarly, he believed he carried responsibility for telling the social work faculty that he should be observed and restricted to working only with male perpetrators.

In his disclosure the student emphasized that when a sex offender is criminally charged and prosecuted, the single incident is only one event in a long history of inappropriate behavior. For example, he stated that he had committed sexually oriented offenses with nearly a thousand individuals.

In response to this information, the chair of the committee requested copies of police records, his convictions, and his incarcerations. The student provided legal documents describing his three felony convictions for indecency with children and attempted rape and distribution of a controlled substance. The student also signed a release of information for his therapist to provide information about his therapy.

The chair of the committee solicited information from his therapist and also asked a nationally recognized expert on sex abuse for his opinion on the issue. The therapist's reply was very affirming of the student's rehabilitation but was very critical of the committee's involvement. He asserted the similarity between sexual and alcohol addiction, and therefore he referred to the committee's concern as "small-mindedness." In contradiction to the student's therapist, the sex abuse expert was rather critical of the student's intended role in social work. While supporting the idea of rehabilitation, the expert was critical of the term *addiction* when describing a history of inappropriate and illegal sexual behavior. The expert's concern was that "addiction" frequently not only implied an explanation but also posed as a rationalization for not controlling sexual arousal. Furthermore, he emphasized the difficulty of rehabilitation for problem behaviors that are so intrinsically reinforcing. Most important, he stated that in no instance should a person with this student's history be placed in a position of trust with the profession's clients.

In subsequent interactions with the student, the latter declared his plan to sue the university and the social work program. He stated that he planned to get a restraining order against the school in order to give him time to complete his education and graduate from the program. As a result of the threats of legal action, the attorney for the university was notified. Furthermore, when the student requested permission to bring an attorney to the meeting, the chair granted permission and asked the university's attorney to attend.

The committee meeting with the student began with a confrontation over the student's intentions to tape-record the meeting. The university's attorney stated that no recordings of the meeting would take place since a secretary was present to write down the major points. The attorney also stated clearly and assertively that the purpose of the meeting was to collect information and ensure that the student received an opportunity to respond to the committee's concerns.

Committee's Rationale and Decision. The committee addressed the first and second sections of the *NASW Code of Ethics* (1994) as these related to the student's situation.

> Section I, A1. The private conduct of the social worker is a personal matter to the same degree as is any other person's, except when such conduct compromises the fulfillment of professional responsibilities.
>
> *(3)*

> Section II, F. *Primacy of clients' interests - The social worker's primary responsibility is to clients.*
> 1. The social worker should serve clients with devotion, loyalty, determination, and the maximum application of professional skill and competence.
> 2. The social worker should not exploit relationships with clients for personal advantage . . . .
> 4. The social worker should avoid relationships or commitments that conflict with the interests of clients. 5. The social worker should under no circumstances engage in sexual activities with clients.
>
> *(5)*

The student treated the deliberations as a judicial action. He criticized the committee for not following every point in the guidelines for academic discipline, guidelines that were clearly inappropriate for the proceedings. For example, the committee's meeting with the student was delayed beyond the fifteen-day time period. The student asserted, therefore, that the issue should be dropped.

He demanded what he considered to be his constitutional right to a face-to-face dialog with witnesses, experts, and accusers. In addition, he wanted to establish the admissibility of every piece of information. The committee informed him that academic proceedings do not require judicial standards of evidence. Furthermore, he did not have a right to face-to-face encounters with other parties who were providing information, and his attorney did not have the right to speak in the meeting unless addressed by the chair of the committee. Finally, the committee chair described how deviations from the guidelines of the committee did not violate the student's right to due process, because the committee was making every effort to be fair and open to his situation and role in the university. The current meeting indicated the committee's interest in providing him an open and fair discussion of the issues.

Prior to the meeting the chair had requested the most recent police report on the student. Much to the chair's surprise, the report included a recent arrest for indecency. In the meeting, the student stated that his behavior prior to entering the BSW program should not be viewed as a violation of the *NASW Code of Ethics* and that only behavior in class should concern the committee. The student was then asked if he was currently involved in legal proceedings or currently under indictment for any new offenses. The student responded that he was only willing to answer questions related to the material contained in the letter that notified him of the current meeting. When a committee member remarked about the relevance of such information, he again refused to respond to the question.

In conclusion, the committee decided unanimously to terminate the student. The decision was based on the generalist nature of the program; that is, graduation from such a program sanctioned students to provide services to all client populations in a vast arena of service settings, a sanction that was contraindicated in this student's case. Once graduated, neither the profession nor the faculty could restrict or monitor his future professional relationship with clients, as he was requesting. Additionally, while supporting the student's efforts at rehabilitation, the committee recognized the strength of the student's awareness of his risk to future clients; however, the risk was unacceptable given the professional role of social workers. The committee reemphasized that even if he were allowed to continue in the program and graduate, he most likely would not be able to secure a social work license from the state because of the established laws forbidding convicted felons from participating in positions of professional trust and licensure.

Ultimately, the student did not sue. His lawyer affirmed that in light of the academically focused proceedings, his client had received due process and his legal options were exhausted.

Student #3

Student History. The third student case involved a student who had enrolled in the undergraduate program. She was a single mother of two children who worked thirty hours a week, and fortunately her financial situation was somewhat alleviated by grants from the state rehabilitation office. She hoped to be a social worker and work with women like herself.

She was very religious, and her fundamentalist church was an important part of her life. She was often offended by more liberal comments by professors or students in the program. While she could be very personable and engaging, she was unsure of her boundaries when she interacted with others. For example, she frequently invaded people's privacy by asking questions that were offensive. She asked about their religious convictions and why they were not married. She even asked a lesbian student why she wanted to "burn in hell." In a much less offensive vein, she typically asked her professors to raise her final grades. Unfortunately, she was largely unaware of the intrusive, offensive, and biased nature of her questions and comments.

The Turning Point. In a matter of six weeks she was terminated from two field placements. In the first setting, she asked staff members if they were saved. If she received negative or noncommittal answers, she inquired why they were not Christians. She also asked about staff members' marital status and their reproductive plans.

Her supervisor in the first placement charged that the student was unwilling or unable to learn from field supervision. For example, she asked for special privileges beyond those given to other field interns, and she became inordinately unhappy when her requests were denied. Her supervisor was frustrated by having to repeat directions and explanations. The student did not take responsibility for her mistakes, and instead she blamed others. On one occasion, she accused a secretary of getting her into trouble and attributed the secretary's behavior to her not being a Christian. In response to her supervisor's criticisms, she became more aggressive and charged that her field supervisor was anorexic, had low self-esteem, and was deceitful.

Upon the termination of the first placement, the student was given a second chance to complete a placement. In the second setting, she alleged reverse race discrimination by her African-American field supervisor. She believed that the supervisor, a Muslim, hated her because she was white and Christian. Later, when the student was told that her supervisor and university field director agreed to terminate her placement, she told the field director that two of her previous professors hated her and that they were behind the charges. She told numerous students that the entire school of social work was anti-Christian. Furthermore, she asserted that if she was removed from the program she would not only sue but she would also take the matter to the press.

The Committee Process. When the committee held the formal meeting, she brought four persons: her two ministers, the student president of the university, and her lawyer. The chair agreed to their attendance with the stipulation that they could not address the committee without permission. In her opening comments, she read from a Muslim tract that challenged all Muslims to hate Christians. The committee was particularly troubled when she asserted that her African-American supervisor was using "voodoo-like" Muslim rituals to rid the agency of her, a white female.

Committee's Rationale and Decision. The committee affirmed her right to her values and opinions. The committee specified that freedom of speech was guaranteed in the program; however, the committee differentiated between her right to hold various beliefs and her attempts to press her beliefs on fellow students, agency personnel, and, particularly, clients. For example, in light of her persistent judgments against persons who were different from her, the committee emphasized that she did not have the right to repeatedly criticize the social work program for admitting homosexuals and non-Christians. The committee also affirmed that the personal lives of her colleagues were beyond the limits of her concern. Furthermore, the committee noted her inordinate fear or concern about being persecuted for her fundamentalist religious beliefs.

Another important concern for the committee was the student's inability to understand her role in the failure of the two field placements. She was unable to objectively assess the offensiveness of her comments about parenthood, personal lifestyles, marital status, and religious convictions. Furthermore, she was unable to distinguish the differences between her opinions and the facts about some faculty members and supervisors. The committee saw her conduct as violating the following NASW ethical standards (1994:7):

> J. *Respect, fairness, and courtesy - The social worker should treat colleagues with respect, courtesy, fairness, and good faith.*
> 4. The social worker should treat with respect, and represent accurately and fairly, the qualifications, views, and findings of colleagues and use appropriate channels to express judgments on these matters.

The committee perceived her aggressive imposition of beliefs as potentially dangerous to clients and unsuitable for the profession. Her slanderous comments about the faculty, the school, and agency personnel were also unacceptable. Consequently, she was terminated from the program and the director of the BSW program assisted her in transferring to a multidisciplinary major.

The shift in major allowed her to graduate in a timely manner, become self-supporting, and work in a field apart from social work clients. The committee refrained from prescribing counseling because of a court case barring such recommendations. The case in point is *Gorman v University of Rhode Island* (1988), discussed in Swem (1987). In this case, the court denied a stipulation in the ruling on a student's dismissal that the student seek and obtain counseling. While social work faculty may be concerned for the troublesome student's future functioning in the practice arena, they do not have a right to mandate therapeutic or remedial actions.

Sound policies and procedures for evaluating students' suitability for the profession enable faculty and administrators to gain a sense of security in addressing problem situations. They feel empowered to critique problem behavior and challenge inappropriate students who often react with threats of lawsuits for discrimination or unfair treatment. At UTA, the published policies enable students to know that their behavior must conform to the profession's established code of ethics. Furthermore, the standards facilitate a sense of respect for social work as a profession that holds its members accountable for their behavior.

The *NASW Code of Ethics* (1996) is the primary set of ethical standards for professional behavior. The code does not fully define all instances of inappropriate behavior; however, numerous sources caution against trying to create a definitive list of unacceptable behavior. Ironically, the general nature of the NASW code allows decision-making freedom and yet increases uncertainty and the burden of responsible judgment. The very nature of ethical determination requires the faculty to exercise their academic and professional judgment, assess each student's behavior in context, and determine his or her suitability.

Committee members involved in the three cases discussed in this chapter believed they were able to provide due process to the students and also to enforce the principles of the *NASW Code of Ethics*. The committee addressed the behavior of all three students, and all three were terminated for violations of NASW's code of ethical conduct. The three case examples are offered here as support and guidance for faculty as they carry out their difficult role as gatekeepers.

The real beneficiaries of clear statements on the purpose, procedure, and process of ethics committee reviews are the countless faculty members, students, and future clients who will have a slight margin of security because a small number of truly unethical individuals are not allowed to inflict their unique problems on vulnerable clients. While this may seem an impassioned statement, those who have had the rare, unfortunate, and challenging responsibility for resolving situations involving an unethical and unacceptable student can fully understand its import.

References

Board of Curators of the University of Missouri v Horowitz. 435 US 78 (1978).

Cobb, N. H. (1994). Court-recommended guidelines for managing unethical students and working with university lawyers. *Journal of Social Work Education* 30:18–31.

Cobb N. H., and Jordan, C. (1989). Students with questionable values or threatening behavior: Precedent and policy from discipline to dismissal. *Journal of Social Work Education* 25:87–97.

Doe v University of Michigan. 721 F Supp 852 (ED Michigan 1989).

Esteban v Central Missouri State College. 277 F Supp 649 (WD Mo 1967).

Gasper v Bruton. 513 F2d 843 (10th Cir 1975).

Gorman v University of Rhode Island. 837 F2d 7 (1st Cir 1988).

Kaplin, W. A. (1985). *The law of higher education.* San Francisco: Jossey-Bass.

National Association of Social Workers (NASW). (1994, 1996). *NASW code of ethics.* Washington, D.C.: NASW.

Stoner, E. N., and Cerminara, K. L. (1990). Harnessing the "Spirit of Insubordination": A model student disciplinary code. *The Journal of College and University Law* 17 (2): 89–121.

Swem, L. L. (1987). Due process rights in student disciplinary matters. *The Journal of College and University Law* 14 (2): 359–382.

PART THREE

Strategies and Processes

13

Academic Standards for Admission and Retention

Patty Gibbs, Eleanor H. Blakely, and Contributors

In recent years, one of the clearest and most important messages to emerge from the literature on gatekeeping in social work education has been that *all* criteria, standards, and performance expectations must be framed as *academic* standards if they are to hold up in court (Cobb 1994; Cobb and Jordan 1989; Cole and Lewis 1993; Madden 1993). A growing body of case law indicates it is essential that academic criteria include not only standards for scholastic performance but also standards for professional behavior, whether the standards are for student admissions, retention, or termination.

Most social work faculty, however, have failed to keep pace with these newer legal requirements and often continue to think of academic standards as including only grade point average, skill acquisition, course completion, and other more cognitive aspects of performance. Expectations for professional behavior, such as conduct in conformity with the profession's ethical standards, are often viewed as "softer characteristics" and therefore are erroneously viewed by faculty and students alike as expectations that should fall into a category known as "nonacademic standards." In fact, even CSWE's current accreditation handbook perpetuates this erroneous thinking in Evaluative Standard 5.8: "The program's policies and practices must include procedures for terminating a student's enrollment in the social work program for reasons of academic and *nonacademic* performance" (CSWE 1994:89, italics added). When constituents raised questions about the differentiation of academic and nonacademic performance, CSWE issued a memorandum in 1996 to clarify the accreditation standard; however, the requirements of the standard remained unchanged and therefore continued to be in contradiction to legal precedents. More recently, CSWE distributed an updated version of the memorandum (CSWE 1999), but the only revision that was made was to change the title from *Guidelines for "Nonacademic" Termination Policies and Procedures* to *Guidelines for Termination for Academic and Professional Reasons.* (A copy of this memorandum is found in appendix 13.) Until accreditation standard 5.8 is revised, the unfortunate confusion between academic and nonacademic standards will remain.

Legal requirements to include expectations of professional behavior in program policies, however, give faculty little guidance on how to go about what has proven to be a particularly troublesome task. In fact, anecdotal information suggests that the development of academic standards reflecting professional qualities and capacities seems to cause faculty significant difficulty in carrying out their gatekeeping function. The difficulty seems to occur at every stage in the development of such standards: identifying and agreeing upon desired professional attributes, transforming these desired attributes into academic standards, and identifying measures that are as readily acceptable as the measures of scholastic standards (e.g., grade point average [GPA]).

A study of screening practices used by BSW programs provides evidence of these difficulties. Based on 207 respondents to her survey, Gibbs (1994) found that criteria for admission to the social work program and the field placement are heavily geared toward scholastic standards (e.g., GPA, number of credit hours, course completion) rather than to desired professional attributes. Only two of the thirteen respondents who sent copies of their gatekeeping policies clearly identified criteria or standards in their program materials that addressed professional qualities, and those that appeared in print were that students should (a) show concern for people and (b) commit to social work and its values. Thus, while there is growing recognition that expected student performance is broader than academics in its strictest scholastic sense (Dunlap

1979; Cobb and Jordan 1989; Moore and Urwin 1990), research indicates that widespread application of this tenet is lacking in BSW programs (Gibbs 1994).

Developing academic standards or programmatic criteria reflecting both scholastic and professional capacities is not an easy undertaking. The initial task for faculty as they engage in developing a gatekeeping policy is to set aside sufficient time to engage in open and stimulating dialogs to explore the full range of possibilities. As is true in reviewing any component of a program, setting screening criteria and/or academic standards is a contextually significant endeavor. Standards and measures cannot be seen as separate from curriculum, governance, student development, and other facets of the program as a whole. Consequently, faculty should expect that discussions will call into question not only many aspects of the program that had hitherto been considered established and stable but also many of their own attitudes and biases about gatekeeping. Faculty should anticipate, therefore, that the thinking brought to the table will not be "of one mind." Lively debate will undoubtedly occur in the course of these discussions, but debate is essential in the development of gatekeeping policies that truly reflect the collective thinking of faculty, who ultimately will carry responsibility for implementing the policies.

The aim of this chapter is to provide information that can aid programs in their efforts to develop sound gatekeeping policies. Because faculty often have difficulty framing screening criteria and program standards, this chapter lists criteria and standards that are currently in use by social work programs across the country, as well as other standards culled from the *NASW Code of Ethics* (National Association of Social Workers [NASW] 1996). A rationale for each of the criteria and standards is included, followed by the types of outcome evidence that demonstrates each criterion has been achieved and measures that might be useful in assessing students against each criterion. Additional information directs readers to resources for learning more about or acquiring some of the standardized measures.

Making the conceptual leap from academic standards grounded exclusively in scholastic potential and achievement to academic standards including professional capacities is often a difficult task for faculty, so this chapter attempts to help make the transition in thinking by classifying academic standards along two dimensions: (a) academic standards of a cognitive, skill, or scholastic nature and (b) academic standards of an affective or professional nature.

It is important to note that the criteria and measures listed in this chapter are neither exhaustive nor universally accepted; rather they are illustrative and suggestive. Some of the measures are not even widely used, for example, portfolios of student work for use in screening for field placement or as an exit measure of a student's achievement and competence. Furthermore, faculty may find some of the proposed criteria and measures in this chapter highly controversial, such as the use of psychometric testing. However, the chapter was developed to identify a range of possibilities that program faculty could explore through intense dialog and careful consideration. To develop effective gatekeeping policies, program faculty must make selections that are acceptable to the institution, agreeable to the faculty who must implement them, congruent with the mission and goals of the program, reflective of the needs of the program's students, and in conformance with contemporary legal requirements.

Attention to legal parameters is an undisputed requirement for responsible gatekeeping, and a few key points provide a good foundation for this chapter on policy development. As noted previously, all standards and criteria to which students are held must be identified as *academic* standards. Judicial precedents for litigation in relation to dismissal from a professional or specialized program, such as social work, show that academic performance is broadly defined by the courts, allowing programs to include areas such as technical and interpersonal skills, attitudes, professional qualities, ethical behavior, and demonstrated knowledge (Cobb 1994; Knoff and Prout 1985). (See chapters 9, 11, and 12 for a detailed discussion of this issue.)

The courts have demonstrated overwhelming reluctance to overturn dismissal decisions made by qualified faculty when evaluation processes and procedures satisfy the legal requirements of due process. Dismissal decisions in these cases, according to the courts, are academic dismissals rather than disciplinary dismissals, the former of which are based on failing to meet academic standards established by the program and the latter of which are based on breaking the institution's rules of conduct. The procedural requirements for academic dismissals are far less stringent than those for disciplinary actions.

A set of guidelines advanced by Cole and Lewis (1993), which are based on case law and federal regulations, should be kept in mind as policies are finalized. Although the guidelines were delineated to assist faculty in screening out or terminating unsuitable students, they have a broader utility in framing all gatekeeping policies and therefore serve as an excellent reference point as faculty shape their gatekeeping policies. Some of the recommendations advanced by Cole and Lewis are as follows:

- Criteria for performance evaluation in classroom and field placement should be clearly stated and presented to the student, including such requirements as attendance. These criteria should be identified clearly as academic expectations.

- Academic decisions, including professional practice appraisals, must be made in good faith, not arbitrarily or capriciously. Decisions of clinical insufficiency or incompetence might be made by a panel or committee to promote uniformity and add credibility to the decision-making process. Subjective grading should be shown to be a rational exercise of discretion by the graders [Editors Note: with clear criteria and uniform application].

- Any student, whose class or field performance makes his or her continuance in the program inadvisable, should be advised of such deficiencies before being dismissed from the program.

- As a matter of fairness and professional courtesy, a system of review and reevaluation should be made available to students who challenge academic decisions. . . .

- Academic and behavioral conduct to which students are expected to conform should be explicated. The *NASW Code of Ethics* could be modified for this purpose.

- Rules governing ethical and behavioral conduct should be articulated clearly, outlining standards and consequences for misconduct. These standards and rules should be included in all appropriate university and social work program publications (i.e., student handbooks, program brochures, university catalogues). (1993:157)

Cole and Lewis's recommendations will assist faculty in meeting legal requirements as they work on developing a policy, and the following list of criteria and standards can serve as a launching point for the discussions that precede policy development. It is important to remember that gatekeeping neither begins nor ends with admissions, and policies and procedures must reflect this reality. Gatekeeping typically commences at the first point of contact with the program, usually when students take the introductory social work course(s), and it continues throughout a student's tenure in the program. The criteria, standards, and sources of evidence suggested below can be included in gatekeeping processes across the program.

Screening Criteria and/or Academic Standards of a Cognitive, Skill, or Scholastic Nature

The following is a list of commonly used criteria and standards, the rationale for inclusion of each criterion, and types of outcome evidence that demonstrate each criterion has been achieved and measures that might be useful in assessing students against each criterion. Some of the tools for implementing the measures, such as the kinds of admissions questions that are useful, can be found in the appendixes.

Minimum overall GPA

Rationale: Ability to maintain good grades reflects (at the very least) motivation, work management skills, and higher order thinking abilities that are requisite to effective practice. Additionally, Cunningham (1982) found high GPA to be the best predictor of success in field education.

Outcome evidence and measures: Studies of BSW program screening mechanisms (Gibbs 1994; Wahlberg and Lommen 1990) show that when GPA is used as an admissions criterion, the usual range is from 2.0 to 2.5 on a four-point scale, with 2.0 being the mode. The second most frequently used GPA level is 2.5. Some programs do require a higher GPA.

Minimum GPA in the major and/or minimum grade in introductory social work course(s)

Rationale: Grades earned in social work courses reflect ability to master the profession's knowledge base and skills and also demonstrate motivation, work and time management skills, and critical thinking skills that are requisite to effective practice.

Outcome evidence and measures:

- Cluster of preprofessional (introductory) social work courses with GPA from 2.0 to 3.0 (on a four-point scale).

- Successful completion of social work courses and skills labs with assignments, readings, exams, simulations, and written work appropriate to realize the objectives of each course.

Sound written communication skills

Rationale: Practitioners are called upon regularly to write a variety of documents and materials that are used to serve clients, fund programs and agencies, plan and develop future services, meet quality control requirements, secure third-party payments, facilitate court actions, and so on. As Simon and Soven (1989) point out, accountability to clients, constituents, supervisors, funding sources, and the public hinges in part on clear and forceful prose.

Outcome evidence and measures:

- Essays, student biographies, personal statements, student self-assessments that demonstrate effective writing. (See appendix 1 for sample essay questions for admissions application, appendix 6 for a sample student self-assessment form, and appendix 10 for a sample grading checklist for evaluating written assignments.)

- Satisfactory scores on the writing portion of the Pre-professional Skills Tests (PPST). These tests are administered through National Teacher Examinations (NTE) Programs by Educational Testing Service (ETS). The writing test, designed to measure basic proficiency in writing as needed for academic success, consists of two separately timed sections: a multiple-choice section and an essay section, each taking thirty minutes to complete. Several test centers are found in each of twenty-seven states. In order to use the PPST, the ETS requires a validity study by a panel of experts. For more information, contact Educational Testing Service Praxis Series, P.O. Box

6051, Princeton, NJ 08541–6051. (Phone: 800/772–9476. Fax: 609/530–0581). There are study guides in most university bookstores, and the guides contain previously used test questions.

- Satisfactory scores on the Test of Standard Written English (TSWE). This test assesses students' ability to recognize standard written English as found in most college textbooks and as expected in college-level written work. For further information, contact Bobbie Goodman, Educational Testing Service, Rosedale Road, Princeton, NJ 08541 (Phone: 609/734–1306).

- Satisfactory scores on the ACT (American College Testing) or SAT (Scholastic Aptitude Test) college entrance exams. These scores are generally made available to faculty when students enter the institution. As a point of reference, students at West Virginia University can test out of their first college-level English composition course if their ACT score is 27 or above on the English section and their SAT score is 580 or above on the verbal section. However, if the ACT English score is 18 or lower or the SAT verbal score is 340 or lower, students must first pass an English placement test in order to register for the first English composition course. Students who do not pass the placement exam must do remedial work before they are allowed entry into the composition course.

- Satisfactory reports of performance on the writing portion of LearningPlus, an interactive computer-delivered instructional program distributed by Educational Testing Service. LearningPlus provides instruction in math, reading, and writing, inclusive of lessons that teach problem solving and critical thinking skills. It is formatted in CD-ROM and 3.5" diskettes and has accompanying handbooks for students who need to improve their skills in any of the three subject areas. Following a series of diagnostic tests, a skills profile is given that shows students' strengths and weaknesses and prescribes specific areas of instruction. Ongoing progress reports assess students' abilities as they proceed through the instructional units. Either or both of these reports provide evidence of the students' writing abilities. For further information call 800/559–7587 or contact the Educational Testing Service (ETS), 33 South Delaware Avenue, Suite 202, Yardley, PA 19067–9507.

- Student portfolio of graded written assignments from specified social work and other college-level courses, which might be used to screen students at the point of admissions or entry to the field as well as to determine competence as part of a more comprehensive evaluation of student performance at the point of exiting the program.

- Positive academic references, usually from social work faculty, that address students' writing skills. (See appendix 8 for a sample reference form.)

- Successful completion of college-level English composition courses.

- Essay questions on exit exams that demonstrate satisfactory written communication skills.

College-level critical thinking skills

Rationale: The ability to make sound judgments and reasoned decisions is an important requisite to effective practice. According to Beck (1996), the most important skills in critical thinking are inquiry, analysis, and communication.

Outcome evidence and measures:

- GPA (i.e., student is in good academic standing).

- Successful completion of liberal arts coursework that involves reasoning, analysis, drawing conclusions, evaluating arguments, weighing evidence, making comparisons, arriving at sound solutions to problems.

- Successful completion of a wide range of activities in critical thinking, such as written assignments (for example, the assignment of comparing codes of ethics found in appendix 14) and the critical thinking workbook for social work students (Gibbs and Gambrill 1999). Appendix 11 has a form for evaluating critical thinking skills.

- Acceptable command of language to express thoughts and ideas (see previous section on written communication skills).

- Demonstrated ability to problem-solve during the capstone field practicum.

- Acceptable skill level on one of the *Tasks for Critical Thinking* tests. These are standardized tests, developed by Educational Testing Service (ETS) and the College Entrance Examination Board, that measure the students' ability to use higher order thinking skills.

Students work through a specific task and scoring reflects abilities in inquiry, analysis, and communication. Scoring is done by local faculty using detailed scoring guides, and a consultant is available for training faculty in scoring. For more information on obtaining individual scores on this test contact Dina Langrana, ETS Higher Education Assessment, Rosedale Road, Princeton, NJ 08541 (Phone: 609/951–1509).

Completion of a fixed number of credit hours, cognate courses, and liberal arts foundation coursework

Rationale: Formal entry to the major generally occurs at the beginning of the junior year. Prior to that students are often viewed as premajors and take the liberal arts foundation and other social science coursework to lay the foundation for the professional courses.

Outcome evidence and measures: Successful completion of fifty-eight to sixty semester credit hours is a common requirement for entry to the social work major; this number of credits moves the student into junior-level rank. Students may be in the midst of completing some of these credits at the time of application, although the liberal arts foundation, as defined by each program, must be completed prior to the professional foundation coursework, according to the Council on Social Work Education's accreditation standards (CSWE 1994:90). Cognate courses are generally in the social sciences, and these courses support and complement the professional curriculum.

Evidence of communication and interpersonal skills sufficient to provide a foundation for building professional interactional skills

Rationale: The ability to communicate effectively and to interact in positive, respectful, effective, and appropriate ways with both clients and colleagues not only is the keystone of professional practice but also meets the ethical standards found in the 1996 *NASW Code of Ethics* (see, for example, section 2.01, "The Social Worker's Responsibility to Colleagues," 15).

Outcome evidence and measures:

- Positive reference letter from instructor(s) of designated social work course(s), work supervisor(s), or supervisor(s) of volunteer human service activity or other field learning experiences. (See appendixes 7 and 8 for sample reference letter forms.)

- Positive feedback from other social work faculty who do not teach courses designated as requiring a reference letter.

- Successful completion of social work skills labs or other appropriate coursework.

- Demonstrated ability to establish and maintain positive relationships with clients and coworkers during the capstone field practicum. (See appendix 9 for a sample evaluation tool for assessing a student's performance in the field setting.)

- Self-assessment by the student that reflects adequate interpersonal skills. (See appendix 6 for a sample self-assessment)

- Interview with faculty at any of the program's screening points that demonstrates satisfactory abilities in interpersonal communication.

- Oral exit exams that demonstrate satisfactory abilities in interpersonal communication.

- Video of interview situation that shows satisfactory interactional abilities.

Screening Criteria and/or Academic Standards of an Affective or Professional Nature

These are the criteria that programs seem to have the most difficulty developing and addressing in the context of admissions and as academic performance expectations for students in the professional and preprofessional curriculum. The following is a list of possible criteria and standards, the rationale for inclusion of each, and types of outcome evidence that demonstrate each criterion has been achieved and measures what might be useful in assessing students with regard to each criterion and standard.

Professional readiness for work with clients and for professional practice

Rationale: Because of the professional nature of social work education, readiness to engage in professional helping activities is essential. Different levels of readiness should be differentiated for different gatekeeping points in the program since one would expect, for example, that professional development, professional identity, skill levels, and the like would increase as a result of engagement with the curriculum.

Outcome evidence: Through preprofessional and professional coursework, advisement sessions, other student-faculty contact opportunities, participation in the student social work organization or other service organizations on campus, human service learning, and any additional feedback mechanisms, the student

- demonstrates adherence to the ethical principles of moral conduct expected of social workers;

- demonstrates respect for the rights of others and upholds the ethical principle of confidentiality as it relates to human service and to classroom activities;

- shows potential for responsible and accountable behavior by observing advisement deadlines, keeping appointments (or canceling appointments if unable to keep them), attending class regularly, etc.;

- demonstrates sound work management skills by completing assignments related to classroom and field activities in a timely manner;

- is able to examine and assess the relationship between his or her personal socialization and its fit with professional helping expectations;

- advocates for himself or herself in an appropriate and responsible manner;

- uses proper channels for conflict resolution;

- demonstrates responsible and self-directed behavior in adherence to the plan of study and the proper sequencing of courses for degree or program completion;

- appropriate to each of the gatekeeping points in the program, demonstrates the capacity to assess strengths, limitations, and suitability for professional practice.

Measures:

- Reference letter from instructor(s) of designated social work course(s), work supervisor(s), or supervisor(s) of volunteer or paid field learning experiences. Appendixes 7 and 8 provide sample reference forms.

- Feedback from other social work faculty who do not teach courses designated as requiring a reference letter.

- Feedback regarding class attendance and participation.

- Student self-assessment and discussion of readiness in essay for admissions. Appendix 6 provides a sample self-assessment form.

- Interviews with faculty.

- Participating or assuming leadership in the social work student organization or other service organizations on campus.

- Capstone field practicum. (See appendix 9 for an evaluation form.)

- Exit exams.

- Psychometric tests such as the Minnesota Multiphasic Personality Inventory-2 (MMPI-2; see chapter 15 for a discussion of its use) or the Basic Personality Inventory (BPI). The BPI Manual reports evidence that the BPI and the MMPI-2 measure similar underlying constructs, with the BPI being half as long. It can be ordered from Sigma Assessment Systems, Inc., P.O. Box 6100984, Port Huron, MI 48061–0984. Phone: 800/265–1285; http://207.176.194.145/default.htm.

A level of self-awareness and maturity that would support professional practice activities

Rationale: This criterion or academic standard closely relates to professional readiness. The nature and demands of professional practice require self-awareness and maturity that would facilitate helping efforts with others in order to resolve their problems, meet their needs, and enhance their social functioning.

Outcome evidence: Through preprofessional and professional coursework, advisement sessions, other student-faculty contact opportunities, participation in the student social work organization or other service organizations on campus, human service learning, and any additional feedback mechanisms, the student

- demonstrates an ability to accurately reflect on his or her strengths and limitations;

- shows a willingness to receive and accept feedback and supervision in a positive manner and to use such feedback to enhance his or her professional development;

- advocates for himself or herself in an appropriate and responsible manner;

- uses proper channels for conflict resolution;

- is able to accurately assess strengths, limitations, and suitability for professional practice;

- is able to examine and assess the relationship between his or her personal socialization and its fit with professional helping expectations.

Measures:

- Reference letter from instructor(s) of designated social work course(s), work supervisor(s), or supervisor(s) of volunteer or paid field learning experiences. (See appendixes 7 and 8)

- Feedback from other social work faculty who do not teach courses designated as requiring a reference letter.

- Student self-assessment. (See appendix 6 for a sample self-assessment form.)

- Admissions essay or biographical statement. (See appendix 1 for sample essay questions.)

- Interview with admissions committee.

- Psychometric tests. See chapter 15 for a discussion of their use and Nurius and Hudson (1993) for a variety of instruments that may be used as part of gatekeeping efforts. The Walmyr Publishing Company, for example, provides a number of short-form scales (The Walmyr Assessment Scales) that focus on personal adjustment issues (e.g., Index of Self-Esteem, Index of Peer Relations). They can be ordered from Walmyr Publishing Company, P.O. Box 12217, Tallahassee, FL 32317–12217. Phone: 850/383–0045; www.syspac.com/~7Ewalmyr/wp01001.htm.

- Exit exams.

- Capstone field practicum. (See appendix 9 for an evaluation form.)

Emotional and mental stability that would facilitate sound judgment and performance in the program as well as generally support the practice of social work

Rationale: According to Section 4.05 of the *NASW Code of Ethics* (1996:23) personal problems, psychosocial distress, substance abuse, and mental health difficulties are seen as potentially interfering forces in relation to professional judgment and performance. To carry out their studies, students must have sufficient emotional and mental stability to complete all aspects of the program and its curriculum. As future helpers, students must have the emotional and psychological resources to render effective assistance to those in need.

Outcome evidence: Through preprofessional and professional course-work, advisement sessions, other student-faculty contact opportunities, participation in the student social work organization or other service organizations on campus, human service learning, and any additional feedback mechanisms, the student

- demonstrates an ability to reflect on his or her strengths and limitations as they relate to professional capacities;

- shows a willingness to receive and accept feedback and supervision in a positive manner and to use such feedback to enhance his or her professional development;

- demonstrates ability to deal with current life stressors through the use of appropriate coping mechanisms;

- demonstrates behaviors in the classroom, the field placement, and with peers that are in compliance with program policies, institutional policies, and professional ethical standards;

- shows a willingness to engage in counseling or seek out support and help if personal problems, psychosocial distress, substance abuse, or mental health difficulties compromise academic performance, interfere with professional judgment and performance, or jeopardize the best interests of those to whom the social work student has a professional responsibility, as outlined in the *NASW Code of Ethics* (1996). Note: If a student is currently addicted to an illegal substance, she or he is not protected by the Americans with Disabilities

Act, but a former addiction, for which student is or has been in rehabilitation, is considered a "disability" and is therefore protected.

Measures:

- Reference letter from instructor(s) of designated social work course(s), work supervisor(s), or supervisor(s) of volunteer or paid field learning experiences. (See appendixes 7 and 8)

- Feedback from other social work faculty who do not teach courses designated as requiring a reference letter.

- Discussion of readiness in an essay for admissions.

- Interview with the admissions committee.

- The Brief Symptom Inventory (BSI). This is a psychometrically strong, fifty-three-item self-report instrument that has been standardized for normal, inpatient, and outpatient populations. It is not in the public domain and must be purchased from NCA Assessments, 5605 Green Circle Drive, Minnetonka, MN 55343. (Phone: 612/939–5000). This inventory is scored along nine symptom dimensions: somatization, obsessive-compulsive, interpersonal sensitivity, depression, anxiety, hostility, phobic anxiety, paranoid ideation, psychoticism, and three global indices. Norms are available for college students. (See Cochran and Hale 1985; Derogatis and Melisaratos 1983.)

- CES-D Scale. This is a twenty-item self-report instrument that can indicate major depression. This scale is in the public domain and may be used without copyright permission. If a program chooses this instrument, the Epidemiology and Psychopathology Research Branch is interested in receiving copies of research reports of its use. (See Radloff and Locke 1986; Radloff 1977).

- The Minnesota Multiphasic Personality Inventory-2. This is an updated version of a standard psychological inventory, which differs from the original version in terms of the norming sample, item content, and, to a limited extent, interpretive guidelines. A variety of clinical scales are directly obtained from the original validating research on the instrument; additional derived scales have been validated by subsequent research. The clinical scales include anxiety, depression, and schizophrenic tendencies. Three validation scales are provided to assist the user in determining the validity of individual response sets. Interpretive guidelines for the MMPI-2 are sensitive to issues of cultural background as well as the possibility of traumatic history, such as being the victim of abuse. The instrument serves as a reasonably objective assessment of the applicant's state at the time of assessment. A sample student consent form signed by students who take the test is included in appendix 5.

- Admissions essay, personal statement, student self-assessment.

- Exit exams.

- Capstone field practicum. Appendix 9 provides an evaluation form.

Current behavior and classroom performance that demonstrates potential for adherence to the ethical expectations and obligations of professional practice as contained in the *NASW Code of Ethics* and as otherwise understood and operationalized by the practice community

Rationale: Social work practice is as much an expression of values and ethics as it is of knowledge and skills. Values and ethics must not be separated from our practice models, professional behavior, and academic performance standards in social work education.

Outcome evidence: Through preprofessional and professional coursework, advisement sessions, other student-faculty contact opportunities, participation in the student social work organization or other service organizations on campus, human service learning, and any additional feedback mechanisms, the student

- is able to effectively relate to and nonjudgmentally work with others who are different from himself or herself (i.e., differences based on race, color, gender, sexual orientation, age, religion, national origin, marital status, political belief, mental or physical handicap, or any other preference or personal characteristic, condition, or status);

- is able to suspend personal biases during interactions with others, including clients, faculty, staff, field supervisors, and other students;

- shows commitment to social justice;

- demonstrates honesty and integrity in all interactions and endeavors;

- shows commitment to the concept of clients' rights to self-determination;

- demonstrates punctuality, dependability, and responsibility in attending class, turning in assignments, meeting classroom expectations, etc.;

- complies with policies, rules, and regulations advanced by the program, the institution, or the field settings.

Measures:

- Reference letter from instructor(s) of designated social work course(s), work supervisor(s), or supervisor(s) of volunteer or paid field learning experiences. Sample reference forms are in appendixes 7 and 8.

- Feedback from other social work faculty who do not teach courses designated as requiring a reference letter.

- Signed contract to adhere to ethical standards of the profession. See sample contract in appendix 3.

- Student self-assessment. Sample self-assessment forms are in appendix 6.

- Admissions essay or introductory social work course assignment that addresses how personal values are consistent with the values of the social work profession.

- Interview with the admissions committee.

- Psychometric tests such as the Jackson Personality Inventory-Revised (JPI-R). See chapter 15 for a discussion of the use of psychometric tests. The JPI-R can be ordered from Sigma Assessment Systems, Inc., P.O. Box 6100984, Port Huron, MI 48061–0984. Phone: 800/265–1285; http://207.176.194.145/default.htm.

- Exit exams

- Capstone field practicum. Sample evaluation forms are in appendix 9.

References

Beck, N. (1996). ETS (Educational Testing Service) assessment measures. Presentation to the West Virginia Higher Education Council on Assessment on April 12.

Cobb, N. H. (1994). Court-recommended guidelines for managing unethical students and working with university lawyers. *Journal of Social Work Education* 30:18–31.

Cobb, N. H., and Jordan, C. (1989). Students with questionable values or threatening behavior: Precedent and policy from discipline to dismissal. *Journal of Social Work Education* 25:87–97.

Cochran, C. D., and Hale, W. D. (1985). College students norms on the Brief Symptom Inventory. *Journal of Clinical Psychology* 41 (6): 777–789.

Cole, B. S., and Lewis, R. G. (1993). Gatekeeping through termination of unsuitable social work students: Legal issues and guidelines. *Journal of Social Work Education* 29:150–159.

Council on Social Work Education (CSWE), Commission on Accreditation. (1994). *Handbook of accreditation standards and procedures.* 4th ed. Alexandria, Va.: CSWE.

Council on Social Work Education (CSWE), Commission on Accreditation. (1999). *Guidelines for termination for academic and professional reasons.* Washington, D.C.: CSWE.

Cunningham, M. (1982). Admissions variables and the prediction of success in an undergraduate fieldwork program. *Journal of Education for Social Work* 18:27–34.

Derogatis, L. R., and Melisaratos, N. (1983). The Brief Symptom Inventory: An introductory report. *Psychological Medicine* 13:595–605.

Dunlap, W. R. (1979). How effective are graduate social work admission criteria? *Journal of Education for Social Work* 15 (3): 96–102.

Gibbs, P. (1994). Screening mechanisms in BSW programs. *Journal of Social Work Education* 30:63–74.

Gibbs, L., and Gambrill, E. (1999). *Critical thinking for social workers: Exercises for the helping profession.* Rev. ed. Thousand Oaks, Ca.: Pine Forge Press.

Knoff, H., and Prout, H. (1985). Terminating students from professional psychology programs: Criteria, procedures, and legal issues. *Professional Psychology: Research and Practice* 16:789–797.

Madden, R. G. (1993). Protecting all parties: A legal analysis of clinical competency and student dismissals. Paper presented at the 39th

Annual Program Meeting of the Council on Social Work Education, New York, N.Y.

Moore, L. S., and Urwin, C. A. (1990). Quality control in social work: The gatekeeping role in social work education. *Journal of Teaching in Social Work* 4 (1): 113–128.

National Association of Social Workers (NASW). (1996). *NASW code of ethics.* Washington, D.C.: NASW.

Nurius, P., and Hudson, W. (1993). *Human services practice, evaluation, and computers.* Pacific Grove, Ca.: Brooks/Cole.

Radloff, L. S., and Locke, B. Z. (1986). The Community Mental Health Assessment Survey and the CES-D Scale. In M. M. Weissman, J. K. Myers, and C. E. Ross (eds.), *Community surveys of psychiatric disorders.* New Brunswick, N.J.: Rutgers.

Radloff, L. S. (1977). The CES–D Scale: A self-report depression scale for research in the general population. *Applied Psychological Measurement* 3 (1): 385–401.

Simon, B. L., and Soven, M. (1989). The teaching of writing in social work education: A pressing priority for the 1990s. *Journal of Teaching in Social Work* 3 (2): 47–63.

Wahlberg, J., and Lommen, C. (1990). An analysis of admissions and termination criteria in BSW Programs. Presentation at the 8th Annual Conference of the Association of Baccalaureate Social Work Program Directors, Minneapolis, Minn.

14

Admission Reviews in Baccalaureate Social Work Programs: Is There a Role for Social Work Practitioners?

Hope O. Hagar

Gatekeeping in baccalaureate social work education has received increased attention in recent years, and it has generally been acknowledged that screening for professionally suitable students begins with the admission review process (Born and Carroll 1988; Cobb and Jordan 1989; Gibbs 1994; Hepler and Noble 1990; McClelland, Rindfleisch, and Bean 1991; Moore and Urwin 1990, 1991; Peterman and Blake 1986; Taylor and Witte 1943). This position is clearly articulated in accreditation standards, which state that "criteria and processes of admission should be designed and implemented to accept from the group of applicants those who . . . are best qualified to become professional social workers at a beginning level of practice" (Council on Social Work Education, Commission on Accreditation, 1994:81). Further, the guidelines specify that "admission standards and processes should reflect an appreciation for the requirements of the profession" (82).

This chapter would not have been possible without the exceptional work of the Adjunct Admission Committee affiliated with the Social Work Program at the University of Wisconsin-La Crosse. Special thanks are extended to Diana Birnbaum, Larry Hagar, Theresa Hengel, Chris McGraw, and Paul Ranum.

Ideally, the faculty's specification of professional requirements is developed in concert with the social work practice community. It is this premise that informed the establishment of an interview panel composed solely of social work practitioners and administrators whose collective judgment regarding a student's suitability for the profession comprised one evaluative component in the admission review process of a baccalaureate social work program. The context within which this screening mechanism evolved, the procedures that were developed, and the responses of both students and practitioners to the experience are summarized in this chapter.

Background

The use of social work practitioners and administrators in the admissions review process of the undergraduate social work program at the University of Wisconsin-La Crosse (UW-La Crosse) is part of a five-year longitudinal research project designed to investigate the predictive validity of admission variables. The predictor variables in the study include scholastic competencies and aptitudes (e.g., scholastic achievement, communication skills, etc.); cumulative GPA and GPAs for particular combinations of courses; professional qualities and behaviors (e.g., ability to relate to others, psychological well-being, identification with social work values, etc.); and alternative screening mechanisms, such as published instruments and coding systems, assessment tools and coding systems developed by faculty, and interviews conducted by social work practitioners and administrators.

Procedures

The panel of practitioners responsible for conducting interviews with applicants to the program was named the Adjunct Admission Committee (AAC). Invitations to serve on this committee were extended to four social work practitioners and two social service administrators. These individuals were selected because their practice competence was greatly respected by the program's faculty and in addition they represented a cross section of the profession in terms of age, sex, number of years in the profession, and areas of social work expertise. All but one practitioner agreed to serve, and ultimately the AAC consisted of two male and three female members. Committee members were told that their work would bring the practitioner's perspective to the admission review process, help identify the most professionally promising students for admission to the program, and be part of a research project designed to investigate admission variables that most strongly predict success in upper-division social work courses and in social work practice after graduation.

Committee members were blind to the specific predictor variables in the research. However, they were given an overview of the application process and its eligibility requirements, a series of tasks, and a timeline for completion of the tasks. In preparation for the interviews, the AAC met on four occasions for approximately ninety minutes each time. During these sessions, members identified qualities and aptitudes deemed essential in social work practitioners, specified the mechanisms and interview questions that would elicit information from students on those qualities, and developed the rudiments of a standardized scoring system that would be used by interviewers to independently rate each applicant on his or her suitability for the social work profession using a five-point scale (1 = not suitable and 5 = exceptionally suitable). This rating form is included at the end of this chapter.

The committee set up four interviewing teams made up of three committee members each. These teams spent two entire days, on a rotating schedule, conducting fifteen-minute interviews with forty-one applicants. The actual interview was conducted according to a standardized protocol, but follow-up questions were tailored to individuals. The following are the standard questions and the order in which they were raised:

1. Tell us about your background and what led you to select a social work major.
2. What qualities are essential to be a good social worker?
   a. What does a social worker do?
3. News article questions (see Interview Statement at end of chapter).

4. Is there anything you would like to share with us that we have not already discussed or is there anything you would like to ask us?

The third interview question addressed an essay written by applicants immediately before their interview. Applicants were instructed to report for their interview twenty minutes early to complete an Interview Statement that consisted of a brief written response to four questions about a recent news article they were given. In anticipation that applicants who completed the essay earlier in the two-day process might discuss the assignment with other applicants, three comparable forms of the Interview Statement were used.

As stated earlier, each of the applicants was rated *independently* by three interviewers. There was three-person agreement (identical scores) in fourteen cases (34.1 percent), two person agreement (identical scores) in twenty-three cases (56.1 percent), and three person disagreement (three different scores) in four cases (9.8 percent). A mean interview score was derived from the three separate ratings. This score was weighed equally with scores on other admission variables in the faculty's determination of admission decisions.

Upon completion of the interviews, committee members participated in two ninety-minute wrap-up sessions with the faculty. The purpose of these sessions was to evaluate the process, summarize the results of ratings of the applicants, give feedback to faculty pertaining to curricular or program matters, obtain a recommendation regarding continuation of the process, recognize the committee's contribution to the program, and bring closure to the group process. In addition to the wrap-up sessions, four members wrote a summary of the committee's planning and interviewing processes, and all responded to four open-ended questions pertaining to their own participation on the AAC.

Practitioners' Comments and Recommendations

Without exception, committee members recommended the continuation of interviews by practitioners in the admission review process. In their judgment, fifteen minutes was enough time to conduct each interview, and they liked the two-day time frame for completing all interviews. Committee members also suggested that the concept of an Interview Statement be retained as a means to assess the writing skills and thinking processes of applicants. Having alternate forms of this statement was deemed valuable in reducing the risk that students might discuss the question with others.

Committee members strongly endorsed the continuation of diversity in the membership regarding such attributes as age, sex, areas of practice expertise, and years in the profession. They also recommended the retention of planning sessions prior to the actual interviews even if the current committee membership would remain the same for another year. This planning time was seen as useful in clarifying their shared expectations and in developing group cohesion.

In terms of the university's coordination of this process, the committee recommended that more attention be given to a review of the applicants' prior exposure to social work courses and social work practice. Although this kind of information was given to committee members at their first meeting, it was not discussed with the faculty convener. The group concurred that a discussion of this nature would have clarified the degree of professional knowledge that could reasonably be expected of applicants.

Given their already busy schedules, why had these community practitioners agreed to serve on this time-intensive committee? AAC members reported being motivated by the opportunity to interact with other professionals ($n = 5$), a commitment to social work education and the profession ($n = 4$), and respect for this particular social work program ($n = 3$).

In terms of the benefits they expected as a result of participation in the committee, gain for themselves was not a predominant motivating factor ($n = 2$) and engaging in an interesting experience with the university and other professionals was also an expectation ($n = 2$). The actual self-reported benefits of having participated in the AAC included interacting with a diverse group of social work professionals ($n = 4$), engaging in complementary group problem-solving ($n = 3$), bonding with other practitioners and making new friends in the professional community ($n = 3$), and learning that high-caliber students are attracted to the social work major ($n = 3$).

In summary, all members of the AAC regarded the experience as worthwhile and were open to serve on this committee during the next admission review process. (One member, though willing to serve, declined participation for personal reasons.) Without exception, they wholeheartedly endorsed their collaborative role in professional gatekeeping through early assessment processes in social work education.

Students' Comments and Recommendations

At an informal level, faculty solicited feedback from *all* students who had participated in the interviews with practitioners. Anecdotal comments indicated that even though the interview process initially provoked anxiety, students liked meeting and questioning practitioners about their jobs and the employment trends in the profession.

All students who were admitted to the upper-division program and who participated in the interviews with practitioners completed an anonymous questionnaire regarding this experience. Of the twenty-nine respondents to the questionnaire, twenty-six students recommended retaining interviews with practitioners in the admission review process. Two open-ended questions elicited what students liked or did not like about the interviews. Not surprisingly, several students experienced the *idea* of being interviewed as stressful ($n = 12$). One illustrative response was: "It seemed so intimidating but once I got there, they were all very nice." Students also thought it was a "good experience" ($n = 11$), an opportunity to ask questions about the field ($n = 11$), and a chance to learn what social workers actually do ($n = 10$). One student commented: "Input from their . . . experiences was appreciated and interesting and led to my reappraisal of myself as a potential social worker."

A few respondents perceived the interviews as an unbiased admission procedure, characterizing them as "very equal in terms of everyone starting on the same level" ($n = 6$). Other students regarded the interviews as preparation for field placement or employment interviews ($n = 6$), exemplification of professionalism ($n = 5$), or linkage to the practice community ($n = 4$). Two respondents said: "I felt I was entering a professional field" and "I liked dealing with professionals, it was different than class." The primary objection to retaining the interviews with practitioners related to the validity of "first impressions" ($n = 3$).

Discussion

This chapter began with a central question: Is there a role for social work practitioners in the gatekeeping function of admission reviews in baccalaureate social work education? The experience of one program that utilized an interviewing panel of practitioners was presented. The results of this experience led to the conclusion that practitioners add a valuable component to the admission process, even if their collective assessment of applicants is not found to be a valid predictor of the students' success. This claim is made for several reasons. Recall that accreditation standards (CSWE 1994) specify that:

> The program should initiate and maintain regular planned exchanges . . . [with] social work practitioners regarding the program's educational goals and objectives, curriculum, student performance, and developments in the field setting that affect student learning. The program should also systematically provide for the participation of field instructors and other social work practitioners in curriculum assessment leading to curriculum revision and development.
>
> *(86)*

Many social work programs rely on advisory councils, guest lectures, routine meetings with field instructors, field selection processes, and evaluations of students' field performance to address this guideline. Another avenue is provided by the admission review process. Practitioners can represent the current demands of practice more authentically than can faculty who are presently not engaged in practice This is helpful to applicants in clarifying their career choice and in gaining other information about the practice of social work. In fact, applicants frequently asked the interviewing panel about what they actually did in practice, how they managed to avoid burnout, and what level of salary one could expect after graduation.

Making use of practitioners during admissions can also provide an "avenue of renewal" for the program, as required by CSWE's

Curriculum Policy Statement (1994:104). The dialogue between practitioners and students can result in feedback to the faculty regarding introductory social work courses, early program requirements, and foundation courses in the institution's general education. For example, practitioners observed that applicants had a very vague and general conception of what social workers do (e.g., help people). This feedback led faculty at UW-La Crosse to increase the number of volunteer hours required of students prior to application to the upper-division coursework. Input of this nature also suggests that some standards should be developed regarding the quality of volunteer experiences that satisfy a program's volunteer requirement. An additional implication could involve strengthening introductory social work courses through the inclusion of considerable case material. Moreover, because the panel of practitioners assessed such qualities as systemic thinking and oral and written communication, their observations become useful in evaluating the institution's liberal studies program.

The involvement of practitioners in admission processes also serves purposes beyond responsiveness to accreditation standards. It brings practitioners and students together and tangibly represents the cooperative linkage between social work education and the practice community. In this instance, it was a catalyst for practitioners to envision ways in which they could help the program address deficits in the curriculum or program that were illuminated by their observations. For example, they recommended the development of a Practitioner Fair for lower-division students. The fair would facilitate interaction between practitioners and students who are interested in a social work major, which would give students another avenue for clarifying the roles and functions of social workers prior to applying for admission to the professional program.

Finally, because the practitioners recorded their impressions of each applicant's strengths and weaknesses as evidenced in the interview process, their notations can contribute to a baseline profile on each student who is admitted to the program. This baseline data could be communicated to students through advisement and could be used to help students develop entry-level learning contracts. The baseline information would also provide comparative data in the assessment of outcomes of the students' learning. For those students not accepted into the upper-division program, the insights of the practitioners may reinforce the faculty's judgment.

It has been the premise of this chapter that baccalaureate admission reviews provide a vehicle for meaningful and systematic participation of practitioners in the gatekeeping function of social work education. Typically, program faculty rely heavily on the observations and evaluation of agency-based field instructors when it becomes necessary to screen a student out during the field practicum. Are not the insights of practitioners an equally valuable resource to faculty who are making admissions decisions? Indeed, anecdotal comments from practitioners suggest that they appreciate participation in gatekeeping at the front end of professional education, before a student is personally and fiscally invested in a social work major. Unfortunately, social work educators are frequently disinclined to ask for yet another kind of program involvement from practitioners. This reluctance does a disservice to practitioners because it fails to acknowledge the depth of their commitment to the profession and to the education of future professionals. This reluctance also does a disservice to social work programs because it fails to capitalize on the synergistic linkage that can be generated through cooperative, worthwhile, and task-oriented endeavors. The interaction that accompanies the completion of this important task in the admission review process sharpens the practice-relevance of social work education, stimulates the professional commitment of those in the practice community, and provides a career-clarifying experience for students.

References

Born, C. E., and Carroll, D. J. (1988). Ethics in admissions. *Journal of Social Work Education* 24:79–85.

Cobb, N. H., and Jordan, C. (1989). Students with questionable values or threatening behavior: Precedent and policy from discipline to dismissal. *Journal of Social Work Education* 25:87–97.

Council on Social Work Education, Commission on Accreditation (CSWE). (1994). *Handbook of accreditation standards and procedures*. 4th ed. Alexandria, Va.: CSWE.

Gibbs, P. (1994). Screening mechanisms in BSW programs. *Journal of Social Work Education* 30:63–74.

Hepler, J. B., and Noble, J. H., Jr. (1990). Improving social work education: Taking responsibility at the door. *Social Work* 35:126–133.

McClelland, R. W., Rindfleisch, N., and Bean, G., (1991). Rater adherence to evaluative criteria used in BSSW admissions. *Aretê* 16 (2): 10–18.

Moore, L. S., and Urwin, C. A. (1990). Quality control in social work: The gatekeeping role in social work education. *Journal of Teaching in Social Work* 4 (1): 113–128.

Moore, L. S., and Urwin, C. A. (1991). Gatekeeping: A model for screening baccalaureate students for field education. *Journal of Social Work Education* 27:8–17.

Peterman, P. J., and Blake, R. (1986). The inappropriate BSW student. *Aretê* 11 (1): 27–34.

Taylor, A. L., and Witte, E. F. (1943). Problems of admission and evaluation in schools of social work. *The Compass* 24 (2): 3–4, 16–18.

Interview Rating Form

Student Name: I.D. #

Evaluator: Date:

Consider the following qualities when rating an applicant:

1. Verbal and written articulation
2. Problem-solving skills and approach to conflict resolution
3. Systemic thinking
4. Commitment to social work
5. Life experience factors that influence career choice
6. Personal qualities such as:
   - self-confidence (self-esteem)
   - poise
   - maturity
   - compassion
   - nonjudgmental attitude
   - humor
   - creativity
   - independence
   - honesty

Rate each applicant's suitability for the social work profession by circling one of the numbers on the following scale:

1	2	3	4	5
Not Suitable	Exceptionally Suitable	Very Suitable	Minimally Suitable	Suitable

Comments:

Interview Statement

Name:	I.D. #

Date:

Please read the excerpt from a recent news article that is provided below and briefly respond in writing to the questions that follow. You may write on the back of this sheet.

Excerpt:

New York Gov. Mario M. Cuomo and California Gov. Pete Wilson, two men who stand at opposite ends of the country and the political spectrum, recently gave surprisingly similar speeches within hours of one another. They both proposed to lock up-for life-any person convicted of three violent felonies.

"Violence and crime have taken on a terrible urgency and we are determined to move quickly and decisively to protect our people," said Democrat Cuomo in his State of the State address. . . . Soon after, Republican Wilson told Californians: "Every Californian has a fundamental right not to become a crime victim . . . and not to live in fear. . . . Put three-time losers behind bars for life." . . .

The speeches illustrate widespread citizen concern that the criminal justice system is too lenient and a growing belief that some people cannot be rehabilitated and need to spend their entire lives in prison. (Thomas, P., "Talking tough on crime," *The Washington Post National Weekly Edition*, January 31–February 6, 1994.)

Questions:

1. What do you see as the central issue in this article and what, if any, conflicts are involved in this issue?

2. What impact do you think this issue has on the practice of social work?

3. What possible interventions or impacts could social work have on this issue?

4. What is your position on this issue?

15

Psychological Testing as a Tool in Assessing Undergraduate Students for Admission to a Baccalaureate Social Work Program

Rose Bogal-Allbritten and Bill Allbritten

The ongoing discussion and debate about the gatekeeping process in social work education raises many questions about the validity of the criteria used in screening out students considered to be unsuitable candidates for the social work profession. While the majority of baccalaureate programs use a formal screening process (Gibbs 1994; Urwin 1991), many programs continue to define admissions criteria in primarily academic terms. Overall grade point average (GPA) and GPA in the major as well as completion of prerequisite courses appear to be the most frequently used admissions criteria. The most frequently cited GPA in Gibbs's (1994) survey of baccalaureate programs was 2.0 ($n = 73$, 46 percent), while 42 percent ($n = 67$) required a GPA ranging from 2.2 to 2.75. Since colleges and universities typically set the GPA necessary for graduation at 2.0, it can be argued that the programs "requiring" a 2.0 for program admission are merely accepting the general standard of their college or university rather than making a deliberate decision regarding an appropriate level of academic performance. Relying on GPA as the primary admission criterion poses another problem: what about the student who scrapes by with an average GPA but does an excellent job in the field and is hired by his or her agency? Or what about the student who goes into the field practicum with a high GPA and is completely overwhelmed by the reality of practice? Just as a high GPA cannot be equated with mental stability and professional suitability, a low GPA does not suggest mental instability and a lack of professional fit.

While a relatively large number of respondents ($n = 70$, 44 percent) in Gibbs's (1994) study indicated that evidence of emotional and mental stability was a criterion in their program's admissions process, there was no further inquiry as to the ways in which this criterion was applied. The application of this criterion is often difficult to articulate. Anecdotal evidence collected from discussions with colleagues at conferences and in other venues suggests several reasons why this difficulty may arise. Program faculty may feel that their hands are tied by legislation such as the Americans with Disabilities Act (ADA), which precludes programs from requesting information concerning a student's past or present treatment for mental illness. They may reject existing assessment tools on the grounds that these tools are inappropriate for use with social work students or that they discriminate against minority groups. These objections may arise from concerns about appropriate norm groups or from lack of information on the part of the faculty about how to use such assessment tools. At worst, faculty might slip out of the role of educator and into that of practitioner, putting the student into the role of client and assuming primary responsibility for the assessment and treatment of the student.

In each of these situations, faculty are limiting their ability to obtain *objective* evidence of a student's emotional and mental stability. Assessment approaches that do not rely solely on faculty observations are needed because faculty observe, at best, a small sampling of a student's behavior. In the case of transfer students, the opportunity to form judgments based on actual observation of the student is further reduced. This need for assessment arises not so much from the likelihood of many unstable candidates seeking admission to the program but more from the following two issues. First, the candidate pool can be expected to reflect the rate of occurrence of significant mental illness in the general population; second, individuals within the candidate pool may bring with them significant unresolved issues within their own lives that, while not indicative of mental illness, represent potential barriers to the candidate's ability to work effectively with clients. When the educator inappropriately assumes the role of therapist in these situations, the goal of assessing a student's appropriateness for the profession may become secondary to that of facilitating the student's personal development. Denying admission to this student may be falsely equated with personal failure on the part of the educator/therapist.

Educators who cite the ADA as the reason for an inability to gather information about emotional/mental stability assume that self-reporting of past or present treatment is the most logical way of obtaining such information, but many students who are applying for admission to a social work program may withhold information they consider damaging. Additionally, it cannot be assumed that those who have not sought treatment are necessarily the emotionally healthy students. Similarly, we cannot assume that students who have been in treatment or are currently in treatment are emotionally unstable.

Finally, negative reactions to psychological assessment instruments may stem from concerns about their misuse as well as from the fear that such instruments discriminate against minority groups. While any screening device, including psychological tests, can be misused, it must be remembered that the screening device is only one tool in the gatekeeping process, in the same way that an examination given in a class is only one tool in the academic assessment process. There are probably few social work educators who would fail a student on the basis of one examination, but many who would assist the student in finding a resource in order to improve the student's performance if this is possible. Additionally, many educators would probably attempt to find out why the student performed poorly; suggestions of more study time or a tutor would not be appropriate if the poor performance is due to illness or family circumstances. Similarly, a psychological test provides information about a student, but the data provided are only a starting point.

The Use of Psychological Testing at Murray State

The social work program at Murray State University has been using psychological testing as part of the admissions process since 1991. This section briefly describes our experience.

Prior to being given the test, the student signs an informed consent document stating that the test is being given as part of the admissions process and that results are viewed only by program faculty and a staff member of the counseling center. Although the psychological test is administered and scored by staff in the counseling center, the score sheets are numerically coded by the program director. Students whose psychological profiles are either valid and remarkable or invalid are asked to make an appointment with a clinical psychologist in the university's counseling center. It should be noted that this is the first point at which the student is identified by name rather than code number.

In the initial interview with the student whose profile is either valid and remarkable or invalid (as discussed later in this chapter), the staff member of the counseling center explores the student's reaction to being asked to come for an interview, collects background information on the student, and shares results of the psychological test with the student. A follow-up interview is scheduled; during the interim between the first and second sessions, the psychologist prepares a report that is shared with the student during the second session. The report follows standard psychological reporting format. The assessment results are objectively evaluated according to established interpretive standards. A brief assessment of the result is made in terms of behaviors likely to be noted in the student. Prognosis and treatment recommendations are included if appropriate. Finally, an assessment of the dynamics taking place in the interview with the student is included. If the report indicates a need to address issues raised in the testing, the student is informed of the opportunities available on-campus and off-campus. The student is also asked to sign a release of information form in order that a copy of the report can be sent to the program director.

The information in the report is addressed in the admissions interview for two reasons: first, to determine whether the student understands the information in the report and, second, to ascertain whether or not the student is willing to participate in the suggested course of action. If the student is willing to accept the suggestions offered in the report, admission is delayed for one or two semesters until the impact of the intervention can be evaluated. The student is informed that compliance will not automatically result in acceptance into the program. If the student refuses, without good reason, to participate in the suggested interventions, the student is denied admission. The student has the option of appealing the decision, but to date only one student who was denied admission has ever filed an appeal; this student failed to appear at the appeals meeting.

On the surface it may appear as if an admissions process that includes the use of a psychological assessment instrument would intimidate students, but the reader needs to be aware that this policy and process were developed with primary input from students as well as faculty, administrators, and the practice community. It is based on the belief that the gatekeeping policy and process should not be imposed from above but rather should reflect the students' rights and responsibilities in having a voice in the development of the program's policy. At Murray State, for example, the policy and process were developed in a senior-level policy class with students seeking input from representatives of regional social service agencies. Students used the original policy and process as a starting point. The original policy used grade point average in the first three social work courses as the primary gatekeeping variable. Much of the impetus for a reexamination of the original policy and process came from reactions on the part of faculty and of students to several students who exhibited "unprofessional" behavior both in the classroom and outside it. This class project resulted in a revised policy that includes, in addition to the assessment being discussed here, an English proficiency examination that is read by a staff member of the university's learning center; a signed agreement to abide by the *NASW Code of Ethics*; an interview process that includes a review of a videotape made in the student's first practice class; and an extended interview with the faculty as a whole. These admissions policy changes were approved by the university's administration and reviewed and approved by the university's legal counsel. Subsequently, specific action of the university's Board of Regents enacted the proposal into official institutional policy. The program faculty recognize the need for each component of the process, as well as the process as a whole, to be evaluated periodically in order to determine whether the process fits the program. A systematic review of the policy by students, faculty, and the program advisory committee takes place each year.

The impetus to initiate some form of psychological assessment as an element in the new admissions policy came from student and faculty reactions to several students who exhibited highly disturbing behavior in and out of class. In one instance, a student refused to disclose any basic information regarding her life outside the classroom. This student claimed as parents individuals who were well-known leaders in psychology and law. At other times, the student fabricated excuses involving nonexistent legal and medical personnel to explain class absences. However, this student passed the preadmission academic coursework in the curriculum at a satisfactory level. When this student was subsequently assessed, the profile was considered to be invalid and indicated an effort to conceal unfavorable characteristics or an attempt to create a false positive impression.

In another case, a student appeared to be always at odds with the academic rules that all students are expected to follow and repeatedly attempted to rationalize why the policy in question was not applicable in her case. This person also indicated a vague intention to transfer to another university and pursue a law degree, therefore implying that program faculty should make an exception regarding the application of these rules to her particular case. The assessment produced results consistent with an individual who might be expected to be hostile, extremely defensive, and easily distracted. Another student with an invalid test score (most likely resulting from an attempt to describe someone whom he or she envisioned as having a perfect, virtuous personality) refused to sign the *NASW Code of Ethics* and rationalized this refusal in terms of career plans that involved religious mission work, rather than social work as a career. Like all students with invalid scores, this student was given the option of retaking the psychological assessment but chose to leave the program.

It has been the experience of one of the authors as a site visitor for the Council on Social Work Education that many programs state that problems such as these are dealt with by the faculty counseling the student out of the program. None of the three students referred to in the above section, however, were amenable to consideration of alternative majors after consultation with faculty nor were they willing to engage in counseling. In all three cases, the faculty recognized prior to the admissions process the inappropriateness of the students' behavior; however, the university's legal staff would not allow involuntary termination from the program without objective measures to validate the concerns of the faculty. Psychological assessment was, on the one hand, an effective way of addressing the institution's legal concern over the absence of objective information upon which acceptance into or denial of admission to the program could be based. On the other hand, assessment provided the program faculty with an additional method of linking students in need of remediation with resources. Several students who were initially referred to the counseling and testing center on the basis of their profiles on the psychological assessment instrument, but whose profiles were, after an initial interview with counseling center staff, attributed to situational factors rather than to pathology, chose to enter counseling to address these situational factors. In fact, the students expressed gratitude for receiving the extra push that was needed for them to seek support services.

The philosophical basis underlying the choice by faculty to use psychological assessments is critical. Very few individuals who have exhibited the academic and interpersonal skills necessary to advance to sophomore or junior class status are affected by mental disorders so profound that the disorder in itself is a disqualifier from the profession of social work. Similarly, it cannot be accurately said that a specific interpretive profile is indicative of future problems in professional practice. A given behavioral problem observed by a program's faculty may have a variety of causes. Assessment provides more accurate insight into what might be motivating the observed behavior. Treatment using appropriate cognitive and pharmaceutical interventions renders many mental disorders manageable conditions that do not overly interfere with functioning. Assessment serves as a useful vehicle for focusing an individual on issues that need correction before the student enters the profession. An approach that uses mental health assessment instrumentation as a means of "screening in" (assessing the student's psychological readiness for admission to the program) rather than merely for screening out students also builds confidence in students as well as a willingness to confront difficult issues in a spirit of growth and change. This is extremely important as defensiveness and nondisclosure doom any helping relationship, whether it be with program faculty or with therapists who are not part of the social work program.

Since 1991, 270 students have gone through the admissions process at the authors' program. Among these, the psychological test results of thirty students raised concern. Five of these students voluntarily left the program after being informed by the program director that unless they pursued counseling, there was no possibility of being admitted to the program. The admission of the other twenty-five students was delayed until after counseling. Twenty-two have been admitted to the program; three others are currently in counseling. An additional twenty-two students presented profiles raising validity questions. Our standard procedure with invalid scores is to have the counselor meet with the student to try to determine a reason for the invalid score (the primary reason is a high level of defensiveness) and then to readminister the MMPI-2. Twenty-one of the twenty-two students who retook the MMPI-2 received valid scores. One student has been involuntarily terminated from the authors' program due to a combination of problematic behaviors and an unwillingness to pursue counseling after an initial assessment with a counselor confirmed the need for counseling.

Choice of Instruments

Since training in psychological testing is typically not included in social work education, most social work educators will have to rely on other professionals, such as psychologists, to make suggestions about appropriate instruments. While this may raise the issue of resource availability, most colleges and universities have counseling centers or other facilities that could provide services *gratis* or for a small fee. Such fees, traditionally charged to the student, could be built into the standard fee structure of the university, in a manner similar to other standard testing and assessment fees.

The social work faculty at Murray State, in conjunction with the staff of the counseling and testing center, considered three widely used instruments as possibilities for obtaining psychological information on candidates for the social work program: the *Minnesota Multiphasic Personality Inventory-2* (MMPI-2), the

California Psychological Inventory, and the *Millon Clinical Multi-axial Inventory-II.* While the MMPI-2 was chosen and is discussed more fully, the other two instruments are discussed only briefly to inform readers of the issues that concerned the program faculty about the two assessments.

The two other instruments considered by Murray State but subsequently rejected are the *California Psychological Inventory* (CPI) and the *Millon Clinical Multiaxial Inventory - II* (MCMI-II). Like the MMPI-2, the CPI is a tool for the assessment of personality. Through a self-report questionnaire, scores on twenty scales representing characteristics of a normal personality can be derived. The scales assess a variety of characteristics, such as socialization, self-impression, and capacity for achievement.

In terms of clinical assessment of psychopathology, the CPI is a derivative of the original MMPI, using 194 items from this other instrument. Bolton (1992) questions the appropriateness of this practice in creating an instrument presumably oriented toward assessment of "normal" personality. Another reviewer (Englehard 1992) submits that the normative basis of the new instrument is seriously flawed, with no presentation of racial, ethnic, economic, social, and geographic representedness of the normative sample. Englehard concludes that the new instrument is an improvement but that the shortcomings of the normative data are a major weakness.

The MCMI-II is a 175-item clinical questionnaire that yields results on twenty-two clinical and three validity scales. It is designed to assess clinical psychopathology and to suggest therapeutic intervention. A review by Haladyna (1992) describes the second edition, last revised in 1987, as the result of continued research and improvement over the first edition, first published in 1976. However, Haladyna criticizes the validity of the current edition, suggesting it is dated, and construct validity is not addressed well in the manual. Other concerns include item overlap between scales and a lack of explanation of the factor analysis upon which the scale identifications are based. Additionally, minorities are underrepresented in the sample (6.9 percent African-American, 4.3 percent Hispanic).

The MCMI-II yields diagnostic information based on the *DSM-III-R* (*Diagnostic and Statistical Manual,* third edition, revised).

This standard reference for the diagnosis of psychological disease has been supplanted by the fourth edition, the *DSM-IV*. Without nonreferral normative data, the usefulness of MCMI-II in a nonclinical population is limited. This factor was a significant contributor to the decision not to use this instrument.

Of the three instruments the MMPI-2 emerged as the most appropriate in terms of underlying constructs as well as in terms of the appropriateness of the interpretive information and normative basis for interpretation as these factors relate to the needs of the authors' program. The other two instruments fell short in both categories relative to the needs of the authors' program.

The *Minnesota Multiphasic Personality Inventory-2* is the result of an extensive renorming and item content analysis of the original MMPI. The family of MMPI instruments is the most widely used psychological assessment device employed by clinicians today (Kramer and Conoley 1992). The original MMPI was published in 1943; the MMPI-2 represents the culmination of a revision process started in 1982 and completed in 1989. An essential goal of the revision process was to insure that the revised instrument's interpretive norms were based upon a demographically representative sample. Reviews in *The Eleventh Mental Measurements Yearbook* (Kramer and Conoley 1992) conclude that this goal was met and that the revised instrument used a norming sample representative of the 1980 census in terms of ethnic, career, gender, and geographic diversity with a slight weighting toward individuals with some amount of coursework at the college or university level. This was deemed to be an adequate sample upon which an instrument used in the assessment of candidates for admission to a social work program could be based. One reviewer concludes that the MMPI-2 incorporates "an appropriate balance between that which required change (norms) and that which required preservation (standard scales)" (Archer 1992). The MMPI-2 offers the clinician a range of clinical information. The interpretation of scores is somewhat dependent upon the demographic characteristics of each candidate. Interpretation also requires knowledge of the interrelations between scales and how various combinations of score values represent specific findings. As mentioned before, specific training in the use of this instrument is necessary for accurate conclusions to be drawn. The standard scales presented on the MMPI-2 include the following (Hathaway and McKinley 1989):

1. Hypochondriasis: High scores may indicate self-centeredness or preoccupation with bodily functions. Classical diagnosis describes individuals presenting somatic complaints with no accompanying pathology;

2. Depression: High scores may indicate symptomatic clinical depression. High scorers present feelings of "discouragement, pessimism, and hopelessness" as well as "hyper-responsibility, high personal standards, and intrapunitiveness";

3. Conversion Hysteria: Loadings on this scale may indicate denial, disorders with no somatic basis, social anxiety, and aggression inhibition;

3. Psychopathic Deviate: Item content reflects absence of acceptance of social and moral norms of conduct;

4. Masculinity-Femininity: In males, may assess stress related to gender role divergence. No similar differentiation for women is suggested;

5. Paranoia: High scorers tend to misrepresent and misinterpret the actions and motives of those around them. High levels of insecurity are also present in many high scorers;

6. Psychasthenia: Significant results on this scale tend to reflect obsessive and compulsive behaviors, as well as neurotic anxiety and fear;

7. Schizophrenia: Item content covers strange beliefs and unusual experiences;

8. Hypomania: Significant results may indicate excessive ambition and extremely high aspirations;

9. Social Introversion: High scores suggest preference for solitary activity; low scores suggest participation as a social person.

The Masculinity-Femininity scale is not used as it is not relevant to the needs of the authors' program. Three additional scales are present to assess the internal validity of the responses of a given candidate.

The instrument requires approximately two hours to administer and another two to three hours per candidate to score and to analyze scores. Automated scoring and interpretive result generation is available. These software programs use computer databases of interpretive information to generate findings. It has been the authors' experience with some of these products that they tend to overdiagnose, that is, produce a significant clinical finding in virtually every profile that is analyzed. Thus, social work programs might wish to rely on local interpretive report generation from the university's counseling center.

Various interpretation guides present caveats for use with various populations based upon experiences unique to those populations. An example would be with regard to young adults in a university environment. While all college students must deal with the pressures of succeeding in or at least surviving in an academic environment, young adults are entering this environment at the same time that they are confronted with the pressures of accomplishing maturational tasks. Therefore, elevations of some scales that in other populations might generate concern, have been found to be of less clinical concern in university student populations and do not indicate problems to the extent that they might in other populations. An example of this may be found in the Hypomania scale. An elevated score may indicate the normal gregariousness and outgoing social behavior that is typical of young people at the traditional college age. A second scale that is interpreted with caution with a college population is the Psychopathic Deviate scale. Elevations may reflect the challenging of authority and identity development typical of many people at the traditional college age rather than pathological problems. This again speaks to the need for using appropriately trained individuals to interpret the results.

Cautions About Using Psychological Assessments

Users of psychological assessment must be aware of the instruments' limitations. As a class, instruments relying on norms can be relatively accurate in identifying cohorts within larger groups that may experience problems related to mental health in practice. However, when attention is focused on a single individual, psychometric issues of error of measurement, sample bias, and other statistical issues must be taken into account in policy formulation that uses instruments for mental health assessment in a gatekeeping process. Some specific cautions should be emphasized.

First, students in social work programs come from diverse family backgrounds. The days are long gone (hopefully) when researchers attempted to identify psychological profiles of abuse victims from the perspective that something in that profile might have "caused" the abuse to occur. In the same light, admissions committees must be aware that a history of abuse causes distortions in perception and response to social stimuli that might be mistaken for underlying psychopathology. Suspiciousness, lack of trust, and inordinate fear may be born out of a terrifying reality rather than being products of psychopathology. It is incumbent on faculty to develop a degree of knowledge of their students' backgrounds so that response to disadvantageous backgrounds can be differentiated from pathology. This is but one example of the care that needs to be taken in distinguishing underlying causes of functional problems.

Second, any normative test by definition cannot reflect all of the cultural nuances of diverse social backgrounds. Some instruments overstate and others understate the level of function and dysfunction in minority groups. It is essential to select instruments with sound norming samples that reflect the larger culture while at the same time exercising caution against forcing all students to conform to a certain normative expectation.

Third, a college or university environment produces, through stress of assessment and other dynamics, its own set of perceptual and behavioral distortions. A sound instrument will, in its documentation, explore the dynamics of these environmental interactions with psychological dimensions.

Finally, testing in itself can distort what is being observed. This may manifest itself in invalid profiles based on analysis of validity scales within the instrument. In these instances, the student is attempting to manipulate the process and in so doing, creates a response pattern on the MMPI-2 that is internally inconsistent. This issue requires attention in that genuineness is a necessary characteristic in the formation of helping relationships. The use of interviews subsequent to assessment can profitably examine the concerns and motivations that might lead to response patterns that result in a student responding, consciously or unconsciously, in a way that creates misleading results. Any assessment tool should have one or more measures of internal consistency as well as representativeness of response patterns to assist program faculty and therapists in judging the validity of a specific set of responses from an applicant.

All these factors point toward a conclusion that psychological assessment is but one tool in the gatekeeping evaluation process. In all cases, assessment results that are in some way unusual should be followed up with interviews with appropriate mental health professionals. It is important to note that psychological assessment done for program gatekeeping functions falls under the stipulations of the federal Family Educational Right to Privacy Act (FERPA), which mandates that adult students have access to their educational records but allows documentation collected solely for treatment purposes to be withheld. This is not the case with assessment data being collected for admissions purposes. Faculty members should be open about results and share all assessment information with the student. Indeed, FERPA requires that student requests for access to academic records, of which this type of psychological assessment is an example, be honored. Faculty should be allowed access to subsequent counseling information only after appropriate waivers of confidentiality have been secured from the student.

The wise faculty also will be cognizant of the variety and diversity of the human experience and, as noted before, not be overly concerned with overemphasis on normative behavior as defined by an assessment instrument. If psychological difficulties are noted in an excessively large number of students (World Health Organization documents suggest that serious mental illness is an issue for no more than 10 percent to 15 percent of a given population at a given time), then the process should be evaluated to determine why an inordinate number of student profiles are being "flagged" as warranting attention.

It is essential to review any assessment element within a gatekeeping process periodically. Program advisory committees can serve as a useful sounding board for policies of this nature. It is extremely important that the faculty communicate with students about the rationale for the assessment. Maintaining some professional distance between faculty and the mental health professionals who interpret the results and provide follow-up services is important. Finally, when students challenge the assessment, their challenges should be met in a forthright and academically honest manner. This may require that some members of the social work faculty become familiar with psychological assessment if none of the department's staff members already have this expertise.

While this familiarity typically will not extend to scoring the instrument or interpreting profiles, social work faculty must understand the strengths and limitations of the assessment instrument as well as the ways in which results should and should not be used. Several discussions with counseling center staff and/or with faculty who have expertise in psychological assessment would be helpful. Similarly, the development of strong working relationships with the counseling center staff can provide a venue in which the students' concerns regarding the assessment process can be addressed.

References

Archer, R. P. (1992). Review of the Minnesota Multiphasic Personality Inventory-2. In J. J. Kramer and J. C. Conoley (eds.), *The eleventh mental measurements yearbook,* pp. 558–561. Lincoln, Nebr.: University of Nebraska Press.

Bolton, B. (1992). Review of the California Psychological Inventory, revised edition. In J. J. Kramer and J. C. Conoley (eds.), *The eleventh mental measurements yearbook,* pp. 138–139. Lincoln, Nebr.: University of Nebraska Press.

Englehard, G. (1992). Review of the California Psychological Inventory, revised edition. In J. J. Kramer and J. C. Conoley (eds.), *The eleventh mental measurements yearbook,* pp. 139–141. Lincoln, Nebr.: University of Nebraska Press.

Gibbs, P. (1994). Screening mechanisms in BSW programs. *Journal of Social Work Education* 30:63–74.

Haladyna, T. M. (1992). Review of the Millon Clinical Multiaxial Inventory-II. In J. J. Kramer and J. C. Conoley (eds.), *The eleventh mental measurements yearbook,* pp. 532–533. Lincoln, Nebr.: University of Nebraska Press.

Hathaway, S. R., and McKinley, J. C. (1989). *Manual for administration and scoring.* Minneapolis, Minn.: University of Minnesota Press.

Kramer, J. J. and Conoley, J. C. (eds.) (1992). *The eleventh mental measurements yearbook.* Lincoln, Nebr.: University of Nebraska Press.

Urwin, C. (1991). Gatekeeping survey of accredited BSW programs. Paper presented at the meeting of the Kentucky Association of Social Work Educators, Pleasant Hill, Ky.

16

Developing a Policy on Sharing Sensitive Information About Students with Field Instructors

Linda Cherrey Reeser and Robert Wertkin

Faculty liaisons and field instructors serve an important function as critical gatekeepers for the profession. Students who do well in the classroom sometimes perform poorly in field placement as a result of unresolved emotional issues, traumas, disabilities, or illnesses. In some instances these issues, problems, and conditions make students unsuitable for working with certain client populations or even for entering the social work profession in general. If relevant personal information about students is kept from field directors, liaisons, or field instructors, inappropriate matches may be made between students and field placements, the student's learning may be adversely affected, and clients may be harmed.

Most schools have no policy for sharing sensitive information about students with field instructors; rather, field directors handle each situation on a case-by-case basis (Alperin 1989). Field directors do not uniformly agree that sensitive information about students should be shared with field instructors (Alperin 1989; Conklin and Borecki 1988; Reeser 1992). The National Association of Social Workers (NASW) *Code of Ethics* (1996) does not

Some of the data reported in this chapter were reported earlier in the following article, used with permission of the publisher: Reeser, L. C., and Wertkin, R. A. (1997). Sharing sensitive student information with field instructors: Responses of students, liaisons, and field instructors. *Journal of Social Work Education* 33:347–362.

provide guidance on this issue because confidentiality is not addressed as it relates to the educational arena. The code neither prioritizes values and ethical principles in a way that would guide social workers through ethical dilemmas nor does it define "compelling professional reasons" for overriding confidentiality (Kermani and Weiss 1989; Moore-Kirkland and Irey 1981; Reamer 1990). In the context of field placements, ethical dilemmas may occur relative to the conflicting interests of students to privacy, of clients to have their welfare protected, and of liaisons and field instructors to have information critical for the learning process and for protection against liability.

Questions of ethics arise if students are assigned to internships and no policies on sharing sensitive information about students with field instructors exist. Making decisions on a case-by-case basis without policies or guidelines might result in inconsistent and inequitable treatment of students and field instructors, with little or no recourse for either. Each of the parties involved must be clear about his or her individual rights; otherwise too much or too little information may be shared, or confidentiality may be violated for noncompelling reasons.

Sharing of information has liability implications. Because of a steady rise in lawsuits against social workers (Besharov and Besharov 1987), information sharing takes on increased significance, all the more so under mounting legal pressures to breach confidences in certain situations (Lindenthal et al. 1988). Social work students, field instructors, and field liaisons are interdependent "on the functioning of each other to achieve success and, thus, create a unique network of collaboration and shared liability" (Zakutansky and Sirles 1993:338). All parties involved may incur unnecessary risks if their interrelationships are not based on accurate knowledge about students and open communication, honesty, respect, and trust (341). Agencies, field instructors, and social work programs share responsibility for the protection of clients and need to do everything possible to ensure such protection, which includes addressing risk factors associated with student interns. A policy and process for sharing information about students must balance the rights of students, faculty, field instructors, and clients (Rosenblum and Raphael 1991).

The primary focus of this chapter is to provide tools for developing a policy on sharing sensitive information about students with field instructors. The first two sections describe a survey of field instructors, liaisons, and students. Findings regarding the type of information that should be shared, who should do the sharing, knowledge about school policies, the information sharing practices between liaison and field instructor, and policy preferences are used as a basis for developing a policy. The third section examines the steps of policy development and approval. The values, moral positions, and special interests of field instructors, faculty liaisons, and students are discussed to enable schools to be responsive to the complexities and the struggles inherent in the development of a policy. In addition, the experience of the School of Social Work at Western Michigan University is discussed. The fourth section presents principles that serve as the building blocks in designing a policy. The next section suggests policy content and implementation issues. Conclusions are drawn about the merits and problems associated with having a written policy advocating the sharing of sensitive information about students with field instructors. At the close of the chapter, documents developed by Western Michigan University's School of Social Work are presented as illustrative policies on information sharing.

Methodology

An exploratory-descriptive research design was utilized to examine the issue of sharing information about students. A survey instrument was distributed to all field instructors supervising students during the 1990–1993 academic years ($N = 573$), the students in field placements ($N = 232$), and the faculty liaisons ($N = 63$) at ten universities in different geographic regions of the country. The sample included BSW, MSW, and combined programs in the Midwest, Northeast, South, and West. The sample was selected based on the willingness of field directors to distribute surveys to their students and liaisons and to provide mailing lists for their field instructors.

Each questionnaire contained items that requested information about current practices regarding sharing sensitive information about students with field instructors, the types of information liaisons should share with field instructors or that students should share about themselves, and perceptions about the types of policies programs should have on sharing information.

Discussion of Findings

The study's findings fell into three major areas: types of information that should be shared, information-sharing practices, and policy and process preferences.

Types of Information

The survey instrument identified twelve types of information that might be shared with field instructors. The three groups of respondents (field instructors, students, liaisons) were asked to indicate whether liaisons should share each of these types of information with field instructors. For example, should the faculty liaison alert a field instructor that a student has been convicted of a crime? Table 16.1 presents responses to these items (in percentages).

Table 16.1

Opinions on Types of Information to Share

Types of Information	% Field Instructors[a]			% Field Liaisons[b]			% Students[c]		
	Yes	No	Maybe	Yes	No	Maybe	Yes	No	Maybe
Inpatient psychiatric	49	18	33	23	34	44	13	57	31
Outpatient psychiatric	31	27	43	13	44	43	8	60	32
Inpatient substance abuse	46	21	33	25	41	34	18	55	27
Outpatient substance abuse	35	26	38	15	46	39	13	55	32
Self-help groups	18	50	32	10	57	34	7	62	31
Family self-help groups	12	60	28	7	61	32	10	62	27
Convicted of crime	49	14	38	11	37	52	16	48	35
Chronic illness	37	27	36	25	39	36	24	49	27
Victim of crime	17	46	37	15	48	38	7	64	29
Disability	45	22	33	39	30	31	28	35	36
Classroom performance	42	25	32	34	20	46	21	46	33
Previous field performance	70	8	22	51	14	36	24	35	40

[a]N = 573
[b]N = 63
[c]N = 232

In general, field instructors had a higher percentage of *yes* responses than liaisons or students, indicating their desire to receive relevant personal information about students. Students had the highest percentage of *no* responses and liaisons the most *maybe* responses. The response differences clearly show how divided these groups are on the types of information that liaisons should share with field instructors and how difficult it is to develop a policy that satisfies all parties.

Response frequencies showed that sharing information about previous field experiences, physical disabilities, and inpatient substance abuse treatment received a higher percentage of *yes* responses compared to all other items rated by each group. The highest percentage of *no* responses for all three groups was for sharing information about individual and family participation in self-help groups and being the victim of a crime. It is important to note that there were substantial differences in the percentage of *yes* and *no* responses across groups.

Students were asked if they would (personally) share each of the twelve types of information about themselves with field instructors. Results are presented in Table 16.2 (in percentages).

Table 16.2

Personal Information Students Would Share with Field Instructors (N = 232)

Types of Personal Information	% Yes	% No	% Maybe
Outpatient psychiatric treatment	18	25	58
Inpatient psychiatric treatment	18	30	52
Outpatient substance abuse treatment	19	30	52
Inpatient substance abuse treatment	19	28	52
Student participation in self-help groups (e.g., AA)	21	27	52
Student's family participation in self-help groups	23	25	53
Convicted of crime other than a traffic violation	12	38	50
Chronic illness (e.g., AIDS, cancer)	29	16	55
Victim of a crime (e.g., rape, domestic assault)	12	26	62
Disability (e.g., dyslexia)	45	10	45
Performance problems in classroom	24	25	51
Performance problems in previous field placement	23	23	54

The most striking finding is the higher percentage of *maybe* responses to all items and a much smaller percentage of *no* responses, compared to the responses to these same items in the first set of questions (when the liaison would share the information with field instructors). The findings suggest that students are more willing to have the information shared if they were the ones who provided the information to field instructors. Perhaps self-determination is the principal value underlying this discrepancy between students' responses to the two sets of items. In two items the percentage of *yes* responses was greater than that of *no* responses: chronic illness and disability. None of the items received *yes* responses by a majority of students. For ten of twelve items, more than 50 percent indicated *maybe*, suggesting that most students might consider sharing this information.

A policy on sharing personal information about students raises legal and ethical questions, and several items explored each group's opinions in these areas. The first of these asked whether personal information abut students must be shared to protect agencies from potential liability risks associated with accepting students and providing services to clients. Two-thirds of field instructors agreed to some extent that the agency's liability is grounds for schools to share information about the students with them. Only 19 percent of liaisons and 28 percent of students agreed.

A second item explored attitudes about lawsuits. Groups were asked if personal information about students should not be shared because of the possibility of lawsuits by students. Of the students, 37 percent agreed, compared to 14 percent of field instructors and 21 percent of liaisons. Thirty-eight percent of the students agreed that they would consider filing a lawsuit against the school if personal information were shared without their permission, and another 23 percent were undecided; 73 percent indicated they would consider filing a grievance against the program if information were shared without their permission.

Is there a belief that sharing information about students without their permission violates the confidentiality clause in the *NASW Code of Ethics*? Seventy-two percent of the field instructors, 73 percent of liaisons, and 90 percent of students agreed to some extent that this would be a violation of the code. With so much agreement, what would compel liaisons to share this information without permission? The answer lies in determining what is the greater good in any given situation, which is the crux of so many complex ethical dilemmas. Sixty-five percent of field instructors, 54 percent of liaisons, and even 40 percent of students agreed that it is more important to protect clients than to hold in confidence personal information about students.

Information-Sharing Practices

In developing a policy about information sharing it is very helpful to assess the respondents' knowledge about any existing formal policy for sharing information and about current practices of information sharing. A key finding was the lack of knowledge among respondents about whether or not their respective programs had a formal policy to guide information sharing. Slightly more than one third of the liaisons, 83 percent of the field instructors, and 74 percent of the students did not know if a formal policy existed in their respective programs. Even in the same program there was considerable variance among respondents. In one program, 30 percent of the field instructors indicated that a formal policy existed while 5 percent said there was none, and 65 percent were not sure. In another program, 31 percent of the students believed there was a policy, 11 percent said there was none, and 58 percent were not sure.

Although liaisons to field placements are usually regular faculty members who should be informed about school policies on sharing information, the findings did not support this assumption. For example, in one program, 7 percent believed a policy existed, 43 percent believed there was none, and 50 percent were not sure. Some variance was found among liaisons in every program surveyed.

Subjects also were asked about informal information-sharing policies. Here, too, considerable variance was found among respondents on whether or not informal policies on sharing information existed—even among respondents from the same program.

In lieu of formal policies to guide practices, decisions are made on a case-by-case basis. Several items queried liaisons about these practices. Liaisons were asked if they share personal information about students without the students' consent. Eighty-three percent of the respondents rarely or never do. A little more than half (54 percent) occasionally encourage students to share pertinent information with field instructors, 36 percent frequently or always do, and only 10 percent rarely or never do. Eighty-two percent stated that the school frequently or always leaves the decision about sharing personal information about students to liaisons; 3 percent said this was rare, and 15 percent did not know. Eighty percent responded that the school occasionally, frequently, or always leaves decisions about sharing personal information to students; however, another 18 percent did not know, and 2 percent said this would be rare.

Of the field instructors, 89 percent rarely or never share personal information about students with liaisons without the students' consent. Forty-two percent occasionally encourage students to share personal information with liaisons, and another 28 percent frequently or always encourage such practices.

About two thirds of student respondents stated that liaisons never or rarely share personal information about students with field instructors without the students' consent. The other third did not know. Seventy-three percent believed their liaison rarely or never encourages them to share personal information with their field instructor. Seventy-eight percent stated that their faculty liaison rarely or never discusses with them what is appropriate to share with field instructors.

Responses by liaisons, field instructors, and students indicated very different perceptions about program policies and practices. Considerable confusion existed about the respective roles of the parties regarding sharing information, the appropriateness of sharing specific information, and the social work program's philosophy and policies on information sharing. The findings show that individual practices of liaisons and field instructors vary considerably. This may be due to the absence of a school policy, the confusion about whether or not a policy is in place, or, in cases where such a policy exists, to the faulty implementation of the policy. These findings support the need for formal policies and methods to assure that all parties know about these policies, understand them, and adhere to them.

Policy and Process Preferences

The opinions of field instructors, liaisons, and students about what type of information-sharing policies schools should have are helpful in developing such policies. Table 16.3 presents the findings on four items that requested these opinions (in percentages).

Table 16.3

Opinions on Information-Sharing Policies

Opinions	% Field Instructors[a]			% Field Liaisons[b]			% Students[c]		
	Yes	No	Maybe	Yes	No	Maybe	Yes	No	Maybe
Share as much information as possible with field instructors	47	42	11	17	75	8	6	83	11
Do not share information with field instructors	12	77	11	20	70	10	50	35	16
Leave decisions about sharing information to the discretion of the liaison	42	47	12	42	47	12	13	79	8
Leave decisions about sharing information to the discretion of students	51	39	10	57	32	12	85	11	4

[a] $N = 573$
[b] $N = 63$
[c] $N = 232$

Should such a policy call for the program to share as much personal information about students as possible with field instructors? Almost one half of the field instructors said *yes*, but 75 percent of the liaisons and 83 percent of the students said *no*. Almost as many field instructors said *no* (42 percent) as said *yes* (47 percent). Conversely, should the policy focus on *not* sharing any personal information about students with field instructors? Seventy-seven percent of the field instructors, 70 percent of the liaisons, and 35 percent of the students said *no*. Findings from these two items suggest that field instructors and liaisons believe that the program should share selected information, but they do not necessarily agree on the nature or kinds of the information. The difficulty in developing a policy that will be acceptable to all parties is evident in the findings that field instructors and liaisons believe a policy should allow information sharing, but many students (50 percent) prefer a policy that would not require the sharing of information.

Field instructors and liaisons were evenly split on whether decisions about sharing information should be left to the discretion of the liaison, whereas 79 percent of the students said *no*. One half of the field instructors, two thirds of the liaisons, and 85 percent of the students believed that decisions about sharing information should be left to the discretion of the student.

Findings from the items in this section further accentuate the serious differences among the parties involved. They also indicate some incongruities among respondents regarding what the best policy might be. For example, 26 percent of the field instructors, 22 percent of the liaisons, and 10 percent of the students who stated the decision should be left to liaisons also said the decision should be at the discretion of the student. It would be difficult to develop a policy that satisfies such conflicting preferences.

Developing a Policy: Process and Issues

The most critical step a program must take in developing a policy for sharing sensitive information about students is to learn about the interests, values, and moral positions of the relevant stakeholders, that is, field instructors, liaisons, and students. This can occur via examining research findings, assessing the roles and responsibilities of all parties, and engaging in a dialogue with field instructors and students. Because the findings of this research indicate clear differences on these issues among students, field instructors, and faculty, it is important to involve representatives from each of these groups in the policy development process in order to ensure that each party's interests will be considered.

This study suggests that field instructors want as much relevant information about students shared with them as possible. Ultimately, they spend more time with the students than faculty, yet they may have less information initially. They believe they should have the same right to information about the students as faculty and that not having the information hurts the students' learning and may harm clients' interests. Field instructors' interests are to avoid lawsuits for harm students may cause, to protect clients, to be rewarded with trust and respect for the time and effort they put into educating students, to have what they need to be successful in educating students and socializing them into the profession, and to have more control over the field placement process (e.g., acceptance or rejection of students).

Faculty liaisons also want an increased amount of relevant information about students shared with them and the field instructors with whom they work. They regard field instructors and the program faculty as critical gatekeepers for the social work profession. Liaisons' interests in obtaining information about students are to achieve success in directing, coordinating, and monitoring the field practicum; to protect students and clients; to teach students to become competent social workers; to socialize students into the profession; and to function effectively as partners with field instructors.

Students take the position that as little information as possible should be shared with field instructors. They want control over what information will be shared. Students' interests in keeping their personal information confidential are to protect their privacy, to succeed in the social work program, to obtain desired internships, to establish good relationships with faculty and field instructors, and to have more control over the field placement process.

One Program's Experience

At the Western Michigan University School of Social Work, a task force was formed to draft a policy on sharing sensitive information about students with field instructors. The task force included the field director, field instructors, liaisons, and students. The values of these groups became evident at the meetings. Field instructors and liaisons believed that the students' self-awareness and self-disclosure are greater goods than privacy. They also believed that the clients' welfare is a greater good than the students' privacy and confidentiality. They chose informed choice for themselves over the students' rights to privacy. They valued empowering students to give permission to share information, but they wanted programs to override students if they refused to share critical information.

Students, on the other hand, started out with the position that they are developing professionals, not clients, and have the right as consumers to keep their personal information private. Although they agreed that the clients' welfare is important, they considered the students' confidentiality and their permission to release information higher priorities. However, after four task force meetings, students agreed that more personal information about students should be shared with field instructors. Dialogue among task force members enabled students to understand the educational benefits of sharing, the liability implications, and the potential harm to clients when information is withheld. Students voiced surprise at what they had discovered by participation on the task force; unfortunately, this subject had not been discussed in their classes.

The moral positions of field instructors and liaisons were closely aligned on this issue because of a belief in the primary importance of protecting the clients' interests. To achieve understanding of and consensus on the issues, all parties must engage in an open, honest dialogue. Field instructors and liaisons clearly have greater power in this situation than the students; thus, the dialogue must empower students so they do not feel invisible or coerced into taking the position of faculty and field instructors.

In sum, the representatives came to agreement about establishing a formal policy so that all stakeholders would know the ground rules, their respective rights and responsibilities, and the consequences for not abiding by the policy. Students were adamant about honoring the value of self-determination and building protections for the students into the policy.

Policy Principles

One principle for developing a policy on sharing personal information about students is to keep a balance between a student's right to privacy and the need of field instructors for information that will enable them to protect clients and to assist students in the learning process. All parties may likely agree to sharing information if the information has a direct impact on the field placement.

Students may be more likely to agree if they are the ones who do the sharing.

Another principle is that the policy should be indeterminate (Flynn 1992); it should not specify issues, conditions, or problems that must be shared but rather should rely on the decision-making process for appropriate outcomes to emerge for individual students. This principle allows for decision making that is specific to the student and situation by focusing on key factors such as the problem's effect on clients, its severity and recency, and the student's capability and progress in working through the issues. Thus, the policy need not set up mutually exclusive and exhaustive categories of information that *must* be shared, because what is relevant may vary. However, some issues, conditions, and problems have primary relevance and always should be shared regardless of the field setting; others have secondary relevance, depending on the setting. For example, a recent felony conviction or a chronic illness may have primary relevance, but an early sexual assault may have secondary relevance unless the placement is in a sexual assault program. It may be helpful for the policy to suggest examples of information that may be shared, depending on the circumstances.

Social work programs may want to request each agency to identify the kind of personal information about students that is relevant to that setting and therefore should be shared. The agency's responses to this request would be given to students, who could then decide whether to apply to certain agencies. Optimally, the policy should empower students to share the information themselves rather than having such information come from a third party.

In the process of developing a formal policy, field directors should consult with university attorneys to be apprised of the legal parameters of the students' privacy. The provisions of both the Federal Privacy Act (1974) and the Americans with Disabilities Act (1990) must be considered. University attorneys may advise sharing as little personal information about students as possible to protect the institution from lawsuits by students. However, another consideration is that potential liability is inherent in the student-client relationship since it is fiduciary in nature. Trust is placed in students to act in the best interest of clients, and students are legally liable in their work with clients.

The doctrine of *respondeat superior*, also known as vicarious liability or imputed negligence, can hold a supervisor legally liable for the actions or omissions of subordinates (Zakutansky and Sirles 1993; Reamer 1989). The doctrine protects clients' rights to receive competent service and the right of supervisees to receive adequate supervision. *Respondeat superior* can be applied to anyone involved in the field placement of a student. Thus, field instructors, faculty, liaisons, and field directors are responsible for preventing harm to clients that may be caused by student interns (Zakutansky and Sirles 1993). Field instructors need to gain accurate knowledge about a student in order to make assessments about that student's appropriateness for particular field placements or social work tasks. Otherwise, everyone involved in field placement may be taking needless risks. The freedom to share information about students must be tempered with protecting the students' privacy and sharing only information relevant for professional purposes (Zakutansky and Sirles 1993).

Policy Content and Implications for Implementation

Policies for sharing personal information about students need to be written in the interests of field instructors, liaisons, field directors, students, and agency clients. The behavior and interests of all these groups, except clients, need to be addressed in the policy to ensure that the policy is adequate in directly impacting the goals of sharing relevant information, protecting students and clients, and enhancing the learning process. Thus, the policy should specify for all parties the responsibilities, rights, and consequences for not adhering to the policy. (For an example, see the Western Michigan University School of Social Work's proposed policy at the end of this chapter.)

The policy needs to address both the formal and informal sources for obtaining personal information about students. It should specify if and how personal information from all potential sources will be used, that is, information obtained from the admissions process, field work applications and interviews, classroom discussions and papers, and informal information that liaisons, field directors, and field instructors may have. A parallel consideration is the need to determine the contexts that require a release of information from students.

To be effective, the policy needs to include a provision that all relevant parties must be informed about and educated on the policy early in the process. For example, students should receive information about the policy in admissions packets, orientations, field applications, and skills labs. Field instructors should be informed via field education manuals and orientations.

Because of poor communication within schools and between schools and agencies regarding sharing information about students, as indicated by this study's findings, policies need to provide guidelines that would increase the permeability of these systems. Guidelines for improving communication channels allow all parties to make decisions and to carry out their functions based on pertinent information about student interns. Informing all parties of their responsibilities also brings more consistency to the process of sharing information. For example, the policy should address the faculty's responsibility for educating students about self-disclosure and the field instructor's responsibility for asking students questions at the initial interview to elicit relevant personal information. Liaisons' and field instructors' responsibilities include informing each other of what students have shared.

The policy needs to identify the hierarchy of power for making the decisions to share information about students and to specify who shares the information. In order to protect a student's right to self-determination, it is recommended that students initially decide whether there is personal information that is relevant to the field practicum. Students should be assisted in this process before they enter the field placement by being educated about appropriate self-disclosure.

The policy also must be guided by information field directors, faculty liaisons, and field instructors consider relevant to the practicum experience. The definition of what constitutes relevant information should be included in the policy, along with examples. In the illustrative policy developed at the Western Michigan University School of Social Work, relevant information is defined as information that has direct impact on the field placement. This includes issues or problems of the student that have an effect on clients, field instructors, or agency staff or would negatively impact that student's learning process.

Having a written policy defining relevancy does not eliminate inconsistencies in its application because individual judgments must be made about whether certain information about a student is relevant and should be shared. Individual judgments based on the conflicting interests and values of the different parties involved may create intra- and intersystem conflicts. To prevent future conflicts, the program should monitor the decisions made about information sharing and the effect of these decisions on students and field agencies. This will enable programs to discern patterns of inconsistent application of the policy. Further discussion could then focus on ways to achieve greater consistency in implementing the policy.

Although it is extremely important that students be empowered via policies for sharing information about themselves, it is necessary for policies to acknowledge the power differential that exists among the parties involved. A policy should indicate who has ultimate power over whether information is shared, keeping in mind the gatekeeping functions social work programs and field instructors perform. Western Michigan's policy gives the school of social work ultimate power over whether information is shared. The field director may decide to override a student's decision not to share personal information or may bar the student from placement if potential harm could result from withholding pertinent information. The field director also has the right to restrict students to certain settings. Faculty liaisons have the right to share relevant information about students obtained from skills labs and field seminars. Students must be informed of the limits of confidentiality in relation to withholding personal information that could cause potential harm.

The field instructors' power also needs to be recognized in the policy. They may be given the power to reject students who choose not to share information, although in their role as gatekeeper for the profession they always have the power to reject students who are inappropriate for the placement. The policy should specify consequences if students hide relevant information from field instructors. One option is to give field instructors the power to dismiss students from the placement if this occurs. This is especially critical if the information withheld causes harmful effects during the placement. In addition, programs may decide, with field instructors' input, that a student's personal issues, problems, or conditions are obstacles to effective social work practice, and at that time the program needs to initiate proceedings to counsel the student out of the program.

The policy needs to provide mechanisms for students to seek redress for unfair treatment that may have occurred as a result of sharing personal information. Examples of possible unfair treatment are the inappropriate sharing or misuse of information, bias against the student as a result of information sharing, and inability to obtain a field placement because of these practices. The Western Michigan School of Social Work's proposed policy suggests establishing a complaint committee, consisting of students, faculty, and field instructors. The committee's charge is to assess the student's allegations or concerns and make recommendations to the appropriate administrative head of the program.

One likely consequence of implementing a policy that encourages sharing of personal information about students with field instructors is bias against a student, who then experiences difficulty in obtaining a field placement. There is a risk of judgmental attitudes on the part of field instructors toward students who decide to share such issues as their HIV diagnosis, mental illness, learning disability, or criminal history. If program faculty decide that a student is suitable for placement, they have an obligation to advocate for that student with agencies who become biased by the information they have received. The program may need to educate the agency about what the student can accomplish with reasonable accommodation, as appropriate. In certain instances, the field director may need to eliminate a field agency or field instructor from the program's approved list because of unaccepting attitudes or behaviors toward students.

Developing a policy for sharing sensitive information with field instructors may seem a daunting task. This chapter's discussion of information sharing provides direction in developing sound policies. To leave the decisions about information sharing to the goodwill of the involved parties is ethically questionable. The existence of a written policy, however, does not eliminate inconsistencies, inequities, and ethical dilemmas. Nonetheless, the policy may serve as a consciousness-raising device and may provide opportunities to monitor decisions and redress grievances. Having a policy that recognizes the right of field instructors to be part of the information loop raises their status in social work programs. It sends a strong message that field instructors have an integral role as educators of students and as gatekeepers for the profession.

Students will likely be very uneasy about or resistive to policies that require them to share personal information with faculty and field instructors. However, having policies that empower students and inform them of the rules, responsibilities, and rights of all parties is preferable to operating in the absence of such policies. One possible adverse effect of the policy is that it may contribute to feelings of low self-worth in the students. Programs need to emphasize that some personal background issues may serve as strengths in field placement rather than present problems. Nevertheless, students who feel they must share personal information that historically resulted in some form of rejection may feel bad about themselves and worry about being stigmatized. These feelings may be exacerbated if they experience another rejection for sharing the information, this time in the form of being denied a field placement. Field directors and liaisons need to assist students in processing their feelings about sharing information and in dealing with the consequences of doing so.

In summary, policy proposals on sharing sensitive information about students need to go through a number of discussions with all relevant parties to enhance the policy's credibility and legitimacy. Feedback should be obtained from the entire faculty, administrative head of the school or program, field director, university lawyers, student organizations, field instructors, and field education advisory committees. Feedback should continue to be solicited after the policy is in force to determine its effectiveness or need for revision.

Western Michigan University School of Social Work's Proposed Policy on Sharing Sensitive Student Information with Field Instructors

Background

Self-awareness leading to effective use of the self is central to good social work practice. By enhancing self-awareness social workers can recognize their behaviors and feelings in interactions with clients, and use this awareness to guide professional responses and decision making. "Only by observing, monitoring, and utilizing their own reactions can social workers construct an objective assessment, develop a helping professional relationship, communicate clearly and directly, and plan an intervention based on client needs" (Bisman 1994:215). Lacking self-awareness, social workers risk employing their power, knowledge, and skills to impose their values, biases, preferences, and needs on clients.

The human problems facing clients are often similar to those that social workers themselves have encountered or currently experience and/or arouse strong feelings within them. Social workers need self-understanding in order to keep their lives and personal issues separate from the lives and concerns of their clients, so that they can intervene in support of the clients' needs and desires rather than advance their own motives and preferences. "Biases and personal feelings are natural responses to clients and their situations; they are a consequence of working with close and intimate matters. . . . Responsible practice involves awareness of their presence and attention to any effects they may have on practice decisions" (Bisman 1994:217).

In an effort to heighten their self-awareness and use of self, students must be able to appropriately self-disclose to the director of field education, faculty liaisons, and field instructors and recognize the need for transmitting sensitive information to them. By acknowledging and discussing any conditions, life circumstances, feelings, and reactions to client situations that impact their practice, students can learn how to utilize this awareness to make disciplined professional decisions that benefit clients. The field practicum is one of the most important avenues in social work programs to evaluate a student's ability to practice.

This policy has not been submitted for approval to the university.

Policy Statement

The school of social work recognizes its responsibility to students, field agencies, clients, and the public to foster the sharing of reasonable and appropriate information about students with field instructors. The school will determine what information will be shared in a dialogue with students. Students will be informed about their responsibility to share pertinent information about their condition or circumstances to enable appropriate field placement, enable informed choice by field instructors, protect clients and the public, protect themselves, and facilitate the learning process. Faculty liaisons may choose to share relevant student information from communications lab and seminars with field instructors. It is expected that field instructors will share relevant student information from the field placement with faculty liaisons. Students are encouraged to be the ones to share pertinent information about themselves. Open and trusting relationships characterized by appropriate information sharing between students, field instructors, faculty liaisons, and field directors are critical to assure continuity and accountability in field education.

The school welcomes the participation of students with disabilities in this information sharing process. The discussion of medical conditions and other circumstances related to disability is encouraged so that reasonable accommodations can be effected. Students, liaisons, and field instructors will be informed about the policy before the placement process begins.

Definition

Relevant information is defined as information having direct impact on field placement. Information is relevant if it may affect clients, the public, field instructors, agency staff, or the learning process.

Procedures

1. The policy will be located in the school bulletin, admissions packet, student handbook, field application, and field education manuals. Students will learn about the policy when they apply to the program. It will be discussed at student orientations and field instructor orientations.

2. Students are expected to sign the policy statement, indicating they have read and understand the policy.

3. Appropriate self-disclosure and possible outcomes of sharing will be discussed with students in communication labs.

4. Field instructors will be encouraged to ask students well-directed questions at the initial placement interview. They will receive suggestions from the school.

5. Field instructors are expected to provide the school with areas in which they consider it necessary for students to share information. Students can then make informed choices about whether or not to apply for placement at particular agencies.

6. Students will prepare a written statement indicating what information may have a direct impact on field placement. This statement becomes part of the field application and is sent to the prospective field instructor. Students may choose to revise their statement after learning more about appropriate self-disclosure in communication lab or if they decide to change their choices for field placement.

7. Students will be given a release of information form to sign after they have been admitted into the program and prior to field placement. The relevant information in their files maintained by the social work department as well as other information relevant to their internship will be shared with the field director, the faculty liaison, and potential field instructors. The information that is requested to be released includes but is not limited to medical conditions and other information that the school believes is relevant to a student's eligibility for and performance during internship. Although the program is committed to respecting the wishes of students regarding the sharing of personal information, there are circumstances that warrant the release of this information without the student's permission. This includes any information that might place the agency and its staff and clients at risk of harm by the student. The university reserves the right to not place the student if in its sole judgment it determines the placement may pose a risk to the student to be assigned, the field agency, the agency's clients, or the general public.

8. Information obtained about students over the course of their stay in the program may be shared with field instructors if it is deemed that withholding it may place the agency and its staff and clients at risk of harm by the student.

9. First-year graduate students will be sent a release of information form when they apply for their second year graduate field placement and will be given the option to decide whether they consent to sharing their first-year graduate field evaluation with their prospective second-year graduate field instructor.

10. If a student is rejected by a field agency on the basis of the personal information he or she has shared, the field director will advocate on the student's behalf or make every effort to obtain another field placement.

11. Students may appeal to the director of the school of social work if they believe their personal information may be or has been misused or not shared appropriately.

12. This policy will be reviewed by the Field Education Advisory Committee after one year and thereafter every two years to make revisions if needed.

Exhibits

1. Student form for sharing sensitive personal information.
2. Examples of relevant student information to be shared.

Student Form for Sharing Sensitive Information

In your field application we have asked you to share your goals and expectations for field placement and your work and volunteer experiences so that we can build on your strengths and assist you in meeting your learning needs. We are now asking you to provide personal information to contribute to our overall picture of who you are so that the school can match you with an appropriate field placement and the field instructor can work with the school to develop an optimal learning experience for you.

Prepare a brief written statement about yourself indicating what personal information may serve as a strength in working in your field internship, may possibly interfere in your learning, or may affect your relationship with clients. Only provide relevant information that may have a direct impact on field placement, that may affect clients, field instructors, agency staff, or the learning process. Is there anything that would hinder you from fulfilling the field education requirements? The following are examples of information that may be relevant to share depending on the type of agency in which you are requesting placement: inpatient psychiatric treatment, outpatient psychiatric treatment, substance abuse treatment, substance abuse problems, conviction of a felony, chronic illness, having been the victim of a crime, and performance problems in class or a previous field placement. Refer also to the examples of relevant student information to be shared found below. Please feel free to share any other personal information that you think is relevant.

Examples of Relevant Student Information to be Shared

This is not an exhaustive list.

1. If you want to be placed in a sexual assault program and you or a member of your family has been raped, you should probably share this information.
2. If you or a member of your family has been hospitalized for a psychiatric illness and you want to be placed in a psychiatric hospital, you should probably share this information.
3. If you have any special needs or limitations that are relevant to participation in field practice, you are invited to share them to enable the agency to make accommodations to these needs whenever possible. Identification of special needs (such as physical, emotional, or learning disabilities) is not required.
4. If you are going through a divorce and you want to do marital therapy or divorce mediation at a family service agency, you should probably share this information.
5. If you or a member of your family received services from child welfare and you want to do your placement in an agency providing child welfare services, you should probably share this information.

References

Alperin, D. E. (1989). Confidentiality and the BSW field work placement process. *Journal of Social Work Education* 25:98–108.

Americans with Disabilities Act of 1990. 42 USCA 12101 *et seq.* (West 1993).

Besharov, D. J., and Besharov, S. H. (1987). Teaching about liability. *Social Work* 32:517–522.

Bisman, C. (1994). *Social work practice: Cases and principles.* Belmont, Ca.: Wadsworth.

Conklin, J., and Borecki, M. (1988). Field education units revisited: A manual for the late 1980s. Paper presented at the 34th Annual Program Meeting of the Council on Social Work Education, Atlanta, Ga.

Federal Privacy Act of 1974. 20 USCA 1232 *et seq.* (West 1990).

Flynn, J. (1992). *Social Agency Policy.* Chicago, Ill.: Nelson-Hall.

Kermani, E. J., and Weiss, B. A. (1989). AIDS and confidentiality: Legal concept and its application in psychotherapy. *American Journal of Psychotherapy* 53:25–31.

Lindenthal, J. J., Jordan, T. J., Lentz, J. D., and Thomas, C. S. (1988). Social workers' management of confidentiality. *Social Work* 33:157–158.

Moore-Kirkland, J., and Irey, K. V. (1981). A reappraisal of confidentiality. *Social Work* 26:319–322.

National Association of Social Workers (NASW). (1996). *NASW code of ethics.* Washington, D.C.: NASW.

Reamer, F. G. (1989). Liability issues in social work supervision. *Social Work* 34:445–448.

Reamer, F. G. (1990). *Ethical Dilemmas in Social Service.* New York: Columbia University Press.

Reeser, L. C. (1992). Students with disabilities in practicum: What is reasonable accommodation? *Journal of Social Work Education* 28:98–109.

Rosenblum, A. F., and Raphael, F. B. (1991). Balancing students' right to privacy with the need for self disclosure in field education. *Journal of Teaching in Social Work* 5:7–20.

Zakutansky, T. J., and Sirles, E. A. (1993). Ethical and legal issues in field education: Shared responsibility and risk. *Journal of Social Work Education* 29:338–347.

17
Portfolio Assessment

Patty Gibbs and Lynn Frantz Adkins

Portfolio assessment is an alternative assessment practice used to document and to evaluate the growth, development, and achievement of students over a period of time (Seely 1994), whether that period is as short as a semester or as extended as the four-year curriculum. If we think of assessment practices as falling along a continuum, portfolio assessment is on the opposite pole from standardized assessment practices. Rather than telling a story of a student's learning over time, as is true in portfolio assessment, standardized assessment provides a single snapshot of a student's knowledge at a particular moment in time (De Fina 1992), with total disregard for the validity, reliability, or representativeness of that single measurement. Standardized assessment makes use of paper and pencil tests that have been devised either by the instructor (e.g., a quiz on a chapter in a textbook) or developed by an outside agency (e.g., state licensure exams). Portfolio assessment, on the other hand, is qualitative and multidimensional, relying on a variety of materials, pieces of work, or types of media as evidence of learning and knowledge. According to Paulson and Paulson (1991), portfolios are

> a purposeful, integrated collection of student work showing student effort, progress, or achievement in one or more areas. The collection is guided by performance standards and includes evidence of students' self-reflection and participation in setting the focus, selecting the contents, and judging merit.

(295)

Despite the rich potential for the use of portfolios in social work education, it seems safe to assume that portfolios are not widely employed, given their absence in reports of gatekeeping mechanisms used by BSW programs (e.g., Gibbs 1994; Wahlberg and Lommen 1990). However, in our view this is a rather glaring omission in the social work educational enterprise. This chapter describes the use of portfolios in social work education as both a method for assessing the students' learning and as a tool for enhancing their learning processes. It explains how portfolios can both increase the students' ownership of their learning and provide data to improve teaching approaches. The chapter also raises questions about current practices in teaching, learning, and assessment and shows the ways in which this qualitative approach to assessment is a more complete and effective approach. It identifies various types of portfolios and establishes the link between the use of portfolios and the program's assessment of outcomes. Finally, the chapter includes a number of practical suggestions directed to faculty members for implementing portfolio assessment.

Assessment and the Nature of Education

The methods used for any kind of assessment reflect assumptions about the nature of learning and the roles of the participants (Courts and McInerney 1993). Testing makes one kind of statement about the nature of the educational enterprise and more qualitative measures like portfolio assessments make a statement that is quite different. Testing reflects an approach to education that Courts and McInerney (1993) identify as the transmission model of education, Freire (1971) called the banking model of education, and Myers (1987, cited in Courts and McInerney 1993) referred to as the "Gas-N-Go" model of education. In all three models the learner is passive in his or her own learning: a vessel to be filled up with the wisdom that pours forth from the learned teacher. Once filled, students regurgitate onto a test what they have learned, and faculty use "objective scales" to put grades on those tests as an indicator of a student's knowledge. But are tests fair and accurate measures of what students know, and, more important, do tests really reflect and assess *learning* at all? Critics of today's educational system say they do not.

Tests (inappropriately) focus on the products or *ends* of learning (what was imprinted on the student's brain) rather than on its *means*. Furthermore, tests attempt to quantify learning rather than facilitate other important aspects of learning, such as its quality and synergy. *Genuine* learning challenges students to think, do, reflect, integrate, and synthesize; that is, students come to know in a more holistic sense. To really learn, students must embark on a journey that develops the thought processes, abilities, and skills that underlie the discipline (Courts and McInerney 1993) rather than collect an odd assortment of facts related to the discipline. On their journey they must be helped to incorporate qualitative, subjective, and interpretive methodologies for understanding their world and their future craft and to arrive at answers not primarily through recall but through a heuristic process that combines the use of insight, personal experience, reasoning, and evaluation. (For a more detailed discussion on alternative ways of knowing, see Schriver 1995.)

Critical thinking is a dynamic process, and the operative word is *process,* not product. Critical or well-reasoned thinking is a form of creation and construction (Gibbs and Gambrill 1996). The ability to engage in critical thinking is essential for helping professionals; otherwise various errors in intervention may occur, for example, focusing on irrelevant factors, viewing behavior as unrelated to its context, selecting inappropriate interventions, withdrawing intervention too soon, and so on (Gibbs and Gambrill 1996:5)

The question arising in this context is how errors in intervention, qualitative approaches to learning, critical thinking, portfolio assessment, and gatekeeping efforts intersect. In order for social work students to become effective practitioners they must possess, for example, a dynamic self-awareness, a commitment to the moral purposes and ethics of the profession, and mastery of well-honed critical-thinking skills. Assessment of these skills and abilities becomes part of gatekeeping efforts, and the use of portfolios is an effective assessment practice.

On a day-to-day basis, social workers find themselves at the front lines of vital decision making across the landscape of practice. If students become practitioners who cannot comprehend the situation in its entirety, do not understand the use of the professional self as an instrument of change, are not committed to the profession's moral purposes, or cannot engage the situation from a variety of perspectives, they will be unable to make informed, reasoned, and appropriate decisions.

Enabling students to make reasoned and sound decisions requires a comprehensive and systematic approach to their education. The learning experience must be holistic, tapping into knowledge and the ways to know, methods and skills and their development, values and their internalization, the helping relationship and the development of the helper's self-awareness, conclusions and the ways in which sound conclusions are reached. In short, the educational experience must provide opportunities for professional growth and development that establish a sound foundation of dynamic proportions on which future learning can be built.

In order to document their growth and development (i.e., their learning) as they proceed through the curriculum, students gather and choose samples of their work to include in the portfolio, examine those samples, reflect on them, revise them, and decide on areas of learning that need further effort. While engaging in portfolio development, students examine their fit with the objectives of the program and the functions of the profession. In short, they engage in the processes of thinking, doing, and reflection that lead to sound critical-thinking abilities and a well-developed sense of professional self. Thus a portfolio is both a tool for documenting and a method for enhancing the learning experience. As part of gatekeeping efforts, portfolios clearly demonstrate the students' mastery (or lack thereof) of the subject matter (knowledge), their acquisition of skills, and their capacity to understand as well as apply professional values to practice.

Types of Portfolios

Once faculty determine the purposes of portfolios in any given course or context, the next step toward implementation is to determine which type of portfolio can best achieve those purposes. The literature identifies many types of portfolios useful in meeting various educational purposes and needs. Courts and McInerney (1993), for example, identify two broad categories of portfolios:

nonselective and selective (98–103). In any given course, nonselective portfolios are used by students to assemble a chronology of all the work they produced in that course, including the assignments and test questions as well as the test answers and all products that respond to the assignments. These all-inclusive portfolios reflect each student's day-to-day performance in the class. A disadvantage of this type of portfolio clearly is its sheer bulk. Selective portfolios, on the other hand, as the name suggests, are a compilation of the student's products that are carefully selected. Selections are made in relation to the purposes of the portfolio. For instance, if portfolios are used as part of admission to the program, students include only the materials that document how the admission criteria are met. On the other hand, a portfolio compiled as a capstone assignment would be more inclusive and reflect the entire educational experience.

Drawing on the work of others, Seely (1994) elaborates four types of portfolios. Two of the most common types are showcase and documentation portfolios. Both are selective portfolios, according to Courts and McInerney's (1993) definition. In showcase portfolios the students, in collaboration with the instructor or advisor, select only their best work to put in the portfolio, and students include written reflections on the reasons for their selection of certain materials or documents over other possibilities. The shortcoming of this type of portfolio is that growth and development are not revealed when only best efforts or products are assembled. Rather, the portfolio reflects what each student is capable of producing (like a test, what *was* learned) instead of how the student went about producing the work (the learning *process*). For admission to the program, however, showcase portfolios might be quite appropriate and would make students feel less threatened than if they were required to include items that showed them in a less than favorable light, from their point of view.

The documentation portfolio shares some of the features of a showcase portfolio but is different because students also include items that document their progress and development. Rough drafts, revised drafts, final papers, works in progress, notes, reflective exercises, brainstorming activities, and the like are appropriate materials to include in the documentation portfolio, for collectively they show the student's progress and growth over a period of time. This type of portfolio reveals the entire journey of the students' learning: where they started, the route(s) they traveled, possibly the rest stops they made, and where their journey has ended for the time being.

Portfolios as a Bridge to Social Work's Lost Art Form

Over the course of its history, social work and social work education increasingly forged an alliance with the scientific model for a variety of reasons too complex to trace in this chapter. (For a discussion of this phenomenon, see Germain 1971; Laird 1993.) The fact remains, however, that both the field of practice and its educational arm have all but abandoned the tradition of social work as an art in favor of the scientific paradigm as a model for framing what social workers do, how they do it, and why they do it. The 1994 version of the *NASW Code of Ethics* (National Association of Social Workers 1994), its revised version (1996), and the past two revised editions of the Council on Social Work Education's (CSWE) accreditation standards (1988, 1994) reflect this long-term trend through increased attention to research. Only rarely do recent texts even allude to the artistic component of social work; a notable exception is Sheafor, Horejsi, and Horejsi (1997).

Early writings on practice and reviews of social work history tie the art of social work to the casework method (e.g., Germain 1971; Ross and Johnson 1950; Strean 1971), which explains why the art of social work is defined in the literature as characterized by humanistic values and the skill in helping (Germain 1971), as skilled use of intuitive, creative, and self-expressive processes (Siporin 1975), as the individual style the social worker brings to bear on the work at hand (Hoffman and Sallee 1994), and as the professional relationship used to effect change (Perlman 1979). Siporin (1975) eloquently elaborates the art of social work and the social worker as an artisan when he describes the dynamic helping relationship through which

> people in need are enabled to realize their capacities, to gain new perspectives and metaphors of reality and truth, to distill complex understandings, to evolve coherent meaning and pattern about them-

selves and their life situation, to achieve balance and harmony of conflicting elements within themselves and between themselves and others. As in other creative endeavors, the social worker tries . . . to enlarge consciousness and self-awareness . . . to [provide] a way of encounter, exploration, and growth in the realms of human spirit and relationship on their deepest levels of meaning and experience.

(53)

Sheafor, Horejsi, and Horejsi (1997) suggest that the art of social work has the following components: "the compassion and courage to confront human suffering; the capacity to build a meaningful and productive helping relationship; the creativity to overcome barriers to change; the ability to infuse the change process with hopefulness and energy; the exercise of sound judgment; the appropriate personal values; and the formation of an effective professional style" (36). Similarly, Weick (1993) ties the nature of social work as an art to its value orientation and therefore holds that preparation for practice must be art-sensitive, regardless of how this may threaten the scientific basis upon which the profession has been so carefully based. Weick's use of analogy in describing the educational preparation for social work as an art provides a lens that brings into sharper focus this often neglected aspect of social work education.

Just as with other art forms, students study about and with other artists. They study painting or music or dance as it has evolved over time. They learn to critically assess works of art. They learn techniques of the art and they practice those techniques until they are no longer conscious of applying them. What they produce is subject to others' comments and views. But through all of this, it is recognized that the performance or product is a creative act which happens in a never-to-be duplicated moment. It is guided by an amalgamation of intentions, knowledge, and experience whose boundaries are lost in the act of doing. Social work, as with other art, is holistic by nature.

(28)

Despite the majority of contemporary arguments to inform practice by way of more scientific rigor, that is, via social work's scientific paradigm, discarding the art of social work is to throw out the baby with the bathwater. At this point in our evolution, it seems counterproductive to continue such binary thinking by continuing to reinforce the notion of an either-or dichotomy—"we must be scientific, and therefore there is no art to social work"—as a good deal of the current literature, the code of ethics, and accreditation standards suggest. Instead, the two components must be reunited to imbue social work with the holism it seems to falsely claim at present.

Portfolios allow faculty not only to resurrect the art of social work but also to gain evidence of its existence in students' learning. When students document the development of their professional selves, they are tapping into the art of social work. When they demonstrate their interactional skills in relationship building, they are entering the realm of art. When they show how they have internalized the profession's ethical canon and wed it to their methods of intervention, they have developed a practice repertoire that transcends the laws of science and emerges in the dimension of art. The creativity they demonstrate, the open-mindedness they develop, the self-awareness they cultivate, and the ethic of caring to which they subscribe are all more closely linked with the art of social work than with its science. The use of portfolios opens up to students this important dimension of social work by allowing them opportunities to engage the learning experience in its totality and to explore and document their learning processes as a synergistic and dynamic whole.

Portfolios: Their Value and Purposes

Before plunging headlong into adoption of portfolio assessment, faculty need to make decisions about why and how portfolios will be used. Although portfolios certainly demonstrate an individual student's learning and development, faculty need to consider other purposes as well because the specific purposes will guide all aspects of how portfolios are implemented in the program.

Throughout their excellent book on assessment in higher education, Courts and McInerney (1993) make a strong case for the purposes of and need for this qualitative assessment tool at all levels of education. They contend that education in general and assessment in particular must become more learner-centered, something current educational practices seldom allow. Fiscal realities have resulted in larger classes, usually large lecture sections, although smaller classes, more writing, and more individual attention to students are needed to improve the learning experience. Courts and McInerney elaborate on how education inappropriately relies on standardized testing, which assesses "a student's ability to take a given exam and little more" (21). Out of their experience with implementing portfolios in their own institution, they provide a broad overview of some of the uses of portfolios:

> to help the learners become integral and conscious participants in their learning processes, by having them recognize both individual responsibility and ownership within that process, and by having them become interactive partners with the teacher in shaping the learning process. Likewise, portfolios provide teachers with the possibility of examining the learning process (and performance outcomes) from the point of view of the learner (what is actually occurring) rather than from some distanced point of view that is reflected in course objectives and syllabi (what is supposed to occur or what we sometimes pretend is actually occurring).
>
> *(85–86)*

One of the advantages of portfolios is that they give students expanded opportunities to demonstrate their learning as well as their achievement of the program's objectives, which other assessment approaches do not provide. An example from Bethany College, which has used portfolio assessment for many years, illustrates this point. After a student turned in her paper on intergenerational day care and received her grade, she made arrangements to visit a company that had such a day care center in order to further increase her understanding of this program's benefits. The experience of seeing the concept in action and talking with people who were involved in the day care center's operation was a valuable source of learning for the student. Through her portfolio, she was able to document her additional learning experience and reflect on its value. Without the portfolio as a vehicle to document her later experience, the term paper itself would have been the only evidence of what she had learned about her topic, and that single bit of evidence painted an incomplete portrait because her learning extended beyond her library research efforts and the graded outcome of those efforts.

Portfolios also are valuable because they allow for both ongoing and cumulative assessment of students, and the work generated is often more creative and therefore more interesting to assess. Because of the nature of portfolios, students tend to work together on projects to a greater extent, and consequently they are less competitive in their efforts.

Value to Students

Portfolios are a valuable method of assessment because they include students in the conversation about their learning in a way that helps them "to better examine what they are learning, how they believe they learn, and what components of the educational system assist or prevent them in coming to know" (Courts and McInerney 1993:27). Through portfolios students become collaborators in their learning. In the process of developing, modifying, and updating their portfolios, students gain insight into the paths of their learning, what they have accomplished and how well they have accomplished it, whether or not they are meeting the requirements of the course or the program, which areas are strengths and which areas need further effort, and what gaps in their learning remain to be addressed. Through self-assessment and corrective action, students become fully engaged partners in their learning experience.

Students also can reflect appropriate extracurricular activities in their portfolios to demonstrate additional learning experiences that are pertinent. Many students belong to service fraternities and sororities that complement and extend the kinds of learning that occur as part of the social work curriculum. As leaders in these organizations, they develop leadership skills they may not have an opportunity to demonstrate in any other context within the program but which are nonetheless important skills that will serve them well when they enter the practice arena. Without portfolios these additional learning opportunities generally remain unknown to faculty and consequently go unrecognized. The portfolio allows students to claim those experiences as appropriate components of their growth and development in achieving a more complete sense of a "professional self."

Portfolios provide students with an opportunity to both document and reflect on all aspects of their learning. Opportunities for reflection sharpen critical- thinking skills and facilitate integration of the curriculum. Students become empowered to become the more appropriate masters of their own educational experience, which shifts ownership of the students' learning away from faculty and onto students (Winograd, Paris, and Bridge 1991). In the course of developing their portfolios, students gain a better sense of how learning is a process "rather than a compilation of decontextualized, isolated products" (Seely 1994). One student, quoted in Courts and McInerney (1993), incisively gives voice to this sense of "disjointedness" in the curriculum.

> I believe that what we term learning is not learning at all. Learning is a process that involves relationships between facts. Most learning, or what we call learning is the memorization of disjointed facts. In real life we see and feel the flow of how things go together. In the class that flow is disrupted and made disjointed. Most of the school structuring I find useless. Most courses teach facts and don't stress putting the facts together. Most courses teach in hunks and sections. The flow of ideas from one section to another is lost or loose. The problem most students have with courses is not the content but trying to understand why they are getting all those disjointed facts. I don't know a better way, but there has to be one.
>
> *(97)*

Students' engagement in portfolio development guides both faculty and students to grapple more effectively with the critical issues expressed in these comments.

While the process of developing portfolios is beneficial to students, the value of the final product cannot be overlooked. When their portfolio is complete, students have comprehensive documentation of their abilities that can be used in discussions with potential employers. Because portfolios represent a complete collection of the processes and products involved in the students' learning process (Jongsma 1989:264), when applying for jobs for admission to graduate programs, students can use concrete examples from their portfolios to discuss their strengths, abilities, and learnings with prospective employers and admissions officers (Courts and McInerney 1993). During job interviews students can bring the portfolio for review by prospective employers who can then gain a more holistic view of the job applicant.

At Bethany College, where portfolios are used in most courses, students prepare a summary portfolio at the conclusion of the educational experience for use during job interviews to document their competence and capability. Appropriate items for inclusion in these summary portfolios are case studies, agency studies, research projects, evidence of work with special populations, field work examples, process recordings of interviews, term papers and other assignments, or evidence of special experiences that document the totality of the student's learning.

In short, as both process and product, portfolios are an invaluable tool for students' learning and, furthermore, portfolios encourage a strengths perspective rather than a deficit-oriented approach to gatekeeping efforts across the curriculum because they allow students to revise, improve, and add to their work materials in order to more fully document their learning.

Value to Faculty and the Program

Because portfolios are a canvas on which a more complete picture of a student's learning is painted, faculty have a rich source of information that is helpful to them in many ways. On the more practical side, faculty have a more holistic sense of individual students' activities, projects, special efforts, skills, accomplishments, abilities, and areas in need of improvement. Consequently, faculty are able to write reference letters that better capture the unique qualities and strengths of each student, and they can more easily identify specific areas that need continued development or refinement. In reference letters, faculty can provide concrete examples drawn from portfolio documentation to support their recommendations for employment or for graduate school admission. In gatekeeping efforts, those same concrete examples show how students have met or not met the gatekeeping criteria or the program's standards.

Collectively, student portfolios clearly indicate the strengths and weaknesses of the curriculum. Furthermore, armed with this information, faculty can make informed instruction and program decisions as part of their assessment of outcomes. The quick, easy, and overly simplistic senior surveys currently employed by many BSW programs to assess program outcomes tend to rely on more quantitative measures and will pale by comparison to the rich information contained in the student portfolio, a more qualitative measure.

The use of portfolios not only aids faculty in determining if they are achieving their objectives by assessing outcomes "at the back end of the program," but also facilitates better front-end decisions when reframing their program and course objectives. In making use of portfolio information to reframe program and course objectives, faculty can escape the trap of identifying discrete, fragmented skills or chunks of knowledge merely because they are easiest to assess (Courts and McInerney 1993:xv). Just as individual students are aided in seeing their learning as a more comprehensive and integrated experience, so too faculty are able to see the learning opportunities across the curriculum as a more integrated whole. Portfolios make apparent the program's coherence, strengths, weaknesses, and gaps.

Finally, another value of portfolios to faculty should not be overlooked. In significant ways, portfolios take the pressure off faculty during gatekeeping efforts. Through portfolios, students clearly establish that they have met the objectives and criteria—both scholastic and professional—or have not met them. The documentation is either there or it isn't. No more guessing. No more hedging. No more wondering. Faculty will worry less about whether or not judgments regarding students' professional capacities are too subjective and impressionistic. Well-designed assignments allow students to demonstrate their abilities—if not on the first attempt, then during subsequent efforts, which is part of the beauty of portfolio use. In an ideal world all students can rise to the occasion or can be provided with sufficient supports for achieving success. However, for most social work educators, the ideal world exists on a fault line, and occasionally it shudders and collapses. Some students, for whatever reasons, will not be successful, and portfolios unveil in a pronounced way the areas of unsatisfactory performance.

Possible Uses in BSW Programs

With the more global purposes and functions of portfolios in mind, how can portfolios be employed advantageously in undergraduate social work programs? Many possibilities come to mind, such as

- for students to document their achievement of admission criteria;
- for students to document progression of cognitive and skill acquisition and achievement (within a course or content area, in the field practicum, or across the curriculum);

- for students to document development of "a professional self";
- for faculty to determine if their teaching assignments are appropriate;
- for faculty to incorporate the students' self-assessment into the educational experience;
- for students to explore and show mastery of the art of social work;
- for students to demonstrate integration of knowledge within a course, among CSWE's nine content areas (CSWE 1994:100–104), and/or across the curriculum;
- for faculty to inform instructional and curricular decisions, as part of outcome assessment;
- for students to demonstrate their mastery of the generalist perspective;
- for students to develop and fine-tune their abilities to think critically;
- for students to use as an expanded résumé when they seek employment opportunities or admission to graduate programs;
- as a tool to help students recognize that learning is a cumulative process that does not end with their degree but continues following graduation;
- as a curricular strategy to facilitate students' ownership of and creative participation in their learning;
- as a vehicle to give students a voice in their own learning as well as in the assessment practices of the program;
- as part of a capstone activity for students to document the fulfillment of their learning contracts and the program's objectives while in the field practicum.

The agreed-upon purposes of portfolios determine the people who will be involved in or contribute to portfolio implementation and the factors that will influence and define the use of portfolios. These sources of input include students, faculty, field instructors, the program's goals and objectives, institutional requirements, and CSWE's accreditation standards. If portfolios are used in conjunction with the field practicum, for example, field instructors will be involved in the development of the students' portfolios. If they are used to document program outcomes, their substance will be influenced by CSWE's accreditation standards.

Student Assessment and Educational Outcomes: The Tie That Binds

Although assessment of student learning is not new to social work education, it has gained increased significance over the years. Early accreditation standards seemed to focus more on what the *curriculum provided*; however, current standards emphasize what the *student learned* in the course of completing the curriculum. Keeping in mind this shift in emphasis, it is clear that the assessment of students and the assessment of program outcomes are not mutually exclusive categories of evaluation in the BSW educational enterprise. Through program assessment faculty must show how the program is achieving the twelve educational outcomes established by CSWE (1994:99), and one way to show that the outcomes are being achieved is by gathering information on what

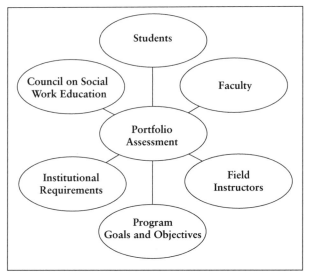

Figure 17-1 Sources of Input Into Portfolios

students learn as they proceed through the curriculum. Thus, evaluation of student learning, that is, their level of competence when they complete their degree, is the smaller unit of assessment embedded in its broader programmatic context.

According to CSWE's Evaluative Standard 1.4, programs "must specify the outcome measures and measurement procedures that are . . . used systematically in evaluating the program, and that will enable it to determine its success in achieving its desired objectives" (CSWE 1994:80). The interpretive guideline for this standard identifies student work products and student self-reports as examples of measures that may be used to document the achievement of outcomes. Portfolios include, among other possible items, student work products and self-reports, the latter of which are often referred to as reflective statements (see, for example, Seely 1994). When used in conjunction with other evaluative methods, portfolios are a valuable tool for demonstrating a program's achievement of the twelve BSW educational outcomes advanced by CSWE.

Helping Students Determine How It Is Conceived and What Evidence Is Included

Some general guidelines faculty may give students are:

- to use a large, loose-leaf notebook with dividers or folders to organize the contents of the portfolio;
- to include a table of contents;
- to number and date the different items in the portfolio;
- to use "sticky notes" on items to label, caption, comment, clarify, or reflect on items in the portfolio;
- to include a checklist of items that are required components of the portfolio.

Portfolios do not need to be paper products. The use of electronic portfolios is an attractive option because it allows students to gain experience with technology and to easily include evidence, such as videos of role plays and actual client interviews, that is more difficult to include in hard-copy portfolios. In some colleges

and universities students not only are submitting materials electronically but also are beginning to cut their own CD-ROMs. At
the conclusion of the educational experience, for example, a student could cut a CD-ROM that documents every aspect of learning during the formal educational process and that could be
updated following graduation to show continued acquisition of
knowledge and skill.

The use of electronic portfolios presents its own special challenges that are helpful to consider ahead of time. Time is needed
to create a program for setting up files as well as to get students
up to speed technologically. Lab time must be available, and
computer-phobic students may require additional attention.
Despite these challenges, the benefits are many. For example,
because students are not shuffling a sheaf of papers, they get less
caught up in how many pages are required. Through the use of
scheduled lab time, work is more up to date. Finally, feedback can
be given to the student more rapidly.

The following is a list of possible items that might be included
in a portfolio, either as a requirement by faculty or at the student's
choice.

- An initial written assignment that can be used to set a baseline
- Paper drafts, revised drafts, completed and graded written
  assignments
- Annotated bibliographies
- Critiques of articles in the literature
- Self-evaluations
- Reflective papers on how a given entry in the portfolio did or
  did not function to enhance the student's growth and learning
- Worst and best test, as well as a reflective paper that discusses
  these items
- Worst and best written assignment with a reflective paper
- Pictures: of agency, of student at work in field setting, of vol-
  unteer work, etc.
- Drawings, diagrams, charts, and the like that support, illus-
  trate, or clarify written work
- An exit paper

To illustrate the use of portfolios in a social work course, a copy of a policy course syllabus is included in appendix 12. In this course, students are expected to gain knowledge of policy assessment and of how social welfare programs impact clients at the micro, mezzo, and macro levels. Portfolios as used in the class allow students to produce evidence relative to both the art and the science of social work practice.

Assessing Student Portfolios

There are as many ways to evaluate portfolios as there are kinds of portfolios and purposes for their use. Some educators contend that portfolios should not be graded—or at least not graded according to traditional grading practices (e.g., Courts and McInerney 1993; Williams 1997). Instead of assigning letter grades, faculty may evaluate portfolios as excellent, satisfactory, or unsatisfactory (or use the less threatening categories of check plus, check, and check minus). Other educators use a numerical equivalent of these categories (e.g., 2 = excellent, 1 = satisfactory, 0 = unsatisfactory). Additional assessment approaches include grading individual products within the portfolio but not assigning a letter grade to the portfolio as a whole or using checklists that assign each criteria or learning objective a certain range of points. Cooper (1977) refers to this latter assessment method as analytic holistic scoring, and we have included a sample grading checklist for assessing portfolios that can be modified as needed.

Sample Grading Checklist

1. All required components of the portfolio are included.

   0 = Several of the components are missing.

   1 = A few of the components are missing.

   2 = All of the components are included.

2. Portfolio is well conceived and well organized.

   0 = Student does not seem to understand how to document learning, and/or the portfolio is disorganized and carelessly assembled.

---

1 = Documentation of the learning process is inconsistent, and/or portfolio is only fairly organized.

2 = Student demonstrates a good understanding of his/her development in meeting the objectives, and the portfolio is a well-organized expression of that understanding.

3. Student demonstrates learning in creative ways.

0 = No creativity demonstrated.

1 = Some creativity demonstrated.

2 = Creativity is demonstrated throughout the portfolio.

4. Student demonstrates integration of knowledge.

0 = Little evidence that student can draw on knowledge from other courses.

1 = Limited application of knowledge from other courses.

2 = Satisfactory application of knowledge from other courses.

3 = Student draws on knowledge, theory, and concepts that span the curriculum.

5. Student has met the first objective (second, third, and so on).

0 = Objective is not met.

1 = Objective is only partially met, and more work is needed in this area.

2 = Objective is fully met.

3 = Student shows exceptional ability in this area.

Total points   ____

Total possible points   ____

Percentage score   ____

Grade   ____

The method of grading portfolios through a grading checklist is also known as a rubric system. Rubric systems provide a scale of verbal descriptions for determining the level at which each criterion, objective, or learning goal is met (Jasmine 1993). The sample field evaluation instrument found in appendix 9 and the sample grade sheet for a written assignment in appendix 10 are other examples of rubric systems. Seely (1994) suggests that faculty collaboratively develop such rubrics with their students so students better understand and are more committed to the assessment process. The process of involving students in designing the evaluative tools for assessing portfolios not only demystifies the evaluation process and helps students to internalize the standards but also allows students to judge for themselves the quality of their work (Brown 1989).

Involving students in the development of rubric systems is not only helpful to them in understanding what is expected but may also save the faculty time later when they evaluate the portfolios. It is sometimes amazing how astute students are about standards and criteria, who is meeting them and who is not, and to what degree those who meet them are doing so. Harnessing that insight and making use of it by enlisting the students' help in developing the criteria and task rubrics that will be used to evaluate the portfolios will be helpful to faculty.

Not all methods of evaluating portfolios involve complex grading constructs. To begin evaluating portfolios, Friedlander (1997) devised a simplistic grading system that may provide some helpful hints for first-time users. Faculty may already use variations of this approach when evaluating complex assignments. To begin with, Friedlander sorted portfolios into three piles: outstanding, pretty good, and "ugh." Then he sorted them again within each category, starting with the best and working from there. Depending on where individual portfolios ranked within each category, A and B grades were assigned to those in the "outstanding" category, B and C grades went to those in the "pretty good" category, and D and F grades went to those in the "ugh" category.

J. Ott (cited in Friedlander 1997) also devised a simplistic system for evaluating portfolios. The highest grade, "superior," was assigned to complete work that went beyond the requirements. Proceeding along a continuum, "satisfactory with minor flaws" was given to complete work with some errors; "nearly satisfactory with serious flaws" was assigned to almost complete work, and "unsatisfactory" was given to work that was unacceptable.

Although views on the evaluative scales or tools employed to assess portfolios vary, educators are in agreement about other aspects of portfolio assessment. First, faculty should meet periodically with individual students to discuss the portfolio, its development, its contents, and the student's learning process. In larger classes, faculty may wish to meet with small groups instead, taking care to constitute groups that would facilitate individual participation. These discussions are centered on the learner, exploring with the learner what is being learned, what learning experiences are valued, and why those particular learning experiences are valued (Courts and McInerney 1993). These discussions are often more fruitful and take different paths than either faculty or students might anticipate beforehand, as the example of Marilyn K. shows.

Marilyn K. Illustration

While discussing Marilyn K.'s portfolio entries with her, her critique of a particularly successful paper she had written led to a discussion of what she perceived to be seriously different, though personally confusing, contradictions she experienced when writing for professors in the hard sciences and social sciences versus the humanities (especially English). Using this particular paper on the economic issues surrounding the institution of slavery in the United States, and comparing this paper with another she had written as a subjective response to *The Scarlet Letter*, she pointed out that her use of the first-person pronoun *I* was encouraged in the response paper and frowned upon in the research paper on slavery. This in turn led us into a discussion of point of view and caused us to examine this question: To what extent does the embracing of a third-person point of view lead to a more "objective" discussion of a topic. Her point—quite legitimate and insightful, I think—was that the use of the third-person pronouns created the "appearance" of objectivity but in many ways was less honest than the use of the first-person pronoun. She also revealed that she had been told by the history professor that she "wrote too much like an English major," which was considered "inappropriate" in the social sciences. When asked what this meant to her, she said that the history teacher was bothered by what he called "flowery" writing. And though she was still not sure what he meant by this because he had not been able to present her with a clear explanation, Marilyn suspected that he was bothered by her use of extended metaphors and analogies based in her own personal experience that she used to identify with some of the issues she was exploring in the paper.

Source: P. L. Courts and K. H. McInerney. (1993). Assessment in higher education: Politics, pedagogy, and portfolios, pp. 92–93. Westport, Conn.: Praeger.

Educators also tend to agree that feedback to students involves more than assigning a grade, regardless of what kind of grading system is used. Students must understand the reasoning behind the grade if learning is to be advanced. Such understanding is facilitated in several ways. The students' involvement in setting portfolio purposes and establishing assessment criteria at the outset helps them, in part, to better understand how and why their work is later evaluated at a certain level. As already noted, assessment conferences with students are a critical element in the assessment process, and these conferences increase the students' understanding of their level of performance. The conferences are invaluable because students have opportunities to reflect on their work and discuss it in light of the criteria, and faculty have opportunities to provide suggestions that can lead to improved performance and increased learning.

Another general area of agreement is in the value of peer evaluators or peer editors. Students can be a support system for each other and can critique one another's work. It does not take a teacher to look at pieces of work and see if they are good or if they fall short of the mark. Students can provide this kind of feedback to each other. Of course, students will need some preparation to engage effectively in this role.

Finally, another area of agreement on evaluation of portfolios involves the view that analyzing performance patterns over a period of time is the most accurate reflection of a student's learning. As is true of individual tests, no single piece of work included in the portfolio provides conclusive evidence of a student's strengths or weaknesses (De Fina 1992), but the entire collection of work assembled over a period of time offers substantial evidence of what individual students have learned, the ways they learn best, and their ability to process and integrate knowledge.

Management Issues: From the Ideal to the Realistic

It is one thing to see the value of portfolios as an educational tool; it is quite another to implement portfolios in the curriculum. One of the major constraints is that they are a time-intensive responsibility. Given faculty workloads, this is not an insignificant issue and requires careful thought. To implement portfolios, determine what is manageable and gauge your plans accordingly. Modify some of the tools provided in the appendix section of this book to make your job easier. Checklists with good descriptors give students as much information as lengthy written notes. If you capture the most common kinds of feedback you typically provide on any given assignment and incorporate these comments into a checklist, you will save yourself a tremendous amount of time in the long run. You may still write additional, individualized comments, but at least you will have the basics in the form of a checklist.

Devote some class time as work periods for students to bring in their materials and organize their portfolios. Sit down and talk with as many students as possible during this period to begin getting a sense of their growth, their strengths, and the areas that need further effort. Ask questions about the learning objectives and how they are achieving them. Ask about how their volunteer activity or field placement helps them meet the objectives. Have them explain how their learning in your class fits with other classes they are taking or have taken already and how they are reflecting those connections in their portfolios. Find out what they think is important to know in order to become an effective social worker. These kinds of exchanges will give you food for thought and provide your students with a less threatening "practice session" that should better prepare them for individual conferences with you. Just as they will be more prepared for those conferences, so will you. In addition to moving around the classroom during these work periods, you might decide to use a portion of the time for conferences with individual students.

You also might assign or let students choose partners who will serve as peer evaluators or peer editors. Be open to experimenting.

Your ideas may not always work when trying new approaches, but remember—they do not always work when you engage in traditional approaches either.

You are probably not the only one to have concerns about the time and energy needed to undertake a portfolio approach to assessment. Students will have concerns too. Allow them to voice those concerns and be responsive to the concerns as you negotiate the expectations. For your and your students' sake, keep it as simple and manageable as possible. Help students to understand that they should not throw everything in the world into their portfolios as if they were about to embark on a paper recycling mission! Many students still adhere to the fiction that more is better: the thicker the papers, the better the grade. Help to dispel that notion by providing the scaffolding that gives insight into the link between various forms of evidence and achievement of the learning goals or objectives.

Portfolios are not magical. They are not a panacea for all of the ills of education. But they are effective in helping students to think about and reflect on their learning. Through the use of portfolios faculty can form a collaborative learning environment to which students may be more responsive. Faculty get a better picture of how students learn, which assignments are helpful and which are not, and what needs to be done in order to facilitate learning in certain areas or to ensure integration of the curriculum threads. This picture allows faculty to make adjustments in their teaching approaches to effect learning in a more holistic sense.

Initially many faculty may view portfolios as a new concept, but it is probably a concept that is only new to their teaching and not to their lives in higher education. Faculty have undoubtedly put together their own professional portfolio for use during annual review of their performance, for promotion and tenure review, or for merit increases. The same principles are at work when faculty develop their own portfolios for personnel review periods as when portfolios are used with students.

At most institutions, faculty assemble materials that demonstrate their abilities, achievements, and effectiveness in teaching, research, and service. In assembling their materials, they make careful choices about what to include in their individual portfolio and why each item is an important piece of evidence. They probably use sticky notes or some other method to comment on and clarify the items they include in the portfolio. To better make their case on how they are meeting the institution's requirements, they probably include a section of narrative reflections, explanations, interpretations, and evaluative comments that will enable reviewers to see exactly how the requirements have been met. To present a positive and clear statement of abilities, faculty make sure the portfolio is well organized. They include a table of contents, numbered pages, and dated entries. Thinking about how portfolios are developed for one's own professional purposes may be a good beginning for thinking about how to engage students in using them for their learning and reflection.

Portfolio use is not a new idea; it is only somewhat new in the educational arena—in particular in certain disciplines in higher education. Professionals have used portfolios for many years as a centerpiece in discussions with prospective employers and customers. Photographers and other artists use them to showcase their work. Designers assemble sketches of their ideas, complete with fabric swatches, to demonstrate their talent and creativity. Journalists collect samples of their various publications to show their growth and the diversity of their abilities. Through a process of self-evaluation during the development of their portfolios, these professionals "come to know what is their best work and what is most valued by the experts in their fields" (De Fina 1992). Social work students can embark on this same journey of learning and documenting and of learning *through* documenting while they assemble the materials that best demonstrate their own growth and development as future professionals.

References

Brown, R. (1989). Testing and thoughtfulness. *Educational leadership* 46:31–33.

Cooper, C. R. (1977). Holistic evaluation of writing. In C. R. Cooper and L. Odell (eds.), *Evaluating writing: Describing, measuring, judging*, pp. 3–31. Urbana, Ill.: National Council of Teachers of English.

Council on Social Work Education (CSWE), Commission on Accreditation. (1988). *Handbook of accreditation standards and procedures*. 3d ed. Alexandria, Va.: CSWE.

Council on Social Work Education (CSWE), Commission on Accreditation. (1994). *Handbook of accreditation standards and procedures.* 4th ed. Alexandria, Va.: CSWE.

Courts, P. L., and McInerney, K. H. (1993). *Assessment in higher education: Politics, pedagogy, and portfolios.* Westport, Conn.: Praeger.

De Fina, A. A. (1992). *Portfolio assessment: Getting started.* New York: Scholastic Professional Books.

Flood, J., and Lapp, D. (1989). Reporting reading progress: A comparison portfolio for parents. *The Reading Teacher* 42:508–514.

Freire, P. (1971). *Pedagogy of the oppressed.* New York: Seaview.

Friedlander, S. (1997). Lessons of secondary-school experience. In J. Barton and A. Collins (eds.), *Portfolio assessment: A handbook for educators*, pp. 61–68. Menlo Park, Ca.: Addison-Wesley.

Germain, C. B. (1971). Casework and science: A study in the sociology of knowledge. Ph.D. diss., Columbia University, Ann Arbor, Mich.

Gibbs, L., and Gambrill, E. (1996). *Critical thinking for social workers: A workbook.* Thousand Oaks, Ca.: Pine Forge Press.

Gibbs, P. (1994). Screening mechanisms in BSW programs. *Journal of Social Work Education* 30:63–74.

Hoffman, K. S., and Sallee, A. L. (1994). *Social work practice: Bridges to change.* Boston: Allyn and Bacon.

Jasmine, J. (1993). *Portfolios and other alternative assessments.* Westminster, Ca.: Teacher Created Materials.

Jongsma, K. (1989). Portfolio assessment. *The Reading Teacher* 42:264–265.

Kadushin, A. (1959). The knowledge base of social work. In A. J. Kahn (ed.), *Issues in American social work*, pp. 39–79. New York: Columbia University Press.

Knight, M. E., and Gallaro, D. (1994). *Portfolio assessment: Applications of portfolio analysis.* Lanham, Md.: University Press of America.

Laird, J. (1993). *Revisioning social work education: A social constructionist approach.* New York: Haworth Press.

National Association of Social Workers (NASW). (1994). *NASW Code of Ethics.* Washington, D.C.: NASW.

National Association of Social Workers (NASW). (1996). *NASW Code of Ethics.* Washington, D.C.: NASW.

Paulson, P. R., and Paulson, F. L. (1991). Portfolios: Stories of knowing. In P. Dreyer (ed.), *Knowing: The power of stories*, pp. 294–303. Claremont, Ca.: Claremont Reading Conference.

Perlman, H. H. (1979). *Relationship: The heart of helping people.* Chicago: University of Chicago Press.

Ross, H., and Johnson, A. M. (1950). The growing science of casework. In C. Kasius (ed.), *Principles and techniques of social casework*, pp. 48–56. New York: Family Service Association.

Schriver, J. M. (1995). *Human behavior and the social environment: Shifting paradigms in essential knowledge for social work practice.* Boston: Allyn and Bacon.

Seely, A. E. (1994). *Portfolio assessment.* Westminster, Ca.: Teacher Created Materials.

Sheafor, B. W., Horejsi, C. R., and Horejsi, G. A. (1997). *Techniques and guidelines for social work practice.* 4th ed. Boston: Allyn and Bacon.

Siporin, M. (1975). *Introduction to social work practice.* New York: Macmillan.

Strean, H. F. (1971). Introduction. In H. F. Strean (ed.), *Social casework: Theories in action*, pp. 5–44. Metuchen, N.J.: Scarecrow Press.

Wahlberg, J., and Lommen, C. (1990). An analysis of admissions and termination criteria in BSW Programs. Presentation at the 8th Annual Conference of the Association of Baccalaureate Social Work Program Directors, Minneapolis, Minn.

Weick, A. (1993). Reconstructing social work education. In J. Laird (ed.), *Revisioning social work education: A social constructionist approach*, pp. 11–30. New York: Haworth Press.

Williams, A. (1997). Using science portfolios in a sixth-grade classroom. In J. Barton and A. Collins (eds.), *Portfolio assessment: A handbook for educators*, pp. 69–79. Menlo Park, Ca.: Addison-Wesley.

Winograd, P., Paris, S., and Bridge, C. (1991). Improving the assessment of literacy. *The Reading Teacher* 45:108–116.

18

The Use of Comprehensive Exit Exams

Lynn Frantz Adkins

Throughout higher education, assessment of students by faculty is a fundamental component of establishing the level of the students' achievement and evaluating the curriculum. Consequently, student assessment occurs at various points in the educational process and for various reasons. On the one hand, evaluation of student performance and learning is an accountability issue, that is, a measure of the degree to which the program is achieving its intended outcomes (see, for example, Slaght, Raskin, and Davis 1995). On the other hand, assessment of students is a gatekeeping issue. Individual students are assessed to determine their readiness to enter the program, to proceed through the sequence of core coursework in the major, to enter the field practicum, and finally to exit the educational program and enter the profession. In order to carry out a program's gatekeeping functions fully, various forms of assessment are needed at the beginning of the program, the end, and at various junctures in between (Moore and Urwin 1990).

Determining who should and who should not be entitled to practice professional social work has been a long-standing concern for social work education and is commonly referred to as gatekeeping. Assessment, as it relates to gatekeeping responsibilities, involves making judgments about *actual performance* as well as about *potential* for accomplishment and success, depending on the point in the curriculum at which the assessment takes place. For instance, during admissions screening, judgments are made about a student's potential for success in the major and in the profession based in part on academic performance at the time of application to the major. Student performance on comprehensive exit exams likewise indicates potential, in this case, readiness to enter the field of social work practice. Thus, the comprehensive exit exam is one type of gatekeeping tool that can be employed to determine each student's level of competence at the time the social work curriculum is completed.

This chapter explores how the comprehensive exit exam, as an assessment tool, relates to gatekeeping concerns. The chapter also identifies the benefits and drawbacks of using exit exams, elaborates some of the considerations that must be explored when developing a comprehensive exit exam, provides an overview of one program's experience with exit exams, and concludes with a sample exit exam for BSW education.

The Exit Exam as a Gatekeeping Tool

Gatekeeping efforts respond to the concern that the public be afforded some protection against inappropriate professional practice and be given some guarantee by the social work program that professional competence has been achieved. In order to address gatekeeping responsibilities, social work programs employ a number of criteria and assessment mechanisms at different points in the curriculum (Gibbs 1994; Moore and Urwin 1991). For example, screening criteria for admission into a program may include documented volunteer experience or an introductory social work course (at the conclusion of which reference letters are submitted), a grade point average (GPA) set by the program, and a certain number of completed credit hours. Assessment of performance occurs in skills labs, in individual courses (exams, papers, projects, and class participation), during the field practicum, and for some programs at the conclusion of the curriculum via a comprehensive exit examination. While the field experience provides students with an opportunity to apply social work theory and concepts in order to demonstrate, at that juncture in the curriculum, a beginning level of competence and skill, the integrative nature of exit exams makes them an ideal tool to assess the depth and breadth of the students' learning from across the entire curriculum.

The use of an exit exam in BSW programs provides final assurance that graduates have acquired the knowledge, skills, and professional values appropriate for entry-level generalist practice. While the substantive focus of the comprehensive exam is on the social work curriculum, the liberal arts requirements should not be overlooked as part of the total educational experience; however, they may not be as readily apparent in the exam due to the broader nature of those learnings. For example, through the liberal arts requirements students develop skills in critical thinking, ethical inquiry, and written and oral communication. The liberal arts foundation also enables students to make critical judgments in a logical and rational manner, to value the continuing search for knowledge, and to deal constructively with the technological, cultural, and social changes that will challenge them throughout a lifetime of learning. While these broad learnings provide the foundation for the social work curriculum, they generally are reflected indirectly rather than explicitly in the BSW exit exam.

The use of exit exams and other gatekeeping tools responds to standards established by social work education's accrediting body, the Council on Social Work Education (CSWE). Accreditation standards include requirements that programs develop various evaluation and gatekeeping activities, specifically as these relate to student development, as outlined in Evaluative Standard 5 (CSWE 1994:87–88). The substantive focus of comprehensive exit exams at the BSW level naturally derives from the program objectives and curriculum guidelines that are advanced in CSWE's accreditation handbook (1994). Students who successfully complete comprehensive exams that are closely tied to those accrediting standards demonstrate not only their achievement of the program's objectives but also their competence for entry-level practice. Consequently, the comprehensive exam as an exit requirement serves a dual purpose of assessing both student *and* program.

Exit exams as one method of student and curriculum assessment have been more accepted over a longer period at the graduate than at the undergraduate level. Historically, graduate programs in social work (MSW), as well as in other professional disciplines, administered comprehensive examinations at the conclusion of the curriculum to ensure students had reached the basic level of competence expected of graduates having completed an advanced course of study. As undergraduate education in social work (BSW programs) came to be accepted as required for entry into the profession, the comprehensive examination became a gatekeeping tool in some BSW programs as well.

A computer search of the literature reveals surprisingly little reference to comprehensive exit examinations in undergraduate programs. Furthermore, recent research on gatekeeping mechanisms in BSW programs shows that only 19 percent ($n = 39$) of the 207 programs surveyed use exit exams, with programs in private, church-affiliated institutions using them more frequently than programs in either public or other private institutions (Gibbs 1994). The paucity of literature on the topic and the limited use of exit exams in BSW-level education underscore the need for further information on exit exams: the benefits and drawbacks of using them; how to develop a comprehensive exit exam, including who has input into its preparation; and finally how the exam should be administered and evaluated. This chapter serves to illuminate these issues.

Comprehensive Exit Exams: Their Benefits

The benefits of exit exams are readily apparent to programs that use them. Some of the benefits relate directly to gatekeeping concerns and others more closely align with a program's accountability and accreditation. One of the benefits in relation to gatekeeping is that the vast majority of students take the exit exam quite seriously and spend considerable time studying for the exam, thereby improving their level of competence. Evidence of increased learning tends to also hold true for students who have not otherwise excelled in their coursework, which may be true in part because studying for the capstone exam tends to be more than a last-minute "cram session." Instead, preparation is an ongoing process throughout the curriculum and typically includes not only individual study sessions but also involvement in study groups. Gaining mastery over the subject matter enhances the students' self-esteem, especially when students pass the exam "with distinction." Finally, in the process of preparing for the exit exam, students are simultaneously reviewing material that will enhance their performance on licensure exams, a gatekeeping tool used by the profession.

Other benefits are tied more closely to accountability issues. First, programs are able to ensure that students have basic entry-level knowledge and competence, and individual students who are unable to demonstrate an acceptable level of competence do not leave the program until they can do so. Second, the results of all exit exams clearly point to the program's strengths and weaknesses. Finally, the use of exit exams serves to document changes in courses and curriculum over time.

Comprehensive Exit Exams: Their Drawbacks

Despite the benefits of exit exams, their drawbacks create difficulties for some programs. The use of exit exams usually involves both direct and indirect costs, particularly in relation to faculty time spent in the development, administration, and evaluation of the exam. Exit exams are a time-consuming undertaking for faculty. Their use involves a good deal of effort not only related to "paperwork" and record-keeping but also in terms of conceptualizing and designing the exam. The larger the program, the greater this time commitment becomes, especially if comprehensives include an oral exam component that is given individually to each student. Despite the substantial increase in the faculty's workload as a result of developing, administering, and grading exit exams, this activity is carried out in the absence of additional remuneration. These drawbacks reflect the more indirect costs. If prepackaged exams are used, the program has to absorb the cost of the exams, which must be considered one of the direct costs.

Some of these drawbacks suggest that the use of exit exams is more suited to small programs located in small institutions that focus on undergraduate-level education than to large programs and institutions that have several levels of education. It stands to reason that management and coordination issues are not as difficult when the number of students and faculty is not unwieldy. Furthermore, since smaller institutions tend to emphasize teaching and individualized instruction, the use of exit exams seems a logical extension of this emphasis. Conversely, larger institutions that include graduate and doctoral-level programs tend to emphasize research rather than teaching (Gibbs and Locke 1989). This research emphasis, coupled with a greater number of students and faculty and with the increased complexity of the educational enterprise, may be seen as a disincentive to employing exit exams as a gatekeeping tool in larger programs.

However, larger programs should not allow such drawbacks to prohibit the use of comprehensive exit exams. Adjustments can be made to accommodate the needs and demands of larger programs without compromising the benefits of using exit exams. For example, designing an exam comprised of true-false and multiple-choice questions will cut down on the number of faculty resources and amount of time needed to administer and evaluate the exam, so using well-constructed objective exams, instead of essay and oral exams, may be a more manageable alternative for larger programs. Objective exams, however, should not be exclusively focused on facts. They should be designed to engage the students' critical thinking abilities in demonstrating what they know. (For a more detailed discussion of this issue, see chapter 17 on portfolio assessments.)

Developing a Comprehensive Exit Exam

Professional social work education requires students to develop practice competence, which is grounded in the knowledge, skills, and values of the profession. The knowledge, skills, and values needed for entry-level practice comprise the fabric of the curriculum design and are translated into the program's goals and objectives. An underlying assumption in developing an exit exam is that students gain knowledge and expertise in the liberal arts, as well as in the core curriculum of social work, as spelled out in the accreditation guidelines and converted into the program's goals and objectives.

Several considerations are important when developing a comprehensive examination: what format will be used; who will prepare the exam; who will administer the exam; what will be the evaluative criteria, and who will be responsible for evaluating the exams.

Format Considerations

Constraints on time and faculty resources must be considered when developing the exam. When adequate time and faculty resources are available, written essay exams, either by themselves or in combination with open-ended oral exams, are possible—and maybe even desirable. In larger programs, written exams that use multiple-choice and true-false questions are more pragmatic. In framing the questions, faculty need to test for both breadth and depth of knowledge. Questions that allow demonstration of learnings from across the curriculum, including the liberal arts courses, can establish the breadth of learning, and questions that allow integration and application of the core social work courses can establish the depth of learning. The greatest substantive challenge in developing the comprehensive exam is to make sure that it is, in fact, comprehensive and integrative in nature rather than merely a repeat of questions from specific course examinations.

Preparation Considerations

Faculty need to determine who will be involved in constructing the exam: social work faculty only? Faculty in other departments who provide the liberal arts foundation? Faculty who teach specific courses, either within the social work program or in the cognate areas? Field instructors who are closely affiliated with the program? Programs located in smaller institutions probably have more cross-departmental interaction and communication, which facilitates collaborative efforts in constructing the exit exam, than those located in larger institutions. However, larger programs need not let their contextual difference interfere with their efforts to develop and implement an effective exit exam. Using the mechanisms already established in larger programs should help overcome some of the limitations those programs face in constructing an exit exam. They can, for example, involve their curriculum, advisory, and field instruction committees in developing the exam. Because the program director generally has ties to faculty teaching cognate courses, input into exam development can be gained by contacting those faculty members.

Whether the program is large or small, the role of the BSW program director in developing the exam must be defined. Is the director, for example, the final authority on the nature, focus, and substance of the exam? Finally, faculty need to decide whether or not—or in what ways—students should be involved in developing the exam. Some programs use feedback mechanisms already in place to gain input from students, that is, through senior surveys, outcome assessment instruments completed by graduates, and the like.

Administrative Considerations

Arrangements for administering the exam must be made, and the party or parties responsible for its administration must be identified. When oral exams are used, a small panel of individuals should be designated to administer the exam. At least one faculty member from a department other than social work might be included, for instance, a faculty member who teaches in one of the cognate areas, that is, those courses in other disciplines (e.g., sociology and psychology) that support the social work curriculum. As part of the oral exam, faculty might want to consider including practitioners who are closely affiliated with the program. Field instructors can be a valuable addition to the team responsible for the oral examination of students for they are well aware of the relationship between the educational program and the practice arena—in essence, the application of theory to practice.

Evaluation Considerations

Issues around evaluation of the exit exams must also be addressed. Faculty must identify who will evaluate the students' performance on the exam as well as what the criteria and standards will be. In addition to choosing the evaluators of the exams, faculty need to determine what constitutes a passing grade on the exam. Other issues related to evaluation also must be addressed in advance. Will special recognition be given to students who excel on the exam? What happens if one area of a student's exam is quite weak although other areas are passing or are quite strong? Will a student be allowed to do some type of remedial work or project to show mastery of the content area on which performance was unsatisfactory? Will students be allowed to take the exam again if they did not do well the first time? If repeat exams are offered, how many times can a student retake the exam? When a student repeats the exam, is the entire exam retaken or just the portion that coincides with the area on which performance was unsatisfactory? In addition to arriving at answers to this list of questions about evaluating the exam, faculty need to establish an appeal process to give students recourse if they want to raise any issues about the process of their involvement with the exam or the outcome of their performance.

The Bethany College Experience

Bethany College, a small, private liberal arts college in West Virginia, has used comprehensive exit exams as a graduation requirement for all students since 1933. Originally, the comprehensive examination consisted of two exams. One exam was taken at the end of the sophomore year to prescribe the future studies of the student. The second comprehensive exam was completed as a graduation requirement at the end of the senior year of study. The exams, consisting of essay questions and a one-hour oral exam, were designed to test general understanding and the interrelationship of all coursework.

Some of the early traditions of the exit exam continue currently. Following completion of the written exams, individual students are given an oral examination by a committee of three faculty members. During the oral exam, the student has an opportunity to provide additional clarification of answers on the written exam. Students are also asked questions that go beyond material covered in the written exam as well as questions pertaining to the liberal arts foundation. The early philosophy underlying the examination and still valid today is that a quality college education is not evidenced merely by the completion of coursework but by the students' ability to master and integrate learning.

For the past several decades the comprehensive exam has served to validate each student's grasp of his or her major field of study by demonstrating his or her ability to reason, synthesize, and communicate a comprehensive understanding of the link between coursework in the major and in the liberal arts. The college catalog describes Bethany's exit exam policies as follows:

A student who has attained senior standing, is completing the requirements for a major and has a GPA of at least 2.0 in the major is eligible to take the Senior Comprehensive Examination. To take the Examination, the student must apply in the office of the Registrar at least two months prior to the first day of the written section of the Examination. The Examination, which is offered in January and in May, is both written and oral. In some majors sections of the Graduate Record Examination are part of or prerequisite to the Senior Comprehensive Examination. The Registrar arranges the oral section as soon as possible after the written section, but in no case more than two weeks later.

Students who have completed all requirements in their majors may take the examination in January with the consent of their advisors. Students failing the examination in January may take it again in May or at any time that it is regularly given within the following twelve months. If the student fails a second time, the student may petition the faculty for a re-examination during the following year. No student may take the examination more than three times.

(Bethany College Bulletin
1995–96:19–20)

Exam Development

The preparation of the exam is up to each department; that is, each department within the larger institution develops its own set of exams. The exams are designed to cover the major field of study from the standpoint of its curriculum outcomes rather than to repeat exam questions from individual courses completed in the major. Some departments use standardized national tests for all or part of the written examination; however, most develop their own questions for both the written and the oral components of the exam. The exams vary in comprehensiveness, depth, and difficulty from one department to the next. However, the Bethany faculty strongly defend these variations as appropriate to the personalized education that small colleges can offer. Surveys sent out by the college indicate that the students accept the comprehensive exams without complaint and most often as a logical conclusion to their education at Bethany.

The comprehensives begin with eight hours of written examinations, taken by all students at the same time. The written exam is divided into three time periods—two morning sessions and one afternoon session. Exams usually begin on Monday morning and continue Monday afternoon and Tuesday morning. The one-hour oral examination is scheduled by the college registrar for later in the week, with three faculty members (the department head of the student's major, another faculty member from the same department, and an out-of-department professor who has taught the student).

As noted earlier, the oral exams are used to allow each student to strengthen or clarify points made on the written exam, so the oral exam provides an additional opportunity to demonstrate comprehension of and proficiency in the major field of study, as integrated with the liberal arts requirements. Because of this additional opportunity, an occasional student is able to pass the entire exam even when performance on the written part of the exam is somewhat problematic, although few students receive passing marks on the entire comprehensive when they perform poorly on the written component.

Evaluation of the comprehensive exam has three outcomes: students can pass, pass with distinction, or fail. If students fail the exam, they may take it a second time without penalty the following semester or at a later date, and faculty may specify additional requirements before allowing the student another testing opportunity. However, a second failure is considered final, although the avenue of appeal to the entire faculty of the institution is available to students. At Bethany, failure is rare. If students leave the college without passing the comprehensive requirement, they may return at a later time to retake the exam, with the provision that they take the current comprehensive examination.

Despite any drawbacks to the use of the comprehensive examination, the Bethany faculty strongly support its use. Furthermore, the college's institutional research reports that 60 percent of the students rate comprehensives as a very valuable part of their experience at Bethany (Bernard 1992).

In addition to using exit exams for the purpose of gatekeeping, Bethany College also employs the exams as an assessment tool to meet requirements advanced by the North Central Association of Colleges and Schools for validating students' mastery of their field of study. The use of exit exams brings students and department faculty to a clear understanding of each student's level of learning.

In the social work program, a satisfactory level of learning involves demonstration of basic competence in the basic knowledge, skills, and values necessary for beginning social work practice.

Comprehensives in Bethany's Social Work Program

When Bethany College established the social work program in 1979, the first comprehensive exam in social work was developed by the college's two social work faculty members. Questions were formulated in relation to the primary program objective of preparing students for generalist social work practice at the entry level. Additional questions were framed to address accreditation standards that required curriculum content in the liberal arts foundation, human behavior and the social environment, policy, research, practice, and the field experience. Since then, the exit exam has been revised with input from the program's field instructors and students. Although the reasons for and means of acquiring feedback from field instructors may be clear, the same might not be true in relation to student input, and thus it bears explanation. In Bethany's social work program, student input into the exam is given as part of the evaluation of program objectives and outcomes. This feedback is used to revise the exam for future use.

The development of the Bethany BSW program's comprehensive exam has always been grounded in the assessment of the program's objectives and outcomes and of CSWE's accreditation requirements. With the advent of the new accreditation standards (CSWE 1994), which stem from the revised Curriculum Policy Statement (CPS), the program is currently in the process of revising the comprehensive examination again. These newer revisions will be based on the program outcomes articulated in the new CPS and will focus on the nine curriculum content areas as defined by the CPS as reframed recently (CSWE 1994).

The model Bethany's BSW program used sixteen years ago to develop the first social work exit exam grew out of the college's requirement for an exam that was both comprehensive and integrative. The social work program's exam continues to follow that original model: the exam begins with foundation knowledge, moves through knowledge gained in the core social work courses, and finally provides opportunities for application of knowledge, skills, and values to practice and to the field placement experience.

The social work exam is developed by all members of the social work faculty, and questions are submitted by key faculty members in the core content areas, such as practice, human behavior, research, and so on. All of the questions on the written part of the exam are essay questions; the essay format allows for more application and expression of knowledge. The exam is administered through the college registrar's office, as noted earlier. Reading and evaluation of the exam are shared by the same group of faculty who provide the one-hour oral examination, and faculty are assigned to these responsibilities by the program chair. The oral examination is used to clarify misinformation given by the student on the written part of the exam and also to enhance and clarify information from the written exam that was not clear to the reader. The oral exam also allows an outstanding candidate to build further on an excellent written presentation.

A Sample Comprehensive Exit Exam for BSW-Level Education

The final part of this chapter provides a comprehensive exit exam for BSWs, which was designed by the social work faculty at Bethany. The exam involves three half-day sessions of essay exams and a one-hour individual oral examination. Students do not receive the entire written exam when the first session commences. Instead, they receive the part of the written exam that was designed for that particular session. The questions for each of the three sessions are increasingly complex, comprehensive, and integrative. The following written instructions preface the exam questions for each of the three sessions of written exams.

> Plan your time before writing. Read the question carefully and think about your response. Outlining your thoughts prior to writing your response to each question is a good technique. Avoid long, rambling discourse, and avoid repetition in your answers. Leave a page or two blank after each question in case you have time to return to the question and elaborate your answer further. Put your name on each blue book, and be sure to identify each question prior to the answer you give. Feel free to use the test sheets and/or an extra blue book for "scrap" purposes: to outline your ideas, jot down key words, and so on. Make sure you turn in all of these notes with your exam.

For the third session the following instructions are added to the basic instructions: "Remember that you are being tested on the depth and breadth of your response, as well as the appropriateness of the answers to the questions posed. Drawing on your knowledge of social work practice gained from both the classroom and the field experience, respond to the following questions."

Social Work Comprehensive Exam

PART I

Three-hour morning session, day one

1. Explain how we define social welfare needs. Give an example from your practice experience that explains how a social worker might work with a client to meet the stated need. Define the social justice issues that ought to be addressed.

2. All social welfare programs are developed from a stated need. Discuss and give an example of the major motivational factors from which social welfare policies and programs are developed. Provide a framework for addressing the issues of social justice and oppression that are created due to the motivational factors you have identified.

3. Discuss the historical issues that have shaped welfare policies and programs. Begin your discussion with the European Inheritance and conclude with the contemporary scene today. Your discussion should concentrate on the development of social welfare history as it applies to policy, program development, and service delivery at the micro, mezzo, and macro levels.

4. Define the generalist model of social work practice and give a case example. Discuss your ability to engage in generalist practice and define what it means to be a professional social worker. How does this definition fit your value, knowledge, and skill development? Include in your answer the strengths and weaknesses you bring to the field of social welfare as a professional social worker.

Social Work Comprehensive Exam

PART II

Two-hour afternoon session, day one

1. Define and discuss the following social welfare programs and provide one or more examples of each type of program.

   Financial programs

   (a) Insurance-type programs

   (b) Grant Programs

   In-kind programs

   (a) Insurance-type programs

   (b) Grant programs

   Social service programs

2. Outline a major social welfare program. Present a model for analyzing this program.

3. In relation to the programs you discussed in #1, what do you consider the most pressing social welfare issue facing contemporary American society? Justify your position through the use of social work knowledge, ethics, values, and policy considerations. Detail how the concepts of social and economic justice impact the issue.

4. Discuss how human behavior is influenced by bio-psycho-social development throughout the life span. Give an example of a problem situation found in social work that involves interaction among these developmental systems. Use several theories to explain your example, giving special attention to how social, environmental, and economic factors impact the problem at the micro, mezzo, and macro levels.

5. Select a research topic relevant to social work practice that you would be interested in undertaking. Explore and explain the research design you would need to follow, the ethical standards you would need to consider, and other research issues such as quantitative versus qualitative research methodologies; analysis of data, including statistical procedures; the research questions that would guide your work, and how you might frame your conclusions in a research report.

Social Work Comprehensive Exam

PART III

Three-hour morning session, day two

Section One

Responses to the first set of questions in this section should refer to the following case example.

Case Example

You have taken a position with the Children's Protective Services Unit of the local human services division. This division's responsibilities include investigation of suspected child abuse and neglect cases. You have just been informed by your supervisor that you have been assigned to investigate the Stone family. On several occasions, anonymous callers have reported observing the Stone children wandering the streets in the middle of the night. The callers also claimed that they have seen "unusual" marks on the bodies of the children (i.e., arms, legs, faces), for which the children give vague and unconvincing reasons. Because you are a new worker, your supervisor makes sure that you are aware of two prior child protective investigations of Mrs. Stone and her children, which stemmed from previous anonymous callers who made allegations similar to the recent allegations. Results of past investigations were inconclusive, so the case was never opened. There are three children in the Stone family: Gerry, age seven; Tina, age six; and Timmy, age four. Mrs. Stone is a single mother who is unemployed and subsisting on public assistance.

1. In completing an initial assessment of this case, what key items or factors would you consider in developing a case management plan (assuming you determine that Mrs. Stone is abusing and/or neglecting her children)?

2. Identify the following systems in this case: change agent, client, action, and target.

3. Discuss how you would engage Mrs. Stone in a helping relationship. Assume that Mrs. Stone is an involuntary client given the social control function of Child Protective Services, so your answer must include a discussion of (a) how to engage an involuntary client and (b) specific social work values that are especially important to consider in working with an involuntary client. Also, remember that Mrs. Stone has already been investigated on two previous

occasions because of similar allegations, so she probably will not greet you with "open arms." Include in your response how you would overcome this negative dynamic in the helping relationship in order to move toward a productive and purposive relationship with this client.

4. Assuming that the allegations of abuse/neglect are substantiated, and that you have to engage Mrs. Stone as an involuntary client, discuss how you would approach working with her; that is, what strategies and techniques might be most effective?

Section Two: Group Work

Propose and design a group experience for students who have lost a parent through death since they matriculated at Bethany College.

1. List the five sections of a group proposal and briefly explain what you would include in each of the sections. Be specific; include examples when appropriate.

2. Prepare an agenda for the first group session. Be sure to include a goal and two objectives for the session. Include a rationale for the activities you have chosen.

3. Drawing on your knowledge of group process, briefly explain what behaviors you would expect to observe in your participants throughout the group experience.

Section Three: Case Example

Develop a case example from your field placement that integrates your learnings from the social work curriculum and demonstrates your critical thinking skills. Be sure that you do not divulge confidential information or in any way identify your client. Use the following guidelines to develop your case example and choose a case that will allow you to address all of the guidelines.

- Define the client system size and type.

- Show how the situation responds to the purpose of social work as a profession.

- Speak to the issue of working with diverse populations.

- Address the issue of professional values and ethics; in particular, explain any inherent value or ethical dilemmas that the case presented.

- Show how social and economic justice were promoted.

- Elaborate on how this case example illustrates working with a population at risk and your understanding of the significance of this issue as you worked with the situation.

- Include an analysis of the case that includes learnings from the following curriculum content areas.

  Human Behavior and the Social Environment

  Social Welfare Policy and Services

  Social Work Practice

  Research

- Develop a summary of how you handled the case situation, giving special emphasis to the generalist roles you carried as the social worker and your professional use of self throughout your work with the case.

Section Four
The *NASW Code of Ethics* is based on the fundamental values of the social work profession. The code embodies standards of behavior that guide the conduct of social workers as they engage in professional relationships with clients, colleagues, and other professionals.

1. Briefly summarize each of the six sections of the code of ethics, giving an overview of the principles of conduct that are contained in each section.

2. Discuss an ethical dilemma that arose during your field experience. It can be one that either you or someone else (another worker or student) encountered. Draw on the code of ethics to show how its application indicates a particular resolution of the dilemma.

Although comprehensive exit exams are currently not widely used in undergraduate social work education, they show merit for partially responding to the gatekeeping obligations of faculty by identifying each student's level of competence at the conclusion of the undergraduate curriculum. While the exams may be better suited to small programs in small educational institutions, they can be adapted to meet the needs and overcome the constraints of larger programs located at large institutions.

Developing and implementing a comprehensive exit exam creates several challenges that must be addressed by the social work program, not the least of which are time and resource constraints. In addition, faculty must address substantive issues in the exam's development as well as issues of constituent input, exam evaluation, and administrative arrangements. Several operative assumptions guide the construction of an exit exam.

- It should be closely tied to accreditation standards.
- It should be comprehensive in its coverage of the entire curriculum, including the liberal arts foundation and cognate courses.
- It should be integrative in nature.
- It should not merely repeat questions from previous course examinations.

References

Bernard, Richard M. (1992). Senior comprehensive examinations: Sixty years of student assessment at a liberal arts college. *A Collection of Papers on Self-Study and Institutional Improvement,* pp. 166–169. Chicago: North Central Association of Colleges and Schools, Commission on Institutions of Higher Education.

Bethany College Bulletin. (1995–96). Bethany, W.Va.: Bethany College.

Council on Social Work Education (CSWE), Commission on Accreditation. (1994). *Handbook of accreditation standards and procedures.* 4th ed. Alexandria, Va.: CSWE.

Gibbs, P. (1994). Screening mechanisms in BSW programs. *Journal of Social Work Education* 30:63–74.

Gibbs, P., and Locke, B. L. (1989). Tenure and promotion in accredited graduate social work programs. *Journal of Social Work Education* 22:126–133.

Moore, L. S., and Urwin, C. A. (1990). Quality control in social work: The gatekeeping role in social work education. *Journal of Teaching in Social Work* 4:113–128.

Slaght, E. F., Raskin, M. S., and Davis, M. E. (1995), Assessing BSW programs: An outcomes-driven approach. *Journal of Social Work Education* 31:17–27.

PART FOUR

Appendixes: Gatekeeping Materials and Sample Tools

Appendix 1

Questions for Student Admissions Essay

The following is a list of sample questions and prompts that may be used by programs in developing guidelines for students to write their admissions essay. These questions and prompts were culled from admissions materials provided by members of the National Task Group on BSW Gatekeeping Standards.

Programs may want to include in the admissions materials a statement to the effect that admissions essays are confidential and will be treated as such. Addressing the confidential nature of shared information not only models expected professional behavior but also encourages students to be more candid in their responses to the questions.

1. Discuss the major reasons for your interest in the profession of social work.

2. Describe some of the successes you have achieved in school, work, and in your personal life.

3. Describe any barriers you have confronted in pursuing your education, work, and personal goals (e.g., physical disability, lack of funds, family crisis, etc.) and discuss how you worked to overcome those barriers.

4. Discuss the life events or experiences that have contributed to your interest in social work. You may wish to refer to family background and circumstances, work experiences; experiences as a consumer of social services provided by social workers, psychologists, psychiatrists, or clergy; influence of education in general or of specific teachers; talents or skills; or

other relevant influences. Be certain to explain why the social work profession is your career choice as compared to other helping professions.

5. Discuss a social issue that is of particular interest to you. What, in your opinion, causes this problem? Describe how you believe our society should address this issue and how you might contribute to its resolution.

6. What do you see as your major limitations relative to a career in social work?

7. What are your career plans and interests? How will an undergraduate degree in social work help you to achieve your goals?

8. The concept of cultural pluralism places an emphasis on respecting a diversity of values, heritages, customs, and lifestyles.

    a. What experiences have you had which make you feel that you can work effectively with people from diverse populations that reflect differences in religion, race, ethnicity, physical abilities, gender, socioeconomic status, and sexual orientation?

    b. What experiences have you had that might present difficulties in working with any of the groups listed above?

9. Identify those skills, knowledge, and value areas that you hope the social work curriculum will assist you in strengthening.

10. Compare your personal value system with the values expressed in the *NASW Code of Ethics.*

11. Discuss your volunteer work or other human service experience and the aspects of it that were most meaningful to you.

    a. What successes did you experience in your work?

    b. What frustrations occurred?

    c. What did you find appealing about being in the helper role?

    d. What did you learn about yourself as a result of this experience?

    e. What did you otherwise gain or learn from this experience?

12. Briefly describe your background, including information about your parents and siblings. Discuss high school and college years, emphasizing extracurricular activities, hobbies, sports, special interests, and achievement. Summarize your employment history.

13. Review your self-assessment. How do your strengths seem compatible with your desire to pursue a career in social work?

14. Based on your self-assessment, identify at least three areas of needed professional development and your plan for improving these areas. Be specific.

15. Provide any additional information that would be helpful for the Admissions Committee to know in order to make an informed decision on your application.

16. What personal qualities do you have that will be useful in serving others as a social worker?

17. Is there any other information you would like to share that would help us to better meet your learning needs?

Appendix 2

Sample BSW Admissions Rating Sheet

Date sent out _____ Date returned _____

Applicant _____ Rater _____

GPA _____ Accumulated hours of human service activity _____

Evaluation

Note: Raters may use middle points of any scale.

Grade-Point Average (GPA)

       4.0 to 3.0 = +10

       2.9 to 2.5 = +05

       2.49 to 2.0 = +00

                                                                                    _____

Letters of Reference

      Very Enthusiastic = +10   Mixed views or average = +00

      All positive   = +05   Basically unsupportive = –10

                                                                                     _____

Personal Statement

Motivation

Strong commitment and enthusiasm (extra human service activity, involved in social service provision or social organization or governance activities)	= +10
Moderate commitment and enthusiasm (met basic criteria; few if any extracurricular activities)	= +05
Not well addressed or questionable motivation	= –05

_____

Career goals and aspirations

Identified, planned, and appropriate to social work	= +05
Not fully discussed or not appropriate to social work	= +00

Quality of written material

Fully articulate with few minor technical errors	= +10
Average writing skills; several minor errors	= +05
Difficulty conveying thoughts and/or lots of errors	= +00

_____

Self-awareness

Knows strengths/weaknesses; maturity shows through	= +05
Moderate ability to articulate understanding of self	= +00
Little self-awareness or not able to express it	= –05

_____

Compatibility with Profession (based on all application materials)

Acceptance of human diversity

Totally nonjudgmental/open-minded; accepts differences	= +10
Usually is sensitive to and respects human diversity	= +05
Some difficulty with accepting differences in others	= +00
Major difficulty in accepting human differences	= –20

_____

If minus 20, describe:

Social work values and ethics

Strongly identifies with ethical standards of social work = +10

No major concerns or growth potential evident   = +05

Major concerns about compatibility with s.w. values   = −20

If minus 20, describe:

_____

Interpersonal skills

Relates well to others, both peers and authorities   = +10

Some minor difficulty with interactions   = +05

May be uncooperative or unfriendly; "attitude problems"   = −05

Ability to interact *or* English competence unsatisfactory = −20

If minus score, describe:

_____

Potential for Professional Development

Solicits feedback; responsive to critique; not defensive; self-directed; shows initiative = +10

Usually responsive to feedback; may be defensive; may require extra direction or prompting = +05

Does not accept or act on constructive criticism; needs constant prompting or attention to perform = −10

_____

Demonstrated Responsible Behavior

Punctual; meets deadlines; dependable; reliable   = +10

Mostly reliable, punctual, dependable, etc.   = +05

Frequently misses deadlines, etc.   = +00

_____

Total   _____

Overall Assessment and Recommendation

[ ] Exceptional   (100 to 90)   [ ] Marginal   (64 to 50)

[ ] Above average (89 to 75)   [ ] Unsatisfactory (49 and below)

[ ] Satisfactory   (74 to 65)

_____Accept into program

_____Minimally acceptable but low priority

_____Reject. Check reason(s).

      Weak autobiographical statement
      Weak letters of reference
      Inadequate competence in English
      Incompatible with social work profession
      Other _____

_____Additional information needed. Specify:

_____Interview with student is recommended. Why? _____

Additional rater comments:

Appendix 3

Student Admissions
Contract and Code of Conduct

Social work is a profession whose members are required to adhere to standards advanced by the National Association of Social Workers (NASW); social work students must also meet standards advanced by the Council on Social Work Education (CSWE). The following behavioral expectations of students were adapted from the *NASW Code of Ethics* and CSWE's accreditation standards for programs of social work education.

1. The social work student is expected to maintain high standards of personal conduct and act in accordance with the highest standards of integrity.

2. The social work student engaged in study and research must be guided by the conventions of scholarly inquiry.

3. The social work student engaged in service delivery holds as primary his or her responsibility to clients.

4. The social work student must respect the privacy of clients and hold in confidence all information obtained in the course of professional service.

5. The social work student is expected to treat fellow students, faculty, supervisors, and staff with respect, honesty, courtesy, fairness, and good faith.

6. The social work student must adhere to commitments made to the social work program.

7. The social work student will uphold and advance the values, ethics, and mission of the profession.

8. The social work student must not participate in, condone, or be associated with dishonesty, fraud, deceit, or misrepresentation.

9. The social work student must not engage in any form of discrimination based on an individual's race, ethnicity, gender, sexual orientation, age, religion, or other personal characteristics, beliefs, status, or conditions.

10. The social work student will continue his or her professional development through regular self-assessment of academic and personal aptitude and performance.

11. The social work student will continue his or her professional development through regular faculty assessment of academic and professional aptitude and performance.

12. The social work student will give his or her faculty advisor permission to discuss the progress in the social work program with the director, dean, other social work faculty members, and field instructors.

Statement of Understanding and Agreement

I understand that although I am admitted to the social work major, if my professional development is not deemed satisfactory by the social work faculty (and/or field instructor), the program has the right and responsibility to request reassessment of my suitability for the major in social work.

I hereby agree to abide by the standards in this document, and I further understand that I must maintain a 2.25 overall GPA and a 2.5 GPA in the social work courses to remain in the program.

Student signature   Date

This sample contract was developed from materials submitted by the social work programs at Ball State University in Indiana and East Tennessee State University.

Appendix 4

Academic Performance Review Policy: Student Continuation, Review, and Dismissal

Policy on Student Continuation

Educational Requirements

For continuance in and graduation from the BSW program, students are required to

- earn at least a C in each social work course;
- earn a "satisfactory" in the senior capstone field practicum;
- maintain a 2.5 cumulative GPA in required social work courses and a 2.5 overall GPA;
- carry out professional activity in conformity with the values and ethics of the profession;
- comply with any contract set forth by the Academic Performance Review Committee to remediate problems and deficiencies.

Policy on Student Performance Review

All students are admitted to the program on the assumption that they have the potential to meet all academic standards, including

This sample policy was submitted by Kathy Byers, Coordinator of the BSW Program, Indiana State University, Bloomington Campus.

scholastic ability and personal suitability for completing the professional program in which they are enrolled. All students in the BSW program are expected to maintain the standards established by the School of Social Work and those held by the social work profession. In order to detect possible academic problems the School of Social Work reviews students' academic performance periodically.

Criteria for Review by Performance Review Committee

Any of the following are grounds for review by the Performance Review Committee:

- Conduct that is not congruent with the values and ethics of the social work profession (e.g., NASW, NABSW, CSWE) and the academic code of conduct for students at Indiana University. Included is behavior that occurs in the student's fieldwork and in the classroom.
- Behavior that interferes with the student's functioning and/or jeopardizes the welfare of those to whom the student has a responsibility, such as clients and coworkers.
- Failure to communicate effectively, both verbally and in written form, including interviewing skills and interpersonal skills that permit comfortable interaction with other people.
- Failure to adhere to agency policies and professional standards during the field practicum.
- Failure to use sound judgment, both in work with clients and in regard to oneself, such as failure to seek professional help for physical and emotional problems that interfere with professional functioning.
- Having more than one "incomplete" at a time in coursework or having received more than two grades of "incomplete" in any courses after admission to the program.
- Academic dishonesty, including cheating on examinations or plagiarism, which involves presenting the work of someone else as one's own.
- Marginal academic performance.
- A request by a faculty member for a review due to the student's poor coursework performance.

Procedures for Student Performance Review

The School of Social Work has established the following mechanisms to respond to requests for performance reviews.

At the beginning of the academic year a Performance Review Committee shall be formed composed of the BSW program director and two faculty members. The BSW program director will be responsible for convening the meeting for the review process. The Performance Review Committee is conceptualized as a mechanism to detect as early as possible any emerging problems with a student's academic performance, which includes both scholastic and professional expectations. The charge of this committee is

- to review students according to the "Criteria for Review by Performance Review Committee";
- to receive faculty requests for student performance review;
- to receive student requests for a student performance review.

When a student's performance is evaluated as deficient, the committee determines what, if any, course of action could bring the student's performance into compliance with program and professional standards. In situations where such action is feasible and desirable, a contract will be created. The contract will set forth problems to be solved, actions to be taken to solve said problems, a time period for completion of designated actions, and a reevaluation of the student's performance. Consequences for nonperformance will also be spelled out in the contract. The committee will work together with the student, her or his advisor, and other relevant parties. If the student fails to fulfill the contract, or, while working on the contract, some serious impropriety or failing academic performance occurs, the committee may decide that the student cannot continue in the BSW program. Discontinuance can occur during any semester of enrollment in the BSW program, including the last semester.

Automatic Dismissal

Under certain conditions, students may be automatically dismissed from the BSW program.

Criteria for Automatic Dismissal

- Failure to earn at least a C in each social work course.
- Failure in the senior capstone field practicum.
- Failure to maintain a 2.5 cumulative GPA in required social work courses or a 2.5 overall GPA.
- Failure to subscribe to and abide by the values and ethics of the profession in carrying out program-related activities and in meeting academic expectations.
- Failure to comply with any contract set forth by the Academic Performance Review Committee to remediate problems and deficiencies.

Notification Procedures

The following procedures are used in the event of automatic dismissal:

If a student is dismissed for any of the reasons identified as warranting automatic dismissal, the instructor of the course or the program administrator will notify the advisor. Also, the student should notify her or his advisor.

Within five working days of receiving the above notification, the student's advisor will send by certified mail a written statement to the student indicating that she or he has been discontinued from the program and inviting the student to meet to discuss her or his academic plans. Copies of the letter should be forwarded to the program director. A sample advisor's letter is appended to this policy.

The advisor will meet with the student, should the student wish to discuss options and reinstatement procedures.

Reinstatement Procedures

Should the student wish to continue in the program, she or he should be instructed to petition the BSW program director for continuance. In the event of a dismissal that stems from a failure to meet conditions to remediate problems or deficiencies, as set forth by the Academic Performance Review Committee, the petition will be submitted to the director of the MSW or the Ph.D.

program, who are parties outside of the original performance review and contracting process.

The petition should be presented in writing and should address two major points. First, any extenuating factors that contributed to the poor performance in the course should be identified. Second, there should be a discussion of the steps that would be taken (a) to alleviate the impact of those factors and (2) to improve academic performance if continuance in the program is permitted.

The advisor will forward a recommendation (with rationale) regarding continuance in the program to the program director. The recommendation should take into consideration the specific situation as well as the student's overall academic performance. The advisor should consult with the instructor of the course the student has failed.

Upon reviewing the student's petition, the program director will review all relevant information, which includes consultation with appropriate individuals, and make a decision.

The program director will advise the student and advisor of the decision verbally and in writing. The director also will advise the student of her or his right to petition for reconsideration by an Appeals Committee.

Petition for Readmission

If a student was automatically dismissed and the petition for reinstatement was not approved, the student can appeal the decision through a petition for readmission. In order to request a review by a School Appeals Committee, the student must present to the dean of the School of Social Work a substantive written statement for an appeal. The committee will make its recommendations to the dean, who will then make a final decision on the matter.

The School Appeals Committee shall be composed and appointed according to the following procedures:

- Upon receipt of an appeal, the dean will appoint a committee of three full-time faculty members. The committee chair will be assigned by the dean.
- The student submitting the appeal may request the appointment of one of the three faculty members (and may also request the addition of a neutral student representative).

- The committee should act expeditiously in order to avoid unnecessary delay of the student's progress in the program.

Appeal Process

Within five days after the Appeals Committee has been constituted, the committee chair will set a date for a hearing. Giving at least once week advance notice, the chair shall inform the student, the student's advisor, and the members of the Appeals Committee of the time and place of the hearing as well as of the issues that will be considered by the committee. The student will be notified via certified U.S. mail. All committee members and the student's advisor must be present at this review hearing.

Role of the Advisor

At the hearing, the student's advisor shall present brief background information about the student. The advisor also will secure from other instructors their evaluations of the student's performance in the previous semester of coursework. The advisor will present information obtained from these instructors and provide her or his own assessment of the student's overall performance. In addition, the advisor will make recommendations that might resolve the student's performance problems.

Appeals Committee Hearing

Fact-finding phase. The student may attend during the fact-finding part of the meeting and may present information to the committee during this time. Prior to the meeting, the student must inform the committee chair of the intent to attend the meeting and/or to speak to the committee. The student must leave the meeting when the committee is ready to begin its deliberation.

The student may ask up to two persons who are knowledgeable about her or his performance to present information to the committee. Such persons are permitted to attend the committee meeting only while they are presenting information, and their statements to the committee must be brief. The committee chair must be informed at least forty-eight hours in advance about those persons who will appear on behalf of the student and the general nature of the information that each will present.

Other faculty members who can contribute information about the student's performance may participate. Such faculty are permitted to attend the committee meeting only while they are presenting information.

Deliberation and action phase. For this part of the meeting, only the committee members and the student's advisor shall be present, although the advisor will not participate in the voting. The committee will deliberate the following: all of the factors in the present and past performance of the student, and alternative plans to address the performance problems. The committee will reach one of two decisions: (a) to develop a plan, which must be completed by the student, to resolve the performance problem or (b) to dismiss the student from the BSW program. The committee's recommendation will be by majority vote.

The Appeals Committee shall prepare a written recommendation for submission to the dean, which will include a statement describing the nature of the performance problem, a summary of the facts as they were presented to the committee, a description of the committee's action, and the reasons supporting said action.

Notification

Within one week after the review hearing, the committee's recommendation will be sent in writing to the dean. The dean may accept, reject, or modify the recommendation of the committee. The dean sends her or his decision to the BSW program director, the student, the student's advisor, and members of the Appeals Committee. A copy of the dean's decision and the committee's recommendation will be sent to the student, with a copy going into the student's file.

Confidentiality

All procedures related to the performance review must be carried out in a manner that assures protection of the student's right to privacy regarding information about her or his academic records, performance, or any of her or his personal affairs. The student has the right to review all written information that is presented to the committee. Members of the committee and other persons who appear at the hearing are expected to maintain confidentiality with regard to all aspects of the hearing. Actions of the committee are to remain confidential and are to be shared only with those persons who are affiliated with this program and institution and are involved with the student in an educational capacity.

Sample Letter from Advisor

Dear (student):

As your advisor, it is my responsibility to notify you concerning your academic status at (institution and school or program). I am sorry to report that the grade of , which you received in (course name and number), does not meet the minimum criteria for continuation in the BSW program.

The applicable educational requirements are described on pages of the school's catalog where it states that each student must achieve a "minimum grade of 'C'" in each required social work course.

You may petition the BSW program director for a review of your status and consideration for continuance in the BSW program. The petition should be presented in writing and should address two major points. First, you should identify any extenuating factors that contributed to the poor academic performance in the coursework. Second, you should discuss those steps that you intend to take to alleviate the impact of those factors and enable you to improve your academic performance if, at some point in the future, you were to be readmitted to the program.

I encourage you to discuss this situation and your options with me right away. Would you therefore please call me at (phone number) to schedule an appointment.

Appendix 5

Informed Consent Form for Psychological Testing

The signature below indicates my awareness and understanding of the conditions under which I am being required to complete the *Minnesota Multiphasic Personality Inventory-2* (MMPI-2).

I understand that:

1. As stated in the admissions policy approved by the Murray State University Board of Regents for the baccalaureate Social Work Program, the results of the MMPI-2 alone will not be used to deny me admission to the program. However, students may be required to seek counseling to resolve issues identified by psychological staff who are charged with interpreting my results.

2. The MMPI-2 will be used only for counseling prior to admissions to the Murray State University Social Work Program. All counseling will be provided by appropriately trained psychological staff with a minimum of master's level training in counseling, social work, or clinical psychology.

3. An interpretation of my results on the MMPI-2 will be made available to me if I request it.

4. Information provided by me on the MMPI-2 will be confidential, with only the following individuals having access to the results:
   a. myself
   b. faculty of the Murray State University Social Work Program
   c. psychological staff providing interpretation and counseling services.

I further understand that exceptions to this confidentiality will be made only in situations in which an individual presents a severe danger to himself or herself (i.e., suicide) or to others (i.e., homicide) or in cases of child abuse or other statutory reporting instances.

_____

Student signature   Date

This sample consent form was submitted by Rose Bogal-Allbritten from Murray State University in Kentucky.

Appendix 6

Student Self-Assessment

The faculty of the School of Social Work at West Virginia University revised the criteria for admission to the undergraduate social work program in order to more clearly articulate our academic requirements and expectations. This self-assessment is based on the revised criteria and will be used during our review of your application. Each criterion for admission is shown in boxes.

Has achieved a 2.5 overall GPA on a four-point scale. (The GPA will be calculated to include coursework transferred to WVU from other institutions. See your advisor for help in calculating your overall GPA.)

Your GPA at the conclusion of the fall semester that precedes your application is _____ .

Will have successfully completed fifty-eight credit hours by the end of the semester that application for admission is made.

By May of the semester I apply for admission, I will have completed ____ credit hours.

Will have successfully completed the liberal arts foundation (English 1 and 2; Clusters A, B, and C; and a mathematics course) by the end of the semester that application for admission is made.

Please show the semester/year that the following requirements were or will be completed.

English 1	200___	English 2	200___
Cluster A	200___	Cluster B	200___
Cluster C	200___	Math	200___

Successfully completes and documents 100 hours of appropriate human service activity (paid or volunteer) by the time of application for admission to the program and receives supportive or generally positive recommendations from supervisor(s).

At the time of application, I have completed and documented ____ hours of human service activity.

Has earned a B or better in SW 47 and 51 (by the time you apply to the program) and receives a supportive or generally positive recommendation from the instructors of those courses. (Students applying to the program through the 2 + 2 arrangement may replace the SW 47 reference with a reference from another approved minority course.)

Grade in SW 47 _____ . Grade in SW 51 _____ .

Use the following scale to rate yourself on each of the admissions criteria that follow, and put your rating in the box to the right of the criterion. In the space that follows each criterion, briefly describe how you meet the criterion.

1 = Outstanding
2 = Above average
3 = Average
4 = Needs work

Criteria	Your Rating
Shows potential for commitment to the National Association of Social Workers (NASW) Code of Ethics.	
Possesses a basic level of communication and interpersonal skills which provide a sufficient foundation for building professional interactional skills.	
Demonstrates college-level writing skills.	
Shows potential for professional development, such as responsiveness to feedback and willingness to address areas that might interfere with effectiveness as a future helper.	

Criteria	Your Rating
Is motivated to pursue a career in the field of social work.	
In general, is sensitive to and respects human diversity, with a basic capacity for nonjudgmental behavior toward individuals whose values, beliefs, and lifestyles may be different from the student's own.	
Is reliable in carrying out responsibilities as demonstrated in classes and volunteer experience (punctual and dependable, observes assignment deadlines, meets attendance expectations, etc.)	
Shows a basic level of self-awareness in assessing strengths and weaknesses as these might impact carrying out professional responsibilities.	

To conclude this self-assessment, identify *at least* three (3) areas of needed professional development and discuss your plan for improving these areas. Be very specific. Continue your answer on back of page if necessary.

Appendix 7

Volunteer Experience Materials

Social Work Human Service Activity: Certificate of Completion and Assessment of Performance

The undergraduate social work program at West Virginia University requires that students complete 100 hours of human service experience prior to entering the social work major in their junior year. This experience is designed to give students an opportunity to work face-to-face in a helping capacity with others. Working in a helping capacity prior to entering the major will help students to determine if social work is a career of interest to them and will give them experience that will make the courses in social work more meaningful.

Given the spirit and intent of the requirement to gain some form of social work experience (which can be paid or volunteer), activities that do not involve face-to-face helping interactions are precluded—such as stuffing envelopes, being a lifeguard at a pool, and other activities that do not involve working directly with people in a helping capacity. Other more appropriate experiences would include being a camp counselor or playground counselor, working with the elderly in a nursing home, tutoring children, and so on.

The 100-hour requirement is not intended to limit students to a single experience in a single setting; multiple experiences in multiple settings are also acceptable, as long as a total of 100 hours is completed. All activities must have been completed since high school graduation.

Or, to give a more specific assignment to students:

The undergraduate social work program at West Virginia University requires students to complete thirty hours of human service experience as part of their social work methods course during the junior year. Every spring semester, this experience is designed to give students an opportunity to work in a helping capacity with larger systems (rather than direct services to individuals), which we refer to as mezzo and macro practice.

Mezzo practice involves practice with families and groups. Task groups, board meetings, advocacy groups, support groups, public awareness/education groups, self-help groups, case conferences with other professionals are some examples that will allow students to integrate their knowledge of group process, dynamics, and roles.

Macro practice includes work with communities and organizations, which sometimes involves the use of groups to create broader social change. Helping students to understand the relationship of the agency and other community agencies/programs working together to meet community needs is a beginning step in helping students develop skills in working with communities. Involvement in interagency activities, neighborhood groups, community education programs, helping to write grants to meet community needs, serving as an agency representative at a community function, and providing feedback on agency services and programs are some activities that will provide good opportunities for student development.

This section is to be filled out by the student.

Student's name   Number of hours completed

Name of agency or organization

Agency   Address

Agency phone number

Inclusive dates of volunteer activity

Brief description of volunteer activities at this setting:

The section on the next page is to be filled out by the supervisor.

Student: I [ ] do [ ] do not waive my right to see this evaluation.

Supervisor: Please complete this part of the form to assess student performance.

Assessment of Performance:

. Behavior was consistent with ethical standards required of someone who helps others.
[ ] Always   [ ] Usually   [ ] Seldom   [ ] Never   [ ] Cannot assess

· Student complied with agency policies, procedures, expectations.
[ ] Always   [ ] Usually   [ ] Seldom   [ ] Never   [ ] Cannot assess

· Student was punctual, responsible, and dependable.
[ ] Always   [ ] Usually   [ ] Seldom   [ ] Never   [ ] Cannot assess

· Student upheld the principle of client confidentiality.
[ ] Always   [ ] Usually   [ ] Seldom   [ ] Never   [ ] Cannot assess

· Student was able to effectively engage the recipients of services.
[ ] Always   [ ] Usually   [ ] Seldom   [ ] Never   [ ] Cannot assess

· Respectful and effective interpersonal skills were demonstrated with clients, agency personnel, and others involved in the helping efforts.
[ ] Always   [ ] Usually   [ ] Seldom   [ ] Never   [ ] Cannot assess

· Student was able to accept and to work productively and nonjudgmentally with others whose background, beliefs, values, etc. may have been different from the student's own.
[ ] Always   [ ] Usually   [ ] Seldom   [ ] Never   [ ] Cannot assess

· Student made appropriate use of supervision and responded to constructive feedback.
[ ] Always   [ ] Usually   [ ] Seldom   [ ] Never   [ ] Cannot assess

Please add additional comments that will help us to determine the student's capacity for helping others.

_____

Supervisor's name (print or type)

_____

Supervisor's signature

Appendix 8

Reference Letter Form

This section must be filled out by the applicant. Please type or print.

Name   SS/ID#

You may waive your rights to see this letter of reference. However, waiving your rights is not required as a condition for admission or receipt of financial aid or any other services and benefits from the university.

I do _____ do _____ not voluntarily waive all rights of access to this letter of recommendation, as conferred by the Family Educational Rights and Privacy Act of 1974 (P.L. 93-380), amended.

Signature   Date

This section must be filled out by the person providing the reference.

Recommender's Name (printed or typed)

Recommender's Signature

Title

Agency or Dept.

Agency or Dept. Address and Phone

How long and in what capacity have you known the applicant? _____

The applicant named above has applied for admission to the social work program at XYZ University. We appreciate your candid assessment of the applicant's current skills, abilities, and personal qualifications, as these might impact the ability to practice professional social work. Although rating forms are rarely sufficient in portraying an applicant accurately, we offer the rating form on the next page to assist you in your evaluation of the applicant.

Please assess the applicant in each area.

	Poor	Average	Good	Superior	Unknown
Academic (or other areas of) performance					
Openness to change					
Written communication skills					
Oral communication skills					
Ability to work well with others					
Dependability, punctuality, reliability					
Ability to accept and respond to constructive criticism					
Ability to relate to people who are different from himself or herself					
Self-awareness					
Maturity					
Ability to establish rapport with others and relate with warmth and empathy					
Motivation to become a social worker					
Integrity, ethical behavior					
Intellectual abilities in critical thinking and problem solving					
Initiative; self-directed behavior					
Performance under pressure					
Leadership abilities					
Ability to maintain confidentiality					
Capacity to follow instructions					

Please describe below and on the back of the page any other factors that might indicate that the applicant either shows potential
for becoming a competent social worker or shows a lack of fit
with a career in social work.

Appendix 9

Field Instruction Tool for Evaluation of Student Performance

This form is to be used in determining the student's field performance at two points: at midterm and at the conclusion of the semester.

To encourage the student's self-assessment, this instrument is designed to allow students to rate themselves on each area of performance. Students should be allowed to complete the form before the supervisor makes his or her assessment. This will provide a rich source of information for use during the midterm and the final evaluation conferences.

Directions: Circle the appropriate number on the scale in each section. If any of the comments at the level you choose do not fit, feel free to cross them out. Likewise, if a comment in one of the other boxes fits, but overall the student is not entirely at that other level of performance, feel free to underline the other comments to indicate their appropriateness. The scale was designed to show the following levels of performance in each of the twenty-one areas:

0 = failure

1 = marginal abilities; unsatisfactory performance

2 = satisfactory performance

3 = above average performance

4 = exceptional performance

On the back of the last page of the form, briefly summarize the student's work activities while in placement, including work with individuals, families, and communities; identify areas in which student needs to demonstrate significant professional growth and include a brief plan for how to meet these expectations.

When you have finished assessing the student in each of the twenty-one areas, total the twenty-one ratings *of the supervisor's assessment only.* Please note that failure in some of the areas, such as ethical behavior, is grounds for dismissal from the program, regardless of student's level of performance in other areas.

42 and above = Pass (60 to 78 = above average; 80 and up = exceptional)

40 and below = Fail

_____

Student's Name

Score _____(assigned by agency supervisor) and final grade (assigned by faculty liaison, in consultation with agency supervisor and student)

Student's statement: I do/do not (circle one) agree with this recommended grade. If in disagreement, I will submit in writing to my faculty liaison an explanation for my disagreement, which will be attached to this performance evaluation.

(Add signatures of all parties)

WEST VIRGINIA UNIVERSITY
DIVISION OF SOCIAL WORK
BSW PROGRAM

Evaluation of Student Performance in Field

Name of student _____ Semester _____ Year _____

Placement site _____ Midterm _____ Final _____

	0	1	2	3	4
Student assessment	0	1	2	3	4
Supervisor assessment	0	1	2	3	4
CRITICAL THINKING SKILLS AND PROBLEM-SOLVING ABILITIES	Frequently misses the "big picture" by overlooking relevant factors. Difficulty in formulating appropriate and/or attainable goals. Frequently reaches wrong conclusions.	Limited ability to examine and sort through relevant factors. Frequently requires direction to stay on track. Difficulty in determining focus of efforts. Reaches wrong conclusions sometimes.	Satisfactory ability to assess situations and formulate interventions. Able to carry out intervention and make adjustments when indicated. Conclusions are sound.	Problem-solving efforts are well-reasoned. Able to identify and weigh opposing points of view. Usually able to engage in independent work throughout problem-solving process.	Demonstrates creativity, reflection, precision, accuracy, relevance, and soundness in problem-solving abilities. Decisions are well supported. Identifies factors that others might miss.
Student assessment	0	1	2	3	4
Supervisor assessment	0	1	2	3	4
PROFESSIONAL VALUES AND ETHICAL BEHAVIOR	Behavior is inconsistent with social work values and ethics. Violations of basic principles occur.	Has some difficulty maintaining a nonjudgmental stance or experiences other value difficulties.	Aware of and satisfactory adherence to the basic values and ethics such as client worth and dignity, confidentiality, self-determination, honesty, and acceptance.	Very committed to social work values. Practice consistently reflects appropriate professional behaviors.	Advanced awareness of and commitment to the profession's value base. Able to identify and address ethical dilemmas with skill.
Student assessment	0	1	2	3	4
Supervisor assessment	0	1	2	3	4
PROFESSIONAL DEVELOPMENT	Lacks commitment to and/or interest in professional development. Inaccurate self-assessment. Ignores feedback on ways to improve. Seems unmotivated.	Has difficulty recognizing limitations and seems hesitant and/or resistant to act on feedback. Responsibility for continued growth is minimal.	Some evidence of commitment to continued professional development and satisfactory level of responsibility for continued growth.	Takes advantage of opportunities for professional development and is committed to continued professional growth.	Is self-motivated. Enthusiastically seeks out opportunities to increase skills and knowledge. Clear sense of professional goals and ways to reach them.

	0	1	2	3	4
Student assessment					
Supervisor assessment					
HUMAN DIVERSITY	Cannot professionally relate to and/or accept and respect certain client populations.	Limited ability to accept, understand, respect, and relate to certain client populations.	Usually is sensitive to and respectful of human diversity in practice and research efforts.	Relates well to various populations. Open to exploring unfamiliar situations and making necessary adjustments.	Skillful in differential assessment and intervention skills in serving diverse populations.
Student assessment					
Supervisor assessment					
SOCIAL AND ECONOMIC JUSTICE	Lacks commitment or is oblivious to efforts that promote social and economic justice. Insensitive to the major issues.	Marginal commitment to efforts that promote social and economic justice. Blind to the public issues found in collective private troubles.	Acceptable commitment to social change efforts and satisfactory skills in advancing clients' rights.	Shows initiative in efforts that advance social and economic justice on behalf of vulnerable populations. Engages clients in these efforts.	Advocacy efforts include a wide range of interventions and focus on smaller and larger systems as both targets and beneficiaries of change.
Student assessment					
Supervisor assessment					
POLICIES AND PROCEDURES	Disregards or manipulates regulations. Procedurally careless. Little awareness of or interest in policies that impact service delivery.	Marginally grasps how policy impacts service delivery. Limited knowledge of relevant policies and marginal ability to observe agency policies and routines.	Understands the importance of policy in service delivery and acts accordingly. Satisfactory knowledge of relevant policies and works within the policies and routines of agency.	Appreciates the policies that guide agency services. Able to grasp influences on policy-making process.	Outstanding ability to apply policy to service efforts. Actively participates in discussions to shape new policies or services. Solid grasp of policy-shaping process.
Student assessment					
Supervisor assessment					
EVALUATING PRACTICE AND PROGRAMS	Has no knowledge of or skill in ways to evaluate practice efforts and programs.	Marginal knowledge of or skill in ways to evaluate practice efforts and programs.	Understands relationship of program and practice evaluation to the problem-solving process. Can carry out basic evaluations.	Comfortable in using more than one approach to evaluate practice and programs. Seeks resources to improve evaluative efforts.	Skillful in use of various designs for evaluating practice and program effectiveness.
Student assessment					
Supervisor assessment					
RURAL CONTEXT	Inability to distinguish the special features of working in rural communities and small towns.	Limited ability to differentiate between rural practice and urban practice.	Satisfactory grasp of practice in rural communities and small towns.	A good understanding of rural areas and small towns. Well able to apply that knowledge to practice.	Advanced ability to provide services in the contexts of rural communities and small towns.

	0	1	2	3	4
Student assessment	0	1	2	3	4
Supervisor assessment	0	1	2	3	4
INTERVIEWING SKILLS	Unable to engage in a purposive and productive interview. Violates principles of effective communication. Unable to establish rapport and engage client.	Minimally effective in the interview situation. Limited ability to apply sound principles of interpersonal communication. Allows client to manipulate or control interview.	Interviewing skills are satisfactory and productive. Able to engage client in an appropriate manner. Usually able to keep interview focused.	Skillful in engaging clients and building rapport. Consistently applies sound principles of communication. Interviews are productive and purposeful.	Superior abilities in the full range of interviewing and communication skills. Strong sensitivity to client needs and good empathic abilities.
Student assessment	0	1	2	3	4
Supervisor assessment	0	1	2	3	4
WRITTEN COMMUNICATION	Lacks the basic skills in effective written communication. Is very careless in written work. Unable or unwilling to respond to agency expectations.	Marginal ability to produce the written work that is necessary. Frequent errors.	Satisfactory ability to produce written work that is necessary. Limited number of errors.	Written work is carefully completed, neat, and conforms to agency requirements. Solid ability to convey information in written form.	Superior skills in written communication. Written work has remarkable clarity and always conforms to agency requirements.
Student assessment	0	1	2	3	4
Supervisor assessment	0	1	2	3	4
USE OF SUPERVISION	Overly dependent on supervision or resents supervisory feedback. Does not understand or appropriately make use of supervision.	Sometimes unable to make good use of supervision. Is sometimes defensive or ignores feedback. Sometimes uses supervision inappropriately.	Appropriately utilizes supervision and responds satisfactorily to information and suggestions.	Is usually prepared for supervisory conferences. Is responsive to feedback; makes good use of supervision.	Appreciates, values, and appropriately utilizes supervision. Seeks input on performance and development. Is responsive to supervisory input.
Student assessment	0	1	2	3	4
Supervisor assessment	0	1	2	3	4
GENERALIST ROLES	Ineffective in many of the generalist roles. Unwilling or unable to expand role repertoire.	Is able to carry several of the generalist roles although effectiveness is often limited.	Is comfortable in most of the generalist roles and is usually effective in each.	Consistently applies the full range of roles appropriate to each practice situation.	Ability to function in a wide range of generalist roles is exceptional.
Student assessment	0	1	2	3	4
Supervisor assessment	0	1	2	3	4
KNOWLEDGE	Little grasp of how theory and research apply to practice. Relies mainly on intuition or trial and error.	Marginal grasp of how theory and research apply to practice.	Draws on and integrates theory, research, and practice satisfactorily.	Consistently demonstrates a sound knowledge base in all areas of practice.	Outstanding grasp of the link between knowledge and practice. Practice is consistently guided by research and practice theory.

Category	0	1	2	3	4
Student assessment	0	1	2	3	4
Supervisor assessment	0	1	2	3	4
RELATIONS WITH CLIENTS	Unable to establish and/or maintain a professional and purposive relationship with clients. Sees clients as friends or is generally disrespectful to and intolerant of clients.	Some difficulty in keeping professional and purposive focus. Benignly ineffective as a helper. Rapport with clients is tenuous.	Able to establish and maintain professional and purposive relationships. Builds rapport and is able to engage client. Dignity and worth of client is valued.	Consistently establishes and maintains professional and purposive relations with clients. Easily builds rapport and generally is able to handle difficult situations	Establishes highly productive relationships. Clients show confidence in the student as a helper. Handles difficult situations with skill.
Student assessment	0	1	2	3	4
Supervisor assessment	0	1	2	3	4
RELATIONS WITH STAFF, COWORKERS, PEERS, AND OTHER PROFESSIONALS	Uncooperative or distant. Attitude problems. Lacks diplomacy and tack in interactions, which arouses resentment.	Has difficulty sustaining a cooperative relationship. Is moody or unapproachable. Sometimes lacks diplomacy and tact.	Generally is approachable, cooperative, and helpful. Respects others and is respected by them, in turn.	Establishes strong working relationships. Is helpful, congenial, and pleasant. Very cooperative in all situations.	Rapport with others is outstanding. Promotes teamwork and is approached by others for assistance. Tact and diplomacy are exemplary.
Student assessment	0	1	2	3	4
Supervisor assessment	0	1	2	3	4
LINKAGES WITH OTHER COMMUNITY RESOURCES	Overly dependent on others for referral information. Ignores appropriate referral procedures. Inappropriate decisions are made due to lack of knowledge in this area.	Identifies and makes use of the obvious resources, but knowledge of resources is limited and initiative in finding resources is lacking.	Satisfactory knowledge of community resources and satisfactory ability to make referrals and to follow through.	Shows initiative in seeking out resources to meet client needs. Has established personal contacts to increase effectiveness of the referral process. Good follow-up.	Firm grasp of resources locally and regionally. Highly effective in preparing client for referral and in conducting follow-up. Has added to agency's referral contacts.
Student assessment	0	1	2	3	4
Supervisor assessment	0	1	2	3	4
WORKLOAD MANAGEMENT	Little sense of how to stay organized. Deadlines are missed. Wastes time. Constant supervision is needed to ensure that tasks are completed.	Performance is uneven and unreliable. Needs occasional prodding to stay on top of workload and meet deadlines.	Satisfactorily organizes work and manages time. Assigned tasks are completed in a timely manner. Faithfully adheres to deadlines.	Is self-directed in completing tasks and assignments. Very organized. Occasionally takes on additional tasks or helps others out. Good sense of priorities.	Remarkable ability to stay organized and on top of workload. Frequently offers assistance to others and volunteers to assume additional responsibilities.

	0	1	2	3	4
Student assessment	0	1	2	3	4
Supervisor assessment	0	1	2	3	4
PROFESSIONAL DECORUM	Pattern of tardiness and absenteeism. May not call in or make arrangements. Inappropriate appearance, dress, and/or behavior. General irresponsibility. Wastes time a lot.	Tardy or absent more than normal. Sometimes calls in and makes arrangements. Appearance, behavior, and/or dress are not always appropriate. Sometimes wastes time.	Fulfills work responsibilities satisfactorily. Seldom misses work and handles absences or lateness appropriately. Appearance and behavior are consistent with agency standards.	Is punctual, dependable, and responsible in all tasks and efforts. Appearance and behavior make a good professional statement.	Outstanding professional decorum at all times and in all situations. Good representative of agency in public situations.
Student assessment	0	1	2	3	4
Supervisor assessment	0	1	2	3	4
SERVICES TO INDIVIDUALS AND FAMILIES	Work with individuals and families is ineffective. Unable to develop supportive relationships. Lacks understanding of and skill for this level of practice.	Limited ability to work with individuals and families. Misunderstands or unable to address dynamics of situation.	Satisfactory practice with individuals and families. Able to identify and make use of client strengths.	Is sometimes creative and resourceful in work with individuals and families. Emphasizes client strengths and maximizes self-determination.	Engages in creative practice with individuals and families. Uses a wide range of strategies and techniques. Can handle complex and demanding situations.
Student assessment	0	1	2	3	4
Supervisor assessment	0	1	2	3	4
WORK WITH SMALL GROUPS	Has little understanding of group use, formation, and process. Avoids consideration of this approach to practice.	Marginal understanding of and skill in working with a specific type of group. Needs considerable support and encouragement to work in the group context.	Satisfactory ability to make use of groups as an intervention method. Has a basic understanding of group theory and acceptable level of skill under supervision.	Has a good grasp of group theory and is well able to make application to practice situations. Demonstrates skill with at least one type of group.	Demonstrates skill in working with more than one type of group. Able to form and plan for group, as well as facilitate group development and process.
Student assessment	0	1	2	3	4
Supervisor assessment	0	1	2	3	4
WORK WITH COMMUNITIES AND ORGANIZATIONS	Displays little or no understanding of the social worker's role in organizations and communities. Unwilling or unable to develop skills at this level of practice	Displays marginal understanding of the social worker's role in organizations and communities. Has few skills to apply to work with organizations and communities.	Has satisfactory grasp of the social worker's role. Able to work with an organizational and/or community group setting with some supervision.	Has a good understanding of the social worker's role with organizations and communities. Can assume a professional role in an organizational or community setting.	Understands and demonstrates exceptional ability to apply assessment, planning, intervention, and evaluation skills in an organizational or community setting.

Appendix 10

Grading Checklist

This grading checklist was developed to grade a student assignment in the introductory social work course. The assignment is to compare and contrast several professional codes of ethics with the NASW code. See appendix 14 for the assignment.

Demonstration of Knowledge (55 points possible. Your score = _____)

1. You were well able to establish conceptual and theoretical connections between the NASW code and the other codes as you analyzed and compared them.

   [ ] high [ ]   [ ] medium [ ]   [ ] low [ ]

2. Your paper demonstrated a good understanding of professional ethics, their similarities, and their differences.

   [ ] high [ ]   [ ] medium [ ]   [ ] low [ ]

3. In general, your analysis demonstrates good critical thinking abilities.

   [ ] high [ ]   [ ] medium [ ]   [ ] low [ ]

Clarity of Expression (25 points possible. Your score = _____)

4. You were well able to communicate your thoughts/ideas clearly and effectively.

   [ ] high [ ]   [ ] medium [ ]   [ ] low [ ]

5. Your instructor did not have to guess at what you were trying to convey. The flow of your thoughts and ideas proceeded in a clear and logical fashion—one thought leading smoothly to the next, with no "jump shifts," gaps, or "disjointedness." The paper was very coherent and "readable."

   [ ] high [ ]   [ ] medium [ ]   [ ] low [ ]

Technical Presentation (20 points possible. Your score = _____)

6. You were attentive to spelling all words correctly and punctuating sentences correctly.

    [ ] high [ ]   [ ] medium [ ]   [ ] low [ ]

7. Your paper was grammatically correct and you used appropriate diction (word choice) in expressing your thoughts and ideas.

    [ ] high [ ]   [ ] medium [ ]   [ ] low [ ]

8. The syntax (word order) of your sentences was correct.

    [ ] high [ ]   [ ] medium [ ]   [ ] low [ ]

9. You proofread your paper carefully to make it free of typos and other mistakes.

    [ ] high [ ]   [ ] medium [ ]   [ ] low [ ]

10. You avoided the common writing errors listed in the syllabus.

    [ ] high [ ]   [ ] medium [ ]   [ ] low [ ]

Total Points = _____   **Grade =** _____

Appendix 11

Critical Thinking Rubric

This checklist was developed for use in assessing students' critical thinking abilities.

1. Ability to make central point and provide supporting arguments

    0 = Identifies central point but has little ability to proceed beyond that step.

    1 = Makes central point but limited ability to provide sufficient supporting arguments.

    2 = Makes central point and provides adequate supporting arguments.

    3 = Makes central point and provides a variety of supporting arguments.

2. Ability to identify and weigh evidence that does not support own position (i.e., other positions or claims; alternative explanations)

    0 = Does not identify or weigh evidence that contradicts own position.

    1 = Presentation and exploration of contradictory evidence is minimal.

    2 = Presentation and exploration of contradictory evidence is adequate.

    3 = Draws on and evaluates several examples of contradictory evidence.

3. Ability to identify premises in own position and position of others

   0 = Inaccurately identifies premises; does not seem to understand concept.

   1 = Limited understanding of concept and ability to identify premises

   2 = Identifies the most obvious premises.

   3 = Accurately identifies premises.

4. Ability to raise appropriate questions or issues related to topic under investigation

   0 = Questions or issues raised are trivial or irrelevant.

   1 = Raises a few relevant questions or issues.

   2 = Raises several relevant questions or issues

   3 = Strong ability to identify the cogent questions and issues.

5. Ability to engage in reflective thinking

   0 = Sticks strictly to the thinking of others; does not identify or explore own cognitive biases or personal experiences that impact reasoning.

   1 = Limited ability to demonstrate own thinking and to relate personal experience to topic.

   2 = Includes own thinking in analysis but unable to relate personal experience to topic.

   3 = Own thinking is evident throughout analysis and appropriate personal experience is included.

6. Integrity of intellectual process

   0 = Reaches conclusions too readily; errors in thinking; makes trivial or irrelevant points; use of language lacks clarity and terms are carelessly used.

   1 = Minimal ability to progress to reasoned conclusions; some errors in thinking; makes some irrelevant points; some errors in language usage.

   2 = Pattern of reasoning is adequate; no or few errors in thinking; sticks to relevant points; language usage is satisfactory.

   3 = Conclusions are well reasoned without thinking errors and digressions; language is highly accurate and effective.

Total points   _____

Total possible points   _____

Percentage score   _____

Grade   _____

Appendix 12

Syllabus Demonstrating Use of Portfolio Assessment

Social Welfare Policy and Services

This course provides a historical and analytical assessment of social welfare as an institution using a framework of problem/need definition, policy goals, program design, and service delivery. Students will focus on understanding policy formulation, analysis, and application for practice. Current policies and services will be studied in order for students to gain a critical understanding of social, cultural, economic, and political factors that influence the current social welfare system. In addition, the following topics will be addressed.

- Evolution of social welfare in relation to other social institutions in the United States seeking to improve social functioning and alleviate suffering.
- Functions of social work as a profession in programs of income security, family and children's services, criminal justice, mental health and developmental disabilities, aging, and other issues.
- Impact of conflicting values, motivation, and stratification on social welfare will be studied.
- Evaluation of the major programs and services comprising the American social welfare system.
- Nature of social welfare policy and implications of policy application for the beginning practitioner.

This sample syllabus was submitted by Lynn Frantz Adkins of Bethany College in West Virginia.

Course Objectives

This course will prepare students to effectively utilize social policy as a generalist social worker. It will incorporate an integrative approach to generalist social work practice that emphasizes intervention on individual, environmental, and systemic levels. Upon completion of this course, students will have acquired the following knowledge and skills.

A. Knowledge of
1. values (professional, sociocultural, personal) and ethics and their role in the policy and planning processes;
2. historical development of social policy;
3. social problems, their impact, and social policy responses to them;
4. major social institutions, particularly the social welfare institution, and the reciprocal impact between them and social policy;
5. a framework for policy analysis and formation;
6. the impact of social policy on people's lives including a focus on oppressed groups and women;
7. effective use of social policy in integrative generalist social work practice, including the reciprocal impact between practice and policy;
8. forces that influence the development, implementation, and outcome of social policies;
9. comparative social welfare systems;
10. citizen participation and power in the policy arena;
11. social planning, social policy, and the legislative process as a source/process of social change;
12. contemporary changes in society and alternative policy responses to these trends.

B. Skills in
1. analyzing, formulating, implementing, and using policy effectively in generalist social work practice;
2. identifying the importance of involving citizens, especially the disenfranchised, in all stages of the policy process;
3. utilizing research skills and professional ethics in planning, implementing, and evaluating policies;

4. facilitating organizational functioning for effective service delivery;

5. clarifying one's own commitment to social justice and social change and assisting others to do the same;

6. valuing diversity when involved in the processes of policy and planning;

7. identifying the importance of facilitating the development of support networks (organizational, community, etc.) in social change efforts.

C. Learning Objectives

Students will

1. develop an understanding of what social policy is, how it is formulated, and what impact it has on social work practice;

2. learn to determine social policy and how it can be changed;

3. develop an appreciation of power and power blocs in the formulation of social policy;

4. understand social policy from a world view;

5. know how their own and other's values and attitudes affect the formulation of social policy;

6. understand how individuals, families, groups, and organizations are affected by social policy;

7. understand that the commonality of the problem-solving approach used in other areas of social work applies equally in the area of social policy decisions;

8. understand the issues of rural life in relation to social welfare policies;

9. understand that policy making is a necessary skill for social workers.

In the area of practice and skills, students will be able to develop a method for analyzing social policies and evaluating them. They also will be able to research, report, and defend in class a particular stance in a field of their choosing.

Course Requirements and Assignments

Assignments to accomplish these objectives will include but are not limited to the following:

- Social Policy Assessment and Class Presentation
- Social Issues Journal (Congressional Quarterly and related readings)
- Two Exams (as scheduled)

Each of the above assignments must be prepared in portfolio form, allowing students a number of options for presenting the materials as well as a number of possible sources for accessing information beyond the traditional library research method. Students could use direct interviews, newscasts, and a number of materials accessible via the Internet.

Course Evaluation: Portfolio Assessment

Portfolio assessment is your opportunity to display your coursework in a manner that establishes your understanding of course content in terms of both the science (theory) and the art of social work practice. All work for which you will receive a course evaluation must be presented in a portfolio to include the following:

1. Two exams—Each of these exams will be an essay exam and will be given during the class period. Your exam will be graded and returned, at which time you may make a further response to the exam in terms of providing additional information or correcting misinformation. This response should utilize critical thinking skills and be prepared in essay form. (40 percent of grade)

2. Social Policy Assessment and Class Presentation—This assignment will span the entire course and will be the center of class collaboration and individual contributions to class discussion. Assessment requirements and guidelines for the assignment are attached. (30 percent of grade)

3. Social Issues Journal—There is a wealth of material available each day on social welfare issues. As students preparing for work in the field of social welfare it is your responsibility to be aware of these issues and to be able to give thoughtful reactions to what is going on in the world in which you live. Through this assignment, it is hoped that you will become better able to analyze policy decisions and to understand the policy making process. (30 percent of grade)

4. Class attendance and participation—To achieve grade of A in this course students must have excellent participation and attendance and assignments must be completed on time. All work that is submitted late or work missed without an official excuse will lower the final portfolio grade. See attendance policy in the next section.

All work required for your portfolio will have an assigned due date and will be evaluated in terms of its submission on that date. Following my review of your work, you may revise any materials presented in your portfolio that you believe can be improved. While rewriting is optional, it is highly encouraged; you may choose to rewrite all, some, or none of your work for the final portfolio. Revision does not guarantee a higher grade but certainly gives you a better opportunity to enhance your grade. The original must always be included with any rewritten assignment.

Portfolios must be electronic and created in the social work computer lab, with a backup disk to be handed in with any supplemental materials that cannot be handled electronically. The course instructor will provide students with color-coded portfolios for inclusion of the course material. You are expected to use materials from the Internet and multimedia software as part of your documentation.

Your portfolio should be developed in a creative manner that reflects your special character and certainly reflects your critical-thinking skills. On or before the designated due date, submit your work to the instructor's office computer under the file name Social Work 220. You can enter and submit your materials as a "Guest" via any campus computer lab. Materials once sent to the professor's file cannot be retrieved until the professor reviews them and returns them either as work completed or work to be revised or continued in another class.

Attendance Policy

Consistent with social work commitments, class absences cannot be tolerated. Excessive absences will negatively affect your grade. Attendance in this field of study is both an academic and professional necessity.

Guidelines for Social Welfare Policy Assessment Assignment

Objectives

Students are to select a topic relevant to the field of social welfare policy and conduct independent research on that topic. This research will be reported in two forms: a written term paper and an oral presentation of key issues and findings to the class. Goals for the project include the following:

- To stimulate students to explore a topic of interest.
- To provide experience in using the library and other information.
- To provide an opportunity to develop and demonstrate writing and public speaking skills.
- To expose students to information and issues not covered in readings or regular class sessions.
- To develop policy analysis skill and ability

Selection of Topic

Any topic relevant to the field of social welfare is appropriate. Topics should address the policy and program aspects of a given issue.

Format of Class Presentation

The class presentation should summarize objectives, issues, and findings of the research. You should not read your paper, but be prepared to discuss relevant aspects of your topic. Prepared remarks should last about twenty minutes and include an additional five to ten minutes for discussion.

Format of Paper

The text of the paper should be approximately ten to twelve double-spaced, typewritten pages. All quotations should be footnoted. Some form of reference or bibliography of resources utilized in the research must be included. On a separate page, include a one-paragraph abstract that summarizes objectives, key issues, and important findings. The paper must be developed in five sections (as outlined in the next section) to include statement of the problem, major motivations, examination of a program, policy analysis and formulation, and summary statements.

Social Welfare Policy Assessment Outline

Part I: Introduction

Social welfare policies are deliberate attempts to achieve goals determined by those designated as policymakers. Policies, in turn, may be of two kinds. There are those that designate the end to be sought and those that dictate at least in part the method to be used.

Example: The goal policy of the former Aid To Families with Dependent Children program was to make it possible for children to grow up without being crippled physically, emotionally, or socially by lack of money. The method policy indicated that the assisted child must be in the home of a relative. Similarly, the goal policy of unemployment compensation is to protect working people from penury during temporary periods of unemployment. The method policy dictates that they should not receive as grants as much as they would receive as salaries if they were working.

Policies in turn are effectuated through social welfare programs, which are attempts to carry out the policies (that is, to reach the goals) through activities.

Select a program or current policy issue of interest to you. Research the current issues associated with your selected topic to include:

· Define the problem and policy issues you will address.
· Provide a historical overview of the development of the issue.
· Discuss the nature and scope of the issue.
· Discuss any possible causes for the problem.
· Provide a general introduction to the problem you wish to research.

This section of your paper will run from five to ten pages and should be typed and footnoted.

Part II: The Major Motivations for Social Welfare

The determination to help meet human needs, is a theme running through all definitions of "social welfare." This desire may arise from a number of motivations, among them:

- Mutual aid
- Religious commandments
- The desire for political advantage
- Economic considerations
- Ideological factors

Discuss these motivations in relation to the topic you have chosen for social policy assessment.

Part III: Examining a Social Welfare Program

You need certain tools in order to develop some intelligent understanding of a social welfare program, some intelligent analysis of its characteristics, and some informed opinion as to its desirability.

First, you need to be able to identify the basic components in any social welfare program. An understanding of the basic structural components will give you a beginning grasp and understanding of what the program is about, what it is intended to do, for whom, and at what price.

Second, you need to know what some of the basic issues are about, alternative ways of organizing social welfare programs, and alternative characteristics that they may possess.

Finally, you need to know what criteria you must apply to any social welfare program in order to evaluate it.

The following schema for examining a social welfare program is drawn from the work of Eveline Burns, Neil Gilbert, and Harry Specht. The models of these individuals have been drawn together or are made similar by Dolgoff, Feldstein, and Skolnik in the book *Understanding Social Welfare*, referenced at the end of this syllabus.

Examining a Social Welfare Program

I. Structural components

A. Goals

B. What is the form of benefit the program produces?

C. Who is eligible for the program?

D. How is the program financed?

E. What is the level of administration?

II. Alternative Program Characteristics

A. Residual, institutional, developmental

B. Selective, universal

C. Benefits in money, service, utilities

D. Public, private

E. Central, local

F. Lay, professional

G. Resources, or engineering as the problem

III. Evaluating the program

A. Adequacy

1. Horizontal

2. Vertical

B. Financing

1. Equitable

2. Priority use of funds

3. Efficient: cost and benefit

4. Cost/Benefit Analysis

C. Coherence

D. Latent consequences

Part IV: Policy Analysis and Formulation

Social work practice and policy are shaped by ideology and values and beliefs held about people, their nature, and what is desirable. Although unproved, values are powerful guides to action that can be tracked through the day-to-day practice of a social worker. An ideology is a value system characteristic of a group; it is tied to political and economic interests. We have previously looked at these issues in relation to our selected social policy. Take an additional look at this issue in relation to social work values and commonly held societal values. Discuss in a page or two the implications of these values as they relate to your topic.

Prigmore and Atherton provide us with a second method of analyzing social welfare policy. Follow the process as outlined and apply the analysis to your selected topic.

Systematic Analysis of Social Welfare Policy

- Considerations Related to Values
    - Is the policy under consideration compatible with contemporary "style"?
    - Is the policy compatible with important and enduring cultural values, particularly equity, fairness and justice?
    - Is the policy compatible with social work's professional value and ethical system?

- Dimensions of Influence
    - Is the policy acceptable to those in formal decision-making positions?
    - Does the policy satisfy relevant interest groups?

- Knowledge Considerations
    - Is the policy based on knowledge that has been tested to some degree?
    - Is the policy workable? That is, can the programs that flow from the policy be carried out in the real world?
    - Does the policy create few problems for both the public and the intended beneficiaries?

- Elements Related to Costs and Benefits
    - Is the policy reasonable effective?
    - Is the policy efficient?

Part V. Special Populations

Consider the impact on special populations in relation to your issue. Document the major concerns, benefits, strengths, and weaknesses. Provide documentation for your stance.

Part VI. Social and Economic Injustice

Throughout history issues of economic and social injustice have prohibited individuals, families, groups, and communities from opportunities to reach their maximum potential. Explore the issues of economic and social injustice as they relate to your topic.

Part VII: Policy Practice

Develop an example of how you might address your policy issue in terms of social work practice at the micro, mezzo, or macro level of practice. Provide insight into how you would incorporate the artistic factors of practice in relation to your stated issues. Illustrate the use of the following artistic factors:

- Relationship
- Empathy
- Warmth
- Creativity
- Imagination
- Flexible Persistence
- Energy
- Judgment
- Personal Values

Part VIII: Summary

You have spent a good deal of time working on an analysis of a major social welfare policy. Now you are ready to make suggestions and develop strategies of implementation of policy development or change.

Write a two- to three-page paper based on the material in the Prigmore and Atherton text to explain what action you would take concerning your social policy issue. Begin your paper with a brief summary of the social policy issue and develop a plan of action for change and implementation.

References

Dolgoff, R., Feldstein, D., and Skolnik, L. (1996). *Understanding social welfare*. 4th ed. Reading, Mass.: Addison-Wesley.

Prigmore, C. S., and Atherton, C. (1986). *Social welfare policy: Analysis and formulation*. 2d ed. Lexington, Mass.: Heath.

Macarov, D. (1995). *Social welfare structure and practice*. Thousand Oaks, Ca.: Sage.

Sheafor, B. W., Horejsi, C. R., and Horejsi, G. A. (1997). *Techniques and guidelines for social work practice*. 4th ed. Boston: Allyn and Bacon.

Appendix 13

Commission on Accreditation Supplement to the Handbook of Accreditation Standards and Procedures: Guidelines for Termination for Academic and Professional Reasons

(Previously distributed under the title *Guidelines for "Nonacademic" Termination Policies and Procedures*)

Accreditation standards (BSW and MSW Standards 5.8) require that social work programs have policies and practices for "terminating a student's enrollment . . . for reasons of academic and nonacademic performance." The interpretive guideline refers to "nonacademic" as "performance or behaviors of students that provide relevant information regarding their likely performance as social work practitioners" CSWE (1994). *Handbook of Accreditation Standards and Procedures,* pp. 89 and 127.

Programs are encouraged to differentially define academic and nonacademic performance in their policies. However, knowledge, skill, and value expectations are all *academic in a professional program* as they relate to a student's "likely performance as a social work practitioner." They are "nonacademic" (in the language of the accreditation standard) to differentiate between termination for deficiencies in academic standing (e.g., student whose

---

This memorandum was mailed by the Council on Social Work Education to social work programs in February 1999.

GPA is less than the required minimum or who has earned more unsatisfactory grades than allowed in the program) and inadequacies in student ability to demonstrate professional conduct and relationship skills and behavior consistent with the values and ethics of the profession.

A. Principles in constructing nonacademic termination policies:

1. Be broad and inclusive in identifying the *framework* for nonacademic termination.

   Example: Failure to meet generally accepted standards of professional conduct, personal integrity or emotional stability requisite for professional practice; inappropriate or disruptive behavior toward colleagues, faculty or staff (at School or field placement).

2. Use behaviorally specific language which links behavior to performance expectations reflected as components of the broader inclusive framework.

   Avoid labeling and general categorizations in identifying criteria (e.g., emotionally disturbed).

3. Ensure that criteria reflect the professional behaviors in the *NASW Code of Ethics.*

4. Ensure that due process procedures are in place, are written and disseminated to program constituents.

5. Ensure that criteria, policies, and procedures are compatible with existing civil rights laws.

B. Suggestions/considerations in the policy development process:

1. Consult with other professional programs at your institution as to policies and procedures which they may have developed for nonacademic termination.

2. Check your state's social work licensing regulations for relevant language which may need to be included in policy.

3. Have your institution's attorney review draft policies and procedures prior to adoption.

4. Review your program's admission criteria, program objectives, class and field objectives, assessment measures (including field evaluation forms), criteria for termination, and criteria for graduation for consistent language regarding expected professional behaviors and capabilities.

Appendix 14

Comparing Codes of Ethics: An Assignment for Developing Critical-Thinking Abilities

This assignment will help you to understand professional codes of ethics in general, and the *NASW Code of Ethics* in particular. In addition, it will help you to develop your critical-thinking skills.

Your objective is to thoroughly review and then compare each of several selected professional codes to the *NASW Code of Ethics,* using each of the other professional codes as paper sub-headings. The comparisons should highlight not only general but also some specific similarities and differences. Think of the following questions as you frame each section of your paper. Are there certain terms, ideas, themes, or concepts that are addressed in the NASW code as well as in each of the other codes (for example, confidentiality)? Are there ways that the NASW code and each of the other codes conflict in the ideas or ideals that are advanced? Are there important ideas or ideals that are elaborated in one code but totally omitted or only briefly mentioned in the other codes? Based on your thorough review of each of the codes, what differences do you see among the professions? Did you find anything that surprised you in any of the codes? Explain. Which code do you think might be the most effective? Explain your reasons for reaching your conclusion.

Remember to be direct when making your comparisons: every time you say one code addresses or does not address something, then you must specify the counterpart comparison in the other code. To help you understand what is expected, you also will be given an illustrative analysis based on the ethics code of the National Association of Black Social Workers to use as a model.

Note to instructors

The following resources each have several of the codes of ethics of various helping profession in their appendixes.

Bloch, S., and Chodoff, P. (Ed.). (1993). *Psychiatric ethics*. 2d ed. New York: Oxford University Press.

Corey, G., Corey, M. S., and Callanan, P. (1998). *Issues and ethics in the helping professions*. Pacific Grove, Ca.: Brooks/Cole.

Herlihy, B., and Golden, L. (1990). *AACD ethical standards casebook*. 4th ed. Alexandria, Va.: American Association for Counseling and Development.

Index